The Sins of the Nation and the Ritual of Apologies

In the last years of the twentieth century, political leaders the world over began to apologize for wrongs in their nations' pasts. Many dismissed these apologies as "mere words," cynical attempts to avoid more costly forms of reparation; others rejected them as inappropriate encroachments into politics or forms of action that belonged in personal relationships or religion. Yet political apologies have gripped nations and provoked tremendous resistance. To understand apology's extraordinary political emergence, we have to suspend our automatic interpretations of what it means for nations to apologize and interrogate the meaning afresh. Taking the reader on a journey through apology's religious history and contemporary apologetic dramas, this book argues that the apologetic phenomenon marks a new stage in our recognition of the importance of collective responsibility, the place of ritual in addressing national wrongs, and the contribution that practices that once belonged in the religious sphere might make to contemporary politics.

Danielle Celermajer is currently a Senior Lecturer in Sociology and Social Policy at the University of Sydney. She was formerly Director of Indigenous Policy at the Australian Human Rights Commission. She was the recipient of grants from the Fulbright Foundation and the Rockefeller Foundation, as well as a Mellon Fellowship. She has written extensively on transitional justice, human rights, religion, and the political thought of Hannah Arendt, and she recently co-edited a forthcoming book on Hannah Arendt and political judgement.

The Sins of the Nation and the Ritual of Apologies

DANIELLE CELERMAJER

University of Sydney

CAMBRIDGE
UNIVERSITY PRESS

CAMBRIDGE UNIVERSITY PRESS
Cambridge, New York, Melbourne, Madrid, Cape Town, Singapore, São Paulo, Delhi

Cambridge University Press
32 Avenue of the Americas, New York, NY 10013-2473, USA

www.cambridge.org
Information on this title: www.cambridge.org/9780521516693

© Danielle Celermajer 2009

First published 2009

Printed in the United States of America

A catalog record for this publication is available from the British Library.

Library of Congress Cataloging in Publication Data

Celermajer, Danielle.
The sins of the nation and the ritual of apologies / Danielle Celermajer.
    p. cm.
Includes bibliographical references and index.
ISBN 978-0-521-51669-3 (hardback)
1. Apologizing – Political aspects. 2. Restorative justice. I. Title.
JC578.C456 2009
320.01′1 – dc22   2008044137

ISBN 978-0-521-51669-3 hardback

For Isaac, Hela, and John before
and Arielle after.

Contents

Acknowledgements

My first thanks go to the people who taught me about injustice, identity, and suffering beyond law and who planted the demand that motivated this work. They are, on one side, my blood family who told me our own Holocaust story from my very beginning, and on the other side my Aboriginal co-citizens who told me their story and showed me how it was also mine. My particular thanks to all the Indigenous and non-Indigenous people with whom I worked at the Australian Human Rights and Equal Opportunity Commission. It was through those relationships that I began to think deeply about the living politics of recognition and identity, and to understand that really addressing human rights violations requires entering deeply into the way we experience each other. Above all, my heartfelt thanks to Mick Dodson, the great Aboriginal leader who allowed me to enter deeply into his very personal political world and at the same time entered into mine.

More formally, I'd like to thank the Fulbright Commission for believing in my aspirations with such enthusiasm and practical support, and in particular Mrs. W. G. Walker, whose fellowship supported the early parts of this work. I would also like to thank Columbia University and the Mellon Foundation, both of which supported me while I worked on this project. Thank you also to the University of Sydney, where I completed the manuscript. My thanks also to my editor at Cambridge, Lew Bateman, who recognized the value of the project and coaxed it through to the final form in which it now rests, and to Emily Spangler, also at Cambridge, for her tireless and graceful assistance.

Bettina Cass, Moira Gatens, Paul Patton, and Jim Tully may no longer recall their connection with this work, but it was their encouragement that supported my shift from front-line political action to more reflective political theory. Without their confidence and passion I could not have taken the plunge. My deepest thanks to Ruti Teitel, who engaged with this project while it was still but an abstract presence across the world on the end of the Internet and who has continued to enrich my intellectual engagement to this day.

At Columbia University, my foremost thanks go to my two principal advisors, Jean Cohen and Ira Katznelson. Their reflections and input enriched my thinking and this project enormously. I am particularly grateful for their having recognized that this project emerged from my own idiosyncratic intersection of interests, and for supporting me in working outside the box. Thank you also to Jeremy Waldron, who opened invaluable doors in my exploration of the link between politics and religion.

At the University of Sydney, I would like to thank Vrasidas Karalis, whose unique combination of humour, irreverence, and brilliance painted a unique intellectual context, and my wonderful colleague Rebecca Scott Bray, whose belief in me was so enriching. Thanks also to Tim Fitzpatrick, who provided important practical support for the completion of the manuscript, and most especially to Kathryn Leader, who went well beyond the call of duty in assisting me to complete the manuscript.

I would also like to acknowledge the contribution several teachers and colleagues made to my thinking: Susan Shapiro (Levinas), Jim Tully (recognition beyond tolerance), Brian Barry (endless fights on multiculturalism), Darius Rejali (for orienting my thinking), and Rabbi Roly Matalon (God). Thank you to Andrew Nathan, Julie Stone Peters, and Thomas Pogge for initiating and running the Human Rights colloquium, which provided those of us working on human rights at Columbia with an intellectual community.

Outside the academy, my undying thanks to Anni Parker, for being our family, for her practical love, and for making it possible for me to know my daughter would always have another home while I buried myself here. Thank you Lois Alexander, Andrew Hahn, Jill Hammer, Shoshana Jedwab, Naomi Meyer, Dinah Pokempner, Lester Ruiz, and Josh Saltzman for being friends who walked with me head and heart throughout this work and deepened my understanding more than they could know.

And of course, thank you to my family, who let me go so far away and supported me in so many ways – my mother, who never allowed me to doubt what I was capable of, and most especially my brother David who bore so much responsibility in my absence. Although he will never hold this book in his hands, my father's presence lies at the foundation of my search for a justice always beyond what we have.

This work would not have been written without the often silent support of Chris de Bono, who once said that he was always on my side, and really meant it. Nor would I have had the loving context in which to sustain the attention years into the project without Leonard McDonald, who both recognized what it means to create thinking and cooked me endless late dinners. Finally, every page would have been far duller without the ever-present colour and luminous love of my daughter, Arielle.

Introduction

The Apology and Political Theory

Picture an image. The lawn of Parliament House, the seat of government and the symbol of the state, is planted thick with thousands of green, red, blue, yellow, black, and white hands, rooted in the earth and reaching up to the sky. Each has been placed there by a citizen to mark his or her apology for the theft of Indigenous land and Indigenous children. In the following five years, tens of thousands more added their 'hands' to a growing 'Sea of Hands' which, like the apology movement, swept across the country, a national ritual saluting the children who had been shoved into institutions and foster homes and the broken families and communities left behind in their tracks.[1] A land marked with a history of violence against its Indigenous peoples was now being reinscribed with a collective apology.

If the scene strikes us as an odd description of contemporary politics, this is hardly surprising, given its dissonance with the fundamental principles and standard institutions of modern secular liberalism. One might well expect to see a ritual of repentance in the church, but not in the world of secular politics. We deal with wrongs of the past through the institutions of justice, by either punishing individual wrongdoers or compensating victims. And if pre-moderns believed that the sins of the fathers were brought down upon the heads of the sons, we secular moderns distinguish ourselves by insisting that our institutions of justice hold responsible only those who personally committed wrongful acts. Besides, we know that a collective is not the type of entity that can apologize; only individuals with an inner life, consciousness,

---

[1] At the time of writing, 250,000 people had sponsored a hand. The Sea of Hands has been planted in different forms in a range of iconic public spaces across Australia, including Bondi Beach, Sydney Harbour Bridge, and Uluru (Ayers Rock).

conscience, and internationality can do that. Yet in late-twentieth-century liberal secular Australia (the site of the coloured hands), the collective apology became the most significant social movement since the Vietnam War.

Apology did not always strike citizens as such an interloper on the political stage; indeed at one time, this type of public repentance in the political realm was not an anomaly at all. President Abraham Lincoln, and before him President John Adams, had declared days of "National fasting, humiliation and prayer" (in 1863 and 1798, respectively), on which the nation as a whole would repent its national sins and recognise its disconnection from the source of its blessings by remembering the God who had created it. The hoped-for outcome of national repentance would be, in Lincoln's words, "no less than the pardon of our national sins, and the restoration of our now divided and suffering country, to its former happy condition of unity and peace."[2]

Today Lincoln's call to repentance strikes us as completely out of place in the political realm, at least in the one we moderns believe we have established. Yet the apology is very much alive in contemporary politics. Far from being an aberrant antipodean moment, the Australian apology was indicative of an astonishing trend that emerged in the last fifteen years of the twentieth century. Whereas only twenty-five years ago the political apology had not even been on the menu of options political leaders considered for dealing with large-scale historical wrongs, from around the mid-1980s, we have seen a spate of apologies across the globe. They began with apologies from European countries for violations against the Jews during the Holocaust and then spread to apologies in a range of other contexts, from colonial and post-colonial nations for violations against Indigenous peoples, from nations for systematic abuses against part of their populations, from nations for their neglect or abuse of other nations and peoples. Some concerned atrocities in the remote or more distant past, others violations in the immediate past. Yet all defied the logic of liberalism's justice. Political realities, and the normative political principles that we have taken for granted, had, it seemed, parted company. By the turn of the century the aberrant apology had taken its place alongside trials, compensation, and truth commissions as one of the basic strategies in the toolkit of 'dealing with the past'.

This sudden and striking shift in modalities raises some fascinating puzzles. What is repentance doing in politics? How did it get there? What does it mean when we, as a collective, apologize for something that happened, often before

---

[2] The context of Lincoln's declaration was the Civil War. He suggests in this declaration that the "awful calamity of civil war, which now desolates the land, may be but a punishment inflicted upon us for our presumptuous sins, to the needful end of our national reformation as a whole People." Abraham Lincoln, "Proclamation Appointing a Fast Day," in Don E. Fehrenbacher, ed., *Lincoln: Speeches and Writings: 1859–1865* ([New York]: Library of America, 1989), 264–265.

many of us were alive? Strangely, these questions have received only scant conceptual analysis.[3] This is odd, given that contemporary social, legal, and political theorists have taken avidly to the study of other institutions for dealing with the past and transitional justice (trials, truth commissions, public memorials, and reparation schemes). Perhaps it is that we theorists too easily fall in with the populist verdict that apologies are nothing but 'mere words' (and probably ingenuous ones at that), and so we relegate them to the 'light' end of the spectrum of strategies for dealing with the past. Or perhaps it is our dogmatically held assumptions about the appropriate modes of modern liberal politics, on the one hand, and our assumptions about the type of act apology is, on the other, that force us to conclude that apology has no place in *our* public, secular political life. To the strict eyes of secular political theory, apology represents an aberrant contamination, one of those unfortunate moments when we lapsed back into primitive ritual, rather than reaching forward to more rational mechanisms of justice. If we theorize apology at all, we approach it as a reminder that the modernist project of rationalizing politics remains unfinished.

What if we are wrong, and in fact apology is a sign of late modern malaise, of our disappointment with the promises of a rationalized politics and indeed the inadequacy of our strongly held model of justice and politics itself? Looking up from the books and around the world, it is clearly premature to dismiss the political apology as a 'mere' or 'mistaken' apology. Indeed, I argue in this book that if we look beyond the confines of our preconceptions of the proper delimitations of modern liberal politics, we are likely to see a world far more enchanted by ritual and story telling and embedded with narratives of sin and redemption than our disciplines counsel us to believe. It is to this gap between our theoretical frameworks and what is actually happening in the world that this book invites us to train our eyes.

Starting here, then, what makes apology so tantalizing and puzzling is precisely that it represents such an unusual approach to 'doing politics'. First, rather than focusing on the individual wrongdoer, its currency is the responsible community; and second, in lieu of justice through individualized punishment or compensation, it suggests the path of repentance.

The first of these turns, from the responsible individual to the responsible community, points to a perennial tension in political theory, but in

---

[3] Nicholas Tavuchis' sociological study on apology remains the key text to which other writers refer when they wish to allude to a study of apology, despite the fact that Tavuchis' concern is almost exclusively the person-to-person apology. Nicholas Tavuchis, *Mea Culpa: A Sociology of Apology and Reconciliation* (Stanford: Stanford University Press, 1991). A notable exception, but approaching the issue in terms of forgiveness, not apology, is Donald Shriver Jr., *An Ethic for Enemies: Forgiveness in Politics* (New York: Oxford University Press, 1995).

contemporary international politics one with a very pressing relevance. In an era where nation after nation is facing its history of systematic, state-sponsored violations, and after the failure of one 'never again' after another, people are becoming increasingly dubious about the efficacy of our conceptions and institutions of justice. Indeed, when we face the systematic nature of the great atrocities of the last century, it is simply no longer viable to argue that responsibility falls entirely on the singular individuals who wielded the machetes or drove the children away. Saying this does not of course imply that we should do away with the institutions of individual justice. Punishing individual perpetrators remains a necessary condition for fully addressing systematic violations, and the expansion of the institutions for doing so at an international level was one of the great (though unfinished) achievements of the twentieth century. The point is rather that even after we have done with *this* justice, we are still left with the sense that the massive body of the society that condoned the violations (albeit perhaps silently) is there in the shadows.

Yet our institutions of justice and the principles they embody, and this intuition that a full justice must reach out to the broader collective, remain in tension. To put that more technically, modern liberal polities and theorists have still not found a way of institutionalizing or conceptualizing collective responsibility in a manner consistent with fundamental principles and institutions of individual liberty. Because contemporary political apologies mark a nod of acknowledgement towards collective responsibility, part of what this book does is theorize from the phenomenon out to suggest an alternative schema we might adopt to make sense of collective responsibility, while remaining faithful to our important commitments to moral individualism, commitments that liberal conceptions and institutions of responsibility are themselves designed to protect. Beyond this, we may need to revise the map we use to plot historical progress from collectivism to increasing individualism. At the turn of the millennium, we seem to be struggling towards a new way of conceptualizing and experiencing the relationship between the individual and the collective, one characterized by neither the gross collectivism we associate with pre-modernity nor the atomized individualism of modernity.

The second turn, from traditional liberal institutions and conceptions of justice to the dynamic of repentance, is more novel to political theory, but equally pressing, given the failure of existing modalities to make good on the promise that ending impunity would curtail crimes against humanity. Admittedly, a good part of the reason why criminal prosecution of individual perpetrators has failed to prevent repetition of crimes against humanity is that perpetrators are tried too rarely and too many still enjoy impunity, thus undermining the objective of general deterrence. But this is only part of the problem.

Even if comprehensively applied, trials would not deal with the whole pallet of responsibility, especially when what we are talking about are systematic, identity-based violations. By focusing on punishing individuals, these institutions of responsibility and justice leave relatively untouched the entrenched patterns of disrespect and misrecognition that underpin the violations that wrack societies and relations between nations.

The problem is, how do we address this level of responsibility? Clearly, punishing 'society' is both absurd and ethically prohibited. Rituals of repentance may strike us as an odd supplement to fill this gap, but if we cast a glance beyond the standard political modalities of the modern secular state to other types of collectives, what we will see is that rituals of collective repentance represent a well-worn strategy for addressing systematic wrongdoing and the normative orientations that underpin it. To be less circumspect, if one looks to the sphere of religion, and in particular the public, regulatory dimension of Judaism and Christianity, one finds that amongst the principal means for addressing systematic wrongdoing in the past was public, ritualized repentance.

This side-step to religious practices will no doubt raise eyebrows in many disciplines as well as important objections about the proper distinction between the appropriate modalities of liberal secular polities and those of religious communities. This book responds to these objections on several methodological and conceptual levels. This begins with a request that the reader suspend his or her preconceptions about 'how we do politics' (and where those rules place religion) so that we might analyze how we are actually doing politics with fresh eyes. And it ends with an invitation to reconceptualize contemporary politics in the light of the evidence. In between, I hope to convince the reader that religious conceptions and institutions of repentance are not adequately captured by caricatured perspectives that reduce them to the ridiculous artefacts of a pre-modern, primitive world, where people were ignorant of the mechanics of causality and insensitive to the moral imperatives of individual responsibility. Though no doubt tainted by religion's institutional abuses, these institutions of repentance speak to important truths about systematic wrongdoing, and we would do well to leave an ear open to them. Correlatively, I hope to show that our own institutions of political justice are harking towards those approaches that we banished into the realm of pre-modern religion.

Indeed, in her bird's-eye analysis of the human condition and the modalities of human sociality, Hannah Arendt characterized forgiveness, a form of action, the invention of which she (mis)attributed to Jesus Christ, as the sole human reaction that makes freedom from the past, and thus politics itself, possible.[4]

---

[4] Hannah Arendt, *The Human Condition* (Chicago: University of Chicago Press, 1958), 236.

While her direct reference was to forgiveness and not apology, Arendt's thesis suggests that this 'repentant mode' of action, apparently so anomalous in politics, might represent the desperately sought-after resource for getting beyond pasts filled with compulsive and entrenched cycles of horrific political and social abuse. Just as Aeschylus dramatized Athena's curtailing the endless cycles of revenge by assimilating the vengeful Furies into the civil institutions of justice, so too civic rituals of apology might put a break on the perpetual insults and injuries that drive collective violations.[5] For apology and forgiveness represent genuinely *new* action, the insertion of something that was neither previously present nor even derived from past action, but actually created, and thus uniquely potent. Of course, whether the appeal to this type of redemptive narrative is ultimately little more than a vain hope that flies in the face of our chronic propensity to abuse and exclude other human beings is another question.

Nevertheless, effective or not, sourcing our political institutions in the Bible is not quite so straightforward a move as sourcing them in Greek tragedy. Unlike the transition from vengeance to justice (which is in keeping with our view of political progress), the suggestion that repentance might constitute a unique and vital *political* strategy challenges the very definition of modern politics. It implies that political action is moving (and perhaps even should move) beyond the standard repertoire of legal and institutional interventions, into the realm of the repentant and the performative.

This suggestion provokes significant resistance on a number of fronts. First, because our imaginary landscape of repentance is dominated by a template of apology in its individual form (the apologizing friend or lover, the confession), we generally assume that apology requires a repenting subject with all the qualities of the reflective individual – a particular identity, a soul, an inner life. With this template implicitly in mind, collective political apologies cannot but strike us as aberrations. They treat the polity as an individual, and an individual

---

[5] The reference is to Aeschylus' third play in the Orestes cycle, *The Eumenides,* where he dramatizes Athena's intervention in the trial of Orestes, casting her deciding vote:

> And nevermore these walls within
> Shall echo fierce sedition's din
> Unslaked with blood and crime;
> The thirsty dust shall nevermore
> Suck up the darkly streaming gore,
> For civic broils, shed out in wrath
> And vengeance, crying death for death!

The Eumenides, trans. E.D.A. Morshead in *The Complete Greek Drama: All the Extant Tragedies of Aeschylus, Sophocles and Euripides, and the Comedies of Aristophanes and Menander, in a Variety of Translations,* vol. 1, ed. W. Oates and E. O'Neill Jr. (New York: Random House, 1938), 305.

in his or her most personal sense: one with an inner emotional dimension that might be transformed through reflection. The inevitable conclusion is that collective apologies are a type of category mistake – trying to match the wrong type of subject and predicate, failing to recognize the ontological difference between a collective and an individual, and failing to distinguish politics from personal relations. Indeed, if we continue to follow Arendt, we would have to say that the repentant mode not only rightly belongs with the individual, but in fact draws on that aspect of the individual's being that is the most 'anti-political' of all, the emotion of love.[6] Things get still worse when the image in the background is the penitent, alone and whispering into the darkened space of the confessional. One would be hard pressed to find a metaphor more remote from the ideal type of modern, rational, secular political behaviour.

Even more damning is the suggestion that our political apologies might be residues of religious collective repentance. Given that we moderns define our politics in self-conscious distinction from the pre-modern, undifferentiated theo-politics that modern liberal secularism displaced, in resuming the discourse of collective apology, it looks worryingly as if we are venturing into the most forbidden zone of all, the zone of pre-modern religion. Here, we imagine that the collective apology turns our entire political community into a mega-subject, within whose undifferentiated body the taint of sin spreads across our darkened bodies like the leprosy of biblical stories. If transposing an individual process onto a collective was a category mistake, the threat here is the far more dangerous one of reifying the collective and losing sight of one of the core principles of modernity, moral individualism.

Approached from either of these habitual frames of reference, the political apology must surely be a faux pas of contemporary politics, indicating either that people fail to understand that political communities cannot operate like individuals or, more dangerously, that they assume that they can, and then seek to regulate them through primitive collectivist rituals. And yet, here it is, in the sphere of contemporary liberal politics, and with a vengeance. This book proposes that we treat this disjuncture with neither consternation nor disapproval, but as a fascinating puzzle, an *aporia*, and an invitation to reconsider the categories that would lead us to predict that it should not be so.

For analytic purposes, we can think of this puzzle as having two parts. On one side lies the empirical data: contemporary polities are apologizing. On the

---

[6] "[O]nly love has the power to forgive. ... [And] love, by its very nature is unworldly and it is for this reason, rather than its rarity that it is not only apolitical, but anti-political, perhaps the most powerful of all anti-political forces." Arendt, *The Human Condition*, 242. Arendt's analysis here follows from her particular understanding of religion as entailing fundamentally otherworldly commitments, the result of her reading religion through Augustine.

other side lie our standard characterizations of justice and politics in late liberal modernity. As we currently see things, the two cannot be pieced together. End of story. I suggest that we approach this failed equation by turning that argument on its head. Rather than assume the validity of the dichotomies that divide our conceptual map into distinct and completely bounded worlds of action and meaning (e.g., religion vs. politics, ritual performance vs. administrative law, crude collectivism vs. moral individualism) and then reject the apology as an inappropriate mode of modern politics, why not look at the practices themselves, as free as possible of presumed classification? No doubt, this poses a challenge to the secular and bureaucratic self-image and trappings of modern politics and to the dichotomies noted above. But why should the modalities of politics be immune to historical transformation now, as they have been in the past? Contemporary political theory would do well to allow that these 'alien' processes can and do partner with modern liberal political institutions and to expand our conception of 'the political' accordingly.

To get to these larger reflections of the character of contemporary politics, however, we need to start with a thorough understanding of what the apology is actually doing. The first and major question this book poses is, then, What is it that we are doing when we apologize collectively?

Methodologically, I pursue this question through a combination of lenses. First, and most traditionally, I consider apologies as speech acts, and use the verbal formulations of contemporary apologies to explore what we are doing *in* and *by* apologizing. Second, and more heretically, I look for the understandings and institutions of collective repentance in Judaism and early Christianity. Third, I analyze the dynamics of contemporary political apologies themselves, focusing in detail on the apology for the forced removal of Indigenous children in Australia.

My using religious practices and understandings to derive the interpretive tropes of contemporary apologies is likely to strike many readers as contentious, not only because methodologically it veers beyond the realm of disciplinary theorizing, but because I might seem to be begging the very questions that are at issue here – the relationship between the spheres of religion and politics, and the problem of a religious practice 'migrating' into secular liberal politics. Certainly, this part of the argument involves a bold assertion. Nevertheless, if we look within the sphere of secular politics itself, we simply will not find the historical roots or the background grammar for apology. By contrast, in the sphere of religion we find those missing tropes and the grammars we need to decode the contemporary practice.

At the same time, I would throw a question back to those who object *prima facie* to practices moving between the spheres of religion and politics. What is it precisely to which they object? The point of this question is not to suggest that the differences are irrelevant or that we might simply go back to theo-politics with no cost. It is rather to insist that we pinpoint the problematic dimensions of religious practices. With these in hand, we can assess with greater accuracy whether what is coming across with the apology are dynamics or commitments we should be worrying about. To my mind, two obvious features of religious practice stand out as antithetical to liberal democratic politics: religions' commitment to the Absolute, or a set of transcendent principles beyond the reach of actual living and changing people, and the thick, unchanging, and particularistic character of the norms that lie at the heart of many religions.[7] By our lights, both of these are completely incompatible with both the democratic idea that political communities must be the source of their own norms and must be permitted to change those norms, and the liberal idea that those norms should be as thin and as inclusive as possible.

Coming back to the religious apology, the question then becomes, Does importing the apologetic form entail importing the substantive moral commitments that traditionally defined sin and the orientation of repentance for religious communities? In other words, is it possible to abstract the *form* of religious apology (understood as a means of addressing what is wrong with our normative commitments) from the *substance* of those commitments? I argue here that it is, and indeed that this formal work of normative reconstitution speaks powerfully to the concerns of contemporary polities. At the same time, religious apologies' orientation around the absolute has not fallen away entirely in the contemporary practice. Now, however, we do not call it God, but rather international law, or peremptory norms, or even the constitution.

In this sense, my return to religious contexts is in the manner of Walter Benjamin's model of the collector, who picks up the fragments of the past that lie broken around his feet to make sense of the present.[8] Though connected with their past, in their present incarnation, these fragments of apology would no longer be thoroughly embedded in the meta-narratives of their original location. They have undergone a sea-change, to become something rich and strange.[9]

---

[7] Whether thick norms lie at the heart of certain religions or whether the regulative dimension of religions is a superstructure subsequent to the initial revelation is itself a contestable point and will be taken up in Chapter Three.

[8] Walter Benjamin, *The Arcades Project*, trans. H. Eiland and K. McLaughlin, prepared on the basis of the German volume edited by Rolf Tiedemann (Cambridge, Mass.: Belknap Press, 1999).

[9] In her introduction to Benjamin's *Illuminations*, Arendt quotes from Shakespeare's *The Tempest* (2,1) to convey Benjamin's notion of the relationship between modernity and tradition. See Hannah Arendt, introduction to *Illuminations*, by Walter Benjamin (New York: Schocken Books, 1969), 38.

That said, it would be naïve to suggest that apology, now transposed onto the political stage, has simply taken on the clothes of thin proceduralism and shed the clothes of redemption. People who believe in a redemptive narrative (dare I say 'have faith' in it) are likely to see our turn to a politics of repentance as the sign of an authentic recognition that we cannot get beyond our pasts of entrenched abuse unless we acknowledge the deep roots of abuse in our collective moral orientations and commit with our hearts as well as our minds to a constitutional reorientation. But if one stands outside it, with a more than justified cynicism, this looks like just another attempt to convince ourselves that we really might be good after all. Indeed, perhaps we are not turning to repentance because we rightly recognize it as the missing link in our transformation, but because we still ache to see ourselves as redeemable at the end of a century where the evidence of atrocity so damns us. Perhaps what provoked this aporaic emergence of repentance is our need to affirm that there is indeed a seed of goodness at the core of our moral constitution, or at least a sheltering oak of goodness at the end of our moral progress. And then again, perhaps it is the hope that this is possible that would make it so.

In the face of these two interpretations, I confess to my own deep ambivalence. In presenting the story to the reader, I would rather leave the decision about which is correct up to you.

CHAPTER PLAN

The book is arranged into four parts, each comprising two chapters. The first three parts (Chapters One to Six) constitute the three lenses for decoding the apology. Thus Chapters One and Two focus on the actual forms of speech of apology, Chapters Three and Four on apologies in the context of religious practice, and Chapters Five and Six on the case of the Australian apology. The final part, Chapters Seven and Eight, then draws on the understanding of the political apology derived from these foundational chapters to pursue the questions about the nature of wrongdoing, responsibility, justice, and politics that apology's political appearance raises.

Chapter One provides the primary data for the whole study, surveying a range of contemporary political apologies, but focusing in particular on the forms of words. It takes the reader through the different types of apologies, including historical and transitional apologies. Chapter Two then considers apologies as speech acts, tracking the linguistic forms set out in Chapter One to derive an Austinian understanding of what we might be doing when we apologize. Using Austin somewhat against himself, I argue that apologies do not (or do not only) express emotion (as 'behabitives') but rather commit the speaking subject to a certain form of action or identity (as 'commissives').[10] In this sense, and again somewhat counterintuitively, they are not simply responses to the past, but importantly, performative orientations to the future, establishing who we will be from here on as a political community.

In Chapter Three, I look in some detail at the stories, texts, institutions, and conceptualizations of repentance in Judaism. The specific concerns of this chapter are to flesh out the distinct trope of the collective apology and decode the type of work it is supposed to do. In particular, I am interested in how this form of action linked the collective with particular acts of wrongdoing, and how the tradition understands the transformative work done by collective repentance. This chapter also looks in some detail at the relationship between repentance directed to the Absolute (God) and wrongdoing between particular human beings, and probes why the former might be relevant in addressing the latter. It also presses some of the standard views of pre-modern religion and the sharp line we draw between it and highly differentiated modern political communities to suggest that the differences we tend to highlight should not blind us to the perennial complexities of the relationship between the individual and the community.

Chapter Four turns to Christianity, beginning with a brief treatment of the early forms of public and collective apology in Christian practice, more or less continuous with the Jewish origins. The key concern of this chapter, however, is the historical shift to the private, individual practice that we now assume has always been apology's essential form (albeit covered over by pre-modern ignorance). In this chapter, I am specifically interested in how the collective form went underground and how it came to be displaced by individual, private apologies in Catholic dogma. The last part of the chapter then turns to the rediscovery of the collective form during the twentieth century and its resumption as official practice in the early 1970s, (intriguingly) shortly before the collective apology was taken up in the political sphere.

Chapters Five and Six then turn back to the contemporary world to examine in detail the apology movement in Australia. Chapter Five locates the particular apology debate and the violation that was its subject against the background issues of race, identity, and the political constitution of the nation to show how dealing with specific injustices against Indigenous Australians evoked and thus required reference to broader questions of political identity and constitution. Chapter Six draws on the arguments raised by proponents and opponents of the apology in the Australian debate to analyze how contemporary actors make

[10] J. L. Austin, *How to Do Things with Words* (Cambridge, Mass.: Harvard University Press, 1962).

sense of apology as a type of political act. Here, we see that while some assumed the individual model of apology, others in fact understood apology as a form of collective commitment, or as a collective statement about the type of political community Australia was committing itself to be. Again, this maps powerfully onto the themes derived using the previous two lenses. Indeed, reading the apology as a form of normative reconstitution (as derived in Chapters Two and Three) allows one to make sense of the explosion of the apology phenomenon in Australia. By contrast, if one insists on seeing apology as a form of individual repentance writ large, it is difficult to understand why it took hold so strongly and captured the popular imagination.

The final two chapters consider how we might need to retheorize contemporary theories and institutions of justice and politics in the light of the findings of the previous six chapters. Chapter Seven looks specifically at conceptions of justice and responsibility and develops a conceptualization of responsibility that takes into account the collective dimension evident in the contemporary apology, while remaining faithful to principles of moral individualism and continuing to protect people from unjust blame. I suggest that in insisting that we attach responsibility to *actions*, liberal jurisprudence has impeded an understanding of (or institutional response to) the role that collectives play in constituting and sustaining the norms that underpin action. Using the empirical material of the Australian case study, this chapter suggests a two-track theory of responsibility, which allows both for individual attribution at the level of action and collective attribution at the level of normative constitution. Building on Jaspers' inventory of guilt, developed in the wake of Nazism, it suggests that we can understand apology as a gesture towards institutionalizing this second dimension of responsibility.

Finally, Chapter Eight aligns and looks back through the different lenses to take up both practical and policy-oriented questions and more abstract questions about the nature of the political sphere. I ask what a successful apology would look like and under what circumstances an apology would be most suitable and potent. More abstractly, I return to the questions raised in this Introduction about the relationship between politics and other spheres of life. Engaging with the range of objections raised throughout the book, I ask whether apologetic discourse ultimately erodes liberal democratic politics or whether it may be compatible with contemporary forms and core liberal principles – or even be a much-needed supplement to them.

Before entering this journey, lest there be any doubt about the overall message of this book, I want to make perfectly clear that I do not see apology as in any way approaching a sufficient response to gross violations of human rights. It would be worse than an insult to suggest that people who have been tortured, parents whose children have been 'disappeared', or the lonely survivors of a genocide might be satisfied with an apology. Their suffering immeasurably exceeds the reach of this response and most likely of any response. In fact, only if we recognize how far beyond apology's reach their violation and experience go can we begin to consider, with integrity and accuracy, apology's work.

I

The Apology Phenomenon

What exactly falls within this class of acts I have called the 'political apology'? As with any family of speech acts, especially a relatively novel one, the boundaries are nowhere clearly set out, so this chapter answers that question empirically by describing a range of apologies from the last twenty years.[1] From this survey, one can appreciate not only the international scope and contagious quality of the trend, but also the linguistic fabric of different apologies, and how the actors who delivered them elaborated the significance of their act.

At a very general level, the apologies included here meet three broad criteria. First, they involve a form of words belonging to the family of apologetic speech acts, which includes, *inter alia*, saying sorry, expressing regret, and asking for forgiveness. As we shall see, this internal linguistic variation is indicative of different meanings, and indeed certain forms of speech may sit at the boundary of the family of acts, implying membership, but not fully or successfully doing the work of apology. Second, they are representative, collective, and public: a leader gives the apology in public on behalf of a collective for which he or she is authorized to speak. This also means that the apology has as its referent a collective that is identified as the victim of the wrong in question.[2] Third, apologies are *political*, meaning that the collective on behalf of which they are given is a political entity, generally a state, but in some instances a sub-state political group, or group that was acting on behalf of the state, or an international entity, or group of states. As we shall see, they are also political in the sense that the political identity of the apologizing collective is tied up with the wrongs for

[1] For another recent survey of official apologies, see Melissa Nobles, *The Politics of Official Apologies* (New York: Cambridge University Press, 2008).
[2] I am not concerned with apologies concerning discrete individual wrongs – for example, the type one sees frequently in defamation cases.

14

which the apology is being given, but this is not itself a criterion for an act to count as a political apology. Finally, they all concern a significant public wrong or wrongs committed against members of a specific group in the past.

In formal terms, the different instances of apology are all variants on the basic structural form: a speaker assumes the role of the one giving the apology, speaking in a representative capacity, and addresses the party to whom the apology is rhetorically directed. The apologies are all articulated (or at least called for) at a public level, and both the 'apologizer' and 'apologizee' are collective subjects. At the same time, they differ along a number of dimensions, including the nature of the wrong, the time lapse between the wrong and the apology, the boundaries of and relationship between the apologizing and victim communities (domestic/international), and the status of the speaker articulating the apology. Notably, the temporal variation means that in some cases the direct perpetrators and direct victims are still alive, while in others they are not. The significance of apologies in the political landscape of the country in question also varies tremendously. Some apologies speak to issues that are very much alive in terms of the stabilization and constitution of the contemporary polity; others raise issues that are apparently of concern only to a minority. In some cases they have deeply engaged the broader community, provoking strong allegiances or oppositions; in others they have been relatively unnoticed sideshows.

For the purposes of organizing the empirical material, I use the dimension of time to classify the apologies into two large groups: first, *inter-temporal* or *historical apologies* dealing with wrongs that occurred in the more remote past, and second, *transitional apologies* dealing with wrongs in the immediate past. Interestingly, although it is more difficult to explain the continuity of agency or basis of responsibility in the case of inter-temporal apologies, it is into the first group that the vast majority of apologies actually fall. This in itself provides a hint about what it is that apology, as distinct from other reparative acts, contributes to the work of dealing with the past.

Notably absent here is any treatment of the apology debate in Japan, both concerning Japanese military aggression and its colonial legacy in Asia from 1910 to 1945 and the issue of so-called comfort women, or war sex slaves. These are excluded because my interpretive methodology rests so heavily on a cultural background rooted in Jewish and Christian rituals, stories, and codes of meaning, which one cannot assume are as applicable in the Japanese context, where norms around honour, for example, are far more significant. This does not mean that the analysis has no application to the Japanese case, but understanding it would require specific attention to the significance of apology in its own cultural context.

I. INTER-TEMPORAL APOLOGIES

Within the first inter-temporal group, I differentiate those apologies concerned with the wrongs committed against Jews during World War II and those concerning wrongs in other contexts.[3] This distinction does not imply a qualitative difference, but rather evidences the historical genealogy typical in the field of institutions for dealing with gross violations of human rights. As in the case of trials for war crimes, public memorials, and reparation schemes, the institutions developed in response to the crimes of Nazism (the Nuremberg trials, German/Jewish reparation schemes, Holocaust memorials) have provided the templates for later institutional developments.[4]

(i) Holocaust Apologies

Post–World War II Germany is often held up as the template for the modern movement of remorse.[5] Indeed, the trajectory from the West German state's reaction immediately following the War to its stance at the end of the twentieth century provides a poignant map of the extent of the shift in the rhetoric of regret. When, in the Bundestag in 1952, a German leader (Chancellor Konrad Adenauer) gave the first official statement of the "attitudes of the Federal Republic towards the Jews", he went only so far as saying that crimes had been committed *in the name of* the German people. In other words, he did not place the German people in the position of being the *active and responsible* subject of those crimes, nor did he express any remorse.[6] The first initiative towards a more repentant 'reconciliation' came from outside government, in a 1965 memorandum from the German Evangelical Church, and then it was dealing with German-Polish not German-Jewish relations. The letter suggested that healing between the Polish and German nations could not be left

---

[3] It is notable that almost all apologies concerning Nazism deal exclusively with violations against Jews. There has been an apology to homosexual victims, but not to other victim groups. Only now at the time of writing is the question of Romani victims gaining a public profile with the emergence of a group action compensation case.

[4] The reference back to the apology is rarely explicit, although in some cases it is. See discussion of the Algerian call for an apology from France below.

[5] See, for example, Peter Novick, *The Holocaust in American Life* (Boston: Houghton Miflin, 1993). As Jeffrey Herf points out, there were in fact two German states. See *Divided Memory: The Nazi Past in the Two Germanys* (Cambridge, Mass.: Harvard University Press, 1997). Overlooking this complexity, the trajectory I draw is from West to Unified Germany.

[6] Frank Stern, *The Whitewashing of the Yellow Badge: Anti-Semitism and Philosemitism in Postwar Germany*, trans. William Templer (Oxford: Pergamon Press, 1992).

to politicians, but rather had to occur between the two societies.[7] One month later, the Polish bishops responded in a letter to West German church leaders: "We extend a hand to you, granting you forgiveness, and asking you for forgiveness."[8]

It took a full twenty years after Adenauer's first tentative statement until a German political leader took the repentant position – and then quite literally. Visiting the Warsaw Ghetto for the first time in 1970, Chancellor Willy Brandt spontaneously went down on his knees before the Memorial to the Victims of Nazi Oppression. His body, though not his words, gestured repentance.[9] Years later, in his memoirs, Brandt commented that he did what people do when speech fails and (again in place of his own words) quoted a newspaper report filed at the time: "Then he knelt, he who had no need so to do, for all those who should have knelt, but did not do so – either because they did not dare to, or could not, or could not dare to."[10] Apologies' internal reference to their own insufficiency, to the unredeemable remainder beyond their reach, is, as we shall see, a common characteristic of political apologies.

The *kniefall,* as it came to be known, was photographed and reproduced all over the world. Perhaps because it represented such a rupture of expectations and stereotypes – the man of power on his knees, the German leader bowed below the memory of the murdered Jews – this symbolic act broke from the sphere of quarantined symbolic performance or personal action and into practical political relations. As one commentator put it, "morality became a political force."[11] Indeed, according to some, the *kniefall,* the simple gesture of repentance, was

---

[7] One sees here the confusion in the appropriate definition or nomination of the entity represented in the apology. I referred above to political apologies involving states as collectives, but the reference here is to nations. The distinction between society and the politicians, however, indicates that in this framing the state and society are seen as two different channels or representatives of the nation.

[8] Norman Davies, *God's Playground: A History of Poland,* vol. 2: *1795 to the Present* (Oxford: Clarendon Press, 1981), 591–3. The interchange did not actually include an apology, which one might suppose should precede forgiveness. This is indicative of the Christian theology from which it emerges.

[9] See Ruti Teitel, "The Transitional Apology," in *Taking Wrongs Seriously: Apologies and Reconciliation,* ed. Elezar Barkan and Alexander Karn (Stanford: Stanford University Press, 2006), 101–14.

[10] Willie Brandt, *My Life* (New York: Viking, 1992), 200.

[11] Peter Bender, *Die Neue Ostpolitik und ihre Folgen. Vom Mauerbau bis zur Vereinigung,* 4th revised ed. (Munich: Deutsche Taschenbuch Verlag, 1996), 182.

not only a turning point in the transformation of German-Polish relations after the War,[12] but a catalyst in reshaping Eastern European politics more generally.[13]

Interestingly, although it is Germany that has, more than any other country, memorialized the Holocaust and paid extensive restitution schemes, it was only in late 1999 that German President Johannes Rau *spoke* the words of apology in a private ceremony marking an agreement on compensation for victims of Nazi forced labour: "I pay tribute to all those who were subjected to slave and forced labour under German rule and, in the name of the German people, beg forgiveness."[14] A month later, at the dedication of the Holocaust memorial in Berlin, Elie Wiesel (himself a symbol of the Jewish Holocaust experience) called on the German Parliament to pass a resolution formally requesting the forgiveness of the Jewish people for the crimes of Hitler. Note the temporality of Wiesel's linguistic formulation: "Do it publicly," he urged, "ask the Jewish people to forgive Germany for what the Third Reich had done in Germany's name. Do it, and the significance of this day will acquire a higher level. Do it, for we desperately want to have hope for this new century."[15] In Wiesel's eyes, the apology was clearly not simply a response to something that occurred in the *past*, but an act that transforms a political relationship into the *future*.

A month later, the German Rau did in fact apologize in an address to the Israeli Knesset (parliament), actively picking up on Wiesel's trajectory into the future: "I ask forgiveness for what the Germans had done, in the name of myself and my generation, and for the sake of our children and grandchildren, whom I'd like to see intertwined with the children of Israel."[16] Using language reminiscent of Brandt's bodily action thirty years earlier, Rau said that he bowed his head in humility before those murdered in the Holocaust during World War II.[17] In just a little under fifty years, the language had shifted from gingerly linking

---

[12] See Adrian Hyde Price, *Building a Stable Peace in Mitteleuropa: The German Polish Hinge* (Birmingham: University of Birmingham Institute for German Studies Discussion Paper, 2000/18), 8.

[13] "[A]fter forty years, the whole rationale of the Soviet Alliance is beginning to fall apart. The key event I think was in 1970, when Willy Brandt went to Warsaw. The sight of a German leader, kneeling in expiation for the crimes of the wartime period, is a sight which no Pole, I think, would ever forget." Norman Davies quoted in Michael Charlton, *The Eagle and the Small Birds: Crisis in the Soviet Empire, from Yalta to Solidarity* (Chicago: University of Chicago Press, 1985), 145.

[14] Johannes Rau quoted in Burt Herman, "Germany Officially Offers Nazi Labor Compensation; Seeks Forgiveness," Associated Press, 18 December 1999.

[15] Wiesel quoted in Roger Cohen, "Wiesel Urges Germany to Ask Forgiveness," *New York Times*, 28 January 2000.

[16] Note here that the victim community is now made synonymous with the state of Israel. This interchange is admittedly in part grounded in the ambiguous status of 'Israel' as people and state, but also evidences the shifting status of the victim community.

[17] "German President Apologizes to Knesset," IPR Strategic Information Database, 20 February 2000. IPR Strategic Information Database: http://www.infoprod.co.il/ (accessed 27 April 2008).

Germany and the Holocaust via the name of the German people to identifying the German people as themselves responsible for the Holocaust and locating them in the aspect of repentance.

In December 2000, the Bundestag also apologized to gays for persecution under a Nazi-era sodomy law: "Parliament is convinced that the honour of the homosexual victims of Nazism must be rebuilt and apologizes for the harm done to homosexual citizens up to 1969 in their human dignity, their coming out and their quality of life."[18] In this case, the wording of the apology does not make its future orientation explicit, but if one keeps in mind the fact that the vast majority of the direct victims of those laws (repealed thirty-one years earlier) were no longer alive, one can see that the apology also has contemporary (and future) German homosexuals in its sight. This is of course not because past laws could compromise the rights of gays today, but rather because a state that remains silent on its past violations of gays as a group leaves ambiguous the status of this group in contemporary political life. Correlatively, its condemnation of past violations affirms that it now recognizes homosexuals as rights-bearing citizens.

The political apology's strange temporality is also evident in the apologies that other European states began to offer for their complicity with Nazism almost exactly half a century after the end of the war. Apologizing for his country's role in the Holocaust was in fact amongst Austrian President Thomas Klestil's opening speech acts when, in November 1994, he made the first official visit by an Austrian head of state to Israel. Addressing the Knesset, he invoked the imagery of the *kniefall* and pointed to the unspeakable remainder we have already encountered: "No word of apology can ever expunge the agony of the Holocaust. . . . On behalf of the Republic of Austria, I bow my head with deep respect and profound emotion in front of the victims."[19] Again, as in Weisel's formulation, the apology for the past was linked here with establishing a sound political relationship into the future.[20]

That future orientation was even more pronounced, and generalized beyond relations with Israel, in Austrian Chancellor Viktor Klima's subsequent apology at the Stockholm International Forum on the Holocaust in January 2000. Uncommonly explicit about apology's purpose, Klima stated: "The aim has to be

---

[18] See Agence France-Presse, "Bundestag Apologizes to Homosexual Victims of Nazis," 8 December 2000.

[19] President Klestil's speech to the Knesset quoted in Karin Laub, "Austrian President: No Apology Can Expunge Agony of Holocaust," Associated Press, 15 November 1994.

[20] Eight years later, in April 2002 Klestil made a more specific apology for the experimentation on mentally ill and handicapped children during WWII. His apology took place during the ceremonial return of the final remains of the 789 deformed or mentally handicapped children who were used for medical experiments and murdered at the children's clinic Am Spiegelgrund.

to clear up the facts without reservation, to reveal the structures of injustice and to pass on this knowledge to coming generations as a warning for the future."[21] The Chancellor's condemnation of the Holocaust as "one of the most monstrous crimes in the whole history of mankind" was, however, no pure deontological statement about ethics but a purposeful performance of his ethical capacities, as he also made explicit when he went on to say that "[a]nyone who does not say this clearly and unambiguously is unsuitable to be entrusted with any responsible public position, either national or international." Given that at the time of his apology, neo-Nazi movements were posing a significant threat to Austria's bid to become a fully fledged member of the European Union, one can surmise that the audience of this performance of repentance and moral condemnation was not, as one might think, the Jewish victims or their children, but other European states, even if they remain unnamed in the dramatic script. Indeed, he said as much openly: "One of the standards by which the next Austrian federal government will be judged internationally is how sensitively and fittingly it addresses these difficult and painful questions of Austria's Nazi past."[22]

When, also as one of his first gestures as President (July 1995), Jacques Chirac of France apologized for the wrongs of the Holocaust, he similarly emphasized the connection between an apologetic stance and the moral-political status of the apologizing nation. In this case, however, France, rather than the rest of Europe, seemed to be its own audience. Like Klestil, Chirac framed his apology by pointing immediately to what lay beyond its reach, acknowledging that his repentant assumption of responsibility only gestured towards a "debt which can never be repaid."[23] Even then, attending closely to what he actually said in his apology, one might well wonder whether paying a debt was what he was doing at all. In one move, Chirac certainly acknowledged the wrong and France's responsibility ("on that day [France] committed the irreparable"), but in the very next, he insisted that in this moment of violation, France had strayed from its true identity as "the homeland of the Enlightenment and the rights of man, a land of welcome and asylum." In a single gesture, he was both assuming the identity of the wrongdoer and distancing himself (that is, his nation) from that identity, in this case not only by condemning a moment in its past self, but also emphasizing that this moment (the Vichy period) was an aberration in French history and

---

[21] As we see in many apologies, Klima explicitly connects the apology with the heart, saying: "And when I now pause in my speech for a few heartbeats, every heartbeat stands for tens of thousands, hundreds of thousands, millions of murdered human beings, fathers, mothers, children." Address given by President Viktor Klima at the Forum on the Holocaust in Stockholm. Available online at: http://www.manskligarattigheter.gov.se/stockholmforum/2000/page955.html.

[22] Ibid.

[23] Editorial, "Mr. Chirac Honors the Truth," *New York Times*, 18 July 1995.

identity. Thus, when he said that "those dark hours dishonor our history forever and are an insult to our past and our traditions", he was effectively realigning contemporary France with those traditions, moving through the assumption of guilt to redemption, a type of return to what France essentially *is*.

Analytically, Chirac's apology is particularly useful because it so clearly illustrates the structural contradiction of every apology. Like his Austrian political counterpart, even as Chirac acknowledged the historical nation's wrong, he redeemed the contemporary nation. In fact *through* acknowledging the historical nation's wrong, he reasserted the essential, true identity of France as the homeland of enlightenment, leaving the ideal self of France firmly intact, perhaps even shoring it up in the face of threat. Even as it is formally addressed to the Jewish victims, the apology speaks far more to France and to the damage *it* has suffered because of these wrongs than to Jews. Once again, despite being the apology's nominal subject of concern, it was not the addressee of the apology (the victim) that occupied the most prominent place in the apologetic gesture, but the national identity of the *apologizing nation*. We should hold this in mind when we come back to ask who the main addressee of the apology is and to locate the site at which it does its most important work.

The French state apology was followed by two sub-state apologies, of interest principally because of how the apologizing group used the apology to redefine its commitments and identity. In the first case, the French Bishops' association issued a statement on 30 September 1997 (the fifty-seventh anniversary of the passage of the first anti-Semitic ordinance by the Vichy government) repenting the Church's official inaction regarding the plight of Jews. The statement, read at Drancy, the holding camp from which thousands of Jews had been deported, said, "The time has come for the church to submit its own history, during this period in particular, to a critical reading, without hesitating to acknowledge the sins committed by its sons and to ask forgiveness from God and from men. . . . Today we confess that silence was a mistake. We beg God's forgiveness and ask the Jewish people to hear our words of repentance."[24] Note here how silence is framed as itself a form of wrongdoing, and apology, the active speech intervention, as a return to a baseline of right.

The following week, the National Union of Uniformed Police apologized for the active role police had played in the deportation of 76,000 Jews from France during the War.[25] Their statement read, "[S]ince then, we policemen have borne

---

[24] World Jewish Congress, "Vichy France and the Jews: After Fifty Years, Regrets Emerge," online at Policy Dispatches, No. 20, October 1997. Note that in this apology, it is God who is the addressee of the call for forgiveness, with Jews themselves accorded the role of witnesses.

[25] The deportations began with the infamous 16 July 1942 'Vel d'Hiv swoop' in which 13,000 Jews were rounded up at a Paris indoor cycling stadium before being placed on trains.

an extremely heavy burden which we must shed without ever forgetting that it existed"[26] and they asked "pardon for those who forgot that *before being police, they were men* . . . pardon for those who said 'I was obeying orders.' "[27] Both here and in the clerical apology one sees a structural shift slightly different from that of Chirac's apology. In these cases, it is not so much a shift from an aberrant moment and back to an essential identity, but rather a renunciation of a prior claim to some special status, literally a uniform, which had rendered the perpetrators immune to criminal prosecution, but not to moral blame. The apology works by stripping away the layers of excusatory identity that had shielded them from fully bearing responsibility as humans who failed to recognize right.[28] In this, they are reminiscent of the classical religious image of the penitent laying himself naked before God, now humble and stripped of all earthly protection.[29]

In May 2001, Polish Bishops apologized for the role of the Church in the persecution and genocide perpetrated against Jews, and in particular for the role of Poles and Catholics in the massacre at Jedwabne, exposed in Jan Gross's *Neighbors*.[30] As part of a requiem service and dressed in black cassocks, the bishops gathered as the Archbishop spoke their collective apology: "[T]he victims of this crime were Jews, while the perpetrators included Poles and Catholics, people who had been baptized", he declared, thus shifting a discourse in which both Poles and Catholics had absented themselves from responsibility. "We grieve deeply at the wrongs committed by those who through the ages, especially in Jedwabne and elsewhere, caused the Jews to suffer and even brought about their deaths." He continued, once again drawing orientations for the present from their reflections on the past: "We also refer to that crime with the intention that we may be able effectively to assume the responsibility for overcoming all evil present in the world today. The effort for the sake of 'cleansing the memory' turns for us into the difficult task of

---

[26] Andre Lenfant, head of the National Union of Uniformed Police Officers (SNPT), reported in Reuters, "French Police Apologize for Jewish Wartime Swoops," 7 October 1997.

[27] Letter of apology by union leader Christophe Gros, reported in "Trial to Revisit French Role in Holocaust," CNN News Online, 7 October 1997. http://www.cnn.com/WORLD/9710/07/papon.trial/(accessed 11 June 2008).

[28] One sees here the distinction between the criteria for criminal guilt, which may be mitigated by excuse or justification, and moral blame, which remains even where such defenses can be brought. This distinction was clarified and articulated by Karl Jaspers in his famous book on collective guilt, *The Question of German Guilt*, trans. E. B. Ashton (New York: Fordham University Press, 2001). I take this up in detail in Chapters Six and Seven.

[29] In the story of David, the first person in the Old Testament to repent, the fact that he was a King and yet repented was particularly important.

[30] Jan T. Gross, *Neighbors: The Destruction of the Jewish Community in Jedwabne, Poland* (Princeton, N.J.: Princeton University Press, 2000).

'cleansing the conscience'. We undertake this task and once more condemn all manifestations of intolerance, racism and anti-Semitism as ungodly."[31]

A month after the church's apology, Polish President Alexander Kwasniewski went to Jedwabne to deliver his own highly publicized and controversial apology: "For this crime we should beg the souls of the dead and their families for forgiveness. . . . This is why today, as a citizen and as the president of the Republic of Poland, I beg pardon. I beg pardon in my own name, and in the name of those Poles whose conscience is shattered by that crime."[32] Again, notice the direction of his attention. As in Chirac's juxtaposition of the essential French commitment to 'the right' and the dishonour of France's lapse at Vichy, here too, it is the Poles who have been damaged by the crime, or perhaps more specifically, it is their sense of themselves as a moral nation that has been damaged. The apology frames the scene in such a way that not only Jews, but also Poles become the injured party and in need of repair/restoration, which is effected here by reshaping the narrative relationship with the Jewish victim. As in the bishops' apology, restoring the integrity and the conscience of the apologizing subject, rather than addressing the injury of the victim, is the principal object of the apology.

Even then, or perhaps especially then because what was at issue was the identity of Poland itself, the presidential apology was highly contentious, with polls indicating that it had the support of only half the population. Critics to the President's political right accused him of "trying to curry favour with Israel and Jewish circles in the West."[33] Meanwhile Cardinal Jozef Glemp, Poland's most senior churchman, opposed the apology by reiterating a traditional Polish accusation that Jews had collaborated with the Soviet occupiers and suggested that they should be the ones giving an apology to the Poles.[34] Beyond these rhetorical displays, the dramatic tension of the apology was heightened when people living in the town where it was delivered made their own symbolic statement, darkening their windows and visibly boycotting the apology ceremony. For the 50 percent of Poles who opposed the apology, Poland's moral identity was not, it seemed, to be placed in question by the years of the Holocaust.

Picking up on this issue of collaboration and the true history or identity of the nation, Croatian President Stipe Mesic initially offered a heavily qualified apology that unmistakably drew a line between the real Croatia (including contemporary Croatia) and the fascist state that ruled its territory between

---

[31] Marcin Mierzejewski, "A Bishop's Apology," *The Warsaw Voice*, 3 June 2001.

[32] "Poland Apologizes to Jews," BBC Online, 10 July 2001. http://news.bbc.co.uk/2/hi/europe/1431339.stm (accessed 18 July 2008).

[33] Ibid.

[34] Jan Repa, "Analysis: Poland Divided on Massacre," BBC Online, 10 July 2001. http://news.bbc.co.uk/2/hi/europe/1431753.stm (accessed 10 June 2008).

1941 and 1945. Thus, when he first apologized before the Israeli Knesset in October 2001, he spoke not in the name of the state that had committed the crimes but rather at one step removed: "I profoundly and sincerely deplore the crimes committed against the Jews in the area controlled during the Second World War by the collaborationist regime which, unfortunately, carried the Croatian name."[35] After it was pointed out to him that Israel expected a fuller apology, he joined these two Croatias, as Chirac had joined Vichy and France, and said to the Knesset: "I take every opportunity to ask forgiveness from those who were hurt by Croatians any time and any place, but first of all from the Jews." Once again, one sees the double move of the apology. By assuming responsibility for the wrong, apology alters the traditional national narrative so as to integrate the previously excluded moment of wrongdoing into a continuous national narrative; but, in identifying the contemporary nation as one that embraces rightful norms (and thus must condemn such wrongdoing), it transforms it into a redemptive narrative.

More than fifty years after the end of World War II a number of other European countries, including Switzerland,[36] Belgium,[37] and Finland,[38] apologized for Holocaust atrocities. Moving beyond the European continent, in June 2000, President Fernando de la Rua of Argentina also apologized for his country's role in providing sanctuary to Nazis after World War II.[39]

---

[35] President Mesic's speech to the Israeli Knesset quoted in Miriam Shaviv, "Croatian President Mesic Apologizes to Jews from Knesset Podium," *Jerusalem Post*, 1 November 2001. Mesic's discomfort can be illuminated by drawing on David Miller's argument that one necessary condition for attributing collective responsibility to a nation is that it be self-determining, a condition that may be absent when it is subject to imperial rule from the outside. David Miller, "Holding Nations Responsible," *Ethics* 114 (January 2004): 259.

[36] In 1995, on the occasion of the fiftieth anniversary of the end of the War, President Kastar Villiger apologized to world Jewry for the 1938 accord with the Nazis and for its wartime actions.

[37] On 6 October 2002, at a ceremony held to commemorate the sixtieth anniversary of the start of the expulsions, the Belgian Prime Minister offered an official apology in his country's name for the collaboration of Belgian government officials in the expulsion of thousands of Jews to the Nazi extermination camps. "There were too many collaborators in Belgium. We must have the courage to say that, recognize this and bear [the responsibility]." "Belgian Prime Minister Apologizes for Nazi Collaborators," *New York Jewish Times*, 7 October 2002. http://www.nyjtimes.com/Heritage/News/OCt0702.htm (accessed 12 July 2008).

[38] Prime Minister Lipponen offered a public apology in November 2001 for the extradition of eight Jews to Germany, exceptions to the general pattern of complete refusal to extradite.

[39] Referring to the way in which Nazis were smuggled into Argentina or received visas, de la Rua said: "I apologize that this was allowed to happen. ... This we regret with a deep feeling of pain." Harry Dumphy, "De la Rua Apologizes for Nazi Role," Associated Press, 13 June 2000.

Given its ambiguous status as a political and religious body, apologies from the Vatican lie on the border of this class of acts; but given the widely publicized proliferation of apologies that were issued under John Paul II's papacy, they undoubtedly form part of this trend. In 1998, in its statement on the Holocaust, *We Remember: A Reflection on the Shoah*, the Vatican expressed its "deep regret [for] the errors and failure of those sons and daughters of the church" for not taking more decisive action in challenging the Nazi regime during World War II to stop the extermination of more than six million Jews.[40] Although the expression of regret broke a long and much criticized silence, in some quarters it was viewed as not going far enough, particularly insofar as the Pope's words fell short of an explicit assumption of responsibility and active apology.[41]

This objection was certainly not baseless. Attending closely to the wording of this apology, one sees that the pontiff took care to distinguish the actions of *people* in the church from the (ideal) Church itself. The apology is made on behalf of the former only, while the Church as the representative of Christ on earth is dissociated from the wrongdoing. This distinction is slightly different from the ones noted in the cases of France, Austria, and Croatia, where the aberrant moment was reassumed into the historical narrative of the nation, but in a manner that redeemed the nation's goodness. Here, the Church itself remains separated from the acts, even as it accepts a type of vicarious responsibility for them, much as an employer might for an employee's individual wrongdoing. In March 2000, however, at a special millennial Mass, the pontiff closed the gap in a powerful assumption of the Church's own corporate responsibility.[42] There he apologized on behalf of the people of the Catholic Church for sins committed in its past, including "sins in the service of truth", sins which have harmed the unity of the body of Christ (the Church). Nevertheless, as in the other cases discussed here, this linguistic formulation allowed

---

[40] William Drozdiak, "Vatican Gives Formal Apology for Inaction During Holocaust," *Washington Post*, 17 March 1998.

[41] Of particular concern here is also the Vatican's defence of the specific role of the Vatican and Pope Pius XII himself, both of which it continues to defend. See James Carroll, *Constantine's Sword: The Church and the Jews* (Boston: Houghton Mifflin, 2001); John Cornwell, *Hitler's Pope: The Secret History of Pius XII* (New York: Viking, 1999); Susan Zuccotti, *Under His Own Window: The Vatican and the Holocaust in Italy* (New Haven: Yale University Press, 2002); Daniel Goldhagen, *A Moral Reckoning: The Catholic Church during the Holocaust and Today* (New York: Knopf, 2002).

[42] The apology was backgrounded by an International Theological Commission report: *Memory and Reconciliation: The Church and the Faults of the Past* (Strathfield: St. Paul's Publications, 2000) and prompted by over 100 requests for apology during the life of the pontificate.

him simultaneously to condemn the actions while confirming and redeeming the ideal identity of the body in whose name he was apologizing.[43]

(ii) Historical Apologies: Race, Imperialism, and Colonialism

Following this proliferation of European Holocaust apologies, the political apology began to be taken up in relation to other atrocities. Although the subject matter of these apologies is more diverse, the vast majority are concerned with wrongs associated with colonialism or other forms of racial, ethnic, or religious discrimination.[44] In some cases, the apologies crossed state borders. In others, they were concerned with domestic wrongs. They all stressed the contemporary importance of acknowledging that actions in the past diminished the social, political, and legal status of the wronged group. At the same time, as in the Holocaust apologies, one sees in their rhetorical formulations how their concern reaches beyond the direct victim to the moral legitimacy of the contemporary nation.

Consistent with his apologetic stance on the Holocaust, Pope John Paul II made numerous apologies for the Church's past imperialist endeavours. On a visit to Benin in 1993 he apologized for the Church's historical ridiculing of African cultural beliefs.[45] In 2001 he apologized to China for "errors" in the Roman Catholic Church's missions there.[46] A month later, he accessed the new global medium of communication, the Internet, to expand his global apologies, posting an unreserved apology to Australia's Aborigines and other Indigenous peoples of

---

[43] Pope John Paul II also apologized for sins committed in actions against love, peace, the rights of peoples and respect for cultures and religions, sins against the dignity of women and the unity of the human race, and sins in relation to the fundamental rights of the person. In this extensive apology, he more explicitly and strongly took up the Vatican's role during WWII. Pope John Paul II in fact made a wide range of apologies. He explicitly apologized to Greek Orthodox Christians for sins of action and inaction committed by Catholics. During a meeting with the Archbishop of Athens and All Greece Christodoulos, the pontiff stated that "for the occasions past and present, when the sons and daughters of the Catholic Church have sinned by actions and omission against their Orthodox brothers and sisters, may the Lord grant us the forgiveness we beg of him." Pope John Paul II quoted in Julian Strauss, "Pope Seeks Forgiveness," *The Daily Telegraph*, 6 May 2001. In his 2001 visit to the Ukraine, the pontiff urged the Catholic and Orthodox churches to ask forgiveness of each other, an appeal underwritten by an explicit apology from the leader of the Ukrainian Catholic Church for conscious and voluntary evil, including collaboration with the Nazis.

[44] An exception, not treated here because of my exclusion of Japanese cases, is the issue of the Japanese apology to 'comfort women' and the Japanese government's apology in May 2001 for the pain and suffering endured by leprosy patients confined to remote sanatoriums decades after a treatment was available. Calvin Sims, "After 90 Years, Small Gestures of Joy for Lepers," *New York Times*, 5 July 2001.

[45] Adu Kwabena-Essem, "A New Look at Ju-Ju; The Pope's Apology to Africans," *Djembe Magazine*, 13 July 1995. http://www.mamiwata.com/pope.html (accessed 11 August 2008).

[46] Pope John Paul II quoted in Melinda Henneberger, "The Pope Apologizes for the Catholic Church's 'Errors' in China," *New York Times*, 25 October 2001.

Oceania for past "shameful injustices" of the Roman Catholic Church, "especially where children were forcibly separated from their families."[47]

Imperial and colonial endeavours have in fact been one of the main subjects of apologies, beginning with President Clinton's expression of regret for U.S. support of African dictators during the Cold War. The way in which Clinton finessed his language to provide the very recognition that he acknowledged had been missing in the U.S. relationship with African nations is particularly noteworthy. What he regretted, he told his audience of school children (and international media), was that the United States had "dealt with countries in Africa ... more on how they stood in the struggle between the United States and the Soviet Union than how they stood in the struggle for their own people's aspirations to live up to the fullest of their God-given abilities."[48] In this act of verbal recognition, he thus began to shift that very dynamic, now recognizing the (colonized) other as a subject with its own aspirations and the right to be a partner in developing social and political institutions, and not simply as an object, a resource for the benefit of the internationally dominant nations. More generally, and in words again reminiscent of the woven future to which Elie Wiesel referred, Clinton said, "perhaps the worst sin America ever committed about Africa was the sin of neglect and ignorance. We have never been as involved with you, in working together for our mutual benefit, for your children and for ours, as we should have been."[49]

France has been less forthcoming in apologizing for its imperial past, although there are indications of a shift in the official narrative about its role in Algeria, including the first official recognition (contained in a 1999 piece of legislation) that France had been 'at war' with Algeria, as distinct from being involved in a conflict or operations for maintenance and order.[50] However, such initial signs that what Robert Aldrich has called "the Algeria syndrome" may be abating have not been translated into an apology[51] despite Algerian President Abdelaziz Bouteflika's explicitly connecting the two sites of atrocity with a correlative apology when he told the National Assembly in Paris that France owed Algeria the kind of apology for its (162-year) occupation of his

---

[47] The first apology came in a report by the special Synod on Oceania held in the Vatican in 1998. "Pope Says Sorry to Aborigines," *The Australian*, 23 November 2001.

[48] James Bennet, "In Uganda, Clinton Expresses Regret on Slavery in U.S.," *New York Times*, 25 March 1998.

[49] Ibid.

[50] See Robert Aldrich, "Colonial Past, Post-Colonial Present: History Wars French-Style," *History Australia* 3, no.1 (June 2006).

[51] Ibid. The reference is to the term the 'Vichy Syndrome', which Henry Rousso coined to describe France's refusal to face up to WWII collaboration. See Henry Rousso, *Le Syndrome de Vichy, de 1944 à Nos Jours* (Paris: Éditions du Seuil, 1990).

country that it had offered for its role in the Holocaust.[52] France has not seen fit to accede to this request, despite the fact that a majority of French citizens think that a formal apology should be issued by the Prime Minister or President.[53]

In January 2004, at the tomb of a leader of the Herero people in present-day Namibia, the German Ambassador expressed his country's "profound regrets" for Germany's role in the brutal massacre of tens of thousands of the Herero people that took place between 1904 and 1907 in what had been German West Africa. Recalling the death of all but 15,000 of a population of 50,000 to 100,000 through murder or subsequent starvation and the enslavement of the survivors, he said that now what was needed was to "give back to the victims and their descendants the dignity and honour of which they were robbed."[54] In response to criticism that the first repentant act had fallen short of a full apology, in August of that year the German Minister for Economic Cooperation and Development told an audience in Namibia that "the oppressors – blinded by colonial fervour – became agents of violence, discrimination, racism and annihilation in Germany's name," asked them "to forgive our trespasses and our guilt," called the act genocide, and made it explicit that "everything" he said "was an apology."[55]

Belgium apologized to the Congolese people for the 1961 assassination of Patrice Lumumba (Congo's Prime Minister) immediately following the release of its own parliamentary commission's finding that Belgium had been 'morally responsible' for Lumumba's death. In February 2002, the Foreign Minister expressed his government's "profound and deepest regrets" for Lumumba's death, admitting that some members of the Belgian government of the time "carry an irrefutable part of the responsibility."[56] Although acts committed in

---

[52] Francois Raitberger, "France, Algeria Struggle to Put Past Behind Them," Reuters, 17 June 2000.

[53] Some 56 percent of respondents were in favour of an official apology. Reported in Jon Henley, "French Politicians in Firing Line for Role in Algeria." *The Guardian*, 11 May 2001. It was against this background that, in 2002, a French general who had admitted torturing and executing dozens of Algerians during the colonial war (1954–62) was successfully sued, not for the acts but for the spoken attitude. The 1968 amnesty precluded criminal charges being brought against him for the acts themselves, but he could be charged with the crime of trying to justify the war. What motivated the action was not simply his publicising his role, but his lack of remorse. David Bamford, "French General in Algerian Torture Claim," BBC Online, 14 May 2001. http://news.bbc.co.uk/2/hi/middle_east/1330576 stm (accessed 12 May 2008).

[54] "Namibia's Hereros, Germany Envisage New Era," Afrol News, 19 January 2004. http://www.afrol.com/articles/10763 (accessed 15 July 2008).

[55] Xan Rice, "Germans Sorry for Genocide," *The Times*, 16 August 2004.

[56] The apology was accompanied by the establishment of a Patrice Lumumba foundation worth over US $3 million, plus a yearly grant of over US $430,000 to be spent on projects in the Congo involving conflict prevention, or in the form of study grants. "Belgium Apologizes for Lumumba Killing," *Washington Times*, 6 February 2002.

the early 1960s were the direct reference point of this apology, its concurrence with contemporary political breakdowns and atrocities in Belgium's former colonies (the Congo and Rwanda) suggests that Belgium's apology for a past moment is not disconnected from its recognition of its ongoing colonial legacy and responsibility.[57]

Turning to the British Empire, in November 1995 the Queen of Great Britain signed an apology expressing regret for the seizure of Maori land in New Zealand by the British colonizers in 1863.[58] Indian groups working in both India and Great Britain were, however, unsuccessful in their attempt to get the British Monarch to apologize for the 1919 Jallianwala massacre during her 1997 visit to India.[59] Closer to home, Prime Minister Tony Blair dabbled with, but skirted, an apology to the Irish, first in the more remote context of the Great Potato Famine and second with respect to more recent violence. Delivered during a period of intense negotiations over the political status of Ireland, his not-quite apology for the famine is particularly interesting for the way in which it tries to manage the issues of continuity of identity and responsibility discussed earlier. In 1997, in a letter to the organizers of a commemoration of the great famine in Ireland, the Prime Minister surgically separated the past and current British state when he wrote that "those who governed in London at the time failed their people through standing by while a crop failure turned into a massive human tragedy ... a defining event in the history of Ireland and of Britain ... that still causes pain as we reflect on it today."[60] One sees here how Blair acknowledges the continued pain, thus bringing the past relationship closer to the present, but carefully holds the distance between the material wrongdoer (those who governed in London at the time) and his own government or contemporary Britain.

---

[57] Mahmood Mamdani explicated this link between colonial histories and the contemporary conflict in Rwanda in *When Victims Become Killers: Colonialism, Nativism, and the Genocide in Rwanda* (Princeton, N.J.: Princeton University Press, 2001). Belgium's exceptionally proactive role in exploiting the concept of universal jurisdiction to prosecute crimes against humanity committed in Rwanda suggests a similar interpenetration.

[58] "World News Briefs," CNN News Online, 4 November 1995. http://www.cnn.com/WORLD/Newsbriefs/9511/11-03/index.html (accessed 20 August 2008).

[59] The Jallianwala massacre, in which hundreds of unarmed civilians were killed by British troops, is considered one of the major events and a symbolic moment in British colonialism and Indian moves to independence. It is no doubt relevant here that the Indian government did not support the campaign. Anjali Mody, "Queen Not Welcome in Amritsar Says Gujral," *The Indian Express*, 18 August 1997.

[60] Toby Harnden, "Blair Apologizes to Ireland for Potato Famine," Electronic Telegraph, 2 June 1997. http://www.telegraph.co.uk/htmlContent.jhtml?html;=/archive/1997/06/02/wfam02.html (accessed 27 April 2008).

Given the living context of violence in Northern Ireland, it is hardly surprising that he was cautious about constructing a historical narrative in which contemporary Britain was linked with historical wrongs against the Irish. Indeed, the next year, announcing an inquiry into the Bloody Sunday shooting of fourteen men in a Londonderry riot in 1972, Blair acknowledged that "Bloody Sunday was a tragic day for all concerned", that "we must wish it had never happened" and that "our concern now is simply to establish the truth, and close this painful chapter once and for all" – but he did not apologize.[61] Interestingly, in 1998, in a little reported act and while on a tour of the United States, Gerry Adams (leader of Sinn Fein, the political wing of the IRA) said, "the IRA have done wrong and I deeply regret that."[62] Subsequently, in July 2002, in a statement in the Republican newspaper *An Phoblacht* (Republican News), the IRA offered its "sincere apologies" to the civilian victims of its campaign of violence. The statement continued, "[W]e also acknowledge the grief and pain of their relatives. The future will not be found in denying collective failures and mistakes or closing minds and hearts to the plight of those who have been hurt. That includes all of the victims of the conflict, combatants and non-combatants."[63]

Moving now from imperialism and colonization to neo-colonialism, a number of post-colonial states have seen intense debates concerning the treatment of Indigenous peoples, including the question of an apology for past violations. In Canada in January 1998, the Federal Minister of Indian Affairs made a formal apology to Aboriginal peoples across Canada for the government's policies of assimilation, and in particular its role in the residential schools' program, where Aboriginal children were removed from their families and communities. The statement read: "The Government of Canada acknowledges the role it played in the development and administration of these schools. . . . Particularly to those individuals who experienced the tragedy of sexual and physical abuse at residential schools, and who have carried this burden believing that in some way they must be responsible, we wish to emphasize that what you experienced was not your fault and should never have happened. To those of you who suffered this tragedy at residential schools, we are deeply sorry."[64] The wide publicity the government gave to its apology and the carefully worded

---

[61] "We Must Find Bloody Sunday Truth – Blair," BBC News Online, 29 January 1998. http://news.bbc.co.uk/2/hi/uk_news/51740.stm (accessed 5 August 2008).

[62] Adams apologized during a speaking tour of the United States. See "Sinn Fein Leader Visits CT," *Yale Daily News*, 20 October 1998.

[63] "IRA Apology a Building Block," BBC News Online, 17 July 2002. http://news.bbc.co.uk/2/hi/uk_news/northern_ ireland/2134320.stm (accessed 23 August 2008).

[64] The Honourable Jane Stewart, Minister of Indian Affairs and Northern Development on the occasion of the unveiling of *Gathering Strength: Canada's Aboriginal Action Plan* on 7 January 1998 in Ottawa, Ontario.

official statement suggest that the state placed significant weight on apology as a political act, but the fact that it was not delivered by Prime Minister Jean Chretien (even though he was in the capital that very day) discounted the statement as an a full apology. In fact, when the Prime Minister (Stephen Harper) did give a full formal apology in June 2008, he said that "The government recognizes that the absence of an apology has been an impediment to healing and reconciliation" and continued, "Therefore, on behalf of the government of Canada and all Canadians, I stand before you, in this chamber so central to our life as a country, to apologise to Aboriginal peoples for Canada's role in the Indian residential schools system."[65] The statement of apology included details of the abuses and their effects on Aboriginal peoples, recognition of responsibility, and reference to the residential Schools Truth and Reconciliation Commission that his government was establishing.

In a wonderful act of irony, the Sahtu Dene (Aboriginal people) of Great Bear Lake in the North West territories of Canada demonstrated the dramatic quality of apology when members of the community travelled to Japan to deliver their apology for their unwitting role in transporting uranium mined from their home and later used to make the nuclear bombs dropped on Hiroshima and Nagasaki.[66] One might wonder why such a small and relatively powerless community would be the one to apologize, in stark contrast to all others discussed in this chapter, where it was the dominant party that came down on its knees. The answer may lie in the fact that the Sahtu Dene's apology came at the same time as they were pressing the Canadian government for an apology for its abuse of their traditional rights, thereby enacting the irony of their being prepared to accept responsibility for a small part in others' suffering, while the more powerful Canada would not accept its responsibility for land theft and systematic non-recognition.

A formal apology from governments and churches for the forced removal of Aboriginal children was one of the key recommendations of the Australian *National Inquiry into the Separation of Aboriginal Children from their Families*. The push and pull over the apology, which culminated in a formal apology a decade after the report, became the centrepiece of the broader racial tensions that dog Australian social and political life, and is the subject of Chapters Five and Six, so I do not elaborate it here.

The Waikato-Tainui Deed of Settlement, signed in October 1995 by representatives of the Tainui (Maori) people of the Waikato District in New Zealand

---

[65] "Prime Minister Stephen Harper's Statement of Apology," CBC News Online, 11 June 2008. http://www.cbc.ca/canada/story/2008/06/11/pm-statement.html (accessed 20 March 2008).

[66] "Deline Leaders Want to Apologize to Japan for Wartime Use of Uranium," CBC Radio, 28 May 1998. The story was told in Peter Blow's 1999 film *Village of Widows*.

and the government of New Zealand, included (alongside land and financial agreements) a formal apology for the confiscation of Tainui land. The second article of the treaty provided that: "The Crown expresses its profound regret and apologises unreservedly for the loss of lives because of the hostilities arising from its invasion, and at the devastation of property and social life which resulted." It went on to say, "[T]he Crown recognizes that the lands confiscated in the Waikato have made a significant contribution to the wealth and development of New Zealand."[67]

In 1993, President Bill Clinton signed Public Law 103–150, the Apology Resolution to Native Hawaiians, marking the hundredth anniversary of the overthrow of the Kingdom of Hawaii. Once again drawing out from the past orientation of apology to a future relationship, the law provided that "the Congress apologizes to Native Hawaiians on behalf of the people of the United States for the overthrow of the Kingdom of Hawaii on January 17, 1893 ... and the deprivation of the rights of Native Hawaiians to self-determination; expresses its commitment to acknowledge the ramifications of the overthrow of the Kingdom of Hawaii, in order to provide a proper foundation for reconciliation between the United States and the Native Hawaiian people; and urges the President of the United States to also acknowledge the ramifications of the overthrow of the Kingdom of Hawaii and to support reconciliation efforts between the United States and the Native Hawaiian people."[68]

Despite Congress so urging, neither Clinton nor any other U.S. President has apologized to (mainland) Native American Indians. The sole gesture towards a state apology was one given in 2000 by Kevin Grover, the Assistant Secretary for Indian Affairs, for the wrongs committed by the Bureau of Indian Affairs. The fact that Grover held an administrative post, and thus the apology was not given on behalf of the executive, and the fact that Grover was himself a Native American, only underscored the absence of a full state apology. Indeed, Grover explicitly commented that he did not and could not speak for the United States, that being the province of the nation's elected leaders. Not surprisingly, to the ears of many Native Americans, this marks a loud silence waiting to be filled, but there is no indication that a further apology is being considered at high levels of government.

Staying with the United States' internal violations, in 1988 and following intense lobbying by representatives of the Japanese American community, President Ronald Reagan signed into law the Civil Liberties Act of 1988 declaring that historical injustices ought to be amended, granting a formal

---

[67] Tom Bennion, ed., "The Tainui Settlement," *Maori Law Review*, May 1995.
[68] *The Apology Resolution*, United States Public Law 103–150, 103d Cong., *Joint Resolution 19*, (23 November 1993).

apology, and authorising $20,000 in compensatory redress to each survivor of America's Second World War program of mass exclusion and detention of Japanese Americans. Two years later, President George H. W. Bush issued a letter of apology to Japanese Americans receiving compensation. Once again, using the words of apology to point to what lies beyond them, it read, "neither a monetary sum nor words alone can restore lost years or erase painful memories, nor can they convey our Nation's resolve to rectify injustice and restore the right of individuals." It continued, now making clear who America is today, "[but] we can take a clear stand for justice and recognize that serious injustices were done to Japanese Americans during World War II."[69] Almost ten years later, surviving Japanese Latin Americans interned by the United States also received compensation and a letter of apology from President Clinton "for the actions that unfairly denied you fundamental liberties during World War II." Again, the apologetic act becomes the moment for establishing an agenda for the America of the future, as if to say, yes, in the past we have gone astray, but from here on, our actions will be aligned with the values at the core of America's essential political constitution and identity: "We understand that our nation's actions were rooted in racial prejudice and wartime hysteria, and we must learn from the past and dedicate ourselves as a nation to renewing and strengthening equality, justice and freedom."[70]

Slavery and the systematic discrimination against African Americans is of course another gaping hole in the record of U.S. apologies. President Clinton did give a specific race-related apology in 1997 when he apologized on behalf of the U.S. government to the eight survivors of the four hundred black men who unknowingly went without treatment for decades in the federally financed Tuskegee experiment on long-term effects of untreated syphilis.[71] This highly circumscribed apology for an event that clearly belonged to a far broader pattern of racial targeting again (like the stunted apology to Native Americans) only drew attention to the absence of a broader apology. Neither President Clinton nor any other U.S. leader has taken up the ongoing demand for an apology to the descendants of slaves.

In 1997, House Concurrent Resolution 96 was introduced to Congress, stating, "Resolved by the House of Representatives that the Congress apologizes to African Americans whose ancestors suffered as slaves under the

---

[69] Letter from President George Bush, October 1990. See James Rowley, "Japanese American Internees Get Apologies, $20,000 Checks," Associated Press, 9 October 1990.
[70] "US to Pay Japanese Latin Americans Held during WWII," *CNN News Online*, 12 June 1998. http://www.cnn.com/WORLD/americas/9806/12/japanese.reparations/index.html (accessed 10 April 2008).
[71] This apology was accompanied by a financial compensation package. Carol Kaesuk Yoon, "Families Emerge as Silent Victims of Tuskegee Syphilis Experiment," *New York Times*, 12 May 1997.

constitution and the Laws of the United States until 1865."[72] The resolution went no further. Indeed, the closest any U.S. political leader has come to apologizing for slavery was Clinton's 1997 reference to the wrongs of the African slave trade, as much of interest for what it did not do as for what it did. Even as he admitted that "we were wrong" in receiving "the fruits of the slave trade", he defined 'we' not as the United States per se but as a 'we' that existed "before we were even a nation".[73] Moreover, the words were addressed to Africans, not to African *Americans*, and were spoken on African, not U.S., soil.

In something of a breakthrough, in February 2007 the state of Virginia passed two bills of regret, one concerned with slavery, the other with the egregious wrongs committed against Native Americans. The bills provided that "the General Assembly hereby expresses its profound regret for the Commonwealth's role in sanctioning the immoral institution of human slavery, in the historic wrongs visited upon native peoples, and in all other forms of discrimination and injustice that have been rooted in racial and cultural bias and misunderstanding."[74] Though the bill fell short of the explicit apology that had been sought, it marked a significant shift in a political field where any move towards apology had been killed before it had reached the state's endorsement.

The transnational violation of slavery has in fact given rise to an appropriately global apology debate, which took place when a collective, international apology for slavery and the slave trade rose to become one of the key issues and points of contention during the United Nations World Conference Against Racism in Durban in 2001. It no doubt strikes us as remarkable that a debate over 'mere words' and not the more predictable points of impasse about concrete conflicts was the one that scattered the nations of the world into patterns of alliance and antagonism, and threatened to bring the conference to a halt in its final days. The final declaration fell short of the explicit apology for which many non-governmental organizations and African states had been pushing. It did, however, acknowledge that "slavery and the slave trade ... were appalling tragedies in the history of humanity ... and crimes against humanity ... and that Africans and people of African descent, Asians and people of Asian descent and indigenous peoples were victims of these acts and continue to be victims of their consequences." The declaration went on to say that the World Conference "profoundly regrets the massive human sufferings and plight of millions of

---

[72] Introduced by Congressman Tony P. Hall of Ohio. See 143 *Congressional Record* H3890–H3891, 105th Congress, 1st Session (18 June 1997).

[73] This was the same speech as the one in which Clinton acknowledged the disrespectful treatment of African nations by the United States.

[74] Tim Craig, "In Va. House, 'Profound Regret' on Slavery; Delegates Unanimously Pass Resolution of Contrition about State's Role," *Washington Post*, 3 February 2007.

men, women and children caused by slavery."[75] One can hardly miss the fact that victim collectives are explicitly named, while the apology remains silent on, and is not specifically attributed to, perpetrator collectives.

Finally, perhaps the most dramatic apology in this group was the Reconciliation Walk repenting the Crusades and more generally the wrongs of Christendom. In this case, there was no representative leader, but rather over 2,150 Christians, mostly evangelical Protestants, who began their new crusade on Easter Sunday 1996 in Cologne, the same city where the Crusades had begun 900 years earlier, and retraced the steps of the original Crusades, going from town to town and offering their apology. To our contemporary eyes and ears, their reenactment and rhetorical flourish may seem comic, but it graphically illustrates and speaks to the theme of performatively re-narrating history and identity we have seen throughout this chapter:

Nine hundred years ago, our forefathers carried the name of Jesus Christ in battle across the Middle East. Fuelled by fear, greed and hatred, they betrayed the name of Christ by conducting themselves in a manner contrary to His wishes and character. The Crusaders lifted the banner of the Cross above your people. By this act, they corrupted its true meaning of reconciliation, forgiveness and selfless love. On the anniversary of the first Crusade, we also carry the name of Christ. We wish to retrace the footsteps of the Crusaders in apology for their deeds and in demonstration of the true meaning of the Cross. We deeply regret the atrocities committed in the name of Christ by our predecessors. ... Where they were motivated by hatred and prejudice, we offer love and brotherhood. Jesus the Messiah came to give life. Forgive us for allowing His name to be associated with death.[76]

Once again at the forefront of this apology is the public assertion (and thereby the reassumption) of the ideal identity of the apologizing party, placed in relief and taken up again by juxtaposing it with a now rejected historical identity. The apology brings the historical community back into alignment with the ideal community; the true Christian community speaking in the name of life now replaces the historical Christian community, which once betrayed its name by speaking in the name of death. It is ironic that just five years later, the President of the United States invoked the name of the Crusades to open a very different kind of journey towards the Muslim world, indicating that by no means all Christians were convinced by or even attracted to this re-alignment.

---

[75] "Final Declaration," *World Conference Against Racism, Racial Discrimination, Xenophobia and Related Intolerance*, Durban, South Africa, September 2001. http://www.unhchr.ch/huridocda/huridoca.nsf/(Symbol)/A.Conf.189.12.En?Opendocument

[76] Jeannine Mercer, " 'Better Late Than Never' for Crusades Apology," *The Jerusalem Post*, 18 June 1999.

2. TRANSITIONAL APOLOGIES

Apologies have also occurred in the immediate aftermath of mass violations, in those periods now known as transitional. In this context, apology occurred as one of the novel or transformed strategies that were developed during the last quarter of the twentieth century as Latin American and Eastern European nations and South Africa began to emerge from periods of totalitarian or despotic rule and faced the challenge of reconstituting themselves as viable, stable political communities. Apologies thus appeared in combination with a range of transitional mechanisms including truth commissions, domestic and international criminal trials, public commemorations, reparation schemes, and lustration.[77] As this survey illustrates, apologies have been less forthcoming when the violations are still part of the living political scene. Indeed, consistent with this distributive pattern, with the lapse of time, we are beginning to see a new round of apologies for violations committed under the violent regimes of the 1970s and 1980s, notably in Argentina and Guatemala.

In one of the rare immediate apologies, in March 1991, at his televised presentation of the findings of the Report of the National Commission on Truth and Reconciliation, Chilean President Patricio Aylwin asked for the forgiveness of the victims' relatives. He also appealed to the armed forces, the security forces, and all who participated in the excesses to recognize the pain they had caused and to cooperate in healing the wounds. In one of the more grandly staged dramas of repentance, he spoke in the very football stadium in which many of the atrocities had occurred, and as he spoke, the names of victims were flashed on a giant screen.[78] The performative power of the scene is striking, particularly in its implications regarding the role of 'ordinary Chileans'. Now, the eyes of all Chile were trained on the names of those who had died at the hands of the military, displayed in the same place that had been 'invisible' to them when those murders were occurring, and in their site of national sport.

Outside Chile, it was only after the turn of the century when the conflicts were no longer so volatile that apologies began to be voiced for pre-transition violations in other Latin American countries. In March 2004, Nestor Kirchner, President of Argentina, offered the first presidential apology for the violations committed during the military dictatorship. Again, this apology was delivered with dramatic

---

[77] While the term 'transitional justice' usually refers to the processes that a particular country undergoes, I include within this category apologies offered by other nations for their role in the conflict, although their intervention does not strictly fall within the transitional mechanisms.

[78] Displaying or reading out the names of victims has become another type of verbal performance of remembrance, seen for example in synagogues like the one in Prague where victims' names are painted over the walls.

poignancy at a ceremony transferring a former torture camp, 'a symbol of barbarism and irrationality' in the words of the head of the Argentine military, to its new role as site of a museum dedicated to the memory of the atrocities and the promotion and defense of human rights.[79] Before the ceremony, the head of the military, Admiral Jorge Godoy, had ordered the removal of the portraits of military leaders associated with the dictatorship, marking the military's symbolic transition from being the principal perpetrator of human rights violations, acting beyond the rule of law, to its new role as a protagonist in building "a prosperous, sovereign nation with social justice." At the ceremony, the President asked pardon in the name of the state for the "sinister and macabre acts"[80] committed during the years of military rule and for the state's "silence over the atrocities during its twenty subsequent years of democratic rule."[81]

On 10 December (Human Rights Day) 2001, Guatemalan President Alfonso Portillo publicly apologized to the families of those killed by soldiers and paramilitaries in the village of Las Dos Erres in 1982. Describing his act as "the beginning of a new step forward for human rights in Guatemala," he said, "Today it's down to me to humbly ask all the victims of Las Dos Erres for forgiveness. . . . I know that life has no price but this is a historical message that the state recognizes its responsibility for these acts that so shame us."[82] In April 2004, following recommendations from the inter-American Court of Human Rights, the government of Guatemala formally apologized for its role in the 1990 killing of anthropologist Myrna Mack. In a ceremony at the Presidential Palace, President Oscar Berger and the heads of Congress and the Supreme Court asked forgiveness for the brutal murder. Although the apology was limited to her death, it implied acknowledgement of the state's role in the more widespread repression.[83]

Despite South Africa's place in the popular imagination as the heartland of reconciliation politics, the representative political apology has not in fact played a major role in that country. There, narratives of repentance have been articulated

---

[79] Speech given by Jorge Godoy on 3 March 2004. The transfer was authorized by the Convenio No. 8/04, Acuerdo entre el estado nacional y la ciudad autonoma de Buenos Aires para la construccion del "Espacio para la memoria y para la promocion y defensa de los derechos humanos" En el predio de la 'ESMA' (Agreement between the national state and the autonomous city of Buenos Aires for the construction of "a space for memory and for the promotion and defense of human rights" on the grounds of 'ESMA') 24 de Marzo de 2004, *Boletín Oficial*, 26 March 2004.

[80] "Americas Argentine President Announces Plans for Victims of Military Dictatorship," VOA News, 24 March 2004.

[81] Martina Noailles and Alfredo Ves Losada, "Godoy mandó descolgar un retrato de Emilio Massera," *Pagina 12*, 7 May 2004.

[82] Greg Brosnan, "Kin Get Apology, Cash after Massacre," Reuters, 11 December 2001.

[83] Sergio De Leon, "Guatemala's Three Branches of Government Apologize for State Role in Human Rights Activist's Slaying," Associated Press, 23 April 2004.

at a more individual level, insofar as truth telling, the confessional aspect of apology, has been at the heart of the South African truth and reconciliation process, and many individuals used the occasion of the Commission hearings to give personal apologies. In August 1993, while still President, F. W. de Klerk did in fact apologize for apartheid, followed days later by Nelson Mandela's apology for atrocities allegedly committed by the African National Congress against suspected enemies. De Klerk apologized again in 1996, this time before the nation for the "pain and suffering" caused by the disgraced system of racial separation, but not in the capacity as head of state. The absence of a post-transition representative apology may be explained by the fact that the new South African government under the leadership of Nelson Mandela was so explicitly identified with the victim group.[84]

In Ethiopia, a country far less well along the way in dealing with its past, there has been no representative apology, but in August 2003 thirty-three former government officials on trial for genocide wrote a letter asking Ethiopia's people to forgive them for crimes they committed during the former regime of exiled dictator Mengistu Haile Mariam.[85] The letter, sent to Ethiopian Prime Minister Meles Zenawi and published by Ethiopia's national newspaper, *The Reporter,* said: "We, the few who are being tried for what had happened, realize that it is time to beg the Ethiopian public for their pardon for the mistakes done knowingly, or unknowingly. ... We are the people who remain from the regime, our actions had the support of the majority of the people who benefited, while we believed it was also the cause of the civil war that has consumed the life of the people and destroyed property."[86]

Apologies have been markedly absent in the political transitions of the former Soviet bloc nations, but have been part of the post-conflict politics of the former Yugoslavia. Heads of the states of the former Yugoslavia have given a number of apologies, beginning with Montenegrin President Milo Djukanovic's apology for the "pain and damage" suffered by the Croatians:

---

[84] In an interesting apology that crossed anti-colonial struggles, in July 1998, the Natal Law Society of South Africa unconditionally apologized for its action, 105 years earlier, in trying to keep Mohandas K. Gandhi from practicing law because he was "not of European descent." Suzanne Daley, "For Gandhi (d. 1948), a Long Due Apology," *New York Times*, 29 July 1999.

[85] This case and the preceding raise important questions about the relationship between apology and other processes for dealing with the past, most notably criminal prosecution. In Chapter Seven I take up this question of whether apology requires or precludes criminal punishment and how one might see them as part of a sequence of justice.

[86] News24.com, "Ethiopians Asked for Mercy," 1 February 2004. http://www.news24.com/News24/Africa/News/0,,2-11-1447_1477313,00.html (accessed 27 April 2008). It is not clear whether this apology is in part aimed at achieving some type of legal pardon. The current constitution bars anybody convicted of genocide and crimes against humanity from benefiting from the presidential prerogative of mercy, but the Ethiopian Parliament is discussing a new bill to empower the President to pardon convicted people.

"On my behalf and on behalf of all the citizens of Montenegro, I want to apologize to all citizens of Croatia, particularly in Konavli and Dubrovnik, for all the pain and material damage inflicted by any member of the Montenegrin people." Linking the distinct crimes with the political consequences of transgressing fundamental norms of international politics, he continued: "We have paid in the lives of our people, the severance of traditional good ties between Croatia and Montenegro and our banishment from the international community."[87] At the same occasion in late 2003, the Presidents of Serbia-Montenegro and Croatia both apologized for the actions of their citizens in the 1991–95 war between those two countries. After Serbian President Svetozar Marovic apologized "as a president of Serbia-Montenegro ... for all the evils any citizen of Serbia and Montenegro has committed against any citizen of Croatia", Croatian President Mesic rewrote his prepared speech to include an apology on the part of his country: "In my name, I also apologize to all those who have suffered pain or damage at any time from citizens of Croatia who misused or acted against the law."[88]

Just two months later, on a visit to Sarajevo, the President of Serbia and Montenegro apologized to Bosnia. Using a form of words very similar to his earlier apology, he apologized for "any evil or disaster" that anyone from his country had caused to anyone in Bosnia. In both apologies, the phrasing was carefully drafted to underline individual responsibility, and Marovic repeatedly emphasized that it was individuals who had committed crimes. This emphasis was no doubt designed to avoid compromising the legal position of Serbia or Montenegro, both of which were facing actions before the International Court of Justice from Bosnia and Croatia for genocide and war crimes and, as such, facing the prospect of huge compensation payments.[89] Still, the fact that he offered both apologies as head of state marked a recognition that even given the pragmatic constraints arising from the legal implications of a collective apology, apology had an important role to play in reshaping relations between these states.

In the following three apologies dealing with living or recent conflicts, one sees how the apologetic act of recognition can finesse the changing boundaries of political identity between violator and victim. In March 2000, on a visit to East Timor eighteen months after the UN-run independence elections, President Wahid of Indonesia offered an unprecedented apology for the violence unleashed

---

[87] "Djukanovic Apologized to Croatia," *AIM Zagreb*, 29 June 2000. www.aimpress.ch/dyn/trae/ archive/data/200007/ 00704-001-trae-zag.htm (accessed 11 July 2008).

[88] "Presidents Apologize over Croatian War," BBC News Online, 10 September 2003. http:// news.bbc.co.uk/go/pr/fr/-/2/hi/europe/3095774.stm (accessed 11 July 2008).

[89] "Belgrade's Cautious Apology," BBC News Online, 13 November 2003. http://news. bbc.co.uk/go/pr/fr/-/1/hi/world/europe/3268405.stm. (accessed 10 May 2008).

by the Indonesian military against East Timorese when they voted in favour of secession. Simultaneous with his words about laying the past to rest, people laid wreaths both at the site of a massacre of Timorese by the Indonesian military and at a cemetery for Indonesian military killed in the 1975 invasion of East Timor: "We as a nation have made mistakes. . . . If we do not apologise as a nation for the mistakes that were made, the problem will never end."[90] Although Wahid's apology was directed to both groups (East Timorese and Indonesians), the structure of his language made clear the different relationships in which he, as Indonesian President, stood to each: "I would like to apologize for the sins that have happened in the past, to the victims or the families of Santa Cruz and those friends who are buried in the military cemetery."[91]

Note here that he refers to the (Indonesian) military victims as 'friends', rendering them part of the Indonesian self, for whom Wahid is also speaking. In contradistinction, the East Timorese are named as the victims, politically distinct from the Indonesian nation. This rhetorical framing is markedly different from the pre-election insistence that East Timor was an integral part of Indonesia. This shift well illustrates the importance of context; under the altered political conditions, a self/other distinction that might have marked the failure of full recognition could have been a gesture towards appropriate respect for the newly established independence.

In her first address to the nation in August 2001, President Megawati Sukarnoputri (Wahid's successor) apologized for Indonesia's rights abuses in two other rebel provinces still part of Indonesia-Aceh and Irian Jaya: "We convey our deep apologies to our brothers who have long suffered as a result of inappropriate national policies."[92] In this case, the apology came not after the conflict had been resolved but amidst ongoing violence. Again, her use of the familial "our brothers" frames Indonesia as a unified and even intimate entity, albeit one with internal conflict. In another ongoing conflict in the same region, during the Bougainville peace talks in 1998, Prime Minister Skate of New Guinea sent an open letter to the people of Bougainville and Papua New Guinea, apologizing for the pain and suffering experienced by everyone involved in the nine-year civil war.[93]

---

[90] "Indonesia Wahid Welcomes Resumption of Timor Air, Sea Link," Associated Press, 1 March 2000.

[91] "Gus Dur's Timor Visit," *Straits Times*, 6 March 2000. Note here that although Wahid apologized to both the East Timorese victims and members of military who were killed in the conflict, he refers to only the latter as 'friends'.

[92] "Megawati's Apology for Rights Abuse in 2 States," Reuters, 17 August 2000.

[93] "Lincoln Agreement on Peace, Security and Development on Bougainville," *The National* (PNG), 22 January, 1998, and *Radio Australia*, 26 January 1998.

Also dealing with complex issues of political identity, in the closing days of a disastrous election campaign in January 2001, President Ehud Barak of Israel apologized for the deaths of thirteen Arab Israelis shot by police during protests to support the Palestinian Intifada.[94] Before an audience of Arab Israelis in the country's largest Arab city he said: "I want to say to the families, I want to meet you and want to tell you as Prime Minister and as an Israeli citizen, the majority of the Jewish people do regret and give their condolences. . . . The blood of Arab Israelis *is the same as ours*."[95] Barak's allusion to blood, ostensibly used here to signify blood spilled, nevertheless has powerful and challenging connotations in a political space where blood differences (racial and religious) lie at the heart of the constitution and identity of the Israeli state itself and have been the site of such intense political and military conflict.

The apology conveys not only a recognition of shared humanity in general, but a forthright affirmation of commonality directly relevant to questions of nationhood and the distribution of political rights and, most importantly, in a manner that challenges historical norms in Israeli politics.[96] The boundaries of shared blood, in Barak's words, are redefined from religious criteria to citizenship criteria, and in turn, religion is removed as the criterion for full citizenship. Those boundaries, however, still clearly exclude the occupied territories, where blood differences still underpin radical differences in citizenship rights.

There have also been a number of debates around apologies from third-party states for their roles in ostensibly domestic conflicts. Most prominent here is the Rwandan genocide, which we now know was no secret to an international community that failed to take any action even weeks into the massacre, despite half a century of promises of 'never again'. President Clinton's apology, delivered in Rwanda in 1998, spoke directly to that silence and retrospectively gave the crime the name that the United States had so strategically refused to give it during the crisis: "[T]he international community, together with nations in Africa, must bear its share of responsibility for this tragedy, as well. We did not act quickly enough after the killing began. We should not have allowed the refugee camps to become safe haven for the killers. We did not immediately call these crimes by their rightful name: genocide. We cannot change the past. But

---

[94] In September 1997, Ehud Barak also apologized on behalf of his party 'over the generations' for the treatment of Jews from Arab countries who immigrated at the founding of the state.

[95] Ned Parker, "Barak Offers Strong Apology to Arab Israelis for Deaths in October," Agence France-Presse, 25 January 2001, emphasis added. In 1997, at the annual Labor Party Convention, Barak, the leader of the Labor Party, had apologized on behalf of the party for the discriminatory treatment of Sephardic Jews during the early years of settlement. See Gil Sedan, "Barak Issues Apology for Sephardim Abuse," *Jewish Telegraphic Agency*, 3 October 1997.

[96] The apology certainly remained remote from the reality of a massive structural gap between the rights of Jewish and Palestinian Israelis.

we can and must do everything in our power to help you build a future without fear, and full of hope."[97] This reference to hope again highlights apology's future orientation and its contribution towards altering the dynamic in the relationship between groups with a history of political conflict.

In April 2000, the Prime Minister of Belgium (former colonizer of Rwanda) begged forgiveness in the name of his country and people for their failures during the genocide. To several thousand Rwandans he said, "I confirm that the international community as a whole carries a huge and heavy responsibility in the genocide. . . . Here before you I assume the responsibility of my country, the Belgian political and military authorities."[98]

In the Guatemalan case, the apology concerned not silence and inaction, but the covert actions of the United States in support of crimes against humanity. In 1999, in the light of the findings of the United Nations' independent Historical Clarification Commission report (*Guatemala: Memory of Silence*) that for decades the United States knowingly gave money, training, and other vital support to the military regime that committed atrocities as a matter of policy, Clinton expressed his regret for the U.S. role. He told Guatemalans, "[I]t is important that I state clearly that support for military forces and intelligence units which engaged in violence and widespread repression was wrong, and the United States must not repeat that mistake."[99] Perhaps not surprisingly, Cambodian students were unsuccessful in their attempt to obtain an apology for China's role in the Cambodian genocide when Chinese President Jiang Zemin visited Cambodia in August 2000. In response the Chinese government issued a statement making it clear that it had no intention of acceding to the request.[100]

So what is it that all of these nations are doing by apologizing at the turn of the millennium? It is already evident that they are not simply trying to make something right for their past victims, nor to repair a long dead past, but are (at least partially) concerned with establishing their own political-moral identity. Certainly, many of the apologies involved recognition of the experience and suffering of a previously excluded or marginalized other, but even then, the identity of the apologizing nation seemed as much at issue as that of the group being recognized. In the following chapter, I turn to the form of words themselves to explore what the actual act of apologetic speech is doing in the political realm.

---

[97] President Clinton's address to genocide survivors at the airport in Kigali, Rwanda, on 25 March 1998, as provided by the White House.

[98] "Belgian Apology to Rwanda," BBC News Online, 7 April 2000. http://news.bbc.co.uk/2/hi/africa/705402.stm (accessed 1 April 2008).

[99] Mary McGrory, "Apologies Are U.S.," *Washington Post*, 14 March 1999.

[100] Peter Harmsen, "History Hinders China's Bid to Play Big Brother in Southeast Asia," Agence France-Presse, 8 November 2000.

2

Apologies as Speech Acts

Words of apology are amongst our most familiar forms of speech, so familiar that we assume we know exactly what they mean, even when they arise in unfamiliar contexts. This type of pre-reflexive interpretive fluency is what makes it possible for us to operate with such ease in a space of shared conventions, but its immediacy gets in the way when a practice shifts and in fact demands a different reading. With a well-worn code at the end of our interpretive fingertips, we import assumptions about the meaning of apology into debates about political apologies, where they shape our evaluations and ability to make sense of the *sui generis* work that political apology might do. In the literature on the political apology one sees this most strikingly in Michel-Rolph Trouillot's influential contention that political apologies transpose what is essentially an individual discourse onto a collective, and his subsequent conclusion that they are thus a type of category mistake.[1] No doubt, if we begin with the template of the repenting, feeling, reflecting individual (standing before his or her friend, lover, or priest) and project that form onto the collective, we are bound to imagine apologizing states as giant sentient beings stumbling around like cartoon characters, absurdly fraught by deep regret. But are we so bound?

The step that this analysis skips is the one of specifying, and even more importantly examining, what type of act a political apology actually is. The critic simply assumes that apology is the type of act that requires a certain type of agency, that is one with internality, emotional depth, and the capacity to

[1] Michel-Rolph Trouillot, "Abortive Rituals: Historical Apologies in the Global Era," *Interventions* 2, no. 2 (July 2000).

43

both feel and reflect. Similarly, it is assumed that an apology is an expression of feeling. Because these qualities are true of the individual apology, they are assumed to be true of the collective apology. But how do we know that to be the case? Is this the extent of the interpretive repertoire available for apologetic speech?

If indeed the assumption is ill founded and this is not the only model of apology, and more specifically if we find that the political, collective-to-collective apology has a different dynamic and is structured around a trope different from the inter-personal apology, then, as Nicholas Tavuchis (who most famously elucidated the inter-personal apology) observed, it would make no sense to evaluate it according to the same criteria; to demand so "is to mistake its task and logic."[2] Indeed, Tavuchis' enigmatic suggestion that collective apologies are caught between two discursive structures with different and at times competing meanings provides a far better explanation for our ambivalent if not confused responses to collective apologies than does Trouillot's categorical condemnation of their confused logic.[3]

What we are lacking is the type of thoroughgoing structural analysis of the collective apology that Tavuchis laid down for the inter-personal apology. This is perhaps hardly surprising, given the difficulty that we have in explicating collective action in general, a problem that becomes still more difficult when we are talking about repentance. Ironically, despite his own insistence on the probable unique nature of collective apologies, the legacy of Tavuchis' highly influential work in the literature is to reinforce the essential place of the individual or inter-personal apology.[4] What we need is a new framework to challenge the assumed model. The later chapters of this book approach this task by looking at the history and hermeneutics of apologetic practices first in the religious context and then in the contemporary context of the Australian apology. In this chapter, I remain with the words themselves, as spoken by political actors, to see what the verbal formulations tell us about what apologetic speech is doing when it is deployed in political contexts.

---

[2] Nicholas Tavuchis, *Mea Culpa*, 108–11. Tavuchis goes little further than this observation of the structural difference between the two types.

[3] Trouillot's argument accords one type of apology, the individual one, the status of the real or essential apology, and sees the other (collective) as deviant. He does not entertain Tavuchis' suggestion that there may be a different type of apology, with a different discursive structure compatible with the collective.

[4] That Torpey refers to this reference in Tavuchis' work as "the most nuanced and insightful analysis of the social alchemy worked by apologies" is not a comment on the weakness of Tavuchis' argument but rather indicative of the gap in the literature. See John C. Torpey, introduction to *Politics and the Past: On Repairing Historical Injustices*, ed. John C. Torpey (Oxford: Rowman and Littlefield, 2003).

In her Amnesty Lecture devoted to political apologies, cultural historian Marina Warner suggests that political apologies unite two forms of speech: the theological/sacramental language of atonement and the psychoanalytic 'talking cure'. Both of these, she argues, are "deeply intertwined with ideas about self examination and self disclosure."[5] In one sense, Warner's analysis defaults to the habitual association between apology and the expression of feeling, and more damningly for political apologies, to the notion of the feeling subject. Her allusions to psychoanalysis and confessional speech also import connotations of apology as therapy, which we will need to scrutinize.

At the same time, however, the metaphors she evokes point to other dimensions of apology that challenge this more traditional reading. In fact, reading beyond the emotional tinge, what these metaphors foreground is the *act of speaking* itself, rather than the internal psyche or soul that might lie behind the words. Both psychoanalysis and the sacraments draw our attention to the work of the speech acts themselves, thus destabilizing our tendency to resort to a dualistic analysis, where the words (on the surface) represent what is really going on (beneath). Moreover, in the case of both sacramental apology and psychoanalysis, the discursive structure of the apology is not a simple dialogic exchange but a more complex type of communication in which the party to whom the apology is grammatically directed, or the party named as the victim of the wrongdoing, is not actually present for the act nor even, it would seem, the principal object of concern. If one thinks about what actually happens in the confessional or the analytic consulting room, it becomes apparent that the scene is in fact one in which a person (the apologizer) is speaking to a third party (the priest/God or the analyst) about what he or she has done to someone else, who is not present at all.[6]

If we take Warner's metaphors as a starting point, what is required then is a more thoroughgoing interrogation of the basic discursive structure of apology and, more specifically, how we map the respective roles of the apology, the apologizer, the apologizee (or victim), and the witness of the apology. This chapter tracks this path, beginning with an analysis of apology as a speech act, then examining the place that the speaker and putative recipient of the apology occupy in apology's work, and finally considering broader questions about the discursive structure of apology.

---

[5] The lectures are reproduced in full on the Open Democracy Web site: "Sorry: The Present State of the Apology," *Open Democracy*, 2003. http://www.opendemocracy.net/democracy-apologypolitics/article_603.jsp (accessed 27 April 2008). An abbreviated version was published as Marina Warner, "Who's Sorry Now: What Apology Means in the Modern World," *Times Literary Supplement*, 1 August 2003, pp. 10–13.

[6] Confession may also concern 'sins against God', a matter I take up in Chapter Three.

I. THE PERFORMATIVE POSSIBILITIES OF SPEECH
AND THE DEVALUATION OF POLITICAL RHETORIC

By examining how speech performs, we can distil our reading of what a speaker is doing with his or her words. This type of linguistic analysis does not eliminate the relevance of actor intention or the history of the practice, but, especially with respect to conventional forms of speech, it does elucidate the structure of the intervention. John Austin's inexhaustible conception of the *performative* dimension of speech, elaborated in the different categories of performatives and the different types of work that they do, provides productive tools for decoding what the political apology is doing.[7]

Even before entering into the different types of performatives that Austin elaborates, the notion that speech is itself action and not merely the contingent representation of what is really going on (paying compensation or feeling sad, for example) already provides a way into responding to some of the major criticisms levelled against political apologies. In its *constative* dimension, speech conveys information or states that something is so, thus always pointing beyond itself; but in its *performative* dimension, speech *itself* brings a state of affairs into being. Approached as a performative, apology then ought to be analysed on its own terms, and not merely as a substitute for what, all things considered, we would really prefer to see happening.

Returning to the site of debates over political apologies for a moment, we see that two of the most common objections to apology take precisely this form. Apology's critics often complain that apology, which demands nothing from our pockets, is a cheap substitute for the money of compensation, or they opine that it is an inauthentic substitute for real sorrow, demanding nothing from our hearts. Jeffrie Murphy and Jean Hampton, for example, allow, in what is a generous concession to apology's revelatory value, that "sometimes, of course the apology is more than mere ritual; indeed, in the best cases it is likely to be a way of manifesting repentance."[8] Our tendency to interpret speech as a contingent label is probably so entrenched that these criticisms strike us as self-evidently true. Austin's notion of the performative dimension of speech invites us to let our attention rest (at least briefly) on the words and the speaking themselves, and not flit immediately over to that referential realm of real things for which we presume they stand.

---

[7] J. L. Austin, *How to Do Things with Words.*

[8] Jeffrie G. Murphy and Jean Hampton, *Forgiveness and Mercy* (Cambridge: Cambridge University Press, 1998), 28.

My (and I presume Austin's) point here is not to argue that intentions and material responses are irrelevant and that speech alone could suffice. Indeed, the other dimensions of reparative action in the wake of systematic violations in the past will also require appropriate attention as part of a repertoire of distinct and complementary dimensions of dealing with the past. What this move towards recognizing speech as constitutive, performative action demands is that we carve out a distinct and irreducible role for speech itself in our map of reparative action. This interpretive shift is not merely a theoretical nicety or aesthetic preference, but a way of making sense of the prominent role that apologetic speech has come to play in the gamut of strategies for dealing with the past. So long as we insist upon the view that speech is but a contingent naming, it is very difficult to account for the proliferation of political apologies or for the obvious weight that they do carry in the political field. Indeed, as I discuss at greater length in Chapter Five, apologies have been recognized at the level of international legal codification as a distinct and necessary component of a full response to gross violations, sitting alongside other forms of compensation and rehabilitation.[9] The relevant United Nations principles call for states to *apologize*, not for them to feel bad.

It is worth pausing to reflect on why we so habitually think about speech as essentially constative, not only in the face of Austin's theory, but also after more than half a century of theories that insist that we ought to revise our habitual word-to-thing hierarchy and recognize that words constitute things.[10] The habitual metaphysical tendency to relegate that which appears (or sounds, in this case) to the status of imperfect being and to imagine it always attached to a truth elsewhere remains in effect, despite Heidegger's initial, and then Arendt's more pointedly political critique of this ontological assumption.[11]

---

[9] "United Nations Basic Principles and Guidelines on the Right to a Remedy and Reparation for Victims of Gross Violations of International Human Rights Law and Serious Violations of International Humanitarian Law," adopted and proclaimed by General Assembly resolution 60/147 of 16 December 2005. The principles were originally developed by Theo Van Boven in 1996 as the *Revised Set of Basic Principles and Guidelines on the Right to Reparation for Victims of Gross Violations of Human Rights and Humanitarian Law*, pursuant to Sub-Commission decision 1995/117, U.N. Doc. E/CN.4/Sub.2/1996/17, 24 May 1996, known as the Van Boven Principles.

[10] The references for post-modernism or post-structuralism are obviously too vast to delineate here, but key figures in this shift would include the linguist Ferdinand de Saussure, the philosopher Jacques Derrida, and the psychoanalyst Jacques Lacan.

[11] See Martin Heidegger, "What Is Metaphysics?" in *Basic Writings*, ed. and trans. David Farrell Krell (San Francisco: HarperCollins, 1997); Hannah Arendt, *The Promise of Politics*, ed. Jerome Kohn (New York: Schocken Books, 2005).

Indeed, the tenacity of this interpretive tendency flies in the face of the way in which politics actually works, where language always has played and continues to play a constitutive role. Words form national constitutions, start wars, name the criteria for membership, declare binding norms of action, and express national identity. National anthems, pledges of allegiance, appropriate forms of public address, formal titles, names evocative of past greatness (Washington, Joan of Arc, Anne Frank) are not the labels for a nation that could carry on quite well without them, but the narrative acts that make that nation real for us at all and give it the qualities by which we recognize it and ourselves as part of it. Nations are not only communities of memory, but also communities of performative speech.

When we place the apology on this *political* list, as distinct from the list of personal and private expressions, it attains a very different gravity, and finds itself in good company.[12] This suggests, as Arendt argued, that the realm of politics does not neatly conform with the metaphysical tradition at all, and to the extent that we interpret it from within this frame, we miss its *sui generis modus operandi*. As the realm of constitutive speech, politics bears the mark of another hermeneutic tradition where words are things and things are words.[13]

The place of words in politics then also points to a more immediate dimension of our tendency to interpret verbal acts with a suspicious ear. On the one hand, one of the hallmarks of modernity is the all-important place that sincerity has come to occupy in our understanding of public life; on the other, we seem to find it less and less frequently.[14] Thus, we think of rhetoric as insincere speech, because we cannot imagine that personal sincerity is not the key criterion by which political speech should be evaluated. Sincerity in politics is of course a problematic matter, complicated in the first instance by the perennial confusion between the personal body of the representative and his or her political body, and in the second by the manner in which contemporary political leaders seem increasingly to try to convince constituents that the former (an appealing personality) is sufficient to the latter (political aptitude). This is only exacerbated by the massive injection of techniques developed for marketing commercial

---

[12] Even at the most personal level, however, anyone who has said, 'I love you', and been met with silence (albeit accompanied by an adoring look), knows that words create a relational space and a meaning-laden world in a way nothing else can.

[13] Arendt's argument is most fully developed in the sections on action in *The Human Condition* and in the "Introduction into Politics" in *The Promise of Politics*.

[14] As Charles Taylor argues so comprehensively, the development of the modern self is deeply tied up with ideas about authenticity and the grounding of one's real being in an individualized self. See Taylor, *Sources of the Self: The Making of the Modern Identity* (Cambridge, Mass.: Harvard University Press, 1989).

products into the business of politics, with the result that we are primed to treat words, *qua* words, with suspicion.

This is not to deny that the ancient Greeks were also alive to the manipulative and dangerous potentials of rhetoric, but rather to insist, with Arendt, that we lose sight of the distinct nature of political speech when we ask only if the speaker is sincere. Certainly, we should be concerned about what happens after a promise is made, or an apology given, but we deprive speech of its constitutive power if we assume that the speaker's feelings rather than the speech itself are the only determinants of such future action. Now, even as our political leaders continue to employ it, we look askance at rhetoric, dubious of it as a legitimate category of action, unsure of the difference between spin and rhetoric and suspicious that it is more likely to be the former than the latter. What we have lost sight of is that rhetoric is not, or at least not only, spin, but is rather *the* political art. The challenge of according political rhetoric its constitutive power, without automatically demanding that it meet the criterion of sincerity, is of course particularly onerous in the case of apology, an act that inevitably carries the scent of intimate relations, that sphere where sincerity is the primary currency.

What we seem to have, then, is a set of associations with distinct interpretive pulls, not only at the more finely grained level of the particular meaning of apology but at the level of the possibilities of political (apologetic) *words*. Even before we get to any particular apology, both apology's ability to work as a pure performative and our analytic ability to acknowledge that it might do so are already hampered, first by the word–thing hierarchy of our metaphysical tradition, second by the devaluation of political rhetoric and the privileging of personal sincerity, and third by the strong association between apology and intimacy. On the other hand, as I pointed out, our political lives are in fact studded with speech's constitutive role, and as members of political communities, we are probably far more engaged with the work of political rhetoric than our theoretical maps allow.

If apology does perform a type of action, what then is apology doing? Coming back to the words themselves, Austin's more detailed analysis of the categories of performatives offers us some greater interpretive scope for de-linking apology from the problematic realm of feeling.

2. CATEGORIES OF PERFORMATIVES

Beyond the basic constative/performative distinction, speech act theory also invites us to specify the type of work done by different forms of speech, designated by Austin as their illocutory force (what one does *in* saying something), and their perlocutory force (what one does *by* saying something).[15] Austin designates five types of performative, defined by their illocutory and perlocutory functions. First are *verdictives*, forms of speech that make some type of judgement, reckoning, or appraisal. 'I rule (that)', 'I diagnose', and 'I take it (that)' are examples of verdictives. Second are *exercitives*, such as 'I appoint', 'I command,' or 'I grant'. These exercise power, right, or authority. Third are *commissives*, which commit the speaker to doing something: 'I promise', 'I guarantee', 'I swear'. Fourth are *behabitives*, such as 'I apologize' (according to Austin), 'I sympathize', and 'I bless'. These are social expressions of attitudes or feelings. Finally, *expositives*, such as 'I quote', 'I repeat', and 'I mention that,' explain how an utterance fits in with the course of an argument or discussion. Austin offers these categories with significant qualification, insisting that they are far from perfect and are inadequately defined and that one cannot definitively classify any particular speech act without knowing the context of its articulation. Nevertheless, the categories provide a powerful analytic tool for getting at how particular forms of speech do their work.

As noted, Austin classifies apologies as behabitives, implying, as per the assumed meaning discussed already, that what one is doing *in* apologizing is expressing an attitude to, or feeling about, certain states of affairs. Linking this back to the examples considered in Chapter One, the form of words used in many apologies, such as 'we condemn our past acts' or 'we wish to express deep regret', certainly seem to fit this categorization. However, as we saw, apologies also take a number of other rhetorical forms, suggesting a wider range of illocutory and perlocutory forces. Moreover, when placed in the context and linked with the political projects within which they are located, their reach certainly seems to go beyond the expression of a feeling. This categorical diversity suggests two things. First, apologies as spoken may be doing things other than expressing emotions, thus (in response to the Trouillot objection) opening possibilities that are not, in principle, incompatible with politics or the repertoire of collective action. Second, it suggests that this class of acts may incorporate different forms of speech that do different and perhaps even contradictory things or can be heard by people as doing different things. This formal linguistic ambivalence helps to explain apologies' uneven reception and the interpretive confusion with which they are often met. Let us now go back to those words with this analytic framework in hand.

---

[15] Austin, *How to Do Things with Words*, 98.

A considerable number of different formulations appeared, including:

1. Apologizing (in one's own name, in the name of the people, unreservedly);[16]
2. Expressing regret *for* the wrongs;[17]
3. Expressing regret *at* or *about* the wrongs;[18]
4. Begging or asking for forgiveness (from God, from the victims, without a referent);[19]
5. Asking for pardon;[20]
6. Confessing;[21]
7. Acknowledging past events;[22]
8. Acknowledging the suffering of the victims;[23]
9. Committing to take responsibility for the ramifications of wrongdoing (into the future);[24]
10. Deploring/condemning the wrongs and the ethical failure they exhibited;[25]
11. Paying tribute to the suffering of the victims;[26]
12. Stating a desire for a certain type of future (involving a different relationship with the victim group, different status for the victim group, or different status for the perpetrator group);[27]

[16] For example, Croatian President Mesic apologized in his own name, Serbian President Svetozar Marovic apologized "as a president of Serbia-Montenegro", and the Pope "apologized unreservedly" to Australia's Aborigines and other Indigenous peoples of Oceania.

[17] The Vatican expressed its "deep regret [for] the errors and failure of those sons and daughters of the Church" in relation to Nazism. Pope John Paul II, *Address to the New Ambassador of the Federal Republic of Germany to the Holy See*, 8 November 1990. See Acta Apostolicae Sedis *(AAS)* 83 (1991): 587–8.

[18] The Prime Minister of Australia expressed regret at or about the history of Aboriginal child removal.

[19] The French Church begged God's forgiveness and asked the Jewish people to hear their words of repentance.

[20] The French union of police asked for pardon for its role during WWII.

[21] Again, the French Church confessed to its role. This language seems to be limited to religious authorities, although Clinton also used the terminology of sin.

[22] Chirac's apology was in the main an acknowledgement of France's role in the persecution of Jews.

[23] The Canadian apology to Indigenous children includes explicit acknowledgement of their suffering.

[24] The New Zealand apology included in the Tainui Settlement includes this linkage.

[25] In his apology to Guatemala, President Clinton said, "[I]t is important that I state clearly that support for military forces and intelligence units which engaged in violence and widespread repression was wrong." President Clinton quoted in Mark Weisbrot, "Guatemala Not the Only Dark Side of U.S. Policy," *Times Union*, 20 March 1999.

[26] German President Rau paid tribute to slave and forced labour.

[27] German President Rau's apology before the Knesset and Clinton's apology to Africans for slavery both explicitly referred to a vision of a different future.

13. Asserting a certain relationship between the act of apologizing and the future;[28]

14. Expressing grief or some other deep emotion about the wrongs of the past;[29]

15. Expressing an emotional response with reference to a bodily gesture of repentance, shame, or humility.[30]

Refining this list, one can identify several basic forms of apologetic speech:

1. Saying sorry;
2. Expressing regret about a situation;
3. Asking for forgiveness;
4. Acknowledging the truth of the past (including the victims' suffering and the role of one's own group);
5. Witnessing;
6. Taking responsibility for the harm or wrongdoing;
7. Articulating and committing to a different future.

Using Austin's performative categories to analyze this list, one sees that in fact they represent a number of types of speech act. This raises several questions. First, is there an ideal type of political apology, and would it, in its perfected form, harmoniously include or integrate as many of the distinct verbal forms as possible? Or are there a number of qualitatively distinct acts, and if so, what is the relationship between them? I come back to these questions in Chapter Eight, but for the moment I want to examine these forms of speech formally to clarify their illocutory and perlocutory functions.

Austin's categorization of apology as a behabitive is consistent with the common interpretation of apology as an expression of feeling in response to something that one has done. If we stay with the actual speech as it occurred in political apologies, however, it is clear that this initial classificatory intuition is insufficient to the phenomenon. In those apologies where the speaker was giving some type of narrative of the past, either by way of simply speaking as a witness or more actively condemning that past, the form of speech more accurately falls under Austin's first category, verdictives, speech that judges or appraises, or under his second category, exercitives, speech that advocates for or favours a

---

[28] Austrian Chancellor Klima explicitly made this link between apologizing and contemporary legitimacy.

[29] The Polish Archbishop referred to deeply grieving the wrongs committed against Jews.

[30] President Klestil of Austria said that he bowed his head with deep respect and profound emotion in front of the victims.

certain course of action. Similarly, apologies that project the apologizing and victim communities into a different future are more appropriately classified as commissives, forms of speech that actually commit to a course of action.

If one thinks about the number of apologies in the inventory that emphasize the reconstitution of the future identity of the apologizing nation and the relations between the perpetrator and victim groups, it becomes clear that this latter classification is particularly pertinent. Again and again, we see that by apologizing, the speaker is stepping out of the previous identity as the one who violated the rights of the victim, now recognizing and acknowledging that violation and thereby establishing a different moral framework or political identity. The expression of an attitude about the past or a feeling about the past is more or less a road to this action of commitment.

This suggests at minimum that political apologies as a form of speech are doing more than expressing a feeling or attitude. Rather, in and by apologizing many of our speakers are passing judgements about the past, publicly establishing or shifting the authoritative truth about the past (one different from the official story henceforth), advocating a public position in relation to the past and the future, and committing to a different identity and set of normative precepts into the future. Once we expand the repertoire in this manner, particularly in the direction of the reconstitutive promise, apologetic speech is no longer, as Trouillot had claimed, a category mistake in the realm of representative politics, but is better characterized as a form of speech bearing typical marks of political action.

Indeed, in describing forgiveness as the two poles of political life, even as she cast aspersions on the political legitimacy of forgiveness, Arendt located promising at the heart of politics because it is the only faculty that allows human beings to predict and rely on each other without imposing structures of domination. Unlike other processes that bind individuals to ongoing commitments from without, mutual promises bind voluntarily and *from within*, thereby creating the stability and continuity that are the condition for law and political community, but in a way that does not violate the freedom of those who participate in the promise.

In Arendt's writings, and indeed more generally in our tradition of political thought, the promise has been associated with the original covenant, or political constitution, or perhaps to laws we subsequently make to bind ourselves into the future, but not with the apology. We might, however, think of the apology as the second promise: the promise one makes after the first has already been broken. Or one might think of it as a corrective promise, the promise one makes when one comes to recognize that the first promise was ill conceived or morally problematic.

This expansion of interpretive apology to the sphere of the promise does not free the apologetic form of its emotive connotations; the more familiar illocutory and perlocutory forces of apology in its individual and personal expression will inevitably continue to provoke the search for the authentic subject. To make sense of this emotive realm will require a thoroughgoing rethinking of political collectives to make sense of the idea of collective orientations or feelings. Rather, what it does is provide a formal template for the apology consistent with its occupying a place in the realm of the political as we already understand it, as distinct from the inherited interpretive template, which would proscribe this transposition.

3. HAPPY AND UNHAPPY APOLOGIES

By elucidating the different illocutory and perlocutory functions of apologies, we are beginning to develop a more coherent explanation of the ambivalent place they occupy in contemporary political discourse. Now we can go a step further and consider how the actual performance of the apologetic act contributes to its success. In the concluding chapter, with a fuller conceptual, historical, and sociological portrait of the apology in hand, as well as a better understanding of the contemporary problems the apology is intended to address, I offer some guidelines for what an ideal apology might look like. At this stage, my intention is the more modest one of applying Austin's evaluative criteria to establish the types of structural performative defects that can stymie the success of apology or, correlatively, the structural conditions that we think apology ought to meet. This expands our evaluative repertoire beyond the question of 'whether he really means it or not.'

Most fundamentally, as performatives, apologies cannot appropriately be assessed as true or false. Rather, they can be evaluated according to the dimensions of 'happiness/felicity' or 'success'. Austin suggested six conditions for assessing the felicity or success of a performative. The first four, which provide the conditions for a performative to be 'achieved', are:

1. There must be a conventional procedure including the uttering of certain words by persons;
2. In the actual delivery or performance the circumstances and the persons have to be appropriate to that convention or procedure;
3. The procedure must be executed correctly by all participants;
4. The procedure must be executed completely by all participants.

If the performance fails to meet any of these criteria, it is not successfully achieved, or it *misfires*.[31] If we apply the criteria to the apologies in Chapter One we can give a structural explanation for our intuitions about those apologies' strengths and weaknesses.

Starting at the most general level, with the first condition, one might say that not one of the apologies was fully successful, because a generally accepted conventional procedure for the political apology has yet to be achieved. In the personal sphere, an apology may fail because the person gives only a partial or qualified apology, or because the wrong person apologizes, but at least we all agree on what is going on when they apologize, and we do so because we are familiar with the apologetic template. In the political sphere, significant ambivalence about what one is supposed to read into apology remains. Nevertheless, the very fact that some political apologies strike us as more successful or more powerful than others suggests that there are at least the beginnings of an accepted common procedure. We might speculate that the establishment of a more robust conventional procedure will require both that the practice itself become more entrenched in the political repertoire and that the significance and boundaries of the convention be more clearly articulated.

Moving down the criteria, one sees how they explain our intuitions about the various apologies. So, for example, the apology to Native Americans 'misfired' because the person apologizing, an administrative officer and not an elected official, was inappropriate to the procedure (criterion two). The apology from the Croatian President misfired because, although the right person was speaking, he did not perform one of the necessary parts of the procedure, which is to actually assume the identity of the responsible party (criterion three or four). Similarly, the U.S. presidential apologies to the victims of syphilis and to African (but not African American) slaves misfired because they were incomplete. One could extend this type of analysis through the whole list.

Notably absent in this first group of criteria is any reference to sincerity or action. Austin places these in a qualitatively different category, which he calls *abuses*. These are captured by the following two criteria:

5. If the procedure involves the expression of certain thoughts or feelings or the initiation of certain actions, the speaker must have those thoughts or feelings or a genuine intention to carry out those actions, and;
6. Where the speech act initiates certain actions, the person must carry them through.

---

[31] Austin, *How to Do Things with Words*, 17–18.

If a speech act meets the first four criteria it is successfully achieved, but if it fails to meet these last two, it is rendered hollow. At first glance, these criteria seem to throw us back into the very characterization of language that the performative category was designed to counter. The claim that an apology involves certain feelings and requires certain actions would seem to imply that in the absence of such authentic feelings, a political apology is fraudulent. Moreover, even as Austin insists that apologies are performatives, bringing about a certain state of affairs themselves, this last condition might easily seem to reduce the apology to a constative, a signifier of the real action, which is yet to take place.

With respect to the question of feelings, things may not be as bad as they first appear. The claim is not that *all* speech acts involve the expression of feelings, but rather that *if* a particular speech act involves such an expression, then the feelings must be present. The relevant question is *whether* the speech act entails the expression of feelings. Moreover, as intimated in the discussion above about the complex quality of political sincerity, what emotional expression means in the realm of political speech should not be assumed to be the same as what it means at the individual/personal level. It may well have been the case, for example, that President Clinton had very sincere and deep feelings when he spoke about the Rwandan genocide, especially in the face of the remnants of the massacre. This is not, however, equivalent to the political community for which he spoke having shifted its categories of recognition in a way that took atrocities against black Africans as seriously as it might take those against white North Americans or Europeans. Properly applying criterion five does not simply mean looking for emotions, but rather asking if emotion is relevant at all, and if so, in what sense.[32] Once again, an unexamined assumption that political apologies are but transpositions of personal ones will elide these two moments.

The second charge is more difficult to answer because undeniably, apology, whether understood as condemnation/judgement or commitment, implies that certain actions will follow. That said, one should approach this demand with considerable care and think through what type of act an apology might imply and the formal relationship between the speech act and other types of action. If the apology is a verdictive, that is, if what one is doing in apologizing is condemning both the acts and the norms of the responsible party (and therefore one's past self), then the judgement and condemnation are themselves forms of action. As we saw, however, apologies also move from a verdictive to a

---

[32] In Chapter Eight, I argue that the emotive field of apology requires that we remap our understanding of the collective and political culture.

commissive dimension, a movement that is both contained in the act itself and implies a movement beyond that act of judgement to a different way of being. The very act of condemning what one was in the past is already a performance of a different normative self; at the same time, one is also announcing that one will be different in the future, thus anticipating future actions and orientations. These future action-orientations should be understood as correlates of the speech act, rather than its referents. Thus, for example, one might surmise that recognizing the experience of the violated other will entail actions such as monetary compensation for losses or the punishment of perpetrators consistent with condemnation of the wrongs committed. These are, however, other dimensions of the commitment it also performs, not what the apology names. In Chapters Three and Four, where we examine Jewish and early Christian practices of repentance, we will see both how those different dimensions were ontologically, epistemologically, and performatively folded into each other and how they came apart.

One way of clarifying the distinction at issue here is to emphasize the modesty of the apologetic act, or not overstretch what we expect of it. Apology is not a substitute for the other actions required, but a *sui generis* approach to recognition. At the same time, it approaches the narrative of wrongdoing and the fabric of the normative relations between perpetrator and victim groups in a manner that the apparently more substantive forms of action do not. Indeed, starting with that first pre-verbal apologetic gesture, the *kniefall*, one already discerns how apology reshapes patterns of relations, power dynamics, and the meanings of subject positions.

To see how this works, one might imagine that before the apology, there exist two subject positions with different perspectives and accounts of truth and history. There is the perspective of the victim, who remembers the violation, protests the injustice, and continues to experience the residues of the injury. There is also the perspective of the perpetrator, who denies (to varying degrees and in different combinations) that the events ever occurred, that they had such a deleterious impact, and that they were wrong and unjust, and who denies his or her own responsibility. When the apology occurs, the dynamic of legitimacy changes; the one who apologizes submits himself to the judgement of the other, allows that the perspective of the other was valid after all, acknowledges the truth of the other, and thereby legitimates his or her subject position. By extension, in situations where one party has the authority over official truths or histories, it is an act of public recognition where the official meanings of different subject positions are altered.

In this vein, Nicholas Tavuchis argues that the first component of a full apology is precisely naming the act as one for which apology is appropriate or required, as something that the parties agree is wrong.[33] Tavuchis has in mind here inter-personal and not political apologies, but his first necessary component of the apologetic speech act fits well with what we see to be the case for apology in the political context. Indeed, it is of the nature of political speech to constitute official national narratives and identities, and at times to reorder the relationship between membership and identity. If one reads through political speeches, particularly at times of transition or during crisis events, one will see that leaders make constant reference to "who we are", what our values are, and who we have been and are to be in the world. In this context, when the political leader or representative of the dominant group narrates the victim's understanding of history as truth, what he or she is effectively doing is ascribing legitimacy to it and giving it the stamp of the state. Speaking this narrative of history and giving voice to the victims' experience of events will be particularly important where there has been a history of denying both the facts and victims' perspectives and suppressing them through other versions of the past, specifically the version that denies any wrongdoing on the part of the dominant group.

Understood in this way, it makes perfect sense that in the United Nations principles of reparation, apology appears under the more general category of 'satisfaction and guarantees against repetition', alongside measures like rewriting textbooks and public commemorations. Apologetic speech, however, as the *kniefall* image conveys so powerfully, is not only narrative of action elsewhere, but also narrative that itself shifts the shape of relations and the significance of identities. It is also a submission or humility, calling not only for a revision of history, but also for reform of the state's own normative commitments and identity.

4. UPTAKE AND DISCURSIVE STRUCTURE

This raises the question of what we think the 'uptake' of or response to the apology ought to be, a question that both Austin and Tavuchis link with the form of apologetic speech. Thus, Tavuchis argues that part of the equation of apology is the response of the injured party, which might be to 'accept and release' by forgiving, to refuse or reject the apology, or to acknowledge the apology and defer a decision.[34] His analysis, in other words, assumes that the

---

[33] Tavuchis, *Mea Culpa*, 22.
[34] Ibid., 23.

objective of the apology is to attain forgiveness. Indeed, this is consistent with his broader understanding of apology as a type of economic exchange, "the symbolic quid pro quo for, as it were, 'compensation'."[35] Thus, according to Tavuchis, one criterion of a successful apology would be the victim's forgiveness.

At first glance, this relationship between apology and forgiveness seems to hold in the class of articulations we are dealing with here. As we saw, the apology is often framed in precisely these terms: as the request for forgiveness, even begging for forgiveness. If, however, one looks to the actual circumstances in which political apologies are given, this link seems more formal than substantive. This becomes apparent if one plays out the drama of apology assuming that the act is only completed by its uptake in the form of forgiveness from the group to whom it is rhetorically directed.

The first and less important set of problems this raises is practical. Who would grant such forgiveness, and how? Would it be another act of representative speech given on behalf of the victim group? Quite apart from any practical problems of representation (who is authorized to speak for the victim group?), demanding this type of uptake will be particularly problematic in cases where the group named as the injured party has dispersed or no longer exists as a group. This of course throws into question the logic of the act itself – how can one ask forgiveness from (or even apologize to) a certain group if there is no substantive group on the other side? One can deal with this, however, by differentiating between those identity requirements for a group to function as a referent of the apology and those required for its granting forgiveness. In the former case, the group need only operate as a subject in a story; in the latter it actually has to *act* as a group *now*. The former is clearly far less demanding and its minimal requirements need not and often do not translate into the degree of contemporary coherence or organization sufficient to provide a definitive uptake.

Still, the fact that there may be no coherent group to grant forgiveness does not in itself indicate that forgiveness is not the ultimate object of the apology from a structural point of view. Far more convincing is the empirical fact that in not one of the actual apologies that have been given was the rhetorical request for forgiveness accompanied by an expectation of actual forgiveness. Despite the extensive orchestration that goes into the linguistic formulation and performance of apologies, in not a single case was the scenario managed to structure in an act of corresponding forgiveness by, for example, inviting (and perhaps prepping) a representative of the victim

[35] Ibid., 33.

group to complete the apology with their forgiveness or refusal to forgive.[36] This is not to say that individuals or representatives may not have some response at a later time, but those responses take place independent of the ritual itself.

This means that if one sees uptake as part of what makes a speech act successful, then, in the case of political apologies, that uptake must be something other than forgiveness from the victim group. This is not to deny that the victim group may be a key participant in the conversation. Nor is it to deny that the speech act of apology may have (and should have) an effect on their status in the political space occupied by both groups. Their presence in the conversation is, however, primarily on the near side of apology, that is, as the main or first advocate for the apology, the one who requests it.

This suggests the more radical proposition that the primary target of the political apology is not the victim group at all, or certainly not the satisfaction of some need that the victim group has. By extension, the economic model Tavuchis suggests, whereby apology would be the reimbursement for wrongdoing's cost, is also rendered inappropriate. Indeed, the metaphor of apology as a form of repayment (which often makes it look so paltry) would not seem to be the appropriate one at all. Linking this with Austin's categories, if one asks what type of *perlocutory* act a political apology is, what one is doing *by* apologizing, it seems that one is not primarily seeking forgiveness from the victim group. How then would one describe its perlocutory force?

Again, going back to the apologies themselves, two main themes appear. In some, for example, German Chancellor Rau's apology in Israel or Clinton's apology in Africa, the speaker referred specifically to his apology's bringing about a shift in the relationship between the groups, looking forward, for example, to stronger links and a greater sense of a shared future. In others, the main concern articulated in the apology was neither the status of the other (victim) group, nor even the relationship between victim and perpetrator groups, but rather the moral status of the political community in whose name it was spoken. Thus, for example, Chirac, Klestil, and the Pope each acknowledged that France, Austria, and the members of the Church, respectively, had committed grave wrongs against certain groups, but framed these wrongs primarily as violations of *their own* essential identities as moral communities. In this context, what the apology was doing was placing a break between what the

---

[36] In the first Canadian apology, five Indigenous leaders were invited to and handed scrolls of the reconciliation statement at the ceremony on Parliament Hill in Ottawa but not given the opportunity to respond verbally. Four of the five representatives in Canada later dismissed the apology as being too weak.

nation did, or who it *was* in its aberrant moment, and who it was declaring itself to be now, or distinguishing that aberrant moment as a historical betrayal of its true or ideal identity. At the same time, in realigning itself with the ideal normative self (the real France as the home of the Enlightenment, for example), the nation was reconciling itself with or reclaiming the ideal identity in historical time. In the act of apologizing, the nation was thus performing and affirming that the historical community and the ideal community coincided.

What we are seeing here is the commissive dimension of apologetic speech, but now it is apparent that the commitment in question is as much about the identity of the apologizing community as it is about its actions in relation to others. It is as much a performative statement directed to the nation itself (as its own audience) as it is to the violated other. Certainly, if the national self is different (and presumably better) from an ethical point of view, it will behave in an ethically superior way *vis-à-vis* its minorities or other types of 'others'. However, this is more a collateral benefit of the shift affected by apology than its primary target. In William Connolly's terms, the difference at issue here is the one between liberal tolerance, which would involve a shifting view of the other, and critical responsiveness, which "involves comparative shifts in the constituencies who offer it ... active work on our current identities in order to modify the terms of relation between us and them."[37]

If one looks beyond the apology itself to the broader institutional context, one sees that apologies are always located within some more comprehensive project of moral reconstruction. Again, this is not to say that the status of the victim group is irrelevant to the apology. Their relevance is, however, not in their power to give or withhold forgiveness, understood formally as the uptake that would form the final stage of the successful apology. Rather, they form a necessary part of the story through which the perpetrator group performs its transformation, a transformation that is effected through its redefining the status of the victim group. The victim 'other' is a necessary part of the speech act insofar as it forms part of the drama where the ethical status of the dominant political group is tested, assessed, and exhibited: we treated them abominably then; we redeem ourselves by treating them respectfully now (the apology); and therefore we experience and show ourselves restored to our ideal normative identity.

Reframing the role of the victim in this way then helps to make sense of what, according to this new understanding, would seem to be an anomalous inclusion of a request for forgiveness. That is, if it does not matter if a

---

[37] William Connolly, *Why I Am Not a Secularist* (Minneapolis: University of Minnesota Press, 1999), 62.

representative of the victim group actually grants forgiveness or not (were this even possible), why would apologies so often include pleas for forgiveness, as they in fact do? The answer is that the perlocutory force of this plea (for forgiveness) is not to evoke a direct response. Rather, by begging forgiveness the apologizing party is making itself vulnerable to the judgement of the wronged other; it is now displaying itself standing before the wronged other with a countenance of vulnerability.

Thus, the judgement itself is less important than the act of submitting oneself to judgement. Indeed, although apologies seem to seek a verdict, everybody already knows it 'objectively': the perpetrator nation is guilty. What the request for forgiveness, and even more, begging for forgiveness provides, especially when combined with an acknowledgement of the others' suffering, is the vehicle for performing one's own reformed status. Nowhere was this more poignantly demonstrated than in the image of the German leader, the one occupying the same symbolic position as the leader who had made Jews into nothing, getting down on his knees before the symbol of the Jew. When I beg the one whom I have harmed and dominated for forgiveness, I am giving over my previous immoral identity not only substantively but also formally. The position of submission, as much as the content of the words, signifies and performs this shift. Moreover, it performs it not simply before the victim, but before a third party, the public witness of the state itself, and in many cases the international community.

Does this mean, in the most unapologetic terms, that the political apology is a self-serving act? In a manner, yes it does. Nevertheless, saying as much neither deprives it of its moral importance or value, nor does it imply that service to the self is irrelevant to the status and experience of the other. Ultimately, the position that the previously denigrated group occupies in the political landscape will, after all, flow from the ethical identity of the dominant group and the degree to which that ethical identity encodes due respect to the other. Indeed, one might imagine a scenario wherein the dominant group paid ample compensation and offered extensive rehabilitative programmes for some wrong committed in the past against, say, Indigenous people, but continued to see them as less than human or to marginalize or discount their experience because the dominant group itself retained its long-held view of itself as above the judgement of the other, as not having violated some value it was committed to honour. In this case, it will only be through 'serving itself' (understood as attending to its normative status) that the dominant group can structurally alter the position of the other.

What this suggests is that in its collective dimension it is not only the content of apology that must be rethought, but also its form or discursive structure, the structural roles that we think the various parties implicated in the apologetic drama play. Drawing on Tavuchis' analysis of the inter-personal apology, apology is generally taken to be a dyadic act, that is, essentially a piece of communication between the perpetrator/speaker and victim/recipient. A communicates to B with a view to bringing about some change in B. If, however, the uptake of the collective apology is not forgiveness from the party to whom it is linguistically directed, this dramatic structure no longer seems to accurately describe its dynamic. Rather, A would be the primary object of A's own communication, with B as a character deployed to play out A's own drama, a far more complex arrangement.

We find a clue about this more complex structure in Tavuchis' reference to Arendt's observation that plurality is a condition for forgiveness (and, by analogy, apology). Oddly, Tavuchis interprets Arendt's understanding as confirmation of his contention that 'the bedrock structure of apology is binary',[38] but this is precisely what she is challenging. Plurality arises not when there are two (as distinct from one), but only where there are more than two. Only then, when there is a public world created by the witness, does plurality arise. What makes this plurality difficult to discern in the drama of collective apologies is that the community in whose name the apology is spoken is also (though not necessarily only) the witness. Indeed, the community occupies multiple roles, as a protagonist in the drama being narrated by the apology (the one who did wrong), the one apologizing, and as witness to that transformation.

Bringing this analysis back to the problem with which this chapter began, it is now apparent that the major structural problems that seemed to render the collective a category mistake no longer apply. Specifically, this reframing allows us to understand apology not simply as the expression of feelings that lie *inside* a subject, but more aptly as a statement that passes a judgement on what the subject has been in the past and one that works to reconstitute the subject's normative identity. If this is the work of apology or, perhaps more accurately, if this is one of the structural possibilities of apology, then it need not, as per Trouillot's critique, automatically demand qualities inconsistent with a collective subject. Indeed, the results of this Austinian analysis provide flesh on the bones of Tavuchis' rudimentary suggestion that the collective apology should not be judged in terms of its success in expressing sorrow or remorse, but for "the remedial and reparative work it accomplishes."[39]

---

[38] Tavuchis, *Mea Culpa*, 46.
[39] Ibid., 111.

What this question leaves unanswered, however, is how does the apologetic act accomplish remediation or reparation of the apologizing collective? If it does not work through a transformation of an inner self, then how does it work? A speech act theory analysis will not provide answers to these further questions, because they demand that we attend to the structure of collective normative identity itself and the dynamics of its transformation. Nor are we going to find answers by going back to the standard inter-personal apologetic form, where the subject has an importantly different structure. In Chapter Seven, when I come back to examine the logic of collective responsibility, I address some of the structural problems raised by the collective apology. At this stage, however, I address that question by looking at the historic practice of apology that has been lurking in the background, that is, apology in the sphere of religion. There we find not only the performative, but, perhaps surprisingly, also the grammar of an essentially collective apology.[40]

---

[40] Interestingly, this was the path that Tavuchis himself identified as the unfinished business of his own study, referring to the spectre of religious confession as "a topic that has haunted our discussion at virtually every point." Ibid., 123.

3

Judaism's Apology

Reconstituting the Community

> Sin is the breaking off of a personal relationship with God. It presupposes the experience of a vis-à-vis whose holiness has been discovered in a retrospective act of reflection and repentance.... [T]he idea of sin is the obverse of the idea of God.
>
> Albert Gelin[1]

I. AN ALTERNATIVE TEMPLATE FOR APOLOGY?

If the dominant images of apology cause us to stumble on the idea that an apology can be genuinely collective, then the Jewish practice of *teshuvah,* or repentance, may well provide the alternative trope we need to rethink contemporary collective apologies. As against the inherited metaphor of apology as an essentially individual event, whose heart lies in an internal process of regret, in Judaism one finds an apologetic form that is essentially public, spoken, and collective. In fact, the collective quality of the practices and theological understandings of *teshuvah* cannot, without gross distortion, be reformulated in terms of the individual 'repentance of the lone heart' model. On the contrary, the Jewish tradition privileges the constructive role of collective symbolic action and speech and encodes it as part of a suite of reparative acts that work in concert to effect not only individual but, more importantly, *collective* transformation. This latter, political dimension of Judaism's apology is particularly pertinent for our purposes, because here we seem to have a model for the work that apology can do in reconstituting the identity of a community as a political

---

[1] Gelin, "Sin in the Old Testament," in *Sin in the Bible,* ed. Charles Schaldenbrand (New York: Desclee Company, 1964), 39f.

entity. Linking this back with the core objections to apology as an effective political intervention, these two features of the Jewish concept and practice, its collective character and the centrality of public speech, make it particularly germane for making sense of the contemporary political apology. The first objective of this chapter is thus to set out and explore the significance of the collective trope of apology in Jewish practice and understanding.

This certainly sounds like a positive move, but as soon as we pause and think about *where* we are looking for this alternative trope, we are likely to be struck by a whole new raft of problems. In this sense, this move may do little more than avoid one set of conceptual dangers by charging into other, more serious, ethical and practical ones. The mere fact that Judaism (or any other religion for that matter) provides an essentially collective trope does not mean that it is a suitable or morally desirable trope for modern liberal political communities. In fact, standard modernist understandings of religious collective practices would maintain just the opposite. Modern political forms, so this argument goes, were established in order to counter the assorted vices of theocratic political forms. In place of their allegiance to a transcendent metaphysics, we limited ourselves to the mundane and human; instead of aligning ourselves with thick, heteronomous values (God's laws), we preferred 'thin' values established by autonomous citizens and always open to revision by a new crop of autonomous citizens; rather than external ritual we chose either authentic individual commitment or rational, 'disenchanted' institutions;[2] and perhaps most importantly, in place of crude collectivism and its failure to respect the unassailable principle of moral individualism, we opted for individual responsibility.

If this characterization of Judaism's apology is correct, then we have now placed the collective political apology between the horns of an interpretive dilemma. If its primary template is the essentially individual apology of the heart, then the collective apology is a category mistake; if it belongs to the class of *sui generis* collective acts, modelled on the religious form, then it is guilty of absolutism, heteronomy, empty externality, and gross collectivism, all of which disqualify it from functioning as a legitimate mechanism in contemporary liberal politics. On the first horn, apology could not be collective or political; on the second, it could be, but not in the 'right' way.

The second objective of this chapter is thus to dispute this characterization or, perhaps more accurately, this caricature of the collective apology as

---

[2] This shift is as much about a move to modernity's self-professed rationalism as it is about a distinction from religion per se, as is evident if one thinks of the starkness of Lutheran churches and the elaborate ritual of certain secular political regimes. On the historical changes in performance in politics, see Jurgen Habermas, *The Structural Transformation of the Public Sphere*, trans. Thomas Burger (Cambridge, Mass.: MIT Press, 1991).

practiced and understood in Judaism. Specifically, by looking at the stories, practices, and philosophies elaborated about *teshuvah*, I suggest a reading of Judaism's collective apology that does not suffer from the maladies associated with a crude understanding that would reduce it to modernity's outmoded other. This is not to deny the general legitimacy of the link between modernity and the processes of individuation and differentiation. It is, rather, to suggest, very much in the spirit of Durkheim's own critique of his earlier contention that there was a sharp division between pre-modern religious forms and modern forms of social organization, that religious logics, and in particular their attention to the collective dimension of social life, are far from absent in modern forms of social organization and institutions.[3]

I am also not suggesting that the interpretation I am offering of Jewish collective rituals as a powerful mechanism of collective normative transformation is the only legitimate way of interpreting the understanding or practice of the collective apology in the Jewish canon. It would be absurd to deny that such religious practices and understandings can and often do degenerate into empty formalism, gross collectivism, and forms of idolatry that deprive actual humans of responsibility for what they must choose to do. My argument rather lies in the space of possibility that the prophets alluded to when they shouted in exasperation that religious practices and theological understandings contain greater potentials than those realized in their degenerated forms. This was, I take it, Isaiah's point when he berated the Israelites for empty formalism and asked, sardonically, "Is it such a fast that I have chosen?"[4]

Specifically, what I believe we can redeem from the practice of collective *teshuvah* are: first, a conceptual framework and actual practice that transcend the apparent contradiction between individual and collective responsibility; second, an understanding of how the work of apology is also the work of reconstituting collective identity; and third, a map of the relationship among speech, action, and being that does not reduce speech to mere representation. Before moving to the stories, practices, and theological debates that support these arguments, a word is in order about their link with the broader project of this book and also the qualifications required for this project to be viable. As I discussed in the Introduction, my contention that there is a formal continuity between the 'religious' practice of apology and the 'political' apology signals the need for a more comprehensive reassessment of the inherited framework that dichotomises

---

[3] For Durkheim's early position, see *The Division of Labor in Society*, trans. W. D. Halls (New York: Free Press, 1979). For his later position, see "De la definition des phenomenes religieux," *L'Annee Sociologique* 2 (1897–8) and *The Elementary Forms of Religious Life*, trans. Carol Cosman (Oxford: Oxford University Press, 2001).

[4] Isa. 15:5.

religion and politics or pre-modern and modern political forms, and represents them as hermetically sealed spheres of activity or systems of logic. Just as, in the case of apology, this dichotomous conceptual grammar prevents our seeing how the ritual form of repentance could speak to modern sensibilities and the demands of modern political organization, so too this logic more broadly impoverishes our understanding of the modern polity and the forms of intervention required to mediate injustice and systematic violation. Thus, whereas that dichotomous framework, when dogmatically applied, would have us ignore and shun any process that seems to belong on the wrong side of the tracks, when we actually attend to the logic and substance of those 'othered' processes, we find approaches, conceptualisations, and indeed practices that may illuminate our own processes and even supplement those we traditionally embrace.

Understood as part of this broader project, the work of this chapter is to unsettle the conceptual dichotomies according to which our map of religion and politics is organized by re-examining the categories that supposedly constitute their religious half. Insofar as the processes of public religious repentance defy clean categorization within one side of each of the various dichotomies noted above, the boundary that would 'exclude' them from the sphere of proper action in modern secular politics also begins to dissolve. Jewish practices and self-understandings concerning repentance and apology are particularly fertile in this regard because they challenge the very dichotomies in question: between human autonomy and divine heteronomy, between the existence of an absolute ground for political or normative order and the ongoing development of political form and norms, between collective and individual responsibility, and between the internal/subjective and the external/performative. Throughout this chapter, as I come to each of these distinctions, I explore how actual practices and understandings in the religious context exceed the container of the dichotomy within which they are thought to sit. The other side of the work is to re-examine the practice in the contemporary secular setting, suspending the strong assumption that this practice must conform with the 'modern/secular' side of the dichotomies and assessing whether some aspects of a collective ontology and performative modality can be reintegrated into our self-understanding. This is the work of Chapters Six, Seven, and Eight.

To recognize this potential compatibility or cross-fertilization, however, it is important to make it clear that it is the *form* of the processes and not the *substance* of the commitments that I am claiming is transferable or relevant for the contemporary context. My attention is on the way in which *teshuvah* can be understood as a process for bringing about social transformation and is not on the issues or, if you like, the 'sins' that gave rise to the call for *teshuvah* or the specific wrongs to which it might have been applied. The fact that religious and modern political communities represent their fundamental commitments and identities in different ways is not what is at issue here, because the *mechanisms* for realizing (and I will argue shifting) fundamental principles of right and identity can be abstracted from the *content* of those commitments and identities. My focus is on these mechanisms, abstracted of content, and it is the former, not the latter, that are transferable from the sphere of religious community to the sphere of secular political community. My argument thus rests on the assertion that Jewish practices provide forms of intervention or processes of societal transformation that can be detached from their content and taken up in the secular setting.[5]

I have organized the material of this chapter into three thematic sections. Together they lay the conceptual foundation for what I am calling the alternative collective trope and elaborate an approach or a logic that makes sense of collective apologies as meaningful and legitimate forms of political intervention. The first section begins with the contemporary practice of collective apologetic speech and looks back to the ritual origins of this practice to draw out its richer significance and the world of meaning we need to draw on in order to make sense of it. The second section takes up the issue of performance, speech, and language and draws on Jewish understandings of the relationship between intention and speech to challenge the subordination of apology to mere representation. The final section then turns to a number of more philosophical and legal Jewish sources to fill out the conceptual scheme already sketched and to suggest how we might answer particular challenges posed by collective political apologies, such as how they work across time as well as the extent to which apology can involve a shift in the normative commitments of a group.

2. YOM KIPPUR: JUDAISM'S COLLECTIVE APOLOGY

In Jewish theology and practice, it is the public and collective forms of apology that predominate. This not only is true in the case of ancient, pre-modern practices, but remains the case in contemporary ritual. One sees this clearly in, for example, the ritual services of Yom Kippur (the Day of Atonement), the annual

---

[5] It is crucial that the reader keep this distinction in mind in what follows, especially in those sections where the sacred content or explicitly religious language, and in particular the reference to God or God's laws, seems to overwhelm the formal process, which is what I am looking to expound. To avoid the type of confusion or conflation that the constant references to Torah or God or God's law are bound to produce, the reader should keep in mind that, structurally, these play the role of the foundational normative commitments and grounds of the normative orientation of the community. In other words, abstracted of their sacred character, they are the fundamental social rules about right and wrong that orient the community.

focal point of apology and repentance in the Jewish calendar.[6] Repentance and, more specifically, apology lie at the heart of the Yom Kippur ritual, when the entire community gathers and communally repents its wrongs. Importantly, when I say it comes together to repent its wrongs, I do not mean that the people gather as a collection of individuals each apologizing for their own wrongs at the same time, but that they repent *qua* community, as the corporate body Knesset Israel.[7]

This corporate form is apparent in the Selichot, or penitential prayers, which dominate the Yom Kippur liturgy.[8] The various prayers are articulated in three basic ways: read aloud by the rabbi on behalf of the community, read privately and silently by each person, and read aloud by all members of the congregation on behalf of all members of the congregation. In the last of these, where each member of the congregation confesses a common list of sins individually, but in unison, the voice of the prayers is first person plural: 'we have sinned against you'. The experience is literally of a single sound as the voices of the pray-ers come together: each person singularly, but also as part of the common voice, speaks his or her responsibility and regret for every sin, whether or not he or she has individually committed it. It is only when it comes to the private silent prayer that individuals are invited to add those sins that they personally wish to repent.

The collective ownership of repentance is also explicit in the content of the liturgy. One Yom Kippur prayer says, for example:

As on this day we examine our individual lives, so do we look at the life of the society around us ... as we would share in the rewards of righteousness, so must we confess a measure of responsibility for the world's evils.[9]

---

[6] As Maimonides teaches, "despite the fact that teshuvah and crying out to HaShem are always timely, during the Ten Days between Rosh HaShanah and Yom HaKippurim it is exceedingly appropriate, and is accepted immediately, as it says, 'Seek HaShem when He is to be found' (Isaiah 55:6)." *Mishnah Torah*, trans. Rabbi Eliayhu Touger (Jerusalem: Moznaim Publishing, 1990); Hilchot Teshuvah: The Laws of Repentance 2.6. The source of this statement for Maimonides is Rosh HaShanah (Talmud) (18a), "Seek HaShem when He is to be found – these are the days between Rosh HaShanah and Yom HaKippurim."

[7] The term *Israel* does not refer to the modern state or land but to the Jewish people.

[8] Over the first eight centuries of the common era, specific *Viduy* (a class of confessional prayers) developed to become the core communal confessional forms used during the period of repentance. The earlier, more simple and general *ashamnu*, dating from the first century C.E., is pure confession, expressing an awareness of sin and the pain of remorse, but making no move towards supplication. The longer, more specific and later *al het* developed gradually in post-Talmudic times, somewhere between the fifth and eighth centuries, and includes both an inventory of sins and a call for forgiveness. See Joseph Marcus, "Confession," in *The Universal Jewish Encyclopaedia*, vol. 3, by Isaac B. Landman (New York: Universal Jewish Encyclopaedia, c. 1939–44), 328.

[9] Cf. Chaim Stern, ed., *Shaarei Teshuvah: Gates of Repentance: The New Union Prayer Book for the Days of Awe* (New York: Central Conference of American Rabbis, 1978), 401.

How can one make sense of this collective form of repentance? What is going on when the community, as a single voice, apologizes for past wrongs? There are several places in which one might seek an answer to this question. First, this modern form of prayer is understood as a substitute for the sacrificial rituals that were practiced before the destruction of the temple, so their significance might be found in the meaning of the ancient practices. Second, Jews tell a number of stories about the origin of Yom Kippur and these provide a window into its significance. Third, in Hebrew, words are themselves rich in significance and cross-reference, so one can look to the etymology of the key terms. In what follows, I take each of these in turn.

(i) Ancient Rituals of Repentance: The Temple-Era Yom Kippur Ritual

While Jewish self-understanding recognizes a definite break between temple-era Judaism and the Rabbinical Judaism that developed after the destruction of the second Temple (75 C.E.), the ancient texts, rituals, and interpretations continue to provide the principal sites of meaning. The collective form of repentant *tefilah* (prayer) and spoken repentance that continues into modern Jewish practice are understood as substitutes for ancient sacrifice and purification rituals. That said, working out the relationship between the two sets of practices is far from simple. This is in part because the very different context in which the ancient practices occurred makes it notoriously difficult to discern the precise significance and in part because our understanding of those differences is itself constituted through our own epistemological and ontological assumptions. Thus we think of the people who practiced the original rituals as having ontological and epistemological understandings of the world and themselves fundamentally different from the ones we hold, but we also imagine those differences within the horizon of our own epistemological and ontological structures. The result is that transferring their meanings to ours entails a complex translation.

A more straightforward problem is that even if it is possible to make sense of the temple-era practices (such as sacrifice) and trace the lines of transmitted meaning, one still has to separate out which part of this meaning apology in particular picks up, because *teshuvah* is just one of a set of practices that substituted those rituals and the apology is just one component of *teshuvah*. As the Yom Kippur liturgy repeatedly reminds us, *teshuvah* (repentance), *tefilah* (prayer), and *tzedakah* (charity) are our substitutes for the now defunct sacrificial rituals, and so specifying *teshuvah*'s piece of meaning will require something of a sifting exercise.[10] I mention this here not only to point to the methodological

---

[10] As stated repeatedly in the Yom Kippur liturgy. See also the Pesikta de Rab Kehana, "Shemini 'Atzeret'" (Buber, 191a; Mandelbaum, 425). ˙

need for a hermeneutic to read off the apology component, but more importantly because it recalls a point that is often forgotten in contemporary criticisms of the political apology. Here, just as in the contemporary scene, apology is always only a component of the comprehensive work of dealing with the past. Consequently, it is a mistake either to look to it to achieve outcomes for which it is not tailored or to criticize it for failing to do so.[11] We might thus take this teaching as a model reminder that apology carries a distinct part of the work, sitting alongside, rather than replacing, material compensation of punishment. The challenge is to specify what apology's part of the work is.

Turning now to the rituals themselves, Jews take the description of the original temple-era ritual set out in Leviticus 16 to be authoritative.[12] Indeed, for Jews, *reading* this text on the morning of Yom Kippur is equivalent to re-enacting it and certainly reinvoking its significance, a fact that in itself speaks to the concern I raised earlier about the continuity between ancient and modern practices.[13] The Yom Kippur portion comes at the end of part IV on defilement and purification, and more generally as part of an extended tract prescribing and describing standard sacrificial practices brought down from older, pre-Mosaic cultic practices.[14] The Yom Kippur rituals fall into the broader categories of guilt (or restitution) and sin (or purification) offerings.[15]

---

[11]   In Chapter Five where I set out the dimensions of reparation specified in the authoritative United Nations Study on Reparation for Human Rights Violations, we will see that apology is understood as one component of reparatory action.

[12]   This portion is set within the book of Leviticus, the book that sets out the rituals and laws that the Israelites were to observe.

[13]   There is a Midrash (see note 61) that addresses this very point. It elaborates on an incident in Genesis 15 wherein Abraham asks God how he can be sure that God will not cut off the people of Israel when they sin in the future, as God did in the time of Noah. When God points to the ongoing practice of sacrifice as a sign that this contract, this relationship, is permanent, Abraham argues that this is fine in the time of the temple, but what about when the temple no longer exists? God replies: "I have already fixed for them the order of sacrifices. Whenever they will *read* the order of the sacrifices I will reckon it as if they are *bringing* me an offering, and *forgive* all their iniquities" (Meg. 31b).

[14]   Lev. 1–7, 14, 17, 27. References to the ritual also appear in Num. 18 and 29. For a treatment of the age of such sacrificial practices, see A. Lods, "Éléments anciens et éléments modernes dans le rituel du sacrifice israélite," *Revue d'histoire et de Philosophie Religieuses* 8 (1928): 399. Gerhard Von Rad, *Old Testament Theology*, vol. 1, trans. D.M.G. Stalker (San Francisco: Harper, 1967), 258–9.

[15]   Milgrom, in his translation and commentary of Leviticus, provides these alternative names. In particular, and importantly for this work, he argues that the term 'sin offering' both is an inaccurate translation and poorly represents what was actually going on, and suggests the alternative 'purification' offering. Accordingly, I use both terms in this text. See Jacob Milgrom, *Leviticus 1–16: A New Translation with Introduction and Commentary*, the Anchor Bible, vol. 3 (New York: Doubleday, 1991), 253ff.

The early ritual is striking as an example of collective and representative repentance. Dramatically, the entire performance centres on the High Priest (predecessor to the rabbi) as the representative actor of the community. It is the priest who will make expiation for all the people of the congregation.[16] The congregation is also expected to "afflict" itself, or practice self-denial (fasting), and abstain from work. However, this is mentioned only at the very end of the portion when the text announces that "to make atonement for the Israelites and for their sins once a year" shall be the law for all time.[17]

The rituals set out Leviticus 16 include animal sacrifice, burning incense, and ritual cleansing of the altar and of the High Priest. The most captivating aspect of this annual drama, and certainly the one that continues to engage contemporary imaginations, is the ritual of the two goats.[18] Here, the text describes how the priest brings two 'he goats' to the entrance of the holy tent, one of which will be marked "as a sin [purification] offering to the Lord", the other – the scapegoat – which will bear the sins of the entire community. Before the High Priest sends away the living scapegoat, he lays both his hands upon the he-goat's head, and confesses over it all the iniquities and transgressions of the Israelites, "putting them on the head of the goat. And it shall be sent off to the wilderness through a designated man. Thus the goat shall carry on it all their iniquities to Azazel." *Azazel* is commonly translated as an inaccessible region, the *other* place, outside the boundary, removed and disconnected from the divinely constituted community.[19]

The text of Leviticus itself is very thin on interpretation or elaboration of the meanings of the offerings, indicating only that the purposes of sin (or purification) and guilt offerings were, respectively, to expiate sins between man and

---

[16] Lev. 16: 30, 32–4.

[17] In fact, in his analysis of the text, Milgrom argues that this last section was an appendix to the primary text. Milgrom, *Leviticus*, 1054.

[18] Lev. 16: 21–2. This rite almost certainly dates back to very early stages of the development of Judaism, and the idea that the goat could carry contamination away from human beings was present in earlier and contemporary pagan practice. For example, during plagues the Hittites sent a goat into enemy territory so that it would carry the plague there, and an Akkadian magical inscription from the city of Assur points to a belief that sickness was transferred from humans to goats. See Ahmuel Ahituv, "Azazel," in *Encyclopaedia Judaica*, vol. 3, ed. Cecil Roth (New York: Macmillan, 1971), 1001.

[19] There has been a great deal of midrashic discussion as to what Azazel refers to. The most authoritative interpretation is that it is a demonic being residing in the desert, but to avoid what would seem to be an acknowledgement of an independent evil power inconsistent with monotheism, many commentators interpreted and translated it as a place, rough ground (Rashi), a mountain near Sinai (Ibn Ezra), or dismissal (the old Greek translation). See W. Gunther Plaut, ed., *The Torah: A Modern Commentary* (New York: Union of American Hebrew Congregations, 1981), 859 and 1735 n. 4.

God and transgressions between man and his fellow. Without elaboration, however, these terms themselves tell us very little and lend themselves to anachronistic readings. Modern commentators have offered a gamut of interpretations of ancient sacrifice, but three stand out: sacrifice as a form of compensation, sacrifice as a form of substitution for retributive justice, and sacrifice as a form of purification.[20] I argue that apology correlates most closely with the third.

According to the first interpretation, sacrifice was a literal act of compensatory renunciation. The agent making the sacrifice was 'giving up' something of value to him, in a way one might see as continuous with the modern legal form of compensation, also including punitive damages.[21] In the case of sacrifice, however, the wronged party is not only another person against whom wrongs have been directly committed, but God, whose will or law the person committing the wrongful act failed to respect. While this attention to God as a wronged party may seem remote from our modern conceptions of wrongdoing or compensation, we might well understand it as equivalent to the modern idea, encoded in criminal law, that when one commits wrongs against another person that contravene the criminal code, it is the state and not the other person that brings the prosecution.[22]

The second understanding of sacrifice sees it as a process of symbolic substitution, where the sacrificial material stands in for the person making the sacrifice. According to strict requirements of retributive justice, what should be done to the wrongdoer is done by proxy to the sacrificial material. One can discern this strand of meaning in the later (post-temple) Yom Kippur custom known as Kapporot (from the Hebrew for atone, the root of *kippur*). In the

---

[20] As Milgrom argues, "[n]o single theory can encompass the sacrificial system of any society." Milgrom, *Leviticus*, 442. For a fuller exposition of sacrifice, see Joseph Dan, "Sacrifice," in *Encyclopaedia Judaica*, vol. 14, ed. Cecil Roth (New York: Macmillan, 1971), 599, and Milgrom, *Leviticus*, 440ff.

[21] In practice, domestic animals as opposed to wild animals were sacrificed because wild animals did not belong to anyone; food offerings took the form of flour or meal, because these required substantial work to prepare: "I cannot sacrifice to the Lord my God burnt offerings that have cost me nothing" (2 Sam 24:24). In the Levitican description of the guilt, the quantity of the offering is measured in terms of the gravity of the sin. The value of the offering is supposed to be equivalent to the value of the transgression, plus one fifth added, presumably by way of punitive damages.

[22] Applebaum writes, for example: "Criminal law is generally considered to be that field of jurisprudence which is concerned with wrongs against society. Such a wrong might arise by reason of an act directed against an isolated individual, but it is the tort against the social structure, resulting from such an act, which is punishable. . . . The purposes of criminal law are rather to punish the wrongdoer for his offense against the mores of society." J. Applebaum, *Military Tribunals and International Crimes* (Westport, Conn.: Greenwood Press, 1954), 9.

traditional form of this ritual, a person swings a chicken over his or her head (a rooster for a man and a hen for a woman), and recites the prayer: "This is my substitute, this is my pardon, this is my atonement, this rooster goes to death and I shall enter a long, happy and peaceful life."[23] Today, a gift of money tied in a handkerchief substitutes for the chicken, still swung over the head while reciting the prayer and later given as *tzedakah* (charity).

The common economy underpinning both of these strands (renunciation and substitution) is one regulated by the principle of exchange, an offering made by way of giving up something that stands in for the 'gain' effected by the wrongful act. Structurally, the operation works by conceptualising the wrongful act as a negative operation or some type of 'negative stuff', whereas the sacrifice (or its later equivalent) is the numerically equivalent, but positively valued, 'stuff'. Sacrifice takes the account from the red back into the black. If one moves from the temple-era to the post-temple-era practices (prayer, charity, and repentance), the most direct successors of this dimension are no doubt charity and those components of repentance explicitly concerned with material compensation. Nevertheless, this trope of economic exchange also infuses understandings of apology, as one sees in Tavuchis' claim that apology "constitutes both the medium of exchange and the symbolic quid pro quo for, as it were, 'compensation'."[24] Along similar lines, recent jurisprudence on processes for dealing with human rights violations has increasingly referred to truth as a 'right' that victims have, rendering it structurally equivalent to other (material) forms of restitution deemed to compensate (however imperfectly) for the loss.[25]

The problem with framing the apology within this economy of exchange is that it distorts the dynamic of the apologetic encounter, or at least conceals from view a dimension of that encounter that is not about exchange at all. When an apology is given, the purpose of the communication is not to pay someone back for improperly acquired goods, but rather to alter the quality of the relationship. More technically, apology's intentional objects are the dynamics of power and recognition between the parties and their respective identities.[26] Thus, when wrongdoers expose their wrongdoing to the world, there may indeed be a type of surrender, but what is being given up is not some *thing*,

---

[23] Rabbi Menachem Davis, ed., *The Schottenstein Edition Machzor for Yom Kippur* (New York: Artscroll, 2004), 4.

[24] Tavuchis, *Mea Culpa*, 33.

[25] For a discussion of relevant cases, see Douglass Cassel, "Lessons from the Americas: Guidelines for International Response to Amnesties for Atrocities," *Law and Contemporary Problems*, 59, no. 4 (Autumn 1996).

[26] Iris Marion Young makes a structurally analogous objection to distributive models of social justice. See *Justice and the Politics of Difference* (Princeton: Princeton University Press, 1990).

but a system of meaning or a position in a relationship. We saw this graphically in the *kniefall*, where the German leader gave up his nation's position of domination and its claim of authority over history. Trying to map this dynamic onto the model of balancing accounts through an economic exchange distorts the complexity of what is actually taking place.

What, then, of the third conception of sacrifice, sacrifice as purification? On first inspection, this trope seems completely inadequate to the task of making sense of apologies in the contemporary context. According to our habitual modern reading, sacrificial purification was a type of magical process that putatively cleansed people and social space of the contamination that was believed to cause individuals to do wrong; yet we think of ourselves as autonomous agents who are ourselves the cause of wrongdoing.[27] Moreover, on this view, sin for the ancients had a quasi-material quality, which, if left unchecked, could spread through the body of the community; however, we see individuals as ontologically and morally distinct.[28] Correlatively, the work of sacrifice would be understood here as a form of external remediation, whereas we would insist on the intentional or conscious involvement of the responsible agent in his or her own correction.[29]

In the background to these readings is a depiction of the ancient worldview and pre-prophetic religious practice that could not be further from the one we hold as an ideal for ourselves.[30] According to this progressive reading of history, we imagine the ancients who practiced sacrifice as a less developed type of human, still lacking a proper understanding of the causes of advantageous or disadvantageous events in their own lives (sickness, shifts in the weather, crop failure) and of the mechanics or structures of causality more generally. They interpreted the success or failure of their endeavours as the independent movement of external forces, transcendent beings (gods and demons) whom they endowed with complete influence over the events in their own lives. In other

---

[27] "The impression is gained that everyday religion was dominated by fear of evil powers and black magic rather than a positive worship of the gods. . . . [T]he world was conceived to be full of evil demons who might cause trouble in any sphere of life. If they attacked, the right ritual should effect the cure. . . . Humans, as well as devils, might work evil against a person by the black arts, and here too the appropriate ritual was required." W. Lambert, "Three Literary Prayers of the Babylonians," *Archiv fur Orientforschung* 19 (1959–60): 55–60.

[28] As Milgrom puts it, sin was understood as "a physical substance, and aerial miasma that possessed magnetic attraction for the realm of the sacred." *Leviticus*, 257.

[29] See, e.g., George Foot Moore, *Judaism in the First Centuries of the Christian Era: The Age of the Tannaim* (Cambridge, Mass.: Harvard University Press, 1958), 497.

[30] This conceptual scheme has been well rehearsed in anthropological and historical literature. For a connection between this worldview and practices concerning sin, see Paul Ricouer, *Symbolism of Evil*, trans. Emerson Buchanan (Boston: Beacon Press, 1967).

words, theirs was a radically heteronomous world in which individuals did not yet understand the ontological and moral priority of individual consciousness, intentionality, or responsibility.

It is easy to see how the ritual described in Leviticus 16, particularly the striking drama of the two goats, lends itself to this reading. Cleansing and purging the individual, the community, and the holy place of the stain of sin are certainly dramatically vivid in this scene. The defilement and contamination of the sin of the entire community are literally transferred onto the goat, which is exiled. Similarly, the text commands the Kohen (High Priest) to sprinkle blood onto the altar, in order to "hallow" and cleanse it of the uncleanness of the people of Israel.[31]

There are, however, strong evidentiary and conceptual grounds for questioning this reading of the purification trope, or at least for suggesting that there are other more sophisticated readings that do not cast the practices as the diametrical opposite to our view of ourselves as rational, autonomous moderns. To start with, there are several 'evidentiary' problems with this interpretation of the ancient rituals. One of the major pieces of evidence brought to prove that the ancient rituals of the Hebrews were formalistic and 'empty' is the prophets' denunciations.[32] However, as I suggested in my earlier allusion to Isaiah, the fact that the prophets berated the people for the emptiness of their ritual practice is not equivalent to an evaluation that those rituals are *essentially* empty. On the contrary, one could well interpret their words as invective designed to highlight the degeneration of practices and inspire the people to reinvest themselves into their rituals.[33] Read this way, the prophetic statements are testament to the abuse of the practices, not proof of their inherent limits.

A second piece of evidence brought to prove the pure externality of the rituals is the absence of any textual reference to the subjective dimension of the practices.[34] But we should be cautious about equating a textual gap with a gap in the processes themselves; that the Priestly Code is crudely materialistic does not mean that this reflects the practice. A more sophisticated knowledge of

---

[31] Lev. 16:19.

[32] The tendency to use the prophets to indict the empty formalism and crude collectivism of Judaism is apparent in some Christian commentary. Redlich, e.g., writes: "[O]ut of the ruins of nationality, in the destruction of the Holy City and the Temple, rose the concept of individual religion." E. Basil Redlich, *The Forgiveness of Sins* (Edinburgh: T & T Clark, 1937), 45.

[33] "I hate, I despise your feasts ... though you offer me burnt offerings ... I will not accept them. But let Justice well up as waters, and righteousness as a mighty stream." 5: Amos 21–4. See also Jer. 7:22.

[34] As Von Rad observes, "the reader looks in vain for firm holds to enable him to rise into the spiritual realm by way of the sacrificial concepts lying behind the sacrificial practices." *Old Testament Theology*, 260.

the way these texts were constructed tells us that the Priestly Code was not the place where this type of elaboration was recorded and that it almost certainly appeared in texts that have not survived.[35] Moreover, as Von Rad argues, if the text contains little indication of "[rising] into the spiritual realm", this is not an indication that the practice was crudely materialistic, nor even simply a short-fall in the text, but rather a signal that we are dealing with an understanding in which "spiritual faith" and "cultic practice" did not belong to two spheres.[36]

Indeed, Von Rad's point here goes to the heart of my critique of the standard portrayal of pre-modern ritual practice. That God is not posited as the abstract object of belief but is immediately experienced through the cultic practice tells us not that the ancients thought of God as belonging to the realm of material objects (as we conceive of them) but that they did not distribute being into two distinct and mutually exclusive categories, spirit and material.[37] Milgrom similarly points out that the ancients did not distinguish between emotional and physical suffering, as one can see in the impossibility of distinguishing between pangs of conscience and physical pain in the language of the primary biblical texts.[38] One did not do something in order to attain a spiritual experience, nor is God reduced to material terms. The faith of ancient Israel cannot be divided in this way. Rather, it was through the sacrificial cult that the faith of ancient Israel (its relationship with God) was maintained and experienced.[39]

A third piece of evidence of the inadequacy of characterizing sacrifice (purification) as crude externality, and one particularly significant for *apology*, is that these early practices always included a verbal dimension, a fact difficult to square with the claim that they involved no intention on the part of the subjects or no engagement with their subjective experience. The Levitican prescriptions

---

[35] A. Buchler, *Studies in Sin and Atonement in the Rabbinic Literature of the 1st Century* (London: Oxford University Press, 1928), 263. As Auerbach pointed out in his classic paper, *Mimesis*, the Old Testament books did not fill in this type of detail but adopted a suggestive, skeletal style. We would be wrong, for example, to move from the observation that the story of the sacrifice of Isaac makes no reference to Abraham's internal state to the conclusion that he had no feelings about this; cf. Erich Auerbach, *Mimesis: The Representation of Reality in Western Literature.* trans. R. Willard (Princeton: Princeton University Press, 1953).

[36] Von Rad, *Old Testament Theology*, 260.

[37] In this context, James Hillman draws a distinction between the abstract belief of monotheistic religions and the direct experience of the divine in myth. In the former, God is transcendent and posited as the object of abstract belief. In the latter, gods are experienced as immediate. James Hillman, *The Terrible Love of War* (New York: Penguin, 2004).

[38] For this linguistic fusion, see, e.g., Jer. 17:14, Ps. 38:2–11, 18–19, 102:4–11, 149:3. Jacob Milgrom, *Cult and Conscienc: The Asham and the Priestly Doctrine of Repentance* (Leiden: E. J. Brill, 1976), 8. Milgrom links this fusion with the fusion between guilt and punishment, which I raise in the etymology section below.

[39] Von Rad, *Old Testament Theology*, 260.

themselves indicate that speech was a necessary part of the sacrificial ritual: "He shall confess that he hath sinned in that thing", "[A]nd confess over him all the inequities of the children of Israel."[40] They also indicate that the prescribed actions had to be accompanied by a verbal pronouncement concerning the meaning of the actions (known as declaratory formula), for example, "it is not acceptable", "it is unclean meat", "it is a burnt offering", or "it is most holy".[41] Without the spoken words, the ritual was believed to be ineffective.[42] According to Von Rad, "only the addition of the Divine word made the material observance what it was meant to be, a real saving event between Jahweh and his people. Only by virtue of the declaratory word of the priest did the sacral event become a gracious act of God."[43]

Moving to the conceptual level, there is a further logical problem with squaring this conception of purification with monotheistic covenantal Judaism. In the polytheistic context, where people saw independent transcendent beings (demons) as the source of impurity, the analogy between sin and impurity was straightforward. Once monotheism became the basis for religious practice, however (as was the case for the Hebrews), there were only two categories: the one God and the human beings themselves, acting freely and in particular ways. There were no other transcendent beings that could fill this role as the source of contamination and correlatively the object to be exorcized. In the absence of these 'external' sources of impurity, it becomes difficult to see how sin can be analogized to contamination and correlatively how purification can be understood as something that *happens to* people. If impurity is no longer attached to another transcendent entity but inheres in human actions and is a function of people's adherence to God's law, then the process of purification cannot but implicate human action and consciousness. In other words, it all has to come from us.

Recognizing this logical problem, Milgrom argues that the sacrificial system must have encoded the principle that, absent a third independent party, Israel itself had to be responsible for its own fate. Human beings, endowed with free will and the capacity to live according to, or in defiance of, God's laws, were

---

[40] Lev. 5:5, 16:21. The scripture itself is silent on the content of the confession, but it is recorded in the Mishnah: "O Lord, your people, the House of Israel, have committed iniquity, transgressed and sinned before you. O, by the Lord grant atonement, I pray for the iniquities and transgressions and sins." Yoma 6:2.

[41] Lev. 19:7, 22:23, 25.

[42] Note an interesting resonance with an observation Arendt makes about the critical role of speech in making action meaningful: "Without the accompaniment of speech, at any rate, it [action] would lose its subject, as it were; not acting men but performing robots would achieve what, humanly speaking, would remain incomprehensible." *The Human Condition*, 178.

[43] Von Rad, *Old Testament Theology*, 261–2.

themselves the sole source of impurity. But if this is the case, one has to think differently about the entire purity/impurity distinction. In this context, Milgrom suggests re-reading the trope of impurity in terms of the fidelity to the covenant. Thus, rather than impurity entering through external corruption, he suggests that we understand it as the direct effect of humans' failing to take up their side of the covenantal agreement to uphold a certain way of living or norms of rightful action. Effectively, the wrongdoing of human beings becomes the force that would "drive God out of his sanctuary" and "out of their lives."[44] When the wrongdoing of the people has reached a sufficient level (read: when the people transgressed the covenant to a sufficient degree by failing to abide by their own agreement to respect certain moral principles), the 'impurity' would drive God away (read: sever the relationship).[45]

In the materiality that characterized ancient practice, a community's orientation in relation to God was understood literally as presence or absence in the temple; recall Von Rad's argument that God was not posited as an abstract object of belief but experienced through practice.[46] The work of purification was to bring God back in. The critical point here, however, is that bringing God in *by definition* entailed reconstituting the holy community of Israel by a collective recommitting to the covenantal norms. That is, God's presence or absence in the sanctuary could not be understood as the independent movement of an autonomous entity, but was always embedded in the covenant that constituted God as the God of Israel and Israel as the community whose being was given by its orientation to God. In this sense, purity and impurity were not 'external' phenomena, but woven into the actions and values of the community and its constitution.

Stepping back for a moment from this reconceptualization of the purity/impurity trope, what is beginning to emerge in this account is an ontological understanding of human beings and God very different from the one we tend to associate with ancient religious practice. God is not an object that can be brought into consciousness independent of the orientation human beings have to God; rather, the proximity of God is a function of human fidelity to the relationship with God. Correlatively, Israel, *qua* Israel, exists only by virtue of its fidelity to the covenant. As the Yom Kippur liturgy puts it: "I am your God if

---

[44] Milgrom, *Cult and Conscience*, 43.

[45] The book of *Lamentations* is testament to this theology: "The Lord has abandoned his altar, rejected his sanctuary. He has handed over to the foe the walls of its citadels." Lam. 2:7.

[46] Milgrom provides a fascinating analysis of the correlation between the severity of the sin and the degree to which the impurity penetrates the sanctuary. Quite literally, the more severe sins move more deeply into the heart of the sanctuary to where God is said to reside. *Leviticus*, 257–8.

you are my people."[47] Driving God away or bringing God back in might thus be understood as shifts in the community's orientation, rather than movements of a transcendent being. Impurity, or the absence of God, is the community's orientation away from the normative principles associated with the covenant, or its core principles of rightful action; repurification (through ritual or repentance) is reorientation. This reading is consistent with the understanding of sacrifice as a means of approaching or gaining access to and fellowship with God, or Holiness.[48] Von Rad, for example, argues that in the sacrificial ritual, "Israel is granted fellowship with Him ... above all here Israel could be reached by His will for forgiveness."[49]

Understood against this background, purification starts to make sense in a way that does not entail crude collectivism and empty externality. What is being purified is not the community, understood as an undifferentiated organism, but the community commitment to a certain normative frame, grounded in the commitment to the covenantal partner. Suzanne Stone addresses the status of the corporate body in very similar terms, asserting that the ground for the Jewish community is a set of collective positive commandments:

In contrast to Christianity ... social solidarity [in Judaism] is not grounded in human nature. Instead, it is a product of a congerie of positive commandments mandating some associations and forbidding others. The legal principles regulating associational life are thus part and parcel of the larger purpose of the law: In biblical terminology, to mould a holy nation; in the philosophic language of Maimonides, to provide for the objective human well-being or happiness of the community.[50]

'The people' is not *naturally* one, that is, by virtue of some pre-political, 'genetic' characteristic that exists before their accession to the covenant.[51] Rather, the people came to be one through their accession to the covenant:

---

[47] The Yom Kippur liturgy includes a prayer called *Ki Anu Amecha* comprising coupled statements about the correlative status of humans and God: "We are your people and you are our god; We are your children and you are our Father"; and so on. Machzor for Yom Kippur.

[48] *Kadosh* (holy) is the most frequently repeated word in *Leviticus*. Indeed if one returns to the original Hebrew, this meaning persists in the language of the text itself. Although usually known in English as Leviticus (from the Greek "of the Levites"), the Hebrew name for the book setting out the sacrificial rites is *Wayyikra*, drawn from the first words of the book: "He is called." Moreover, the Hebrew word for sacrifice is *Qorban*, which derives from the root קרב, meaning 'close' or 'near'. Sacrifice, in Hebrew, means to approach, to bring near, or to come near (to the altar, literally, and then to God). This significance is minor but nevertheless still resonant in the English word *sacrifice*, derived from the Latin, which means literally to 'make holy'.

[49] Von Rad, *Old Testament Theology*, 260.

[50] Suzanne Stone, "The Jewish Tradition and Civil Society," in *Alternative Conceptions of Civil Society*, ed. Simone Chambers and Will Kymlicka (Princeton: Princeton University Press, 2001).

[51] This would be the case if, for example, the claim were that Jewish identity was grounded in an essential pre-social characteristic like race understood biologically.

an act with legal and political as well as religious dimensions. What is more, the action that constitutes the covenant – the giving and receiving of Torah (the law and guideline for the nation's orientation) – was not a singular event in history, resulting in the formation of a corporate body that then existed independent of human action. On the contrary, the giving and accepting of Torah as the constitution of the people of Israel is something that has to happen continually, with the active participation of the living people identified as Jews.[52] The people must, in other words, continually recreate their (collective) identity. This reading of sacrifice destabilizes the dichotomies underpinning the modernist/pre-modernist framework I discussed earlier.

Indeed Milgrom develops the argument in precisely this direction, using this interpretation to link the collective character of the ritual to the nation in a manner that resonates powerfully with apology's contemporary deployment in political processes and national discourses. Using the analogy of *The Picture of Dorian Gray*, he argues that "while the sin may not scar the face of the sinner, it does scar the face of the sanctuary", where the sanctuary is the seat of God and as such the source of Israel's identity as the people of this God.[53] What in the priestly scheme is represented as the sanctuary being corrupted, Milgrom reads as society being corrupted. What is represented as God being driven out of the sanctuary is the nation being destroyed. Again, underpinning this reading is an understanding that Israel exists by virtue of its acceptance of the covenant and, correlatively, that driving God out is equivalent to the death of Israel.

This also establishes how the collective's relationship with God is the key determinant of purity or impurity. Infidelity to the covenant, that is, failing to uphold its norms, brings impurity and at a practical or manifest level becomes the context within which members of the community, no longer oriented by the norms of rightful action, systematically commit violations. Return to the covenant purifies and re-grounds or re-sanctions respect for those norms. Thus, Milgrom argues that the collective is responsible for driving God away not because sin is transmitted like a contagion within the organic community, but rather because those who 'allowed the wicked to flourish' did not pay sufficient attention to protecting what was, in symbolic terms, the sanctuary or, in more abstract terms, the normative, constituting principles of Israel. Linking this with the foundational Jewish principle "*Kol yisrael arevin ze bazeh*" (the Jewish

---

[52] So, e.g., the blessing recited when the Torah is read in synagogue is in the present: "Blessed is God who *gives* us Torah."

[53] Milgrom, *Cult and Conscience*, 51ff.

people are collectively, not just individually, responsible before God), we now have a different way of understanding this co-responsibility.[54]

Perhaps most significantly for our purposes, what this implies is that *teshuvah* is not 'added on' to the process of identity formation and constitution but is an essential part of the process through which the covenantal relationship is constantly renewed and the people kept in existence and oriented according to its core normative commitments. It is through recognizing that one has strayed from the path that one cannot only return to it, but also identify it as one's path at all, or for that matter redefine it. In this case, where we are talking about a corporate body, Israel, the process of being confronted with and accepting its own transgression is what allows Israel to identify a set of principles expressly as its own and *practically* to recommit to them.

This means that it is logically impossible to think of someone as a Jew or of his or her obligations to Jewish laws or relationship with God entirely outside the corporate body, Israel. Because law logically requires plurality, no single abstract person could abide by the laws outside the fact of the body of Israel. If one insists on starting with the individual at this level, there could be no law. This does not rule out evaluating substantive laws in terms of their effect on individual rights or distinguishing between laws on the basis of how well they allow for or suppress the expression of individual personality or aspiration. But 'the law', *qua* law, as an authoritative organizing system, logically precedes specific laws. And at this level the law, like the grammatical structure of a language or the notion of property, exists only if it is held up at a number of locations.[55] At the point of origin and thereafter, the law and parameters of right are a collective endeavour. Absent general respect, the law cannot work as a meaningful and authoritative mechanism for regulating social relations, and so cannot work for any single individual. Without this structural starting point, only anarchy, not autonomy, is possible.[56] The sages expressed this conception

---

[54] This understanding is spelled out in a number of Talmudic laws, e.g., "All Jews are responsible for one another. They are like one body and like a guarantor who repays the debt of a friend." Ritva, Babylonian Talmud, Rosh Hashanah 29a.

[55] The idea that law requires at least three has been argued from a number of disciplinary perspectives, including Lacan's linguistic psychoanalytic analysis of the necessity of the third for the establishment of law, a symbolic order, and identity. Cf. Jacques Lacan, "The Function and Field of Speech and Language in Psychoanalysis," in *Écrits: A Selection*, trans. Alan Sheridan (New York: Norton, 1977).

[56] This notion was beautifully expressed by the literary character of Sir Thomas More in *A Man for All Seasons*: "And when the last law was down, and the Devil turned round on you, where would you hide ... the laws all being flat? This country's planted thick with laws from coast to coast ... and if you cut them down ... d'you really think you could stand upright in the winds that would blow then?" Robert Bolt, *A Man for All Seasons* (New York: Vintage Books, 1960), 66.

metaphorically: "It can be compared to people on a boat. One took out an awl and began boring a hole in the boat beneath his seat. The others said to him, 'What are you doing?' He replied, 'Is that any concern of yours? [I am not boring a hole beneath your seat] but only under mine'. They said: 'But you will sink the whole ship, and we will all drown.'"[57]

If *teshuvah* is understood as part of the process of sustaining this foundational covenant and its cognate norms, its collective dimension is not necessarily opposed to but may in fact be one of the conditions for individual rights. Of course, the degree to which this is the case will depend on the substantive content of the law and the processes whereby law is defined and redefined. Again, however, the structural foundation is logically prior to the substantive content. In his commentary on the category of sin, Von Rad similarly draws attention to the social aspect of sin in its Old Testament usage. In Old Testament theology any offence against the sacral order implicates all members of the community, not simply because of the deep ties of blood and interconnection, but more importantly because the offence threatens the order itself, the possibility of cultic activity, and the set of relationships that organizes the community and its social function.[58] Sin, understood in this latter sense, is not attached to a number of individuals by virtue of their proximity to the wrongful action, but rather rests at the level of the set of relationships and organizing principles in which they, *qua* collective, are located, that is, in the covenant.[59]

Coming back to my initial note of caution about whether one could legitimately transfer the meaning of rituals in this pre-modern setting to modern practices, we now find ourselves in a more hospitable framework. As reframed, those practices no longer suffer from the standard maladies of a caricatured pre-modernism. Indeed, understood as ritualized means of renewing and re-enlivening the foundational covenant, they are not so remote from modern secular politics, where norms are also not abstract objects of belief but the grammars that organize practices and institutions. Indeed, though we often like to think of them otherwise, our modern political norms also have a transcendent or symbolic *and* an action-oriented dimension. Norms are articulated in laws or written codes, but encoded as the *community's* norms through its active ascription to them. Here, too, in the secular political, the internal/external

[57] Attributed to Rabbi Shimon bar Yochai, Vayikra Rabbah (Margaliot), 4.

[58] Von Rad, *Old Testament Theology*, 263ff.

[59] As we shall see when I come to discuss contemporary theories of collective responsibility, this claim strongly resembles Karl Jaspers' argument that it is the "moral failings", the "countless little acts of negligence, of convenient adaptation of cheap vindication, and the imperceptible promotion of wrong" that make evil possible and "cause the conditions out of which both crime and political guilt arise." Karl Jaspers, *The Question of German Guilt*, 34.

and the collective/individual dichotomies break down; individuals can experience or recognize themselves and others as subjects of rights and make subjective judgements about right and wrong only because they are interpolated into the grammar of norms of the political community.[60] The individual experiences political normative judgements as *his or her own*, but these norms are certainly not his or her own creation. Indeed, it is largely through their performance at various public rituals that he or she comes to experience these norms as his or her norms.

(ii) Stories of the Origin of Yom Kippur

Like all Jewish holy days, Yom Kippur is said to mark and recall an event or story that is constitutive of the principles of Jewish belief and practice and of *B'nei Israel* (the people of Israel). Accordingly, one way to understand the principles embodied in the ritual practice is to ask the historo-mythological question, What does Yom Kippur recall or memorialize?

According to the Midrash, the first Yom Kippur took place as part of the drama of Moses receiving the Torah (the law or the way of living) and accepting the covenant with God.[61] When Moses first climbed Mount Sinai to make a covenant with God, he commanded the people to wait for him and to not turn to any other gods in his absence. When he returned with the tablets (which we presume contained the original commandments), he found that the people had not waited and, in defiance, had made a golden calf that they were now worshipping, an idolatrous act signifying their lack of faith in the one God of their new religious identity. Moses pleaded with God for forgiveness on behalf of the people, and on the first day of the month of Elul, he again ascended the mountain for a second set of tablets.[62] This time, in his absence, the nation fasted from sunrise to sunset. On returning, on the tenth day of the month of Tishri, Moses found the nation truly repentant and announced that God had forgiven them. He then decreed that this day would remain a day of atonement

---

[60] In making this claim, I am not staking out a position with respect to the existence of absolute norms, or natural laws that lie outside social organization. There may be a limited list of norms that preceded social institution. Even then, however, the list will be far shorter than those considered fundamental in different societies.

[61] The Midrash is the general term for the stories that the sages and rabbis told to elaborate the thin descriptions contained in the actual written Torah. According to some interpretations, the Torah given at Sinai contained not only a set of laws and prescriptions, but also all future commentary. Whether called Torah or commentary on Torah, the body of Jewish thought comprises a series of interpretive layers and conversations; see Ta'anit 30b.

[62] Judaism follows its own calendar. The months of Elul and Tishri (approximately August and September, depending on the year) are the months of the phase of repentance.

for all generations. The forty-day period between his return from the first and second ascents marks the forty days of repentance in the Jewish calendar, and the tenth of Tishri, the day of Moses' return and bringing the law to the waiting people, is Yom Kippur.

If one reads this story as a clue to the meaning of Yom Kippur, it hardly tells the story we might expect. Rather than recalling a seminal moment of repentance and correlative forgiveness, narrowly understood as direct responses to particular wrongful actions, it locates Yom Kippur within a narrative about the primary covenant that brought the Jewish people into being as a distinct people, whose identity and civil order were organized around a set of laws and principles of association and civic behaviour. The ritual does not represent a *quid pro quo* for a violation, but rather the people's return to faith after a period of faithlessness, their turn back from infidelity to the principle of God, in this case a turning back that is also the first moment of its constitutive relationship. Certainly, in Moses' story there is an event involving repentance and forgiveness, but these are not singular acts or processes. They are embedded in the broader drama of the covenant. In fact, in the narrative of this story, *repentance and forgiveness comprise the process whereby the covenant was forged*. The initial agreement to form a covenant with God slips away very quickly in the absence of sustaining proof, and it is only the retrospective recognition of the loss, which occurs when the community faces the consequences of its having turned away, that brings it to the point of being able to enter the covenant. The period of repentance and the subsequent declaration of forgiveness coincides with the delivery of the Ten Commandments, with God's and the people's accession to the covenant. Already, in this first narrative of origin, the moment of repentance and the moment of covenanting coincide.

More specifically, if one looks at Moses' actual communication with God (the communication that the contemporary representative 'apology' is said to recall), what one sees is that he was not asking for 'forgiveness', understood as a singular act, but for the restoration of the relationship with God and the covenant. Or perhaps forgiveness and the covenant were inseparable. And what Moses got by way of forgiveness was the covenant, in the form of both the law (the tablets) and a set of revelatory words, setting out the attributes of God. When Israel recites these words, it brings itself back to the covenantal relationship. Israel's repentance is its affirmation of God's norms as its own.

One might ask, from a narrative point of view, what the text achieves by telling the story in this way. Surely an omnipotent and omniscient God would have no need or desire to allow the people to make a mistake. What is served by locating the covenantal moment after the people's 'sin' and recognition of their sin? The answer lies in the particular nature of this relationship and in what political covenanting means. On one side there are orienting laws and norms, norms that are not purely subjective. But on the other there has to be a community that actively takes on those norms, not as external laws but as its own, those that it affirms, even those that it desires. Only the experience of loss, the experience of God's absence or the absence of a normatively constituted community, can create this experienced sense of desire, embrace, and attachment. Repentance, in this sense, does not logically follow ascription to norms but always precedes it.

Taken as a whole, the repentance/forgiveness drama is a performative reaffirmation of the principle of God and of the covenantal relationship, a reaffirmation that occurs by *our* speaking them ourselves.[63] This last point is particularly important in thinking about the apology as a particular type of practice. Indeed, the Talmud teaches that human beings can receive the revelation of God by reciting the "*Shelosh Esre Middot*", the thirteen divine attributes that were spoken by God when Moses asked for a divine revelation.[64] According to this story, the recitation is not a *means* of obtaining the revelation but is a form of revelation itself. Far from 'standing in' for the authentic process of dealing with the past, the performance itself is the process of dealing with the past. It is the affirmation that re-covenants the instantiated (as distinct from the abstract or historical) community. Repentance, encounter, and the covenant are not distinct spheres but are one and the same moment.[65]

The original scriptural descriptions of these practices refer to 'confession', but in these early forms, that term marked something broader than self-exposure and is more in the nature of naming or witnessing: profession rather than confession understood narrowly. Indeed, this conflation of affirmation and remorseful expression is still apparent in the form and content of the (post-temple-era) Yom Kippur liturgy, which integrates repentance and recognition or praise of God. In the Yom Kippur liturgy, the plainly penitential prayers (those confessing sin and seeking forgiveness) are interspersed with

---

[63] This reinforces my argument in Chapter Two that the principal form of uptake is not the forgiveness of the other, wronged party, but a reorientation of the one who has him- or herself done wrong.

[64] When Moses asked God to reveal God's self, the response was God's name, and the *Shelosh Esre Middot*, or thirteen divine attributes. According to the Talmud (Rosh Hashana 17b), recitation of the thirteen divine attributes brings about forgiveness.

[65] This analysis is consistent with the movement from demonic to human sources of sin that Milgrom linked with the development of monotheism. If human beings are the source of sin, and sin arises from a movement away from a relationship with God, then overcoming sin is the same as moving back into a relationship with God. Moreover, this is a relationship that is forged through both actions and words, hence the need for both rightful action and apology in the act of *teshuvah*.

prayers affirming the greatness and mercy of God, the divine attributes, giving thanks, and confirming the close, covenantal relationship between God and God's people.[66] Over and over again throughout the day of Yom Kippur and during the approaching month, the community recites the *"Avinu Malkeinu"* ('Our Father Our King'), a prayer that affirms the unique status and capacity of God to receive this repentant community and that calls or recalls various dimensions of God's being and the covenantal relationship.[67]

Stepping back from this dense textual analysis and returning to the original reason I looked at the ancient rituals and stories of the origin of repentance, we can now draw together their implications for the significance of *teshuvah*. As normally read, the ritual forebears of the apology tend to be understood as magical processes of cleansing the impurities that cause sin, but if we re-embed the processes into their narrative context they now look like the practices the community adopted in order to establish, or re-establish, proximity to the Divine, where this is understood as an orientation to a certain set of normative principles. Indeed, reversing our habitual understanding, it is not the case that one achieves purity by approaching a transcendent God; rather, humans re-approach God through the work of purification (repentance), where this is the expression of sorrow for our infidelity to the principles of the covenant. Again, recalling Milgrom's point, it is not only human beings, singularly or as a collective, who are 'purified', but also the sanctuary, the place where God can reside and the seat of the community's life. The performance makes literal what it means to approach God: one removes the defilement so as to make possible the encounter with God, otherwise understood as the foundational relationship and the possibility of the ethical polity itself. In Milgrom's terms, through repentance we are acting directly to restore the portrait that has been damaged through sin, and thus to connect ourselves with the foundational vision for ethical action.

(iii) Etymology

In Hebrew, words are never just labels; through their etymology and metaphoric resonances, words constitute rich resources of significance. To get to those meanings, two methods are generally employed: first, looking to the

---

[66] I refer here, *inter alia*, to the recitation of the modified *tefillah*, the recitation of Psalm 27 as well as the thirteen divine attributes. The integration of praise and repentance is complex throughout the liturgy. For example, during the month leading up to Yom Kippur, and in the Yom Kippur liturgy itself, a number of insertions and modifications explicitly referring to mercy and God's remembering his people are made to the daily *tefillah*.

[67] See Abraham Milgrom, *Jewish Worship* (Philadelphia: Jewish Publication Society of America, 1971), 226.

shoresh, or root, and second, identifying 'the atmosphere' of the stories or poems in which the word appears in sacred texts.[68] Here I look at the Hebrew words translated as 'repentance' and 'sin'.

The key term for what we would call repentance *in toto* (including apology and other dimensions of compensatory action), *teshuvah*, comes from the root שוב (*shuv*), meaning to turn, to turn back, or to return. The metaphor of turning comes through strongly in the elaboration of the concept. The rabbinical understanding, for example, holds that the 'turning' of *teshuvah* has three dimensions: towards God, towards the community and other people, and towards one's self. Rabbinical commentary emphasizes the idea that what we are doing during the period of the "Days of Awe", known as *chesbon hanefesh* (accounting for the soul), is returning to the principles of correct relationship with God, with other people, and with ourselves as ethical beings.[69]

The context of the term makes clear that the turning or returning is not understood as moving back on an imagined line of time; one is not called to return to an event in the past, but rather one turns towards God or God's law or God's way. So, for example, the prophet Hosea calls for the people to return "unto the Lord", just as Jesus calls out for them to "Repent and return to the Gospel."[70] The movement, then, is not back to a place that once existed, but forward towards a yet-to-be fulfilled principle. Moreover, almost without exception, the word is constructed only in its verbal form, emphasizing that *teshuvah* is a process.[71] This grammatical preference transmits the idea that *teshuvah* is not "a quality which man could possess as his own; there are no converted men in the Old Testament but only men who are forever being converted."[72]

Teshuvah's dynamic quality stands in contrast with the English words *repentance* and *penitence*, both of which have their root in the Latin *paenitentia*, meaning to regret, or the Latin *paene* or Greek *poenere* (to suffer, to feel pain). Interestingly, *poen* originally referred to a payment of money to get rid of pollution connected with manslaughter; it is cognate with, or derived from,

---

[68] Gelin, "Sin in the Old Testament," 18. As Levinas comments in his Talmudic readings, "ideas are never separated from the example that both suggests and delimits them." Levinas, "Towards the Other," in *Nine Talmudic Readings*, trans. and ed. Annette Aronowicz (Bloomington and Indianapolis: Indiana University Press, 1994), 21.

[69] See Chaim Stern, *Shaarei Teshuvah*, ix.

[70] Hos. 14:1, 2; Mark 1:15.

[71] It appears as a noun only in Isaiah 30:15. Gelin also points out that the word is constructed with a preposition, which accentuates the movement of rupture and return. Gelin, "Sin in the Old Testament," 33.

[72] E. Jacob, *Theology of the Old Testament* (New York: Harper, 1958), 289 n. 2.

Greek *poine*, blood money (and also the name of a goddess of vengeance). When the Hebrew was translated into Greek, *teshuvah* was rendered *metanoia*, from the two terms *meta*, meaning beyond, and *nous*, meaning mind. This translation carried with it two significant conceptual shifts. First, the action orientation of the Hebrew was replaced by an inner transformation, a state of mind.[73] Second, the sense of a turning or spiralling movement was replaced by a movement forward or beyond or above.

The English word 'sin' is generally understood as a breach of a fixed (usually sacred) law for which repentance is due, thus making it one half of a sin/repentance equation. In translation, it stands in for a number of Hebrew words used in the Torah and foundational texts, the three most common being חטא (*chet*), עון (*avon*), and פשע (*pesha*), all of which have quite different meanings to the English word. In its literal usage, *chet* means 'missing', or missing the mark or goal or way, or failing or failing someone.[74] For example, slingers from the tribe of Benjamin are described as being so good with their weapons that they can "aim at a hair and not *chet* (miss)."[75] Similarly, in the phrase in Proverbs usually translated as "he that hasteth with his feet sins", the term *chet* means, more literally, he who stumbles or falls or misses the way.[76] When King David is on his deathbed his wife Bathsheba comes to him and says, "If Solomon does not become king after you then Solomon and I will be *chataim*", the usual translation is that they will be counted as sinners, but the phrase literally means that they will not reach their potential.[77]

Interestingly, *chet* is used to refer both to the sin and to its consequence: incurring guilt or penalty or forfeiting something as a consequence of sin, for example, "I shall incur the blame (*chet*) of sinning against thee all my days"[78] or "I bear the loss (*chet*) of it."[79] Similarly, Moses' warning about what would happen to those who did not abide by God is usually translated as "if you are disobedient you will have *sinned* and you will meet with your *punishment*."[80] In fact, the root of the words translated variously as sin and punishment is the same.

---

[73] Maimonides, for example, insisted that full *teshuvah* occurs only when the same person does not act the same way when placed in an identical situation of temptation (Mishnah Torah, *Hilkhot Teshuvah* 2:1).

[74] Used with respect to God, it appears in the Torah more than 500 times, e.g., Lev. 4:3, Lev. 5:1, 11, 17, 21, 23; but only 36 times with respect to man, cf. Exod. 5:16; 1S.26.21.

[75] Judg. 20:16.

[76] Prov. 19:2. See also Prov. 8:36, "The one missing me is one wronging himself."

[77] 1 Kings 1:21.

[78] Gen. 43:9.

[79] Gen. 31:39.

[80] Num. 32:23.

To the modern reader, for whom sin/guilt and punishment are distinct moments, indeed moments that stand in a causal relation, this confluence seems illogical. Yet this linguistic fusion is consistent with the interpretation that is emerging throughout this chapter of sin as a breach in relations and organizing principles. Understood in this way, it makes perfect sense that the wrongful act and the consequences be designated by the same word, because the breach is both the act and the problem. If we understand the covenant as a living bond, sustained only by active observance, then every infidelity is damage to the covenant, not merely the cause of damage to the covenant.[81]

The second root, *avon,* is usually rendered 'iniquity' in English. *Avon* literally means to be distorted, to go astray or to act perversely. In its more common nounal form, *avon* means a trespass, and always involves the guilty party's intentional transgression. As with *chet,* while *avon* is usually rendered 'iniquity' or 'sin' in translation, it is in fact linguistically ambivalent, standing for sin or guilt, and the consequences of sin (penalty). When Cain's murderous deed was found out and cursed by God, his exclamation "[m]y *avon* is greater than I can bear" is usually translated to render *avon* as 'punishment', but the phrase might equally be taken to mean that he could not bear his sin.[82]

These etymological metaphors and plays, particularly those in which sin conveys the idea of missing or breaking a relationship, are consistent with the argument of Old Testament theologians that sinning always signified the breach of the sacral order, and further signified a direct insult to God.[83] As Gelin writes, as cited at the opening of this chapter, "Sin is the breaking off of a personal relationship with God. It presupposes the experience of a vis-à-vis whose holiness has been discovered in a retrospective act of reflection and repentance. . . . [T]he idea of sin is the obverse of the idea of God."[84]

When placed together, the etymologies of *teshuvah* and the two terms for sin reinforce the interpretation I derived from my analysis of ritual and stories.

---

[81] As Von Rad puts it, "the 'recompense' which catches up with evil is certainly no forensic event which the sin evokes in a completely different sphere, that is with God. It is the radiation of evil which now continues on; only so does the evil which the sin called out reach equilibrium." Von Rad, *Old Testament Theology,* 256. Like Ricoeur, Von Rad connects this linguistic fusion with what he calls the synthetic view of life in which people do not understand actions and their consequences as two separate events.

[82] Gen. 4:13.

[83] This understanding of sin resonates with the Jewish, as opposed to the Pauline or Augustinian, understanding of the significance of the Fall in the narrative of the garden of evil. The original sin is understood not as the violation of a law, but rather as a departure from the primal harmony between human beings and God, an act of separation, or infidelity. See Samuel S. Cohen, "Original Sin," *Hebrew Union College Annual,* 21 (1948).

[84] Gelin, "Sin in the Old Testament," 39.

The idea of sin and repentance as economic relations to a law, where sin marks a deficit and repentance rebalances the accounts, is far less apparent than the idea of sin and repentance as movements in a dynamic relationship. Wrong-doing and repentance work here as humans' movements away from or towards the place from which the sense of right and wrong emerges. The return of repentance effects a reconnection with this place of orientation, from which the person is resourced for ethical action.

3. THE SIGNIFICANCE OF SPEECH: EXTERNALITY AND INTERNALITY

The original function of speech consists not in designating an object in order to communicate with the other in a game of no consequences but in assuming towards someone a responsibility on behalf of someone else. To speak is to engage the interests of men. Responsibility would be the essence of language.[85]

In Jewish thought and practice, the public declaration of a normative stance plays a constitutive role in establishing that norm. Thus, from within the community, it is through declaring what it holds to be wrong and what it aspires to be that abstract principles are transformed into living values. This scheme differs considerably from the 'mere words' view of apologies that has been so prevalent in contemporary debates. Once again, if we look at how the tradition itself understands these practices, one finds a very different logic, and one we might find useful in making sense of the strangely important role that public speech plays in contemporary politics.

As we saw in the descriptions of sacrifice, for the ancient Hebrews the spoken word was intrinsic to the ritual. Absent the priest speaking the words, the ritual was ineffective. Words, like the action into which they were woven, were *sacramental,* the embodiment of repentance rather than its proxy. Commentators on the use of language in the ancient context have sought to convey the special weight carried by words. Redlich, for example, writes:

When they used a word, they saw in it its results as well as its immediate meaning. Hence to remember included action as well as recalling to memory, to love included the consequences of the sentiment, to save meant actual deliverance, to cover a sin meant reconciliation following the covering. So also abstract ideas were embodied in narrative.[86]

---

[85] Emmanuel Levinas, "Towards the Other," in *Nine Talmudic Readings*, trans. Annette Arono-wicz (Bloomington: Indiana University Press), 21.

[86] E. Basil Redlich, *The Forgiveness of Sins*, 8. See, also Von Rad: "[T]he word has a different and much more primitive way of acting: on solemn occasions it can release meanings and establish mental affinities which lie at the deeper level of its magical matrix and which apparently have little or nothing to do with its obvious and every day meaning." *Old Testament Theology*, 82–3.

The inter-dependence of the dimensions of *teshuvah* is evident in Maimonides' systematized teachings on its necessary conditions or components.[87] In answer to his question 'what is complete repentance?' he listed six necessary components: (1) abandonment of sin, (2) removal of the sin from thoughts, (3) resolution, (4) regret, (5) expression of sincerity before God, and (6) oral confession. Throughout these teachings, *teshuvah* is understood simultaneously as attitude, action, and most importantly here, speech. Following the rabbinic teachings, Maimonides emphasizes that, even if all the other conditions necessary to achieve *teshuvah* are fulfilled, they will not be sufficient, save the spoken words of apology. The sinner must "confess in words, with his lips and give voice to those matters he has resolved in his heart."[88] The *sine qua non* of *teshuvah* is verbal confession, words offered to the other. One must address oneself to the other and with spoken words identify oneself as a wrongdoer, confess the specific sin, expose one's shame, and promise not to repeat the sinful act.[89] Indeed, in Jewish law, if the injured party has died, the perpetrator must still speak the words of apology, not to the victim's face but at the side of his or her grave.

This emphasis on the spoken word is remarkable when compared with the common conception of apology as a mere representation, the signifier of an elsewhere signified. Clearly, what is being gestured at here is an interdependence of language and relationship that our habitual schema fails to encode. As the twentieth-century Jewish philosopher Emmanuel Levinas observes, in Jewish thought, the material form of expression is not arbitrary, a trapping that might be shed so as to get to the essence that it contains, but is itself a site of significance. Speech has real weight.[90] More specifically, Levinas sees in Judaic teachings on repentance an implicit understanding of the interdependence of inside and outside. He, too, places himself in the line of Maimonides, arguing

---

[87] Maimonides, *Mishnah Torah, the Hilchot Teshuva* (Treatise Concerning Repentance), Book 1, V, Chapter I.

[88] Ibid., Chapter 2. Also, "Even though a man pays (the offended person) he is not forgiven until he has asked pardon." Mishnah Baba Kamma 8, 7.

[89] "How is the verbal confession made? The sinner says thus: 'I beseech Thee, O great Name! I have sinned; I have been obstinate; I have committed profanity against Thee. Particularly in doing such and such. Now behold! I have repented and am ashamed of my actions; forever will I not relapse into this thing again'." Maimonides, *Mishnah Torah: Treatise Concerning Repentance*, Book 1, V, Chapter 1.1. Maimonides refers back to several tracts quoted in the section on *tefilah*.

[90] "Ideas do not become fixed by a process of conceptualization which would extinguish many of the sparks dancing beneath the gaze riveted upon the real. I have already had occasion here to speak of another process which consists in respecting these possibilities. . . . Ideas are never separated from the example which both suggests and delimits them." Levinas, "Towards the Other", 21.

that "all that is said of God in Judaism signifies through human *praxis*."[91] Repentance cannot be correctly understood as essentially disembodied, and then 'named'; it is in the naming that it exists.[92]

The philosophy that Levinas here attributes to Judaism is a particularly valuable tool for making sense of the apologetic act because it does not simply champion the value of the performative, but presents a more profound challenge to the modernist dichotomy and hierarchization of inside/outside.[93] Ritual, the *mitzvot* (laws), and specifically those brought down in the tradition for seeking forgiveness do not stand outside a sealed consciousness, which might or might not authentically repent.[94] Rather, "originating communally, in collective law and commandment, ritual is not at all external to conscience. It conditions it and permits it to enter into itself and stay awake. It preserves it, prepares it for healing."[95] This is not to say that healing is the end of the process: the healed consciousness is only the one that is continually open to responsibilities towards other persons and the world. Healing is this process of opening, not a sealed end.[96] When the damaged consciousness reconquers its integrity, this is at once the work of social morality and the basis for a living, embodied moral sociality. If the concept of the healed or repentant consciousness makes sense at all, it is not in the ethereal realm, but insofar as one acts with respect for the concrete other.

Thus, the multidimensional quality of *teshuvah* should be understood neither as a composition of distinct and independent parts nor as a dialectic that will ultimately resolve itself into a higher order common term. *Teshuvah* is rather an irreducible movement against which interior and exterior (and, for that matter, individual and collective, vertical and horizontal) are static points,

---

[91] Ibid., 14.

[92] Levinas goes even further in seeing apology not simply as an example of the interdependence of inside and outside, but rather as the heart of what he calls the conversational relationship between two persons, thereby making it the fulcrum of the *religious* bond itself. By religion, Levinas means the realm in which self and other come into relationship but are not collapsed into a "totality." See Levinas, *Totality and Infinity*, trans. Alfonso Lingis (Pittsburgh: Duquesne University Press, 1969), 40.

[93] Levinas was no doubt also influenced by Nietzsche's scathing critique of the assumed distinction between surface and depth, seeing it as an artefact of modernity: "The 'apparent' world is the only one. The 'real' world has only been lyingly added." Nietzsche, *Twilight of the Idols*, trans. R. J. Hollingdale (Harmondsworth, England: Penguin Books, 1968), 36. This affinity, which one finds also in Heidegger, raises important questions about the relationship between Jewish thought and the radical ideas of Nietzsche and Heidgger that laid the foundations of post-modernism more generally. Cf. Marlene Zarader, *The Unthought Debt*, trans. Bettina Bergo (Stanford: Stanford University Press, 2006).

[94] Mitzvot are the laws required by Torah, also thought of as the blessings.

[95] Levinas, "Toward the Other," 17.

[96] This is reminiscent of the observation I made earlier concerning the absence of the nounal form *teshuvah* and the presence of only the verbal form *shuv* (turning) in the *Pentateuch*.

constructed by the observer who wishes to name them. Performance does not belong to the realm of 'external action', as if there is a hidden internal behind it, but is itself meaningful action, even more so when that action is speech, which by its very nature cuts across the divides between internal and external, self and other. Nevertheless, acknowledging the performative dimensions of speech is not equivalent to naiveté, and one must remain alive to the instrumental dimension of speech and the ever-present possibility that the words we speak to each other may not be words of respect and recognition but attempts to preserve and promote our own positions. The point is not to deny speech's instrumental dimension or the possibility of a split between speech and intention but rather to remember that dimension of speech that constitutes intention and orientation.

Levinas' most detailed examination of the critical role of speech takes place in his reading of Yoma 85a-b, a passage from the Talmud dedicated to the theme of *teshuvah*.[97] The text takes as its paradigmatic case of wrongdoing not, as one might expect, a grave act of physical harm, but a verbal injury, harmful words. To ground its teachings, the Talmudic commentary refers back to the words from Torah: "You are snared with the words of thy mouth; thou art taken with the words of thy mouth."[98] And why is it that we are ensnared by our speech? Because it is the quintessentially social act. When we speak, we both place ourselves in and draw on a social world.[99] Not only do the words I speak bind me to the person to whom those words are directly addressed; they also bind me into that broader phenomenon of the social web:

Speech, in its original essence, is a commitment to a third party on behalf of our neighbour: the act *par excellence*, the institution of society. The original function of speech consists not in designating an object in order to communicate with the other in a game of no consequences but in assuming towards someone a responsibility on behalf of someone else. To speak is to engage the interests of men. Responsibility would be the essence of language.[100]

If this is so for speech in general, it is even more pronounced in the case of apology, where my words throw out in front of me a different form of social

---

[97] This in itself should not be too quickly dismissed as mere coincidence given that, as Levinas reminds us, in Jewish teachings the example is never just a particular shell for a more universal meaning but is itself constitutive of that meaning.

[98] Prov. 6:2.

[99] A similar theme appears in Castoriadis' work on the institution of society and is discussed in Chapter Seven.

[100] Levinas, "Toward the Other," 21. Here again, Levinas draws this teaching in part from the particular example chosen by the *Talmud*. The injury it deals with is not simply a verbal injury, but in fact involves a case where a person has made a promise as a guarantor for a third party.

relations. What I feel inside is a matter for me only, but what I say to others is what gives shape to our relations. By defining the apology as a social act that constructs and does not simply reflect social relations, the analysis is forced to move beyond the depth and surface paradigm. Certainly, social relations are structured by what people do, as reflected in the requirement that one alter one's behaviour. But they are also structured and organized by what people say and specifically by what people say about what they did and said in the past.

Well and good, one might say, so religious practice sanctifies speech, but do we? Yes, we do. Despite a modernist bias away from the constitutive power of speech, if one turns one's attention to the political realm, one finds that it is precisely the public use of language that steers outcomes. True enough, laws would probably lose their full force to bind people's actions if they were not ultimately backed by some form of sanction, but the existence of sanctions is not the only reason people feel obligated to and act in accordance with the word of the law. Even in his often-misquoted definition of the state, what Weber emphasized was that the key defining characteristic of a state was its *claim* to the legitimate use of force, not its actual ability to use force.[101] When it comes to the public speech of representative leaders, the social, binding power of words is crucial in relation both to the substance of what they are saying and to their legitimacy as political representatives.

More specifically, at the heart of almost all of the apologies I discussed in Chapter One lies a violation of the rights of a group of people selected because of the public significance of their ascriptive identity, be it Jewish, Indigenous, or African American. If we remember that for most members of the dominant group, the significance of those identities is entirely constituted by social meanings (as distinct from direct experience), then we should also allow that those meanings can be reconstituted. And politically sanctioned speech, as one of the principal mediums through which public meanings and social relations are constituted, will have a significant part to play in this drama. The fact that speech has too often been rendered as empty in the mouths of contemporary political leaders (as were the rituals Isaiah decried) does not devoid speech of all potential. It requires a prophetic reminder of what has been lost.

4. APOLOGY, THE ABSOLUTE, AND TIME

Beyond providing an alternative trope for making sense of collective apologies, Jewish practices and understandings also offer some useful resources for

---

[101] Max Weber, "Politics as Vocation," in *From Max Weber: Essays in Sociology*, ed. H. H. Gerth and C. Wright Mills (New York: Oxford University Press, 1946).

addressing two remaining problems posed by a collective apology. The first concerns the normative basis for apology and, specifically, whether apology entails a set of absolute moral standards, fixed in time, or whether apologizing can in fact be a way of shifting normative understandings and commitments. The second, which flows from this, is the problem of time, and how we can make sense of the notion that something one does in the present can address the past.

At the beginning of this chapter, I mentioned several qualities of religious worldviews that we tend to think of as unattractive from the point of view of modern, secular political principles. One, which I have not explicitly dealt with so far, but which is clearly going to be problematic in any claim to move from the religious to the secular liberal democratic context, is the thickness and absoluteness of the moral values to which religions ascribe and indeed around which they organize their identity. If we were to do a quick free association around 'religious norms', most likely, when we heard that term, we would immediately think of a fixed set of divinely sanctioned unimpeachable rules about permissible and impermissible associations and activities.

I suggest we leave to the side the particular content, and focus solely on the ahistorical and divinely sanctioned character of these norms. If, indeed, the religious form of apology is essentially oriented towards preserving existing and, worse still, non-revisable norms grounded in a transcendent absolute, then my argument for transferring the model to the contemporary political context is in trouble. This is because a closed essentialist and static moral code is structurally incompatible with two core principles of contemporary liberal democratic politics: first, that political cohesion and identity should not demand a single conception of the good, and second, that the moral commitments of citizens should be able to change over time. Perhaps more damningly, if the orienting principles are unchangeable, the aspiration of moral progress through history is ruled out.

What then is the ontological status of the norms relevant to religious apologies? Logically, the very concept of apology implies a continuous set of norms; otherwise, it would make no sense to admit that one's past actions or laws had been wrong.[102] But this logical requirement of continuity is not equivalent to a further requirement that those norms be thick, absolute, or impervious to revision. The logical requirement of continuity of commitment can be rendered compatible with the liberal democratic insistence on moral fluidity by orienting apologies around open-ended, revisable norms. But if we adjust apology in this

---

[102] In this sense, apologies always imply a prior promise, which, as Arendt points out, stabilizes relations into the future. Cf. *The Human Condition*, 243–7.

direction, are we not moving it beyond the scope of the religious model that forms our template, where the orienting norms were, apparently, literally carved in stone? My earlier caveat, that what I was abstracting was the *form* of *teshuvah* and not any particular content, will not work here, because the form is itself imbued with the idea of the absolute; *teshuvah* is at essence a return to God and the covenant.

In fact, one might say that my analysis so far makes this problem even worse, given how much I have spoken about return, the covenant, and the basic constituting principles of the people of Israel. If apology is always about coming back to the thick moral principles set down once and for all, it would seem to be an essentially conservative process, impermeable to new information or sensibilities. Now this is not so much of a problem if we are talking about certain norms, like the prohibition of killing or torture. There is no different perspective and no new information that could call us to progress beyond fidelity to those norms. But my claim goes further, because I have spoken about return to the principles that made a community the particular community that it is.

What if, in the light of experience, or encounters with other types of people, or closer attention to how *all* members of our community are affected, some of those principles turn out to be wrong, because they are discriminatory or limit human freedom? There are numerous textual proscriptions against homosexuality in the Torah, and yet in a contemporary context, and given our commitment to the principle of equal respect, many observant Jews would insist that discrimination on the basis of sexual preference is morally impermissible. Apology should also provide the scope for moral learning, or the expansion of norms, not simply a return to what we once thought was right and are now bound to for time immemorial.

This is, of course, no abstract argument. As we shall see when I come to discuss the apology to Indigenous people in Australia, and as we saw to some extent in the apologies in Chapter One, nations have frequently been constituted around norms that are exclusionary and discriminatory. If apology is bound to those norms as the fixed moral standard against which it judges contemporary actions, then removing Aboriginal children, using African Americans as slaves, or excluding women from political participation will never be something for which we need to apologize. As we saw with de Gaulle's Vichy apology, states may well claim that their wrongdoing represented an aberration from their core moral commitments and moral identity, but often even then, some type of story about moral learning will accompany this claim. To permit ethical progress, apology must structurally allow for some type of dialectic.

Caricatured conceptions of God as an absolute transcendent source of heteronomous rules would seem to place the religious apology in the worst-case basket, and there is doubtless abundant grist for this mill on the side of both aggressive atheists and religious fundamentalists. A more sophisticated reading for the elaboration of the meaning of religious norms and of God, however, gives rise to a very different framework. To get at it, let us first read from the *Mishnah Horayot*, a piece of Talmud that elaborates the procedures that people in the post-temple era (when sacrifice was no longer permitted) should follow when individuals or the entire community sins.[103] The argumentation in this *Mishnah* is of particular interest in thinking through political apologies because it considers situations analogous to those that become the subject of transitional and historical justice, that is, violations committed under the colour of the law or with the sanction of the state and later condemned as wrong according to some more universal or enlightened standard.

Already the first line of this text – "If the *court* ruled to transgress any one of the commandments of the *Torah*" (emphasis added) – makes it clear that the norms relevant for a community exist at two levels and that they can be in conflict. If they do come into conflict, this text makes it clear that Torah trumps the provisional judgement of the court. Now, if we substitute constitutional law or international law for Torah, this provides an appropriate model. The Nuremberg trials, for example, used international law (in that case relatively amorphous international customary law) as the standard against which to condemn not only individual actions, but also state laws. If, however, Torah is the stone tablet of an ancient law, we are back to the problem I raised above. There can be no gap between the legitimate court's legal pronouncement and the truth of Torah. Let us probe this *Mishnah* and the tradition more generally then to ask two questions: What is the relationship between these two levels of law, and How do we understand Torah?

The implication in this *Mishnah* is that the two levels of law have an intrinsic connection. The immanent authority draws its norms, albeit partially and imperfectly, from the absolute. In fact, in Hebrew this internal connection is even conveyed etymologically; *horah* (the court) shares its root with Torah. But it would be incorrect to think of them strictly as the ideal and the actual, or template and exemplar, because although *horah* is derived from Torah it is by no means equivalent to it, and so can deviate from and violate Torah. This then opens to the second question, the ontological status

[103] Mishnah, Tractate Horayot Chapter 1, published in Hanoch Albeck, *Shisha Sidrei Mishna* (Jerusalem, Bialik, and Tel Aviv: Devir, 1952–9). The Mishnah is the redaction of the oral law, put into written form in approximately 200 C.E. but collecting oral debates over previous centuries. Translations of this Mishnah used here are by Natan Margalit, in his doctoral dissertation, "Life Containing Texts: The Mishnah's Discourse of Gender, A Literary/ Anthropological Analysis," Ph.D. diss., University of California, Berkeley, 2001.

of Torah. Torah, this *Mishnah* teaches, does not exist as a fully articulated object in itself, but only articulates itself in time through human interpretation. Were Torah or absolute law already available and fully accessible, the court's function would be limited to enforcement and there would be no need for it to act as a creative jurisprudential body.[104] At the same time, if there were no moral compass beyond the particular court (and the particular moral expression of a historical political community), it would be altogether unhinged from any correcting device. Thus, the law as given by the *horah*, accessible but fallible, provides explicit, specific judgements. Torah, infallible but inaccessible, does not furnish individuals with a fully articulated code of behaviour, but represents the ultimate moral compass. Again, however, that compass becomes accessible only through the particular, which is always revisable. As with the individual/collective dialectic, what we have here are two inter-dependent terms that stand not in a causal relationship but rather in a dynamic co-constitutive relationship.

Indeed, despite the more populist conception of Torah as a set of commandments, Jewish teachings also transmit a conception of Torah as an ongoing project that requires the open-ended participation of historical subjects – hence the notion of the living God. Jews are not directed by a complete set of rigid, heteronomous God-given laws. Nor are they totally free to act according to the whim of the moment. Rather, the ideal normative frame, which one might call Torah, is co-constituted by an ongoing inter-penetration of human ethical exploration and background orienting norms. In this sense, this hermeneutic challenges not only habitual conceptions of God's law and indeed God, but also the idea that what distinguishes theocratic from secular political orders is the heteronomy of the former's laws.

This alternative conception is poignantly illustrated in two traditional debates. The first concerns the question, already raised in the Talmud, about what precisely was transmitted at Sinai: all 613 commandments, the ten of the tablets, or some lesser number.[105] At one extreme is the position that God revealed the entire Torah on Sinai: every letter, word, and prescription was the literally revealed text from God. In this view, living according to the precepts

---

[104] Gadamer's understanding of the interpretive relationship between courts and law, and indeed his correlative understanding of religious law, makes the same point: "A law is not there to be understood historically but to be made concretely valid through being interpreted. Similarly a religious proclamation is to be taken in a way in which it exercises its saving effect. This includes the fact that the text, whether law or gospel, if it is to be understood properly ... must be understood at every moment, in every particular situation, in a new and different way." See Hans-Georg Gadamer, *Truth and Method*, trans. Joel Weinsheimer and Donald Marshall (London and New York: Sheed and Ward, 1975), 275.

[105] Bavli (Babylonian Talmud) Makkot 24a.

of Judaism permits no deviation from a set of fixed laws, no progressive interpretation, and no human involvement in shaping Jewish faith or norms, only
acceptance and obedience. A second position holds that only the Ten Commandments were given on Sinai, but these comprise an absolute normative/legal
frame. The third holds that only the first two of the Ten Commandments were
given at Sinai: "I am the Lord Your God" and "You shall have no other Gods
before me", and after this, the message was too overwhelming for the people to
bear. Still another sage declares that only the first commandment was given.
According to this reading, what was given was not a law at all, but a point of
orientation, a talisman of where loyalty should reside. Yet another proclaimed
that it was only the first word of the first commandment that was spoken at Sinai:
Anochi (I), orienting us not even to a thick conception of God but to another
subject point outside our own immanent human location. As one moves through
these progressive stages, paring down the Sinai transmission, not only the law,
but also the conception of God, becomes less substantial.[106]

The final position is attributed to the Galician Hasidic master Menahem
Mendel of Rymanov, who held that all God actually said was the first letter of
the first word: aleph.[107] Aleph actually makes no sound at all, but is the proto-
sound, the necessary precedent to any sound a person utters. Aleph is the
potential from which all actuality, and all actual speech, conversation, and
moral debate emerge. This latter position implies that what was given was
not the substantial laws themselves, but the capacity to make laws: constructive
autonomy. Metaphorically, if what was given (or acquired) at Eden was being –
ontology – and what was acquired at the expulsion was morality, then at Sinai
what was given and acquired was the capacity to create law and a new form of
social organizations oriented around law and moral principles: social morality
and politics. God, or God's law, in this case represents the universal ground
that the very idea of law requires, as per Laclau's observation that "the
impossibility of a universal ground does not eliminate the need for it: it just
transforms the ground into an empty place which can be filled in a variety of
ways."[108]

Achieving the balance between ground and interpretation is no doubt a
delicate task. The less content one ascribes to this universal ground, the more
easily one can fall off the other end of the scale, abandoning the idea of a

---

[106] See also Franz Rosenzweig, "A Note on a Poem by Judah ha-Levi," in *Franz Rosenzweig: His Life and Thought*, ed. Nahum N. Glatzer (Indianapolis and Cambridge: Hackett Publishing, 1961), 285.

[107] As transmitted by Gershom Scholem, *On the Kabbalah and Its Symbolism*, trans. Ralph Manheim (New York: Schocken Books), 30.

[108] Ernesto Laclau, *Emancipation(s)* (London: W. W. Norton, 1996), 59.

continuous normative framework altogether and opening the door to individual caprice and social anarchy.[109] Yet this is certainly not what the original sage, nor those who draw on his authority, had in mind. They are gesturing towards an idea that allows for open-ended creativity with respect to norms, yet preserves an orientation to some other point, here called God. In this sense, they do not simply present an alternative position, but are suggesting a more profound structural challenge to the autonomy/heteronomy dichotomy. As David Hartman puts it, "when Jews built their civilization around a sacred text, they viewed the text not as a closed and final word, but as a starting point for creative interpretation."[110]

There is a second famous story in the Talmud in which a number of rabbis are arguing on a certain point of Torah interpretation.[111] Rabbi Eliezer, who stands alone in his position against all the other rabbis, calls out: "If the Law agrees with me, let the carob tree prove that I am right." The carob tree is uprooted and flies one hundred cubits into the air. He then calls out: "If I am right, let this stream of water prove that I am right", and the stream begins to run uphill. Similarly, when he looks to the house of study for a sign, the walls lean inwards, and when he speaks to heaven, a *bat kol* (heavenly voice) calls out that the law always agrees with him. Still, the others do not change their minds. Rather, one of them (Rebbe Joshua) argues that the laws given at Sinai now belong in the human domain, that human reason trumps the heavenly mandate, authorising his claim with the source text from Deuteronomy: "The commandment that I command you is not hidden from you, nor is it far. It is not in heaven that you should say: 'Who will go up to heaven and bring it to us that we can hear it and do it?' . . . But the word is very near you, in your mouth and in your heart that you may do it."[112] When the sages vote, they voted with Joshua, despite the 'signs' of God's position. The Talmudic story does not finish there, but goes on to report that after the scene, God laughed and said, with obvious pleasure, "My children have defeated me."

Coming back to my initial dilemma about what type of norms orient the religious apology, what we have here is a conception very different from the one with which I began, and indeed one that breaks the heteronomy/autonomy or

---

[109] "If autonomy runs the risk of introducing anarchy, heteronomy runs the risk of legitimating fanaticism." Kenneth Seeskin, "Ethics, Authority and Autonomy," in *Cambridge Companion to Modern Jewish Philosophy*, ed. Michael Morgan and Peter Eli Gordon (Cambridge: Cambridge University Press, 2007), 198.

[110] David Hartman, *A Living Covenant* (Woodstock, Vt.: Jewish Lights Publishing, 1997), 222.

[111] Baba Metzia 59b. See also Hermann Cohen, *Religion of Reason: Out of the Sources of Judaism*, trans. Simon Kaplan (New York: F. Ungar Publishing, 1972), 78–9.

[112] Deut. 30:11–14.

absolute/immanent dichotomies that divided the religious apology from secular political principles. Earlier, I referred to Von Rad's claim that particular wrongs against other people are simultaneously offences against the sacred order, a claim I related to the contemporary legal reasoning that criminal offences against individuals are actually offences against the state. We are now coming to this same inter-penetration of the absolute or universal and the particular, but from the other side. Here, the claim is not only that the universal is damaged by sins against particular others, but that the universal is itself recognized and even articulated through our historical confrontation with our own infractions and that this universal is constituted historically through the process of apology. The transcendent cannot be abstracted out and conceived, removed, and 'decontaminated' of its trappings in human relationships.[113] Rather, it is in the particular trappings that the transcendent has being-in-the-world, and through the particular trappings that it is reached. That is why, in religious terms, divine forgiveness is required for sins against other people or, in less abstract terms, why the process of confronting particular wrongs committed against concrete others provides a way into renegotiating our relationship with general orienting norms.

As Levinas presents it, Judaism rises up against "the overly virile proposition ... which puts the universal order above the inter-individual order."[114] Judaism insists that God's forgiveness, or the forgiveness of history, cannot be given unless and until the relationship between persons has been honoured.[115] But in saying so, Levinas is not just honouring the sanctity of individuals. He is pulling us towards a conceptual scheme that brings together the plane of universal moral values and the plane of particular, local infractions against other people, yet without collapsing them. By retaining the idea of the absolute (God), Levinas places a ballast against the tendency to fall in the other direction, reducing the transcendent to the interpersonal or allowing that abstract norms can be reached only by attending to a closed personal morality.[116] The inter-penetration of the abstract and the concrete is what allows the parochial and one-sided historical understanding of right to expand. At the same time, it is history that gives form and thus reality to the abstract norm.

---

[113] Levinas goes even further in his analysis, in a manner resonant of some of the scholastic discussions of grace and the order of forgiveness. It is not quite correct to say that God forgives a person because that person has attained forgiveness from others. Rather, one's forgiveness of others presupposes that one has God's forgiveness. Forgiveness of others is both a manifestation and an outcome of this implicit divine forgiveness.

[114] Levinas, "Towards the Other," 20.

[115] Levinas writes: "God is perhaps nothing but this permanent refusal of a history which would come to terms with our private tears." Ibid.

[116] This is strongly echoed in the Castoriadis work, discussed in Chapter Five.

Perhaps most importantly, what drives this ethical progress is the recognition of the claim of the other, the one who had been excluded from the conversation through which the law is interpreted. Norms are universalized when they are brought face to face with the suffering caused by their limited interpretation; when women demand the right to equality, when blacks demand the right to dignity, when Indigenous people demand the right to family integrity. This is perhaps the heart of Hillel's teaching, "Whatever is hateful to you, do not do to your neighbour. That is the entire Torah, the rest is commentary; go and learn it."[117]

But we *do* in truth do what is hateful to our neighbours, and sometimes we do so because our understanding of what is right, in an absolute sense, fails to take into account what that action means to the other person. When that happens, what needs to be set right is both the particular act and the imperfect interpretation of the universal that underpinned it; we are obligated to do *teshuvah*, both to our neighbour and on the plane of the absolute. By implication, the pieces may not be ordered in quite the sequence we thought, where the absolute universal comes first, followed by particular actions (which are right or wrong according to the universal standard) and then *teshuvah* (which applies the universal to the particular).[118] Apology does not follow from a complete ethical system but is part of the process of creating and completing it. Only through being faced with the consequences of the actions that we assumed were right do we come to revise our evaluations of their moral status in the first instance, and beyond that, our evaluations of the norms that defined them as right. Absolute ethical progress is dependent on concrete history.

This, then, suggests both how the *teshuvah* model addresses the apparent paradox of apology and explains apology's unique quality as an intervention in social relations. The paradox is that apology seems to involve a reversal of the normal order of time because it rests on an assumption that it is possible to do (or say) something at one point of time that will alter what occurred at an earlier point of time. Certainly, as Levinas points out, there is only one path between the events of the past and the present, already marked out and incorruptible, but there are also many paths between the present and the future, and these are yet to be carved out by our treading them. It is freedom at this place, looking and moving forward, that makes possible another type of

---

[117] Shabbat 31a. Shammai and Hillel represent the two great schools of interpretation.

[118] A similarly interesting argument is made by Arendt in her reading of Kant's distinction between reflective and determinate judgements. *Lectures on Kant's Political Philosophy*, ed. Ronald Beiner (Chicago: University of Chicago Press, 1992).

recommencement of the present, and therefore of the past.[119] Here "the destiny of an actually lived life recommences at each instant, receiving a new sense starting from the inimitable novelty of the present which opens upon the unforeseeable future."[120] True, the past, understood as an event in the world, is not touched by the recollection, but the past, understood as a determinant of the future, is. This, as Levinas puts it, is "only constituted in the *future* of a recollected being."[121]

Although Arendt is not (or at least not explicitly) writing within the Jewish tradition, her writings on forgiveness are remarkably close to and elucidate this conception. For Arendt, forgiveness opens the possibility of breaking the absolute determinism of past events. Forgiving, as she writes, is "the only reaction which does not merely re-act but acts anew and unexpectedly, unconditioned by the act which provoked it and therefore freeing it from its consequences both to the one who forgives and the one who is forgiven."[122] Forgiveness as used by Arendt, and pardon as used by Levinas, marks this possibility of human beings' adding something new to a chain of events otherwise conceived like Newton's billiard balls: cause, effect, effect, effect. 'I' or 'we' and what we experience need not simply be the product of fate, the passive outcome of the passage of moments following upon each other mechanically and inexorably producing each other. Pardon or forgiveness interrupts or corrupts this path, opening the space for what Levinas calls 'fecundity': the creation of something new.

Crucially, for both Levinas and Arendt and within Jewish philosophy more generally, this freedom with respect to the past is not located inside the individual consciousness. What makes it possible to bring in something new is not an attribute of the sole human person. It is not that 'I' have a distance to myself, as if I were able to determine myself in some regards but not others. If the future is still indeterminate, open before us as the possibility of calling up the past as memory and giving it new meaning, this is only by virtue of the presence of another point of view. It is the *relational* dimension of repentance that makes possible this freedom or fecundity. The infinity of the future that allows for the recommencement of the past cannot be my work alone. The other must accompany me in my re-visitation of the past, and only in this space between one and the other can the continuous flow be broken.

---

[119] Levinas writes that this rupture, achieved through pardon, is "the very work of time." *Totality and Infinity*, 282.
[120] Ibid., 130.
[121] Ibid., 166.
[122] Arendt, *The Human Condition*, 241.

The freedom that apology opens up does not, however, imply that we have the capacity to rule over history and so change the event in itself. For both Levinas and Arendt, what is distinct about human life is its movement between two poles; for Levinas, the incorruptibility of the past and the fecundity of the future; for Arendt, promise and forgiveness. Life is lived between the historical narrative of my life, with all the fixity and finitude this implies, and the moral creation of the I, whose "horizons [are] more vast than history."[123] The former provides the continuity necessary for identity and the latter the possibility of its transformation, and together, they function in creative tension. The pole of pardon or forgiveness does not annul the pole of determinism, but at the same time promises cannot bind meaning. The creative tension between these two poles resembles the conception of Torah as the ongoing product of human creativity that continues to evolve in an open-ended future, yet always tied to a point of origin. Linking this back to the thinking of *Mishna Horayot*, Torah is the anchoring point, but it is *horah*, the voice of the living community that gives content to, and has the capacity to breathe life into, the ethics for lived situations.

Understanding repentance as a constructive process throws a bridge over the apparent gulf between religion as the sphere of heteronomous law and democratic politics as the sphere of human autonomy, but still we should not too quickly pass over the more habitual understanding that sees foundational laws or norms as thick and resistant to change. This is especially significant in the context of the current project, because not only religions, but also nations draw their distinct identities from precisely such particularistic norms. What this raises is the tension not simply between religious identities or normative commitments and liberal principles, but also between the process of constituting nations and liberal principles. If apologies do indeed take their orientation from values that are embedded in the identity of the political community, and those norms themselves involve exclusionary or hierarchical categories, they may involve a conservative, and not simply a progressive, dynamic.

This chapter has suggested that in Judaism's practice and understanding of apology as a collective, reconstitutive act, we find a model that better makes sense of the contemporary practice than the individualistic internal models of apology that dominate our habitual interpretive frames. Here, what we see is a notion of apology as the publicly spoken declaration of who we have been and who we aspire to be, a declaration that does not simply name a process that is taking place elsewhere, but itself allows a political community to recommit to

[123] Levinas, *Totality and Infinity*, 246.

and revise key normative principles. If this is so, what happened to this understanding and practice? How did it go underground as a template for our own understandings and practices, and how was it replaced by the model we now assume to be the essential apology? In the next chapter, I look for that answer by tracing the trajectory of apology in Christianity.

4

The Privatization of Repentance in Christianity

> The focus ... shifted from the well being of the community and the reintegration of penitent sinners to enabling sinners to make satisfaction for their sins and experience forgiveness. The ministry was less and less perceived as community ministry – the ministry of the community to penitent sinners with the goal of restoring the integrity of the community – and instead regarded as an individual ministry of the priest or spiritual expert for the sinner who sought healing.
>
> James Dallen[1]

In line with the commonly held image of Christianity as a religion emphasizing an individual's salvation relationship with God, one usually thinks of the Christian model of repentance as essentially individual and private.[2] The communal and collective dimensions that remained central in Jewish understanding and practice seem alien in concept and absent in practice. It is almost inconceivable to us that, in fact, the corporate model is not so remote from Christianity at all, but lies at the heart of early Christian practices and understanding, and indeed remains a central form of religious practice and understanding in

---

[1] James Dallen, *The Reconciling Community: The Rite of Penance* (New York: Pueblo Publishing, 1986), 101.

[2] Arendt, for example, sets her attempt to conceptualize collective responsibility in relief against what she assumes to be the essentially individualistic lens that is part and parcel of the Christian heritage. "With the rise of Christianity the emphasis shifted entirely from care for the world and the duties associated with it, to care for the soul and its salvation." Hannah Arendt, "Collective Responsibility," in *Responsibility and Judgment*, ed. Jerome Kohn (New York: Schocken Books, 2003), 151–2.

some churches. This is, however, no innocent invisibility, but rather the product of the triumph of the individual form. If we cannot see the collective apology in Christian practice or theology, that is because it has been overshadowed by the dominating image of the individual, privately murmuring his or her sins in the darkness of the confessional, sanctioned by Trent, and immortalized by a historical erasure of the fact that any other form existed. In fact, in the first centuries after Christ, the church's penitential practices were highly public and involved the entire community, but from the Council of Trent (mid-sixteenth century) until Vatican II in the 1960s, the sole sanctioned rite of penance in the Catholic Church comprised an individual, private ritual, wherein the penitent exchanged words of contrition for forgiveness and absolution. The Roman Catholic concept of repentance and this form of practice have been considered synonymous, and there was no recognition of the fact that there had been or that there could be other forms or conceptualizations.

This changed with the call from Vatican II to develop new rites of penance that would better embody the communal and reconciliatory dimensions of repentance that were now resurfacing in the church's memory of itself. Subsequently, in 1973, three new rites of penance, now (significantly) named Rites of Reconciliation, were promulgated and entered official church practice. One of these remained exclusively individual and private, one combined private penance with a public and collective ritual, and the third eliminated the private part of the rite altogether. What makes this shift particularly fascinating in the context of this project is that it occurred shortly before the emergence of the public political apology. This temporal proximity is certainly not sufficient evidence to argue that the two stand in a causal relation, but it does suggest a more general shift in conceptualization and practice, manifest in each of these spheres.[3] Shifts in both the religious and political spheres evidence a growing recognition and acceptance of the communal or social dimensions of wrongdoing and the consequent pressure to accommodate this alongside the dominant individualistic conception of responsibility.

This chapter looks initially at the early forms of penitential practice in the first centuries of the church's existence, then at the development of private penance in the Celtic church and its subsequent export and ascent. My main focus is on the trajectory from early Christianity through the dogma and

---

[3] Nevertheless, the fact that doctrinal and institutional change occurred and was experienced in the Catholic Church in the years immediately preceding the emergence of the political practice supports my weaker thesis that religious practices of repentance provide the alphabet or the grammar with which political actors then work. Moreover, the institutionalization of this form of collective repentance in the Church at this critical juncture provided a concrete experience that could then support its development in a new sphere.

practice of the Roman Catholic Church.[4] In particular, I concentrate on the two turning points: first, the dogmatic declaration of private confession as the sole valid form of practice to the exclusion of all others and, second, the Roman Catholic Church's reintroduction of collective repentance.

In reviewing this history, I want to draw particular attention to the Roman Catholic Church's positive concealment and repression of the early practices and the alternative, public conception of repentance that these practices embodied. The shift in practice and the move towards privatization and individuation signified and perpetuated important re-conceptualizations in the nature and concerns of religion as a distinct sphere of life, of individual and communal responsibility, and of the work of repentance with respect to each of these. In the words of one contemporary Catholic theologian: "the form of the administration of the sacrament is not harmless; it favours one aspect of reconciliation. The private form favours reconciliation with oneself in the interior of one's own conscience, sole seat of authentic relationship with God. Other human realities, and notably economic and political relationships, escape all interference from Christianity."[5] Correlatively, one might infer that as the collective form of repentance once again becomes part of standard practice, so, too, those other human realities that concern structural inequality and collective denigration can more easily emerge from behind the singular story of individual responsibility.

The chapter also looks briefly at the Protestant Churches, where repentance has had a very different trajectory. In this case, Trent was not the beginning of a new dogma in the form of privatized penance, but the formation of a new Church, and with it a rejection of the sacrament of penance altogether, largely because of the abuse of mediation that had sullied the Church. The story of Protestantism's reaction to this degeneration in the role of the Church is well known, that is, getting rid of mediation altogether and making the relationship with God entirely personal and private. What is less known is that there was another side to this reaction, which was to make the mediation entirely transparent and public by getting rid of the private dimension altogether and putting in its place a public general confession. Thus, as the continuous practice of general, public confessional forms in the Anglican Church testifies, the template of the apologizing collective has remained alive; the prose, rhythms, and voice

---

[4] Other than looking at early forms of practice, this chapter does not discuss the eastern or Orthodox churches.

[5] Christian Duquoc, "Real Reconciliation and Sacramental Reconciliation," in *Concilium Religion in the Seventies*, vol. 61: Sacramental Reconciliation, ed. Edward Schillebeeckx (New York: Herder and Herder, 1971), 36.

of collective repentance have remained at the centre of religious ritual, etching a template for the collective apology, albeit unmarked as such.

I. EARLY CONCEPTIONS AND FORMS OF PENITENTIAL PRACTICE

(i) Jesus and the Gospels

The call to repentance lay at the heart of Jesus' teaching and formed a major key in the Gospels, beginning with the invitation to "repent and believe in the Gospel" (Mark 1:15) and concluding with the command "in his name repentance and forgiveness of sins is to be proclaimed" (Luke 24:47).[6] The stories and parables about repentance provide the richest elucidation of what it actually signified. Continuous with Judaism, their predominant note is not repentance as a specific legalistic response to particular transgressions, but rather as return and commitment to a relationship with God and the holy community.[7]

Amongst the parables about sin and repentance, the prodigal younger son poignantly illustrates the most important New Testament themes.[8] In this story, the younger of two sons asks for his inheritance early, takes it, and leaves his home and his father. When he all too quickly squanders the money, he discovers himself desolate and without support, and resorts to working as a swineherd, a deeply humiliating situation for a Jew, for whom pork was unclean and forbidden. It is only at this point, standing in this remote place, that he contacts his sense of deep alienation and meaninglessness. Only from here does he experience the impulse of connection to his father that moves him to choose to return home.[9] His father welcomes him compassionately, accepts him unconditionally, and even calls for the finest robes in which to adorn him and the fattest calf to celebrate his return.

If we wonder why this son, the one who rebelled and only then returned, attains a status that his brother, who simply stayed in his father's home, never attains, we might turn back to the Jewish teaching that the one who sins and repents stands where not even the righteous stand, for the latter lack the

---

[6] There is a plethora of references to forgiveness and repentance in the Gospels, prominently, Luke 24:47; Matt. 6:14, 12:32, 16:18–19; John 20:22; 5:14–17; Mark 3:29; 2 Cor. 5:18–20.

[7] This is hardly surprising given that Jesus was a Jew and the early Christian community emerged directly out of Judaism. Nevertheless, the relationship was complex. As James Dallen puts it, "[e]arly Christians were reluctant to borrow from rabbinic Judaism while competing with it." Dallen, *The Reconciling Community*, 10.

[8] Luke 15:11–32. Other key parables on repentance are at Luke 18:9–14, 15:1–7, and Matt. 18:23–35.

[9] As noted in Chapter Three, one of the meanings of the Hebrew root *chet* is to be beside oneself.

penitent's intense yearning.[10] As was the case for the Hebrews, who could only really approach God at Sinai after they had experienced what it was like to lose God, so too the son only really attains the conscious connection with the father once he has experienced himself out of connection. Once again, sin is not a violation of a law but a breach in relationship, change in orientation, or departure from a way of being in the world, and repentance is neither repayment nor regret, but return to relationship. Relationship and commitment, not law, define the decisive moments.

Indeed, despite our habitual reading of Eve and Adam's original sin as a breach of God's law and the punishment that follows, this story, retold by Paul in Romans, can also be read as a commentary on the attempt to gain independence at the expense of symbiotic connection and naïve reverence. Recall that they ate the fruit forbidden them by God after the serpent told Eve that if they did, they would not die, as God had warned, but the fruit would make them "as the Gods", knowing (and hence able to discern between) good and evil.[11] As a result of their decision and subsequent act, Adam and Eve acquire self-consciousness and shame and are expelled from the place of undifferentiated harmony.[12]

As in the story of the prodigal son, the legalistic reading is but a thin veneer over the far richer narrative on the constitution of human beings as creatures who discover the existence of their own will and with it acquire the capacity to reflect morally on the consequences of exercising that will. The choice is the occasion for experiencing themselves as individuals and correlatively having a positive, as distinct from an assumed, experience of moral commitment. Without the choice, as Kant observed, the idea of morality is empty, and hence it is only from this place that return and commitment become possible as moral choices, manifest in repentance.[13] Of course, the return cannot reconstruct the situation *ex ante*; the untrammeled

---

[10] Berachot, 34b. As set out in Yoma 86, repentance out of love transforms sins into *mitzvoth* (blessings), because they bring the sinner closer to God.

[11] The serpent's promise was, "For God doth know that in the day ye eat thereof, then your eyes shall be opened, and ye shall be as gods, knowing good and evil." Gen. 3:5. The observation that God makes subsequently is, "Behold, man is become as one of us, to know good and evil." Gen. 3:22.

[12] Within this story is another with the same structure: the story of the serpent or Satan. The name Satan is derived from a root meaning to 'oppose', and extra-biblical commentary fills out the identity of the serpent as the angel who fell from God as a consequence of his bold assertion of independence. Like Adam and Eve, it was his desire to be out of the original form of relationship with God that was the core of sin and the cause of his expulsion. There are a number of sources explaining the identity of the serpent and Satan. For example, Isa. 14:14; Babylonian Talmud, Baba Bathra, 16a; and *The Life of Adam and Eve*, an early Jewish Apocryphal text.

[13] "If our will is not free, if the soul is divisible and perishable like matter, moral ideas and principles lose all validity." Immanuel Kant, *Critique of Pure Reason*, trans. Paul Guyer and Allen W. Wood (Cambridge: Cambridge University Press, 1998), 499.

innocence of the original state has gone. But the recognition of alienation can form the foundation of a positively chosen reconciliation (as distinct from symbiosis), re-entry into relationship, and subjectively experienced commitment to being 'good'.

Interpreting the implications for New Testament theology of these key stories, Monika Hellwig gives a reading strikingly close to the one offered in the previous chapter:

> Sin can never be reduced to the breaking of rules and commandments. It cannot even be reduced to a collectivity of specific, discrete destructive deeds. Sin is deliberate or unrecognized detachment from God, orientation of human striving away from God. It is the placing of ultimate trust in anything other than God, even placing of trust in moral behaviour or good conduct according to the law of God.[14]

Hellwig's all-important distinction between trust in God and adherence to the law of God points to Paul's essential distinction between love and law. The heart of the religious bond lies not in legal compliance but in an orientation and commitment to that orientation. What these stories narrate is the process whereby human beings make that commitment. They do not do so 'naturally', but acquire a subjective experience of commitment to a certain way of being only through a retrospective recognition attained through loss, or straying from the path. The call to repentance in the New Testament is a call to come back into a rightful relationship with God, and by extension with the *ecclesia* – the holy community, which is God on earth. It was this conception of repentance that was taken up in the early formation of Christian communities.

(ii) The Early Patristic Church

The earliest Christian communities that formed in the first century after the death of Christ were fervent, small, and tightly knit and believed that the ultimate judgement was imminent. Their sense of urgency about the imperative to be close to God and on the right side of redemption, combined with the fact that most members were baptized as adults and so had already been through an exacting process of conversion, initially made additional intervention to counter sin superfluous, and so little attention was paid to post-baptismal penance. Post-baptismal sin was nevertheless unavoidable, and the New Testament and

---

[14] Monika Hellwig, *Sign of Conversion and Reconciliation: The Sacrament of Penance for Our Times* (Wilmington, Del.: Michael Glazier, 1984), 21.

early documents provide evidence of the types of penitential rituals developed at this stage to deal with it.[15]

Initially, these processes of repentance were not formalized, but there appear to have been two main ways of dealing with sin. The first was through a combination of fraternal correction, the prayer of the community, and a form of public verbal confession.[16] Second, and in the case of especially serious and public sins, the person in question was separated from the community, corrected in order to move him or her to conversion, and then reintegrated into the community.[17] Communal prayer and mutual correction were common practice, understood within the context of a strong sense of the corporate body and the social character of sin. In both cases repentance was not a solitary process, but rather one in which the entire community was directly involved. Moreover, this corporate quality did not simply reflect a sense of mutual concern or responsibility, but flowed from an understanding that the church was the embodiment of God on earth and from the conception of sin as directly affecting the community per se.[18]

Preserving the righteousness of the Church (the gathering of Christians) was a particular imperative because Christians saw it as the witness to the reality of God's being in front of Jewish and pagan communities. As such, the reintegration of the individual through penitential processes was not merely a service to the individual, but also a way of once again making whole and holy the Church as the living proof of God.[19] Repentance was an integral part of constituting the Christian community – a community whose identity was founded on certain normative orientations.

The collective dimension of repentance also grows from the early Christian emphasis on horizontal relations between members of the Christian community.

---

[15] See J. Murphy-O'Connor, "Pêche et communauté dans le nouveau testament," *Revue Biblique* 74 (1967). Letters of the Roman bishop Clement and a Syrian document from the late first or early second century, the *Didache*, provide key testimony. See *Ancient Christian Writers*, vol. 1: *The Epistles of St. Clement of Rome and St. Ignatius of Antioch*, trans. James A. Kleist (New York: Newman Press, 1946).

[16] "Confess your faults one to another, and pray one for another, that ye may be healed." Jas. 5:16; 1st Epistle of John, 1:9: "If we confess our sins he is faithful and just to forgive us our sins, and to cleanse us from all unrighteousness." Cf. Also Matt. 18:15–17, 19–20; Gal. 6:1–2; 1 John 5:16.

[17] 2 Thess. 3:6–15; 1 Tm. 1:20.

[18] "Know ye not that a little leaven leaveneth the whole lump? Purge out therefore the old leaven, that ye may be a new lump, as ye are unleavened." 1. Cor. 5:6; see also Rom. 14:7–8, 2 Cor. 2:5.

[19] This is evident, for example, in Ignatius of Antioch's letter to Polycarp, which insists that the sinner be reclaimed "so that you may preserve the whole of your community intact." *The Epistles of St. Clement of Rome and St. Ignatius of Antioch*, 11.4.

The Gospels, the Acts of the Apostles, and the writings of St. Paul and John the Evangelist indicate that love of God was equivalent to love of neighbour. Early Christian communities then understood being without sin as being in a relationship with God, and this in turn meant living as a holy community that embodied God's being in this world (and not only the world to come). The return to God through conversion or repentance was a community enterprise, not by virtue of the support it offered, nor even because acting well to others was the means for achieving a return to God, but because creating and sustaining this normative community was what it meant to return to God.[20]

The two central terms designating repentance in these early documents are *exomologesis* and *metanoia*. *Exomologesis* is usually translated as confession, but (as in the case of the early Hebrew) it signified praise of God as well as admission of wrongdoing and appeal for forgiveness.[21] *Exomologesis* was a necessary but insufficient element of a holistic penitential practice that effected *metanoia*, the general term for conversion. Importantly, *metanoia* was understood as a process, a shift in the person and his or her relationship with the community, and not an institution.[22] Most critical in this process was conversion of faith and realliance to God enacted and evidenced through word and deed. In practical terms, this included self-abasement, confessional prayer, fasting, alms deeds, and the humble acceptance of ecclesial punishment.[23] Expiation proportionate to the wrongful act and active reconciliation between people were also required.[24]

The emphasis on orientation as opposed to legal compliance comes through strongly in early views about forgiveness. Like later Christians, these early writers were already concerned about what was required for forgiveness; but whereas in later doctrine this question was answered by classifying sins themselves as remissible or irremissible, in the early teachings what was relevant was the orientation of the sinner himself. If there were limits on the possibility of forgiveness, this was not because the sin carried an objective level of punishment under God's legal system but because its gravity was indicative of the person's orientation away from God. Such informality became untenable once the circumstances of the Church changed and specifically as the Church grew from a small group of

---

[20] Using the same reasoning, Hellwig places the Eucharist at the center of early Christian life and connects it with the early understanding of repentance. Hellwig, *Sign of Conversion*, 91.

[21] Didache 4:14; Clement, Letter to the Corinthians 26:2, 48:2, 51:3, 52:1–2, 61:3. See G.W.H. Lampe, ed., *A Patristic Greek Lexicon* (London: Oxford University Press, 1961), 1: 499–500.

[22] Dallen, *The Reconciling Community*, 22.

[23] "The Shepherd of Hermas", an apocryphal Roman work dating from the later first and early second centuries, witnesses the contemporary practices of repentance. A translation of the Shepherd of Hermas by J. B. Lighfoot in 1891 is available at http://www.gnosis.org/library/hermas.htm.

[24] Didache 14:1–2.

fervent adult converts to a new demographic of people born into the group. This demographic shift, in combination with the influence of Roman legalism, led to the hardening of repentance into a formal institution. Already in the early second century, there is evidence of the incipient formalization and ritualization of what had been loose processes of repentance, and of appeals against such hardening, stressing the processural rather than institutional nature of *metanoia*.

By the beginning of the third century, penitential practices very similar to those that were to become the formalized order of the penitents were already common in the Latin-speaking North African church, known variously as restoration, reincorporation into the church, peace, return to the Church's camp, and reception into communion.[25] The highly public performance started with *exomologesis* or *confessio*, public speech in which the penitent spoke of his or her sinfulness and acknowledged God's mercy and his or her desire to return. As in the Jewish practice, people were also required to reconcile with those against whom they had committed wrongs.[26] The wrongdoer donned sackcloth and ashes, fasted, abstained from delicacies and comfort, groaned and wept in public, prostrated before the priests, and knelt before the congregation of the faithful to beseech their prayers.[27]

Hermas' five visions (written in the first or second century) recorded in "The Shepherd of Hermas" poignantly capture the corporate dimension of the early understandings of the penitential process.[28] In the first two visions, Hermas is sinning and then learning from an old woman (who represents the Church) that he can gain forgiveness by repentance. In the third vision a great tower built on water (the water of baptism) appears, surrounded by stones (representing people) at differing distances, with fire at the edge of the water. Those professing faith are warned that unless they commit while the tower is in the process of being built they will be cast away. Those most remote from the tower, with no connection with the Church, are falling from the water into the fire. In the fourth vision the aged woman, seeing that her warning has been heeded, becomes a bride, and in the last vision she departs and sends the shepherd, the angel of repentance, in her place. Repentance, personified by this angel, represents the reconstitution of the corporate wholeness or the moral integrity of the holy community, where all members share a normative orientation.

---

[25] The most important witness here is Tertullian, born in North Africa in around A.D. 155. His key works are *De Paenitentia*, written while he was still a Catholic in 203 or 204, and *De Pudicitia* (On Purity), a polemic against Catholicism, written when he had become a Montanist.

[26] Tertullian, *De Paenitentia*, Chapter 11. Original documents in Oscar D. Watkins, *A History of Penance, Being a Study of Authorities*, 2 vols. (London: Longmans, Green, 1920).

[27] Tertullian, *De Paenitentia*, Chapter 9.

[28] Hermas' text was widely cited in early documents, though his identity remains unknown.

This strong ecclesial understanding comes through more formally in the writings of Cyprian, Tertullian's successor as the Bishop of Carthage (A.D. 249–58).[29] Cyprian teaches that penitential works achieve divine forgiveness, but only through reconciliation with the Church. Driving out evil means adjusting one's priorities to make fidelity to God paramount. This is done through penitential acts that achieve and witness conversion, and in turn involves reintegration into the corporate body of the church.

To make sense of the dynamics of these rituals and the conceptualization of repentance that they embodied, one has to map them against the complex structural connection that held between the idea of God, the holy community of the church, and the individual as sinner or penitent. Most importantly, that map is misconceived if we think of God as the abstract, transcendent term to which the individual sinner is oriented via the necessary mediation of the Church as God's proxy. Rather, as with the social conception of sin, the relationship with God was grounded in the constitution of the Church as the community of God. If we assume a hard conceptual or ontological distinction between the abstract transcendence of the divine and the materiality and mundane character of the ecclesial community, we will miss this inter-penetration. Think, for example, of the practice of laying on hands to infuse the penitent with the spirit of the holy community. The performance does not represent God, as if physics stood in for metaphysics, but is rather brought about by the embodied ecclesial infusion and the transmission of *pax cum Ecclesia*.

Understood in this context, repentance was not simply about bringing the individual back into a community, but reconstituting the community itself, because the community only existed as God's body by virtue of the fidelity of individuals who composed and affirmed it. Moreover, as was the case in Judaism, the existence of the community and its normative orientation are not two separate moments, where the community exists first and then it acquires a normative character. Rather, the church was constituted as a distinct community only through its ethical orientation, an ethical orientation that correlatively exists only insofar as it is the ethical orientation of actual people.[30]

---

[29] See Bernhard Poschmann, *Penance and the Anointing of the Sick* (New York: Herder Press, 1964), 53–62.

[30] It is interesting in this context to reflect on the Pope's apologies and his care to distinguish between the sins of the sons and daughters of the Church and 'the Church' itself. He was clearly asserting the ongoing existence of the Church as a corporate entity faithful to its ethical orientation. One might wonder at what point the loss of this ethical orientation in the actual practice of members of the historical church would constitute its demise and not simply its deviation. This was presumably part of Luther's criticism.

(iii) The Eastern Church and the Shift to Inwardness

In the Eastern Church, contemporary testimony indicates similar forms of public penance, with the additional distinct emphasis on private counsel and spiritual direction.[31] Although not a substitute for public penance, ministers in the Eastern Church played a distinct role as healers and spiritual guides, mostly at the beginning of the process of public penance or in the case of lesser sins that would not require the full penitential journey. These guides, who were required to be not church officials but rather holy persons, would provide spiritual counsel concerning how to return to a holy life through repentance. They were referred to as physicians, helpers of Christ the supreme physician. Following this metaphor, sins were thought of as the wounds that must be shown to God and to God's priest.[32] One finds resonance of this metaphoric frame in many of the references in contemporary apologies to the healing work of repentance and the wound of wrongdoing.

Although this distinct modality differs from the private form of confession that was later to become the sanctioned sacrament of penance, it can nevertheless be seen as an early antecedent of the monastic penance that developed into the sacramental form.[33] The resemblance lies not only in its formal privacy, but also in the emphasis on internal moral striving and conscience. In this encounter, the core purpose of confession was the manifestation of conscience, as distinct from the public revelation of sinfulness. Inwardness, the transformation of the soul, was paramount here, and the work of confession focused on the individual person who sinned (purgation) rather than on the public display and relationship. This medicinal or therapeutic dimension of repentance was to become the mark of the Greek Church, and later the dominant tone of the church per se.

Even then, the emphasis on internality and conscience in this context did not go along with a detachment from the ecclesial aspect of repentance. The constitution of the holy community remained intrinsic and public penance was still standard practice. St. Gregory of Neocaesarea (known as the Wonderworker, third century) left us a vivid picture of the topography of the penitential process.[34] He describes five grades of penitents, each located literally further or closer to the heart of the holy community and communion. The 'mourners'

---

[31] Key documents here are the testimonies of Clement of Alexandria (d. A.D. 215) and Origen (d. A.D. 254), and the Didaskalia, a North Syrian document from the early third century.

[32] Poschmann, *Penance*, 90; Watkins, *A History of Penance*, vol. 1: 246, 472.

[33] Scholars disagree about the relationship between this early eastern practice and the later Monastic and Celtic developments. Cf. Dallen, *The Reconciling Community*, 104–5.

[34] Poschmann, *Penance*, 90; Watkins, *A History of Penance*, vol. 1: 246, 472.

were located outside the church altogether, seeking the prayers of the faithful and readmission; the 'hearers' were allowed to stand just inside the entrance hall, but only during the early part of the service; the 'fallers' or 'prostrators' were permitted inside the nave, but in a position of self-abasement, and again only for the first part of the service; the 'bystanders' were present for the entire liturgy, but were excluded from communion; and the 'faithful' were fully admitted to communion. In this very graphic and literal way, the relationship of the members of the church to God, or holiness, or the ideal of the church as the holy community was mapped in the grammar of repentance. The space between the reality of the lives of the church members and ideal of the church as the holy community could be measured through the grades of repentance – and in turn, the process of repentance provided the vehicle for closing the gap.

(iv) Canonical Penance from the Fourth to Sixth Centuries

The Peace at Constantine at the beginning of the fourth century transformed the Church from a persecuted 'community apart' to a politically tolerated religion with legal status. This political legitimation in turn influenced the development of practices within the Church, including the penitential system. So long as the Church had been defined as a 'community of saints', and the contours of Christian identity had been given by the mandate to distinguish the Christian from Jew and pagan, sin had primarily been defined as public offence against, or infidelity to, this holy community. Once this strictly oppositional identity fell away, structure had to come from within.

Mainstreaming Christianity and assimilating it into civil models of administration had two types of effect. First, as the Church adopted Roman models, legal formalism replaced the informality and spontaneity that had characterized its early life. Whereas sin had been an experiential category, and responses to sin had been developed in the context of closely knit communities of people who knew and responded to one another, sins and the appropriate responses now became legally defined and impersonally regulated. This movement towards formalization had already been happening, but now it took on a legal character.

In Rome during the fourth century, bishops acquired the right to act as judges in civil suits and their judgements had legal force. The structure of the role carried over; as judges they acted in the name of the Emperor, as bishops they acted in the name of God. Their role in the church became that of legislators and arbiters, promulgating rules and adjudicating compliance. The themes of obedience and penalty in turn came to take over from those of bringing individuals back to and strengthening the corporate body of the church. Sin, which had been regarded as a break in the relationship of love and trust between members of the community, and a breach of the covenantal relation between the community and God, was increasingly conceived in legal terms, as a violation of a divine or ecclesial law. Correspondingly, repentance, which had been understood as the change of heart required to re-enter the holy relationship, was now regarded as the penalty imposed for violating the law. In turn, the notion that penance was satisfaction to expiate or pay for the offence started to be abstracted from its other roles, and this strand became predominant.

This reflected a deeper theological shift. The early fathers had conceived of repentance as the means by which sin was eliminated in the sinner and forgiven by God, just as sin was *itself* the estrangement and not the cause of estrangement as a separate event. In this later period, penance becomes the prelude to a forgiveness that occurs as the final act of reconciliation. Repentance/reconciliation, which had originally comprised an integrated process, now became a linear succession of detached acts – repentance/penance/forgiveness. Separating the moments into discrete events meant that the penance could be measured economically, so as to assess whether it would be a sufficient causal agent.

The tension between these two conceptions is evident in the writings of Augustine, who provided the most comprehensive picture of the penitential system during this period.[35] He still held the view that sinfulness was in principle a matter of conscience, and believed that the classification of sins should be based on the attitude of the sinner. In practice, however, since no one can look into another's heart and assess the degree of sorrow, the gravity of sins had to be judged according to some external measure according to which sins could be graded.[36] Of course, this change did not happen in a single historical moment, but was built on the incipient formalism already noted. Nevertheless, it was during this period that a series of conciliar decisions, papal decretals, private counsels and directives, and the penitential letters became the basis for rigid legal forms. These canons strictly regulated practice, hence the term *canonical penance*. The mechanization and legalization that is evident at this period became only more pronounced right up to the council of Trent in the mid-sixteenth century.[37] The formalization of canonical penance marks one of

[35] I complement them here with other contemporary writings, including testament found in Ambrose and Pacian's vindications of the capacity of the church to forgive, written in the face of extreme Novatianism.

[36] On the opacity of the heart, see Augustine, *Confessions*, Book II, chapter VIII.

[37] See Kenneth E. Kirk, *The Vision of God, the Christian Doctrine of the Summum Bonum: The Bampton Lectures for 1928* (London, New York: Longmans, Green, 1941), Lecture 3, 130–7.

the most important shifts in the conceptualization and practice of repentance and apology.

Augustine notes three categories of penance: pre-baptismal penance, which was the initial process of conversion; penance for sins of daily occurrence, whereby the Christian was constantly brought to a more holy life; and penance for grave sins – *paenitentia maior* – which required canonical penance, the ecclesial public ritual.[38] Notably, there was no category of private ecclesial penance.[39] The public penitential procedure was essentially the same as that set out already by Tertullian, Cyprian, and Origen in the preceding century. It was initiated by the request to do penance, which included acknowledgement of the sin and verbal confession, followed by laying on hands and formal admission to the Order of the Penitents. Entering this order entailed becoming part of a special body with inferior legal standing and literally occupying a distinct physical location within the church.[40] Penitents were excluded from the Eucharist, but were allowed to be present during the service, and there was a special rite of blessing of the penitents, which included the laying on of hands before the congregation.

Once in the order, penitents were to wear ignominious clothing, crop their hair, and neglect their personal care.[41] A series of rigours and restrictions characterized the life of the penitent: fasting, almsgiving, prayer, renunciation of the pleasures of body and mind, curtailment of sleep, sexual abstinence, and the abandonment of the struggle for worldly honours. The period of penance for ordinary sins of the flesh was probably reasonably brief, about forty days, but for more serious sins there is evidence that periods of ten, twenty, thirty years, or even lifelong penance were imposed.

Reconciliation at the end of the period of penance was again a public, dramatic, ecclesial rite. On a raised platform sits the bishop, below him the penitents, prostrate and in tears, around them the congregants, bowing in prayer, weeping in compassion and joining in the reconciliation. Though it is the penitents who are being brought back in, the whole body of the church is involved in the act of making whole. This strong corporate ecclesial dimension is graphically portrayed in Jerome's description of the bishop's ministry:

---

[38] De Fide et Operibus, 26 in Watkins, *A History of Penance*, vol. 1: 442.

[39] This question has been the subject of controversy in Church history, but Poschmann argues that the first evidence of private penance is found in the eleventh canon of the Synod of Toledo (589), which branded it an abuse that had crept into practice in some Spanish churches. See Poschmann, *Penance*, 86 and 116ff.

[40] Augustine refers to this as the *locus paenitentium*; Serm. 232, 7, 8.

[41] Cf. Ambrose, *De Paenitentia*, 1,8,37; Jerome Ep. 77, 2.

The priest offers oblation for the layperson; he imposes hands on the one subject to it; he prays for the return of the holy spirit, and thus by the other public prayer he reconciles the people to the one who had been handed over to Satan for the destruction of the flesh so that the Spirit might save. And no sooner is *one member restored to health than all members come together as a whole.* The father finds it easy to pardon his son when the mother begs on behalf of her flesh and blood.[42]

Three related aspects of this passage are particularly pertinent to our considerations. First, notice the powerful metaphor of the family. The father represents the transcendent God; the mother the Church or God's immanence; and the son the human individual or community.[43] The Church is the partner of God and the human child is their flesh and blood, partaking in both and inconceivable out of this relationship. Second, the publicity and community of the act are not incidental, or helpful, as they will soon come to be portrayed, but essential. Third, one sees the extent to which the priest is steeped in the body of the community. Certainly, he is a representative actor, but of the embodied Church and not a transcendent abstracted God who acts on the sinner through the representative figure. Again, these observations point to the theological puzzle of the respective roles of God, the Church, and the individual in the work of forgiveness and the relationship between them. Dallen sets out the core terms of the theological problem:

The assembled church in its diversity of orders, functions, and responsibilities, received the penitents and then celebrated the Eucharist as the ultimate sign that the penitents were reconciled to God, in the Body and the Blood of Christ. The laying on of hands seems not so much to give the spirit directly as to restore access to the Eucharist through which the penitents are once more filled with the Spirit. It is this *ius communicationis*, the right to share, which is primary: solidarity with the Spirit-filled community, expressed particularly in its Eucharist.[44]

The Church, as an active community, occupies a direct and not an incidental role in the work of repentance and forgiveness. The moments or dimensions of God as the source of forgiveness and the church as the body within which reconciliation occurs may be distinguished analytically, but they are not separate. From a theological and not simply a practical point of view, repentance is necessarily about the body or the constitution of the Church as a community oriented to a certain way of being, and it is in this context that repentance and

---

[42] Contra Luciferianos 5 quoted by Dallen, *The Reconciling Community*, 72. Emphasis added.

[43] Jerome's gendering is notable here: the Church, represented as the mother, is the body, the ground of being, while the father stands above, the inspiration.

[44] Dallen, *The Reconciling Community*, 73.

reconciliation as public communal processes make sense. Correlatively, as sin and repentance came to be seen in individualized, internal, and legal terms, the publicity and collectivity of the institution became relatively superfluous. The quote at the beginning of this chapter is Dallen's commentary of the shift during this period: "The focus had now almost totally shifted from the well being of the community and the reintegration of penitent sinners to enabling sinners to make satisfaction for their sins and experience forgiveness."[45] The role of the community becomes one step removed: standing beside the process rather than being its primary subject.

This is evident in the incipient shift in the descriptions of the role of the community and congregational prayer. The prayer of the community moves to the role of helpful support for the individual in his or her journey.[46] No longer were communally based repentance and reconciliation moments part of a process grounded in the body of the church. Rather, confession and penitential works came to be seen as the cause of forgiveness, and reconciliation became the public declaration of forgiveness that had been obtained.[47]

This loss of connection between the practice of public penance and the experience of sin and repentance provides the internal reason for the demise of the practice. Deprived of a compelling and connected meaning, it lost its hold. More practically, public penance's extreme rigour made it unsustainable in a Christian community that no longer comprised only staunch devotees. Particularly abhorrent were the life-long restrictions that were imposed on penitents even after they had been reconciled and which most people avoided by delaying canonical penance until the last days of their lives. By the sixth and seventh centuries, the end of Christian antiquity, canonical penance had fallen into disuse.

2. THE PRIVATIZATION OF PENANCE THROUGH THE MIDDLE AGES

The modern penitential system, centred on the act of private confession, has its roots in practices developed in the Celtic Church from around the sixth century.[48] Initially developed as monastic practice and as a form of spiritual

---

[45] Ibid., 101.

[46] Caesarius of Arles (501) writes that while satisfaction for certain sins can be made alone and secretly, the prayers of others are helpful (Sermo. 261).

[47] This shift can be traced further back, in, for example, changes in the use of the term *exomolgesis* from Tertullian, for whom the term encompassed the whole procedure, to Cyprian, who used it in the more restricted sense to designate the final act of liturgical penance undertaken before reconciliation. Already here there is a shrinking back or isolation of confession to a specific moment in the process.

[48] See Watkins, *A History of Penance*, vol. 2: 603–31.

guidance, confession became the first instance of a private and individual form of penance that spread through the Celtic and Anglo-Saxon churches in the sixth and seventh centuries. Irish missionaries took the new private form of practice to the continent from about the end of the sixth century where it quickly took hold, although it also met with significant resistance on the part of the church hierarchy. The Carolingian reform councils of the ninth century condemned it as contemptuous of ancient law and tried, without success, to ban the penitential books.[49]

In the face of its expansion across the continent, Church officials attempted to reach a compromise, at first offering private penance as an option for sins not subject to canonical discipline, and later suggesting that public sins be subject to public canonical penance and private sins to penance based on the Celtic model.[50] Through these doctrinal debates and the interaction of practices, the private form underwent a number of profound changes before it was crystallized as the sacramental rite sanctioned by the Church at the Council of Trent in the mid-sixteenth century.

Turning now to the actual substance of this new form, right from its early Celtic inception, private penance began with a distinct type of confession. Confession had, of course, been an integral part of the earlier public process; now, however, confession was not a public act before the church community but a private communication with the priest. Following the confession, the priest assigned penance or satisfaction, which was then performed by the penitent. Notably, the community had little or no role in the process; the confessor regulated entry into the process, the performance of penance and provided reconciliation.

In the early stages of this practice, reconciliation was granted only after the performance of penance, but even then, in contrast to the canonical form of public penance, there was no formal ritual of excommunication following confession. The penitent was excluded from receiving communion, but not excluded from the community, and the end of the process entailed lifting legal restrictions, not re-integration and reformation of the community. Indeed, though the term was still used, *reconciliation* now seems inappropriate, or at least it has significantly changed its meaning, because the earlier corporate significance has fallen away. By the year 1000, confession and reconciliation had collapsed into one scene – a change that generated troubling questions about the role of satisfaction (acts of penance) in forgiveness – given that forgiveness was granted before any satisfaction was actually performed.

---

[49] Notably, the councils at Tours (813), Reims (813), Paris (829), and Mainz (847).

[50] Canon 26 of Arles; Canon 31 at Reims.

In the Celtic context, and then in the spread of private penance through the continent, an inventory of the correct penitential satisfaction required for any particular sin was set out in penitential books that proliferated from around the sixth century.[51] The most commonly prescribed penance was fasting joined with fervent prayer, but it might also entail abstinence from marital intercourse, renunciation of weapons, and even, for more serious crimes, exile. Again, as time progressed, the amount of penance assigned and performed decreased and the "shame, humiliation, and self-punishment that were seen as freeing a person from sin's consequences were [being] transferred from the penance to the confession."[52] In this, one can see the two distinct types of roles that the confession played: first, an instrumental, legalistic role, providing information or evidence on the basis of which the priest could properly prescribe penance, and second, a healing or medicinal role in itself, the means of cleansing through admitting sinfulness. In the ancient eastern monastic tradition confession had primarily served as a means of healing and purification – a trope that became increasingly central as penitential work all but dropped out of the process altogether. In the meantime, this evidentiary role came into play for the first time.[53]

Clearly, the passage from the work of sacrifice discussed in the previous chapter to this conception of the work of repentance involved a significant narrowing of meaning. Recall that the repentance that emerged from the early sacrificial system served variously as a form of compensatory justice, substitute for retributive justice, purification, approach to God, and recommitment to the holy principles that gave form to and oriented the community. Here, the work of confession is cut off from the broader communal context and has become very much focused on purifying the individual, where purification means exorcising some stain of sin, as distinct from restoring a connection with God and the holy community. It also works as a type of punitive compensation, where the individual pays for his or her sinfulness with his or her shame. In a completely novel way confession combines an economic model of compensation and a medicinal model of purification; repentance has become a type of compensation for damage to the soul.

This comes into sharp relief if one compares this form of penance with the form of justice that operated in the Celtic context in which it emerged. According to Celtic tribal law, *Wergeld*, taxes, fines, and lesser substitute

---

[51] The earliest was the Penitential of Finnian (sixth century) and the best known the Penitential of Theodore dating from around the middle of the eighth century.

[52] Dallen, *The Reconciling Community*, 117.

[53] See John T. McNeill, "Medicine for Sin as Prescribed in the Penitentials," *Church History* 1 (1932).

penalties had to be made as expiation for crimes. By analogy, the relationship with God came to be seen in similarly economic terms. Penance represented the satisfaction to be paid for the sin, and the metaphoric frame shifted, from medicine for the illness of sin to penalty for a crime. Now operating within this frame, sin and penance had a positive quantifiable value and could be measured against each other in order to ensure economic parity. A shorter, more severe and intensive penance (for example, a complete fast of three days) could substitute for a longer, less severe penance (a partial fast of a year), provided they both entailed the same 'amount' of self-denial. Located within this context, confessing a list of sins became a way of outlining the evidence, which then provided the priest with the information he required to allocate satisfaction. One can miss this shift if one looks only to the outward forms, which were to a large extent similar; both for example regularly entailed fasting, but whereas in the former this was understood as the process through which the penitent *lived* conversion, in the latter it was payment in exchange for sin.

This shift in meaning infiltrated even those more public forms that survived beyond the demise of canonical penance, namely, crusades, flagellation (which was mostly a monastic, but also a lay practice), and *paenitentia Solemnis* (a yearly ritual of the Lenten season, which originated in the mid- to late eighth century and eventually became standard practice for all Christians).[54] Although these practices were still 'public' and retained an outwardly collective dimension, they had now become little more than individual practice in the public domain, rather than practices implicating the public domain per se. The significance of publicity shifted from its being a necessary aspect of a process that was integrally communal to its being a means of intensifying the punishment.

Confession itself also underwent significant transformations during this period. First, the meaning of *confessio* narrowed from profession of faith to inventory of wrongs and expression of regret for the wrongdoing. At the same time, confession increasingly moved to the centre of the whole process. As already noted, at the early stages of the development of this form, it was still seen as a prelude to the penitential work that was the effective cause of forgiveness, and served mainly by way of allowing the priest to set the correct satisfaction. Over the next three to four centuries, however, confession itself

---

[54] Beginning the Wednesday marking the beginning of Lent, penitents entered a series of rigours that remained in place until they were reconciled on Holy (Maundy) Thursday. The practice of giving them ashes, which became central in the tenth century, is the origin of the term Ash Wednesday.

became the effective cause of forgiveness (insofar as the penitent contributes to this),[55] effecting its work through the humiliation it brought: "Shame covered him wholly like the fine glowing ashes falling continually. To say it in words! His soul, stifling and helpless would cease to be."[56] The focus or the goal of the process narrowed in on the guilty individual anxious for salvation, and forgiveness was the resolution to guilt.

One can see evidence of this abstraction from community in the Scholastics' struggle to explain the role of the priest in the process of repentance/forgiveness through private auricular confession. Explaining the role of the priest became a problem *now* because repentance and forgiveness were understood as processes that took place inside the individual, albeit in relationship with God. The fact that this even became a question, let alone such a central one, is indicative of how far the understanding and practice of repentance had come from its origins as reconciliation with the living God: the Church as a community of the faithful. Whereas earlier it would have made no sense at all to abstract the transformation from the ecclesial context, which was a way of being in community, now theologians had to find a necessary link between the priest (the Church) and the transformative process. Now that the inwardness of the soul and the outwardness of the church were distributed across different orders of being, it became necessary to explain their relationship.[57]

In Chapter Three, I discussed the difficulties that emerge when we try to map ancient practices according to our modern understanding of the distinction between external and internal, or individual and communal. What comes through in the Scholastics' debates is that it was precisely during this time in history, the late medieval and dawning modern period, that these categories were undergoing important transformations and being consciously rethought and re-articulated. So, for example, in the Scholastics' attempts to articulate the operation of the sacraments and to formulate the categories within which they could be understood, we can see how practice and intention are drifting apart. The eleventh-century founder of scholasticism, Peter Abelard, emphasized *contritio* (sorrow) as the decisive agent in the process of repentance and attaining forgiveness. On first reading, his claim may seem no different from those

---

[55] I am referring here to the Scholastic debate about the relative contribution to forgiveness of the confessant, the Church, and God. No amount of repentance on the part of the sinner would be sufficient to forgiveness in the absence of Divine grace.

[56] Saint Bonaventure, "Confession: Du concile de Latran au Concil do Trente," cited in *Dictonaire de Théolgie Catholique* (Paris: Letonzey et Ané, 1911). S.v. Confession: du Concile de Latran au Concile de Trente, 3: 920.

[57] Given its complexity I omit any discussion here of the important theological debate about the *claves ecclesiae*, the keys of the church, and the relationship between attrition, contrition, grace, and the Church. See Jose Martos, *Doors to the Sacred* (New York: Doubleday, 1981).

offered by Augustine, or for that matter Maimonides, both of whom placed 'repentance of the heart' at the centre of the process. Now, however, this is a sorrow that can be abstracted from the outward work through which conversion is effected and experienced: an abstraction that only became possible when internality was constituted as a separate category.

Before the early Scholastic period, one never saw the question of sorrow treated as a distinct subject outside the broader question of satisfaction; the notion that sorrow, as such, might be an effective agent would have been nonsensical within this framing.[58] It is during this period that penitential work becomes the evidence of the sorrow, not the external dimension of a movement, where sorrow is the internal dimension. Internal sorrow becomes a functionally independent category and thus detachable from penitential work that would, in time, virtually drop out of the picture altogether. It is this detachment that makes possible the critique of apology as 'mere words' and the accusation of insincerity or partiality, accusations that continue to haunt our assessment of apology as a response to wrongdoing.

Along with this shift came a sharp split in the understanding of forgiveness. At this stage in history, one can clearly see the contours of the distinction between forgiveness as the remission of debts or punishment, on the one hand, and a more abstract forgiveness of the soul, on the other. This is explicit in Abelard's teaching that sincere contrition out of the love of God will automatically annul sin and eliminate the cause of eternal damnation, but that temporal punishment must be expiated by satisfaction – or if not then this takes place in purgatory.[59] Forgiveness now has two distinct meanings: one abstract, the forgiveness one *feels* towards the person, and one concrete, the forgiveness of debts.

The Scholastics tried to explain how the process of repentance resulted in forgiveness by combining the different parts of the repentant process (confession, contrition, satisfaction, absolution) with the different levels of forgiveness (internal/external, temporal/in the after-life). The idea was that if the right match could be made, the combined contributions of the different components would be sufficient to complete forgiveness. Looking back at these attempts, what is most interesting is not the veracity of the permutations that the different Scholastic writers proposed, but rather how the writers are beginning to draw distinctions that continue to inform our understandings of what it is that repentance, as opposed to, say, punishment or material compensation, is supposed to do.

Recall in the discussion of the Hebrew words translated as sin – *avon* and *chet* – I noted that there was an indeterminacy in their meaning, a fluidity of

---

[58] Poschmann, *Penance*, 157.
[59] Peter Abelard, Sermo. 14. See Poschmann, *Penance*, 158 and n. 3.

movement between sin, guilt, and punishment. Here, in the writings of the early Scholastics, the distinction between guilt – *culpa* – and punishment – *poena* – is introduced into theology. Through this lens and within this grammar it becomes possible for the first time to be absolved of guilt through a penitential process, as if guilt is something like a colour of the soul, and still be liable for temporal punishment. Within this split frame the former branch, the 'inner', came to be defined as the proper sphere of religion. Religious practice accordingly intensified its focus on guilt as a condition of the soul, as distinct from a guilt that encompassed both the state of the soul and the person as an actor in the world. As repentance became more and more strongly associated with this branch, and institutionalized in the private form of confession, it became 'natural' to think that this was its essential sphere of application, distinct from the business of changing action or making concrete adjustments, both of which now came to belong to a different sphere: politics and law.

3. THE SACRAMENTAL RITE OF PENANCE TO VATICAN II IN THE ROMAN CATHOLIC CHURCH

From around the year 1000, private auricular confession had become virtually the sole and universal form of penitential practice in the Church. The legal status of this form had been hardened through a number of canonical decrees, most significantly those of the fourth Lateran Council (1215) requiring that all Christians (of age) undertake annual private and secret confession to a priest.[60] As part of this process, the priest was instructed to interrogate the penitent in order to tease out all sins, and the failure to confess entailed refusal of a Christian burial and threatened hell.

The private form of penance was definitively sealed as the sole authoritative form of the sacrament in the Roman Catholic Church at the Council of Trent (1551). The Council was itself set up to establish and declare Church doctrine in the face of reformers and in particular the reformers' putatively heretical anti-ecclesial stance. Because Luther's and Calvin's critique of penance was so closely connected to the heart of their overall critique of Church doctrine and practice, the rite of penance was one of the more important subjects of Trentine pronouncement.[61] It was also a place where the split in the church led to very different practices. I return to the Protestant trajectory later in this chapter.

---

[60] Chapter 21 of the decrees of Lateran IV (DS 812). On this, see M. Gy, "Les bases de la pénitence moderne," *Maison Dieu* 117 (1974): 79.

[61] Neither rejected the process of confession outright. In his earlier and less polemic work Luther recommended it, and Calvin recognized it as a useful institution, though he rejected its divine origin. Both explicitly rejected obligatory confession; Calvin called it mental torture. See Calvin, *Institut. Rel. Christ.* III, Chapter 4.

The key doctrines concerning penance set out at Trent were designed to deal with the reformers' two major critiques of contrition, the first concerning the role of the penitent, the second the ecclesial power and its role in absolution.[62] Specifically, Luther had claimed that by giving contrition (the penitent's personal merit) and the church causal roles, the church was undermining the work of Christ as the effective cause of salvation. In response, Trent firmly asserted the judicial power of the Church in the work of absolution, directly countering the reformers' denial of the priestly power of the keys. Trent explicitly defined absolution as a judicial act.[63] This judicial power, 'the power of the keys', derived its authority from the Gospels, which were seen as vesting power to grant absolution in the church, a power transmitted to priests through ordination.[64] The Trent doctrine also recognized that satisfaction had educative and medicinal roles, but it clearly established its primary identity as retribution and judgement. This is both in keeping with the trend we have been tracking, and establishes this as the metaphoric frame for the next four hundred years of church practice and doctrine.

As well as its doctrinal pronouncements, at its final session in 1563, the Council entrusted the Pope with the task of liturgical reform. This work culminated in the *Rituale Romanum* promulgated on 17 June 1614, which became the basis for the rite of penance throughout the Western church and essentially remained the standard penitential practice in the Catholic Church right up to the time of Vatican II, more than four hundred years later.

To grasp the extent of the journey that repentance had travelled to get to this point, one might call to mind the images of penance in the early church described above, and juxtapose these with the penitential scene in the late medieval period as solidified at Trent. Recall the spectacle of the different orders of penitents, distributed, as in Hermas' vision of the tower, with human souls swimming or drowning around it, at varying distances from the altar, and gradually moving back into communion and community as they underwent the process of conversion. The repentance one envisions there is a fully and necessarily corporate process, taking place literally in the body of the ecclesia.

The rite sanctioned by Trent looks very different.[65] In this scene, there are only two actors, the penitent and the priest. The latter's role is distinctly defined, primarily as judge but also as physician. The single penitent enters

---

[62] These were by no means the only criticisms. Reformers also took issue with more practical matters, such as the abuse of church practices through indulgences. I am concerned here, however, more with doctrinal matters than with their misapplication.

[63] Council of Trent, Session VI, Canons 9 and 10.

[64] Matt. 18:18 and John 20:23.

[65] The details given here track the 25 regulations of the *Rituale Romanum*.

the church, kneels, and makes the sign of the cross. He sits in a confessional in an open place in the church, separated from the priest by a screen.[66] The verbal exchange that constitutes the process then takes place. The priest inquires about the penitent's status, his last confession, and whether he has examined his conscience. The penitent then gives a general confession (the *confiteor*), followed by a more specific enumeration of his own sins. At this point, the priest may ask the penitent to be more explicit about the number, type, and circumstances of the sins. The priest then offers some verbal counsel and support for contrition and amendment, and imposes penance (satisfaction) to assist the penitent in renewal, remedy his weakness, and punish his sins. In theory, satisfaction could include almsgiving and fasting as well as prayer. But in practice, the fact that the penitent would most likely not get around to performing the penitential acts the priest prescribed led priests to demand only what could be performed before the penitent left the church: that is, prayer alone.

Finally, and in the same scene, the priest gives a brief and formulaic absolution, followed by a (non-obligatory) prayer for the penitent. Repentance has become a single scene, a private scene, a primarily verbal exchange between two parties, the penitent and his judge/confessor. Its focus is now exclusively on the inner conversion and reflection of the penitent, and the assessment, attribution of punishment, and judicial forgiveness by the priest. The community is nowhere to be seen, let alone included in the process. There is some remnant role of another person in the prayers of the priest, but now this is a matter of another, 'professional' person praying for, as distinct from praying with, or even in communion with, the sinner. Inwardness, individuation, and legalism have taken the place of communal integration and the re-establishment of the holiness of the Church. Indeed, there is no remnant of the collective form of repentance. Trent did not simply authorize one form of the rite; its dogmatic claim was that the authorized form captured the eternal essence of the process of repentance. All other forms were now defined as deviations.

To fully understand the significance of this relegation of repentance to the realm of the individual's relationship with a transcendent God, one has to widen the lens to take into account the shift that the Church itself was undergoing in the socio-political landscape. In the pre-modern context, the church had been the single site of normative regulation and indeed there had been no distinction between the public, social, and political and the transcendent. With the emergence of the modern state, however, this undifferentiated authority was split. On the one hand, the state took over the role of organizing the public sphere and

---

[66] In late medieval practice the penitent had kneeled in front of the priest (women kneeled to the side). The screen was introduced in the fifteenth century and prescribed in the 1614 *Rituale*.

regulating the norms that would orient public life. On the other, the focus of the Church's attention was increasingly the state of the individual soul, the quality of spiritual sinfulness as opposed to the externalities of action, punishment, and relations between persons, the space now regulated by secular institutions. The crucial point is that this historical shift did not simply entail a redistribution of different spheres of authority to different institutions. It reframed the way we thought about those spheres, drawing new distinctions and thus creating new ways of thinking about the different parts of our lives and selves.

One might think of these levels of change, the conceptual and institutional, as two dimensions of a more comprehensive shift in the social imaginary. The institutional differentiation of the spheres that marked the development of the modern state was both made possible by, and brought about, a restructuring of concepts and indeed the very concepts that defined religion or theology. One might start either with the institutional or the conceptual differentiation, but the two dimensions are in fact mutually constitutive. At the institutional level, one sees the separation of church and state and a reallocation of the work that had previously come under a single head, the inward individual soul to the church, and the outward, public, collective life to the state. At a conceptual level, the state of the soul becomes distinct from the concrete ordering of relations between persons. Thus, in this specific domain of church practice, the privatization of the penitential process was both made possible by a shifting understanding of the site of sin and conditioned the individuation and the inwardness of subjectivity.

Certainly, the secular state developed its own public rituals to orient the community around its constitutive norms and consolidate its authority. Not only formal laws, but also flags, national anthems, public ceremonies, national myths and stories of origin or great acts, war memorials, and the public display and rhetoric of the symbolic head of state continually converted individuals into members of a nation. In this sense, one can see the formal relationship between apology as a means for organizing the collective and those forms adopted by the modern state, but collective apology and public repentance were decidedly not amongst such political forms of secular symbolic constitution. That the proper sphere of influence of the apology is some inner or spiritual quality of the individual person appears perfectly natural to us because the grammar of apology had narrowed to its transcendental individual dimension. Yet this naturalness was historically constituted.

It is this assumed naturalness that lies (in part) behind Trouillot's argument that the political apology mistakes the state for the modern liberal individual writ large. It is what makes it so difficult to think about a collective apologizing without projecting a particular type of subjectivity onto that collective. It is also what creates a difficulty for making sense of the relationship between apology and the modern state's more habitual mechanisms for dealing with wrongdoing: punishment and compensation. When apology re-emerged on the public stage as a response to grave violations committed in the sphere regulated by the state, we no longer had the grammar of the public apology, so were not sure what to make of it. If it is concerned with the inner soul, what place does it have dealing with serious violations? If it is supposed to deal with the temporal consequences of those violations, is it not a poor substitute for punishment or material compensation?

4. COMMUNAL REPENTANCE IN THE PROTESTANT CHURCHES

At this point, I briefly interrupt the narrative of the trajectory of the Roman Catholic Church to look at forms of repentance in the Protestant churches that did not follow the Catholic prescriptions; these churches developed their own understandings and practices of repentance. This discussion is in no way intended to comprehensively treat the vast array of practices in the plethora of churches that have emerged since the Reformation but rather to point to the apparent anomaly that while virtually all post-Reformation Protestant forms of Christianity identify the individual conscience as the valid interpreter of Scripture and thus the individual as the site of sin or repentance, the collective and public ritual forms of repentance have remained a mainstay of worship.

As noted earlier, one of the reformers' main criticisms was that the Church's ministry had been corrupted, so that its mediation was no longer a clear path between humans and God.[67] The commonplace characterization of the subsequent split is that Protestant churches eliminated or minimized mediation, replacing it with a direct relationship between each Christian and God.[68] What this portrait leaves out is the other side of the response – which was to make that ministry public and general. This alternative is manifest in the forms of confession and repentance Protestant churches adopted. In both the Anglican and the Lutheran churches, for example, one still finds strong and robust forms of communal repentance.[69]

---

[67] Luther's 1520 sermon, "The Babylonian Captivity of the Church", represents a powerful criticism of the medieval sacramental system.

[68] The degree to which the church's mediation was eliminated differs significantly in different churches, from the High Churches to the congregationist churches.

[69] In fact, Luther did practice and preach the importance of private confession, and included a liturgical form in his Short Catechism, albeit opposing the Roman Catholic form. See P.H.D. Lang, "Private Confession and Absolution in the Lutheran Church: A Doctrinal, Historical, and Critical Study," *Concordia Theological Quarterly* 56, no. 4 (October 1992).

The introduction to the morning and evening services in the *Book of Common Prayer*, for example, begins with a penitential service where the whole congregation expresses a general confession:

Almighty and most merciful Father we have erred, and strayed from thy ways like lost sheep. We have followed too much the devices and desires of our own hearts. We have offended against thy holy laws. We have left undone those things which we ought to have done; and we have done those things which we ought not to have done.[70]

In response, while the congregation remains kneeling, the priest pronounces absolution or remission of sins:

Almighty God, the Father of our Lord Jesus Christ, who desireth not the death of a sinner, but rather that he may turn from his wickedness and live; and hath given power, and commandment, to his ministers the absolution and remission of their sins: he pardoneth and absolveth all them that truly repent and unfeignedly believe his holy gospel. Wherefore let us beseech him to grant us true repentance, and his Holy Spirit.[71]

In fact, in the 1928 edition of the *Book of Common Prayer*, based on the liturgies of 1549 and 1662, and used by the Episcopal Church in the United States until the latter half of the twentieth century, the Holy Communion included a collective representative form of repentance spoken by the priest:

Almighty God, Father of our Lord Jesus Christ, Maker of all things, judge of all men: we acknowledge and bewail our manifold sins and wickedness, Which we, from time to time, most grievously have committed, By thought, word and deed against thy Divine Majesty. . . . We do earnestly repent, And are heartily sorry for these misdoings. The burden of them is intolerable. Have mercy upon us, Have mercy upon us most merciful Father; For thy Son our Lord Jesus Christ's sake, Forgive us all that is past; And grant that we may hereafter Serve and please thee in Newness of life, To the honour and glory of thy Name; through Jesus Christ our Lord. Amen.[72]

Collective forms of repentance are in fact found throughout the liturgy, for example in the Exhortations, calling all who come to communion to fully repent, and the Litany. In the Litany, the refrains, "Have Mercy upon us",

---

[70] Morning and Evening Services, *Book of Common Prayer*.

[71] An alternate response is: "Grant, we beseech thee, merciful Lord, to thy faithful people pardon and peace, that they may be cleansed from all their sins, and serve thee with a quiet mind; through Jesus Christ our Lord."

[72] *The Book of Common Prayer* (With the Additions and Deviations Proposed in 1928) (London: Cambridge University Press, 1928), 314.

"Good Lord deliver us", and "We beseech thee to hear us, good Lord" form repetitive tropes, woven through like a drumbeat driving the prayer.[73]

In this liturgy one also sees, in a manner reminiscent of the Jewish prayers of repentance, a close interlacing of confession of sin and profession of faith in God. This fusion evokes the original understanding of confession as profession and is indicative of the theological understanding that turning to God (Christ) is itself the path of redemption. Here again, the liturgy uses the first person plural: it is 'we', the community, who acknowledges God as the condition of possibility of its existence.

Within the churches themselves, there is a range of interpretations of the theological significance of this use of the first person plural. In her commentary on the theology of her father, Reinhold Niebuhr, Elisabeth Sifton remarks on the use of the first person plural through much of the liturgy. She notes both that there is "an entire school of thought that says that's the only kind of prayer that makes any sense" and that even as he himself wrote prayers in this plural mode, her father thought of prayer as essentially individual, even when people prayed together.[74]

While it is certainly relevant whether those partaking in the service interpret the use of the first person as a mere remnant, and not actually indicative of the corporate quality of repentance, or whether they understand themselves as actually speaking as a collective, the force of the form is not equivalent to this conscious self-understanding. The rich prose and the affecting rhythms, the persistence and heavy repetition of the trope provide templates of collective repentance, part of the assumed grammar. It may even be the case that they would not stand up to a rational analysis in search of a properly constituted subject; but they are nonetheless affective for this.

5. TWENTIETH-CENTURY ROMAN CATHOLIC REFORM

Moving back to the Roman Catholic trajectory, the four centuries between Trent and Vatican II saw only minor theological and doctrinal shifts concerning penance and the occasional, albeit unsuccessful attempt to re-infuse penance with a more corporate understanding.[75] The Trentine template with its essential judicial orientation, its focus on lifting the transcendent punitive

---

[73] Ibid.

[74] Elisabeth Sifton, *The Serenity Prayer* (New York and London: W. W. Norton and Company, 2003), 184–5.

[75] See Leonard Swindler, *Aufklärung Catholicism, 1780–1850: Liturgical and Other Reforms in the Catholic Aufklärung*, AAR Studies in Religion No. 17 (Missoula, Mont. Scholars Press, 1978).

consequences of sin for the individual, and its assumption that the internal soul was the medium within which sin and repentance took place essentially persisted unchallenged throughout those four centuries, and this was what we inherited at the end of the twentieth century.

One might then wonder how, after four hundred years of stasis, reform came so radically in the second half of the twentieth century. The answer lies beyond the specifics of penitence itself, belonging in part to a general recognition of, and dissatisfaction with, the distance between what had become archaic rites and the experience of contemporary Catholics and the sense that not only the people but also the rites had to shift to close that gap. This sense of distance was captured by the popular slogan "The signs should signify."[76] But it was not only this dissatisfaction with the church's archaism that brought about a push to reform the rites of penance. Reformers in the church recognized that there were a number of specific ways in which this rite – in its privacy, its abstractness, and its emphasis on the individual – was 'out of sync' with important social, political, and theological trends of the era. Several factors working in combination help to explain the shift in awareness and consequently in practice.

First, the more open political and intellectual environment in the Church in the twentieth century supported more thoroughgoing research into the history of repentance and rendered permissible its influence on theological and doctrinal debate.[77] Church historians had been rediscovering the penitential practices of the early church and, for the first time, documenting them in a scientific manner. Initially, and into the mid-twentieth century, the ideas suggested by this historical work were considered modernist (a term of invective) and threatening to the Church's claims to absolute and eternal truth, and so staunchly resisted by the Church hierarchy. However, as the Church started to open to the influence of other intellectual disciplines, resistance softened and debate became possible. Catholic historians and theologians began to call into question Trent's absolute doctrinal claims and started to acknowledge the more variegated history of repentant rites. As the discursive space within the church broadened, the notion that it had a history and that this history contained a more social conception of sin and repentance was able to take hold.

More broadly, the ascent of structural analysis in the intellectual environment and its infusion into at least some parts of the Church provided a foothold

---

[76] Cf. Hellwig, *Sign of Conversion*, 105; Martos, *Doors to the Sacred*, 147.

[77] Karl Rahner, "Forgotten Truths Concerning the Sacrament of Penance," *Man in the Church*, vol. 2: *Theological Investigations* (Baltimore: Beacon Press, 1963); Edward Schillebeeckx, ed., *Sacramental Reconciliation* (New York: Herder Press, 1971); and Michael G. Lawler, *Symbol and Sacrament: A Contemporary Sacramental Theology* (New York: Paulist Press, 1987).

within the Church for a social conception of repentance. Those members who had already been insisting that injustice and sin were social and not merely personal welcomed these 'forgotten truths' about church practice and embraced them as support for their argument that social injustice or social sin should themselves be concerns of the Church, and not simply relegated to extra-religious political activity. Christian Duquoc, a twentieth-century Catholic theologian, points to the two-way link between political views or interpretive frames and support for, or dissatisfaction with, existing rites. The institutional forms were at once symptoms of what had been a highly individualistic conception of responsibility, and the practices that transmitted this conceptual frame.

[T]he form of the administration of the sacrament is not harmless; it favours one aspect of reconciliation. The private form favours reconciliation with oneself in the interior of one's own conscience, sole seat of authentic relationship with God. Other human realities, and notably economic and political relationships, escape all interference from Christianity.[78]

This critique of the private form of penance then had a highly political thrust. Those who framed their societal analysis in collective terms argued that the private form "robs sacramental penance of its social character", whereas in fact part of the work of the sacramental symbol was to give concrete expression to the social function of forgiveness.[79]

On instruction from Vatican II, a liturgical commission was established to investigate the history of the rite of penance and develop options for reform, leading in 1973 to the official promulgation of the New Rite of Reconciliation, which set out three new forms of the rite.[80] The change of name from penance to reconciliation announced and marked the change in focus and import, from a narrower concern with an individual's sins to a broader ecclesial process.[81]

The first form (Form A) was consistent with the fully private rite sanctioned at Trent, while Forms B and C both incorporated some of the corporate/communal and public dimensions of the earlier Christian practices. Form B is a hybrid rite, moving from the communal to the individual and then back to

[78] Christian Duquoc, "Real Reconciliation and Sacramental Reconciliation," in *Sacramental Reconciliation*, 36.

[79] Ibid., 30–5.

[80] For a background on the preparation of this new rite and the work of the liturgical commission established to investigate the rite, see Martos, *Doors to the Sacred*. The new rites themselves were not implemented until 1975.

[81] Cf. Kenan B. Osborne, *Reconciliation and Justification: The Sacrament and Its Theology* (New York: Paulist Press, 1970), 205.

the communal. It starts with open, communal greeting and prayer, silent examination of conscience, and communal recitation of a general confession and prayer. Each member then moves separately to individual confession and absolution. They then re-form as a community for the final communal declaration of God's mercy, giving thanks, blessing, and dismissal.[82] Form C is fully communal. Whereas in Form B the community separates out for individual confession and absolution, in this final form they remain together as a community, where both confession and absolution occur.[83]

There is a debate within the Church about whether the new forms reflect a genuine shift in the understanding of repentance or are simply a pragmatic if grudging concession to the unfortunate realities of Catholic communities that impede the effective reach of confession in its essential and correct form.[84] Those who maintain that penance remains a rite concerned with the individual soul argue that even though communal forms are now included, they are carefully circumscribed by strict canonical restrictions, and the rite makes clear that they are to be used only in exceptional circumstances.[85] Arguing the very opposite case, others insist that these restrictions are but a sign of the doctrinal lag and that in fact the communal forms are the model rites – closer to the essence of repentance, now understood as a fuller ecclesial reconciliation.[86] They too can draw support from the text setting out the rite, which elsewhere recognizes and affirms the way in which the communal form unites the community, knitting it together through the common process of coming to awareness of sinfulness.[87] Moreover,

---

[82] Cf. Canadian Catholic Conference, *Rite of Penance* (Ottawa: Publications Service, 1975), secs. 22–30.

[83] Ibid., secs. 31–35.

[84] In particular, it is argued that communal confession provides a pragmatic response to the practical difficulties involved in ensuring that individuals actually get to confession given its negative associations and the high ratio between congregants and confessors in some communities.

[85] The first paragraph of the collective form states: "Individual, integral confession and absolution remain the only ordinary way for the faithful to reconcile themselves with God and the Church, unless physical or moral impossibility excuses this kind of confession." *Rite of Penance*, sec. 31. Further, the restrictions include the requirement that individuals confess grave sins in private within a year of taking part in this communal form.

[86] See Dallen, *The Reconciling Community,* and Hellwig, *Sign of Conversion*; Ralph Keifer and Frederick R. McManus, eds., *The Rite of Penance: Commentaries: Understanding the Document*, vol. 1 (Washington, D.C.: Liturgical Conference, 1975), and James Crichton, *The Ministry of Reconciliation* (London: Geoffrey Chapman, 1974).

[87] Para. 5 of the *Rites of Penance*, for example, reads: "By the hidden and loving mystery of God's design, men are joined together in the bonds of supernatural solidarity, so much so that the sin of one harms others just as the holiness of one benefits others. Penance also entails reconciliation with our brothers and sisters who are always harmed by our sins." See also para 22.

Vatican II itself explicitly expressed a preference for communal over individual celebration of the sacraments.[88]

The communal forms allow for expression of the social nature of sin and repentance, reinstitutionalizing and thereby reinforcing a thread of theology and religious praxis that dropped away after Trent. Lucy Thorson, a theologian who has tracked the reemergence of this communal form, argues that far from being a deviation or pragmatic accommodation, it recaptures an essential dimension of repentance that had long been lost:

Like the practice of public penance in the early Church, Form C of the rite can be understood to be powerfully sacramental in effecting what it signifies, and indeed in effecting it in a way that is accessible to common experience. The sign and the symbols, such as communal confession of sins and communal absolution, are effective in signifying that the community is in solidarity in their recognition of sins and sinfulness and in their recognition of the need for common forgiveness and healing.[89]

Translating this language into more secular terms, the communal form performs and effects the idea that the community in question shares and affirms together a common set of values and allegiances. In their acting together, they are enacting a set of precepts that bind them, and to which they rebind themselves in the act of corporate repentance. This corporate dimension remains even though the sins that are the subject of confession are sins committed by the individual.

The documents themselves will not resolve the disagreement about which rite embodies the true nature of repentance, because they are themselves the result of compromise between different interpretive communities within the church. Thus, the ambivalence of the text is most accurately read as symptomatic of church dynamics. The tensions in the final documents evidence the continuing unresolved disagreements between those who support the doctrinal strictures of the Trentine rites and those who wish to re-enliven the communal dimension of repentance. More important, they evidence the tension between these different tropes of repentance, a tension that had been concealed until Vatican II. Now that there is a doctrinal debate, the two readings of the

---

[88] See Article 26 of the *Constitution on the Sacred Liturgy*: "whenever the particular character of the rites suggests a community celebration, with a congregation present and actively taking part, it should be stressed that this sort of celebration is to be preferred, as far as possible, to a celebration of them by one person alone, as it were, in private." Printed in Walter Abbott, ed., *The Documents of Vatican II* (New York: American Press, 1966), 161.

[89] Lucy Thorson, "A Call to Communal Repentance, Jewish and Christian Liturgical Experiences: A Dialogical Approach," M.A. thesis, University of St. Michael's College, Toronto, Ontario, 1993.

'essence' of repentance do not simply exist as part of an abstract or esoteric debate, but are carried by different personalities in the church, with each party pushing for its interpretation, and the final documents reflecting the compromise position they have been able to reach at a particular point in time.

At this point, one might assess the shifts by observing that while the understanding of repentance as a public collective practice and concept that directly implicates the entire community has gained significant ground, it still falls far short of universal acceptance in the Church. Nevertheless, the significance and impact of the forms should not be reduced to their intellectual interpretation. In fact, to insist that their only effect is the one that passes the muster of rational scrutiny is to miss the unique dimension of ritual practice. As practical templates, they work on us, and often beyond what we might think we are doing.

6. COMMUNAL REPENTANCE IN THE CHURCH AND POLITICAL APOLOGY

What is the relationship between the emergence of the political apology and this re-emergence of the communal dimension of repentance in the church? Certainly, I have no evidence to suggest a direct causal connection, but their temporal simultaneity is certainly remarkable. At the most general level, their coincidence evidences a general shift in the last quarter of the twentieth century towards recognizing that repentance also works as a communal practice, and away from the insistence that its sole legitimate concern is the inner soul of the individual. Going a step further, one might suggest that the re-emergence of the collective form as a living and sanctioned praxis in the Catholic Church drew attention to this model and gave people an experience of this type of repentance. True, they experienced this as Catholics, but insofar as they were also citizens, the model also became a live possibility with no fixed address. In the Protestant churches this experiential base had long been available as ritual form, albeit without the same degree of conscious reconstruction or explicit connection with collective responsibility. In both cases, the presence in the religious context furnished the opportunity for this performative mode to be experienced, and thus to become part of the repertoire available to those looking for ways to deal with the wrongs of the past in other spheres of their lives.

These models also became more salient at a point in history when political actors were looking for effective ways of dealing with systematic violations in the course of reconstituting their political communities. As the limitations of prosecutorial strategies and other traditional liberal strategies that had been the mainstay of political strategy for wrongdoing became more evident, and the need to deal with violations more pressing, the search for alternatives intensified. If the collective form of repentance in the church became a live ball thrown up in the air in the early 1970s, political players had their gloves out, ready for the catch.

Nevertheless, one should not underestimate the barriers to translating the practice from one sphere to the other. The grammar of apology we have inherited remains deeply inscribed with the form of the individual and strongly marked as belonging to the distinct sphere of religion, cordoned off from public politics. Even though apology had once been part of public regulation of norms (politics), and could still be understood as playing this regulatory role, the sharp differentiation between the sphere of modern secular politics and that of religion entailed an implicit ban from politics on the modes now associated with religion. In this context, re-appropriation of repentance as a tool in the *political* repertoire was highly problematic. The split between the transcendent and the mundane and the inner and the outer that had characterized the constitution of both religion and the state meant that it was not simply a matter of re-admitting apology into the sphere of politics. Against the background of formal legal and material institutions, apology stood out as an anomaly.

5

Australia's Divided History

Inattention on such a scale cannot possibly be explained by absent mindedness. It is a structural matter, a view from a window which has been carefully placed to exclude a whole quadrant of the landscape. What may well have begun as a simple forgetting of other possible views turned under habit and over time into something like a cult of forgetfulness practiced on a national scale.

William Stanner[1]

When the apology burst onto the stage of Australian politics, during the closing decade of the twentieth century, the nation found itself poised between two national debates, one over the treatment and status of Australia's Indigenous peoples, the other over a new constitution for a nation entering the new millennium. Both of these processes involved and invited profound reconsideration of the political and social map of the Australian nation, although they apparently moved in opposite temporal directions. The constitutional debates sought to clarify the fundamental values of the Australian nation and articulate them in a legally binding constitutional document for the future, while the debates around Indigenous issues principally sought to deal with Australia's troubled past. Nevertheless, the two are best understood as inter-dependent processes. If Australia needed a new constitution, it was largely because the existing one represented neither the demographic and geopolitical character of the contemporary nation nor the aspirational values and political principles that would carry it into the new century. Yet this movement forward was stymied by a past of systematic violations against Australia's first peoples, a past that had not been adequately resolved politically, legally, socially, or

[1] William Stanner, *After the Dreaming: Black and White Australians: The Boyer Lectures* (Sydney: ABC Press, 1969), 67.

culturally. For Australians to articulate who they wanted to be and to declare their normative political personality, they needed to deal with a past that had fallen well short of this ideal nation.

In this chapter and the one that follows, I suggest that it is precisely because the normative status of the Australian nation was such a pressing concern during this period that so much energy was drawn into the apology question. If the Australia of 2001 (the centenary of federation) was to declare itself a nation constituted according to principles of equality, diversity, and respect for human rights, it had to find a way of positively distinguishing itself from the Australia of the twentieth century, which had now incontrovertibly shown itself to be one characterized by systematic inequality, intolerance, and human rights violations against its own Indigenous peoples.

A standard political theoretic or institutional analysis would suggest that what was required to draw this distinction was legal reform, appropriate compensation, and economic redistribution, specifically through the legal and institutional recognition of Indigenous land rights and the full promulgation of anti-discrimination laws and programs. No doubt, interventions at this institutional level were necessary, not only to effect justice, but also to promote a different set of norms about citizenship and identity; but they were not sufficient. The Australian people *themselves*, the 'subject' dimension of the nation, also had to undergo a process of 'reconstitution', from the inside as it were. They too had to recognize themselves and others – most notably, Indigenous others – as full subjects of citizenship rights and national membership and to recognize the way in which equality and identity had been systematically linked in the nation's past, and linked in a way that belied the nation's self-image. Justice, as Teitel observed in her genealogy of transitional justice, had to move "beyond legal notions of guilt and responsibility, towards a political theology, building on a discourse that incorporated moral imperatives."[2]

This need for a 'social reconstitution' was recognized and embodied in the large-scale reconciliation project that the federal government sponsored beginning in 1991, to be completed in 2001 for the Centenary of Federation.[3] Largely through public education and civic participation, the reconciliation process was intended to take the strands of a racially divided Australia and weave them together in a manner reminiscent of Bishop Tutu's image of the Rainbow Coalition of South Africa. This desire to move forward as a differently constituted

---

[2] Ruti G. Teitel, "Human Rights in Transition," 83.

[3] For details on the constitution and functions of the Council for Aboriginal reconciliation, see *Council for Aboriginal Reconciliation Act* 1991, available at http://www.austlii.edu.au/au/other/IndigLRes/car/1994/7/56.html.

nation also required an honest eye to the ugly past and, more than that, a willingness to take responsibility for that past and to own it as part of the nation's history. To quote Michael Walzer, Australia needed to "find some ritual processes through which the ideology it embodies ... can be publicly repudiated."[4] It was this scene that set the stage when the forced removal of Aboriginal children hit the headlines in 1997 and the question of an apology became the focus of national debate in the closing years of the century. This chapter steps back from that debate, which I consider in detail in Chapter Six, to examine the racial constitution of the Australian nation in which apology took such a powerful hold.

I. AUSTRALIAN NEO-COLONIALISM: THE INVISIBILITY AND EMERGENCE OF BLACK AUSTRALIA

By the end of the twentieth century, the human rights situation of Aboriginal and Torres Strait Islander people had long been a blight on the record of a country otherwise known for, and confident about, its relative wealth, stability, and respect for human rights. Constituting just 1.6 percent of the population, their presence on the Australian socio-political landscape was accentuated by their consistently inferior status according to all measures of socio-economic well-being. Of all Australians, Aboriginal people were the sickest but the least well served by the healthcare system. They were the most frequently homeless or poorly housed and the poorest. They had the worst access to institutional education, but overpopulated Australia's prisons by a factor of up to twenty-six.[5] At the beginning of life, they were twice as likely to be low-birth-weight babies and more than twice as likely to die before their first birthday than non-Indigenous babies.[6] During their lives, they suffered chronic and infectious diseases at rates far higher than non-Indigenous people and still suffered diseases long eradicated or rare amongst non-Indigenous Australians.[7] At the end

[4] Michael Walzer, ed., and Marian Rothstein, trans., *Regicide and Revolution: Speeches at the Trial of Louis XVI* (New York: Cambridge University Press, 1974), 88.
[5] A survey of statistical studies across a range of socio-economic indicators including health (mortality and morbidity), housing, education, imprisonment, and deaths in custody, education, income, and employment is available at http://www.hreoc.gov.au/social_justice/statistics/index.html#6.1.
[6] Australian Bureau of Statistics (ABS) and Australian Institute of Health and Welfare (AIHW), *The Health and Welfare of Australia's Aboriginal and Torres Strait Islander Peoples 2005* ABS Catalogue No. 4704.0 (Commonwealth of Australia: Canberra, 2005), 80.
[7] Australian Institute of Health and Welfare, *Australia's Health 2004*, AIHW Catalogue No. AUS 44; ABS Catalogue No. 8903.0 (Commonwealth of Australia: Canberra, 2004), 197, Tables 4.6, 7.34, and 7.37.

of life they could expect to die eighteen years younger than non-Indigenous Australians.[8]

When people sought to make sense of this astonishing pattern of disparity, a range of contemporary inequalities and institutional failures appeared as evident causes, but they were certainly not sufficient to explain the persistence and depth of the problems. To explain this, one had to look further back to the legacy of a long past of discrimination, denigration, and exclusion.

Up until the 1940s and 1950s, all Australian states and territories still enforced laws that were overtly discriminatory.[9] Aboriginal people were not allowed to vote, to drink, or to travel, or to marry without permission, and while they provided much of the menial labour in rural and remote Australia, the state generally held their (already unequal) wages 'in trust', giving them a trickle of pocket money, and holding onto money that few ever saw.[10] Absent any constitutional protection, domestic avenues for Indigenous Australians to contest the myriad insults to their status and violations of their humanity were virtually non-existent, and Indigenous peoples in neo-colonial contexts had yet to make effective connections with the incipient international anti-racism and decolonization movements.[11] Besides, most white Australians were either unaware of their plight or indifferent to it.

There was something of a formal shift starting in the 1950s and early 1960s as some of the most explicitly discriminatory laws were repealed. Nevertheless, still into the mid-1960s some states upheld voting restrictions, and Aboriginal people did not occupy an equal place within the Australian Constitution. It was this constitutional disparity that brought the broader issue of Aboriginal disadvantage onto the national stage for the first time when, in 1967, a referendum was held to amend the discriminatory provisions of the constitution.[12] Although, in fact, the proposed amendments were of a relatively technical nature (to give the Commonwealth power to make laws regarding Aboriginal

---

[8] ABS, *Deaths 2004*, ABS Catalogue No. 3320.0 (Commonwealth of Australia: Canberra, 2005).

[9] Note that Australia does not have a Bill of Rights, and the constitution does not proscribe racial or other forms of discrimination. For a history of legal discrimination, see Andrew Markus, *Australian Race Relations 1788–1983* (Sydney: Allen and Unwin, 1994).

[10] See Rosalyn Kidd, *Trustees on Trial: Recovering the Stolen Wages* (Canberra, ACT: Aboriginal Studies Press, 2006).

[11] There had in fact been early attempts to bring international attention to the situation of Indigenous Australians, in particular through Jesse Street and Faith Bandler's work with the Anti-Slavery Society. See Marilyn Lake, "Citizenship as Non-Discrimination: Acceptance or Assimilationism? Political Logic and Emotional Investment in Campaigns for Aboriginal Rights in Australia, 1940 to 1970," *Gender and History* 13, No. 3 (2001).

[12] Bain Attwood and Andrew Markus, *The 1967 Referendum or When Aborigines Did Not Get the Vote* (Canberra: Australian Institute of Aboriginal and Torres Strait Islander Studies [AIATSIS], 1995).

people, and to have them counted in the national census), the referendum was presented and understood as a national vote between discrimination and exclusion/ segregation, on the one hand, and bringing Aboriginal people into mainstream Australia, on the other.[13]

In the lead-up to the referendum campaign, dramatic images of Aboriginal camps, infested with mangy dogs and populated by dirty and deprived-looking children were broadcast across the media, successfully provoking shock amongst 'ordinary' (non-Indigenous) Australians. The campaign was highly successful, at least in its narrowly understood objective of influencing the vote: the referendum passed with an unprecedented 90 percent majority. Aboriginal people, who not so long ago had actually been classified as flora and fauna, were now to be counted alongside other Australian citizens, marking a symbolic shift towards civil equality. Yet this burst of interest was not sufficient to sustain the effort required to address substantive inequality. Soon the concerns of Aboriginal people all but disappeared from the mainstream media and the public agenda, much to the distress of Aboriginal people who had been assured that 1967 marked a genuine turning point in national policy.[14] When, in 1975, the progressive federal government passed race discrimination legislation, bringing Australia into conformity with its obligations under the United Nations' Convention on the Elimination of All Forms of Racial Discrimination, the general assumption (not shared by Indigenous people, of course) was that now that civil/political and legal parity had been achieved, functional equality in other areas of life would follow.

Parallel with these legal and constitutional developments, and also starting in the 1960s, recognition of traditional land rights emerged as another site of struggle. The ostensible problem was that most Aboriginal people had been moved off their traditional lands and forcibly relocated to missions or reserves where they had no choice but to sell their labour, usually at a pittance, to retain a livelihood. The underlying issue was, however, more deeply rooted in the political constitution of the nation. Aboriginal people had not merely been removed *qua* individuals. Rather, the legal status quo, known as the doctrine of *terra nullius*, denied Indigenous peoples any right to a legitimate claim to property on the basis of prior or traditional title. According to this legal fiction,

---

[13] See Australian Federal Parliament, *Constitution Alteration (Aboriginals) 1967: Argument in Favour of the Proposed Law, the Case for Yes* (Commonwealth of Australia: Commonwealth Government Printer, May 1967).

[14] The gap between the rhetoric of the referendum and the institutional changes that did not follow was provocation for intense activism, most dramatically manifest in the 'tent embassy' established on the lawns of Parliament House in 1972 by Aboriginal Australians, symbolically claiming their rights as a sovereign people to be dealt with as would any other country.

when the British colonized Australia in the late eighteenth century the land was unoccupied (at least as far as property title was concerned), and as such, on attaining sovereignty, the Crown simultaneously acquired legal title to all land. According to the new colonial law, all the land belonged either to the Crown or to those to whom it had sold or allocated title according to its own internally valid procedures.[15]

Although the land rights movement ran parallel with the efforts to eliminate discrimination and obtain substantive equality, it represented a struggle for a different type of recognition. The aim of the equality movement was recognition as co-citizens, or colour-blind treatment, the right to be treated in the same way as everyone else under Australian law. Successful resolution of the land rights struggle, by contrast, required recognition of the distinct and separate rights of Indigenous peoples, rights deriving from their status as prior land owners and, even more radically, as prior sovereigns. Underpinning the land rights movement was a far more comprehensive political position that held that the post-colonial Australian state was legally and morally required to recognize Aboriginal communities as themselves sovereign, and as such a source or arbiter of legal rights and political authority. Tracking the post–World War II decolonization process, from the mid-1960s Aboriginal people agitated more vigorously for political recognition of their independent political status as Indigenous nations (self-determination), the legal recognition of their land rights, and substantive return of their traditional lands.[16]

Aboriginal communities had of course long been keenly aware of the impact of the legal and functional obliteration of their political and land rights, and political campaigns had already been launched, without success, in the nineteenth and early twentieth centuries.[17] It was, however, only with the election of a progressive government in 1972 that they obtained a partner in mainstream politics, and their claims could move from the periphery to the mainstream political agenda. The government officially shifted from a policy of assimilation to one of 'self-determination', which, though far from adequate in its execution, did mark a nod of acknowledgement to the political claims of Aboriginal peoples. More substantively, it passed powerful land rights legislation for the Northern Territory and made a further commitment to national

---

[15] A challenge to this doctrine was mounted, but rejected, by the federal court in *Milirrpum v. Nabalco Pty. Ltd.* (1971) 17 FLR 141.

[16] See Frank Hardy, "This Bin Gurindji Country," in *The Aborigine Today*, ed. Barbara Leach (Sydney: Paul Hamlyn, 1971).

[17] David Lowe, *Forgotten Rebels: Black Australians Who Fought Back* (St. Kilda: St. Kilda Permanent Press, 1994); Henry Reynolds, *Dispossession: Black Australians and White Invaders* (St. Leonards: Allen & Unwin, 1989).

land rights legislation. Absent broad political support, however, and in the face of strong objections from the powerful mining and farming lobbies, further progress on this front was truncated after the initial promise. Then, with the ousting of this government just three years after it had won office and the return to a conservative government, the 'Aboriginal issue' was once again sidelined from mainstream politics.

Aboriginal issues came back onto the national agenda in the 1980s, principally because of two major developments, the publication of the *Royal Commission into Aboriginal Deaths in Custody* and the High Court's recognition of common-law Indigenous land rights.[18] More than simply reviving the issue, both drew attention to the intrinsic connection between the failure to recognize Aboriginal people as co-equal citizens, and the failure to recognize their distinct rights and political status. In 1987, and in response to increasing agitation about the disproportionate number of Aboriginal people dying in custody, the federal government established the Royal Commission into Aboriginal Deaths in Custody. Although the Commission was specifically established to investigate the deaths of those Aboriginal people who had died in police lock-ups or prisons since January 1980, the commissioners interpreted the terms of reference extremely broadly as a mandate to inquire into how Indigenous people in particular came not only to die in custody but to be there in the first place. In its final five-volume report, accompanied by an additional five volumes on the states and territories and eighty-six volumes on the individual deaths, the Commission laid out before Australia (and the international community) the first comprehensive picture of the historical abuse of the rights of Aboriginal peoples and their contemporary disadvantage measured against every socio-economic indicator.[19] The Commission's report not only covered the disadvantage suffered in the context of the administration of law, policing, and the penitentiary system, but linked this problem with the systematic disadvantage of Aboriginal people, documenting their situation with respect to education, housing, health, employment, and infrastructure. Notably, the report documented the fact that of the ninety-nine Aboriginal people whose deaths had been investigated, forty-three had been removed as children from their natural families through intervention by the state, mission organizations, or other institutions. This fact, and the brief history of the forced removal of

---

[18] Royal Commission into Aboriginal Deaths in Custody (RCIADIC), *Report of the Inquiry into the Death of Malcolm Charles Smith* (Commonwealth of Australia, Canberra, 1991); *Mabo and Others v. Queensland* (No. 2) (1992) 175 CLR 1.

[19] The full RCIADIC report is available online at www.austlii.edu.au/au/special/rsjproject/rsjlibrary/rciadic.

Indigenous children that the report provided, was noticed by some but largely lost within the broader sweep of the report.

Importantly, the Royal Commission contextualized these specific disadvantages within the *political* history of colonization: the policies of integration and assimilation, the non-recognition of land rights, and civil and political inequality and exclusion. It framed them not as discrete acts of discrimination or inequality but as part of a pattern of non-recognition. Moreover, the Commission authors argued that the problem was not merely that Aboriginal people had not been recognized as full citizens of the post-colonial Australian state, but more radically that they had not been recognized as sovereign peoples with pre-existing rights. To this end, the report's recommendations went beyond specific 'welfare' interventions to advocate a more comprehensive shift to recognizing the right to self-determination. Of course, it did so only in a limited way, never suggesting that this go so far as challenging the legitimacy of the sovereign claims of the state or Australia's territorial integrity.

For a brief time, the report brought the issue of Aboriginal disadvantage, broadly understood, onto the agenda of the press and public policy. All governments (federal and state) provided comprehensive responses outlining the measures they would take to address the report's 339 recommendations.[20] In the main, these were framed as measures designed to ensure full equality, but the Commonwealth did make some gestures towards self-determination, principally through a structural reform of the central administrative body, whereby a black elected arm was grafted onto what had been a white-dominated, largely paternalist bureaucracy. No doubt this safely circumscribed form of self-determination fell well short of the political independence entailed by a full-scale recognition of collective political rights.[21] Nevertheless, by opening the way for the organizational philosophy and policy priorities to be shaped not by parliament or white bureaucrats but by an independently constituted body of Indigenous commissioners, each elected by a regional Aboriginal community, the reform provided institutional recognition of the connection between

[20] Royal Commission Government Response Monitoring Unit and Aboriginal and Torres Strait Islander Commission (ATSIC), "Five Years On: Implementation of the Commonwealth Government Responses to the Recommendations of the Royal Commission into Aboriginal Deaths in Custody," *Australian Indigenous Law Reporter* 50 (1997). Available online at http://www.atsic.gov.au/issues/law_and_justice/rciadic/five_years_on/Contents.asp or http://www.austlii.edu.au/au/journals/AILR/1997/50.html.

[21] W. Sanders, *Towards an Indigenous Order of Australian Government: Rethinking Self-Determination as Indigenous Affairs Policy*, Centre for Aboriginal Economic Policy Research, Australian National University (ANU) Discussion paper No. 230 (2002). Available online at http://www.anu.edu.au/caepr/Publications/DP/2002_230.html.

socio-economic inequality and the non-recognition of the distinct political rights of Indigenous peoples.

As a result of the findings of the Royal Commission, the Commonwealth also established the Council for Aboriginal Reconciliation and the office of the Aboriginal and Torres Strait Islander Social Justice Commissioner, a member of the Commonwealth Human Rights and Equal Opportunity Commission mandated to monitor and report annually on Australia's compliance with human rights obligations and to make recommendations towards greater compliance.[22] These measures, and the continuing work of the three bodies highlighting the ongoing concerns of Aboriginal people, sustained a degree of public and political attention, and certainly assured that the Aboriginal issue was known domestically and internationally to be a stain on Australia's human rights record. However, to the extent that the Australian public was engaged in the situation of Aboriginal people, the issue was still mainly seen in terms of inequality and the remnants of historical discrimination, both of which, it was presumed, would be overcome in time through welfare programs and effective anti-discrimination laws.

This changed suddenly and significantly in 1992 when, in the case of *Mabo v. Queensland* (No. 2), the High Court belatedly recognized that Indigenous Australians retained distinct land rights.[23] As noted above, the long campaign to gain recognition of land rights through the legislative arm of the state had repeatedly faltered under the vagaries of political expediency and pressure from powerful interest groups. This motivated a small group of Aboriginal activists, aligned with (Aboriginal and non-Aboriginal) historians, anthropologists, and lawyers, to shift their strategy to the judicial arm and specifically to mount a case seeking to overturn the 200-year-old common law doctrine of *terra nullius*.

Eddie Mabo, a member of the Meriam people (in the Torres Strait Islands off the north coast of Australia), successfully argued, using a wealth of historical and anthropological evidence, that contrary to myth and legal doctrine, Indigenous people did have a distinct form of land ownership prior to colonization. He was also successful in arguing that colonization, while giving the Crown sovereignty over the territory (a political right), did not automatically

---

[22] For a full discussion of the powers of the Commissioner, see chapter 5 of Aboriginal and Torres Strait Islander Social Justice Commissioner, *First Annual Report 1993*, available at http://www.austlii.edu.au/au/special/rsjproject/rsjlibrary/hreoc/atsisjc_1993.

[23] The decision was belated not only in terms of how long it took in the Australian context, but also when compared with other common law jurisdictions. The independent land rights of native Americans had already been recognized in the Marshall decisions in the early nineteenth century, and in Canada in *Calder v. Attorney General of British Columbia* [1973] S.C.R. 313.

extinguish native title.[24] Finding in favour of the plaintiff, the Court ruled more generally that in certain cases, subject to subsequent grants of title, the descendants of the original owners retained their original rights to land, derived from a *sui generis* form of title known as 'native title'. Moreover, because these rights predated contemporary forms of title, they called into the question the watertight validity of the land title system introduced with colonization. In the words of the leading finding: "the Meriam people are entitled as against the whole world to possession, occupation, use and enjoyment of the island of Mer."[25] Certainly, the justices made it clear that the existence of this title would be annulled in cases where there had been a valid act of extinguishment by the Crown, but their judgement raised troubling questions about where such valid extinguishment had in fact occurred.

What made the decision so stunning to the Australian public was not only that it opened the possibility for Indigenous groups to make claims on land held by the Crown (and possibly under certain other types of title). Rather, it was that it set out in such clear and authoritative terms the links between the doctrine of *terra nullius* and the constitution of the Australian nation, and correlatively the link between the ideological underpinnings of this doctrine and the denial of the more general citizenship rights of Aboriginal people. The *Mabo* decision brought to light not only Australia's systematic failure to recognize the rights of Indigenous Australians, but also the political motivation for that failure, and as such exposed the link between non-recognition and the constitution of the nation. In this fashion, it also smoothed the way for people to argue for the link between the failure to recognize the distinct and prior rights of Indigenous peoples, the failure to accord them equal citizenship rights, and the normative character of the nation.

In their detailed arguments, the highest justices in the land showed how the doctrine of *terra nullius* had been ideologically justified by the claim that Aboriginal society was so low on the scale of social organization as to have no legal system capable of giving rise to land rights as recognized by the common law.[26] Justice Gerald Brennan, in his lead judgement, discussed this nexus between the way Aboriginal people were seen and the rights they were accorded in some detail.

---

[24] Critics saw this failure to recognize the political dimension of Indigenous rights as a significant setback. See Noel Pearson, "204 Years of Invisible Title," in *Mabo: A Judicial Revolution*, ed. M. A. Stephenson and S. Ratnapala (Brisbane: University of Queensland Press, 1993).

[25] *Mabo*, 2 (Mason CJ, Brennan, Deane, Toohey, Gaudron and McHugh JJ).

[26] A position originally articulated in John Locke's "On Property," in *Two Treatises on Government*, ed. Peter Laslett ([1698]; rpt., London: Cambridge University Press, 1967).

The supposedly barbarian nature of indigenous people provided the common law of England with the justification for denying them their traditional rights and interests in land, as Lord Sumner speaking for the Privy Council said in *Re Southern Rhodesia* ... , The estimation of the rights of aboriginal tribes is always inherently difficult. Some tribes are so low in the scale of social organization that their usages and conceptions of rights and duties are not to be reconciled with the institutions or the legal ideas of civilized society. Such a gulf cannot be bridged. It would be idle to impute to such people some shadow of the rights known to our law and then to transmute it into the substance of transferable rights of property as we know them.[27]

This being the case, the Crown's declaration of universal title did not constitute theft, because there was no *subject* deemed capable of a legitimate form of ownership. Classifying Aboriginal people as un-civilized then also formed the basis for their exclusion from the reach of the new citizenship regime.

The justices' comments made it clear that they understood this decision about property rights within a broader context of national identity and Australia's standing before itself and the world. Indeed, by explicitly condemning the deeper underpinnings of the doctrine of *terra nullius*, they went beyond a strictly legal brief and threw back onto Australians the responsibility for confronting their retention of a profoundly discriminatory culture. More positively, it was an invitation for contemporary Australia to move its house so as to shift the window through which it viewed the Australian politico-historical landscape and cast its eye on what had been systematically shielded from view. Not only legal recognition but a cultural recognition would be necessary if Australia were to put behind it its history of racial superiority and discrimination and actively raise itself to the standards of equality set out in the norms of international law. As Justice Brennan set out in his leading judgement:

The fiction by which the rights and interests of indigenous inhabitants in land were treated as non-existent was justified by a policy which has no place in the contemporary law of this country. . . . Whatever the justification advanced in earlier days for refusing to recognize the rights and interests in land of the indigenous inhabitants of settled colonies, an unjust and discriminatory doctrine of that kind can no longer be accepted. The expectations of the international community accord in this respect with the contemporary values of the Australian people.[28]

This reflection, especially coming from the highest court in the land, provided the impetus for a far more piercing examination of Australia's history,

---

[27] *Mabo*, 39 (Brennan J).
[28] *Mabo*, 42 (Brennan J).

constitution, and national character. As the Aboriginal and Torres Strait Islander Social Justice Commissioner, Mick Dodson, described the decision in his first annual report:

The deepest significance of the judgement is its potential to hold a mirror to the face of contemporary Australia. In the background is the history of this country. In the foreground is a nation with a choice. There is no possibility to look away. The recognition of native title is not merely a recognition of rights at law. It is a recognition of basic human rights and realities about the origins of this nation: the values which informed its past and the values which will inform its future.[29]

The mirror metaphor, with its false promise of a perfect correspondence that "in no way displaced, dimmed or distorted" reality, was itself somewhat misleading, but Dodson's point was that the judgement provided another mirror, displaying a reflection that now portrayed the excluded image.[30] The power of the invitation, to look where the people had not been willing to look, remained.

The most far-reaching implication of the decision was that this generalized *terra nullius*, the 'cult of forgetfulness', had itself been the condition for the establishment of the post-colonial Australian nation. The High Court's declaration that there had been rights-bearing people in Australia prior to colonization and that they had not relinquished their collective rights on colonization caused the imaginary map of Australia to tear open. Underneath was revealed a previously suppressed subterranean layer of rights and claims that were now not only demanding attention, but also doing so with the stamp of legitimacy from the highest court in the land. The institutional shift both reflected and demanded a shift in the national imagination and in turn in other institutions. In this sense one can locate it as a high point – at the level of formal institutions – in an ongoing conversation about the core norms of the nation, and the relationship between those norms (as both ideals and institutions) and 'Australia' as an imagined and institutionalized nation.

The significance was evident to the then Prime Minister, Paul Keating, who used his office to elevate the demand. Launching the International Year of the World's Indigenous People on 10 December 1992 in Redfern, the heart of the Aboriginal community in inner-city Sydney, he placed before the nation

---

[29] Aboriginal and Torres Strait Islander Social Justice Commissioner, *First Annual Report* 1993, 12.

[30] The words are from Gerard Johann Vossius [De Vos], *Ars Historia* (1623), quoted and critiqued in Reinhart Koselleck, *Futures Past: On the Semantics of Historical Time*, trans. Keith Tribe (New York: Columbia University Press, 2004), 132.

the unprecedented challenge of looking squarely in the mirror. The speech merits quoting at length:

This is a fundamental test of our social goals and national will: our ability to say to ourselves and the rest of the world that Australia is a first rate social democracy, that we are what we should be – truly the land of the fair go and the better chance.

It is a test of our self-knowledge.

Of how well we know the land we live in. How well we recognise the fact that, complex as our contemporary identity is, it cannot be separated from Aboriginal Australia. How well we know our history. .... How well we know what Aboriginal Australians know about Australia.

And, as I say, the starting point might be to recognize that the problem starts with us non-Aboriginal Australians.

It begins, I think, with the act of recognition. Recognition that it was we who did the dispossessing. We took the traditional lands and smashed the traditional way of life. We brought the disasters. The alcohol. We committed the murders. We took the children from their mothers. We practiced discrimination and exclusion.

It was our ignorance and our prejudice. And our failure to imagine these things being done to us. With some noble exceptions, we failed to make the most basic human response and enter into their hearts and minds. We failed to ask – how would I feel if this were done to me?

As a consequence, we failed to see that what we were doing degraded all of us.[31]

Keating's framing of the issue represented a remarkable act of recognition and assumption of responsibility. In terms of form, it also represented a bold willingness to speak on behalf of the national collective. His employment of the subject 'we Australians' went well beyond the institution of the state and reached very personally to the Australian people, appealing to them in a very personal way to re-examine their relationship with the past and to accept a continuity between violations in the nation's history and their contemporary identity.

Although the official apology debate began five years later, only after the issue of the removal of Aboriginal children came on the national agenda, Prime Minister Keating's speech was, in a sense, the first or proto-apology. It was Keating who named the wrongdoing, took responsibility for it, and expressed national shame. And it was Keating's speech that did what I have claimed an apology can (potentially) do: it threw down the gauntlet for a national normative reorientation. As became all too obvious, however, when he resoundingly lost the next election, Keating's deep reform agenda was not universally shared

[31] Paul Keating's speech has become known as 'The Redfern Address'. It is available at http://apology.west.net.au/redfern.html.

by his fellow Australians. What, from the point of view of Aboriginal people and the Prime Minister, had been an opportunity for fuller recognition was, from the point of view of many non-Indigenous Australians, an unwelcome threat to the nation as they knew it, and to their own identity.

While the federal parliament was debating legislation to codify the common law established by the court in *Mabo*, populist radio disc jockeys were getting significant mileage from a fear campaign vilifying Keating and the High Court as ringleaders of an assault of Indigenous extremists wanting to push ordinary Australians out of their suburban homes, off the beaches, and out of the cities. The National Farmers' Federation and the mining lobby, with clear financial interests at stake, fuelled the fear with incendiary advertising campaigns showing Aboriginal people building fences to keep out white farmers and Aboriginal children cheating white children at play. Keating's apology had forced Australia to come face to face with the normative conflict in their history, but many wanted to turn away.

It was in this context that the issue of the forced removal of Indigenous children from their families and the apology entered the public sphere.

2. BRINGING VIOLATION INTO THE FAMILY: THE REMOVAL OF ABORIGINAL CHILDREN

> So in their brothers' bodies again and again
> They butcher the lesser wildness that's their own.
> Franz Berman Steiner[32]

In the mid-1990s, the status and rights of Indigenous Australians held an ambiguous status in the national imagination. On the one hand, the repeated recitation by both government and non-government organizations of the systematic and politically based violation of Indigenous rights by the state had left white Australia with no option than to see its part in the drama of recognition. On the other hand, many non-Indigenous Australians now identified land rights and health as the main concerns for Aboriginal people and technical/legal measures as the main mechanisms for resolving them. Once the grosser caricatures of Aboriginal native title claimants clearing the suburbs of all white folk and embezzling Australia's mineral wealth had been dispelled, most Australians saw the resolution as remote from their lives or identity.

---

[32] Franz Berman Steiner, "Elephant Capture," trans. Michael Hamburger, *Modern Poetry in Translation* 2 (August 1992): 31.

This sense of distance and complacency was shattered in 1997 when *Bringing Them Home*, the Human Rights and Equal Opportunity Commission's nearly 700-page "National Inquiry into the Forced Removal of Aboriginal and Torres Strait Islander Children from Their Families", hit the public stage.[33] Here was a story of children, many of whom were the contemporaries of the politically active public (in their thirties and over), who had clearly done nothing other than be born to an Aboriginal mother, but who had suffered horrors anyone could relate to in a very personal way. Perhaps even more staggering was the national silence that had accompanied the practice, and the complicity this implied.

Against this national silence, the report spoke the history of Indigenous people's experience in graphic detail, laced with personal testimonies. Over the course of a little under two years, the Commission had examined documentary evidence and taken written and oral submissions from government departments, non-government agencies (principally churches), expert witnesses, and, most important, hundreds of Aboriginal people who had themselves been removed or had been directly affected by removal.[34] Part of what lent the report its particular power was the way in which this text, the official report of the Australian Commonwealth, built its history and its policy arguments from the first-person testimonies of Aboriginal people. Each section of the report was suffused with the voices of Aboriginal people telling the very stories that had been excluded from the official story of the Australian nation and, critically, telling them with their own voices – the voices that had not qualified as legitimate *subjects* (as distinct from objects) of history. Their memories became our history and, critically, part of the history of the nation.

When the report was released amidst a storm of media activity, Australians learned that from about 1910 up until 1970, between one in three and one in ten Aboriginal children had been taken under the sanction of the state, against their will and against the will of their families (usually their black mothers), in most cases never to see their families again. Unlike their white counterparts, Aboriginal people did not enjoy the protection of the 'private sphere' of family because, until the late 1930s, 'protectionist legislation' gave the Chief Protectors of Aborigines or Protection Boards virtual total control over Aboriginal people, including the legal guardianship of children. Aboriginal children could

---

[33] Human Rights and Equal Opportunity Commission (HREOC), *Bringing Them Home: Report of the National Inquiry into the Separation of Aboriginal and Torres Strait Islander Children from Their Families* (Sydney, April 1997). Report available online at http://www.hreoc.gov.au/social_justice/bth_report/index.html.

[34] The Inquiry took evidence from 535 Indigenous people around the country affected by removal. Significantly, not a single mother whose child had been removed came forward to give evidence.

be, and commonly were, simply removed from their families without need to show cause, and there was no legal recourse for their families. This ostensibly changed from around 1940, when Aboriginal children were placed under general welfare legislation, which required that neglect or uncontrollability be proven, but in truth it made little difference, as welfare departments and the courts alike held that the poverty and the lifestyle of many Aboriginal communities were synonymous with neglect. In any case, the requirement of proof was often moot, as Aboriginal people were denied access to due process, both directly and indirectly through the *de facto* barriers of poverty, distance, cultural difference, language, and lack of knowledge about the legal system.

Aboriginal parents who attempted to make inquiries about their children were denied access to all information. Communication that relatives sent, intended for their children, was not passed on but held in files in welfare departments and was passed to the children only when they came of age and were released from their status as wards of the state. In one particularly poignant testimony, a young Aboriginal man, born in 1964, tells of the day when, at age eighteen, he was given his very thick file, including letters from his mother pleading for his return and information about him, as well as photos and a birthday card for every year of his estranged life.[35]

Once taken from their families and communities, children were placed in institutions run by the state or churches or in foster homes, or they were adopted by white families. Arrangements were made to ensure that many were sent as far as practicable from their home community, sometimes several thousand miles across the country. More than half of those who gave evidence had experienced multiple placements. Many told stories of being repeatedly fostered or adopted, and each time returned to the institution because the white family was not satisfied, or because of the problems they had in adjusting. Photographs show the children lined up in rows, like puppies in a pet shop, waiting to be picked out or left.

Many recalled living under extremely harsh conditions, poorly fed and clothed and with education sufficient only to prepare them as cheap labour on farms or as domestics, where most were sent to work from a very early age. Their wages, save a small amount of pocket money, were handed over to the Protection Board, putatively to be given to them when they came of age. Here, as elsewhere in the administration of Aboriginal affairs, however, fraud was an institutionalized practice and the wages were rarely properly distributed.[36]

[35] HREOC, *Bringing Them Home*, 68ff.
[36] See Kidd, *Trustees on Trial*.

Many revealed histories of physical as well as sexual abuse, both in institutions and in foster homes.[37]

Abhorrent as these abuses were, what set the experience of Indigenous children apart from that of other children who were institutionalized and similarly mistreated during this period was the particular denigration and annihilation of identity that they uniquely suffered.[38] Certainly, the damages inflicted included physical neglect and abuse, the failure to provide a decent standard of education or care, and sexual abuse in some cases. The heart of the specific damage, however, coincides with the basis for the practice: the denigration and destruction of Aboriginality. From the point of view of the Australian nation-state, Aboriginality was a racial impediment to be eradicated; from the point of view of the individuals who were removed, it was their identity. It is at this point that one can locate the nexus between the particular violations experienced by the children and communities affected, the broad policy objectives of the state, and the political culture in which those policies emerged.

In the nineteenth century, under the sway of social Darwinism, the colonial population generally believed that Aboriginal people were not simply an inferior, but also a dying, race.[39] Correlatively, the colonial state felt little need to directly intervene because the 'pure blacks' would, so it was believed, simply die out, and 'half-castes' would naturally merge into white society as the weaker black blood was subordinated to the stronger white.[40] The problem was that by the early part of the twentieth century it was becoming clear that Aboriginal people were not dying out at all, but living on, even in the face of the colonial onslaught. As a 1937 article from the Brisbane *Telegraph* put it: "Mr. Neville [Western Australian Chief Protector of Aborigines] holds the view that within one hundred years the pure black will be extinct. But the half-caste problem was increasing every year. . . . The pure blooded Aboriginal was not a quick breeder. On the other hand the half-caste was. In Western Australia there were

---

[37] By 1940 the NSW Board's record with respect to Aboriginal girls placed in service was well known and even condemned in Parliament, but nothing was done to stop the abuse. HREOC, *Bringing Them Home*, [11].

[38] Recent work on the experience of British child migrants sent to Australia in the 1930s to 1950s indicates similar patterns of abuse and harsh treatment. See Margaret Humphreys, *Empty Cradles* (London: Doubleday, 1994).

[39] "The Australian nigger is the lowest type of human creature about. . . . But having one splendid point in which he is far ahead of the chinkie. He'll die out and the Chinkie won't." G. Inson and R. Ward, "The Glorious Years," in *Boomerang*, 17 December 1887.

[40] "There is no biological reason for the rejection of people with a dilute strain of Aboriginal blood. A low percentage will not introduce any aberrant characteristics and there need be no fear of reversions to the dark Aboriginal type." Norman B. Tindale, "Survey of the Half-Caste Problem in South Australia," in *Proceedings of the Royal Geographical Society, S.A. Branch, Session 1940–41* (Adelaide: Royal Geographical Society, S.A. Branch, 1941), 67.

half-caste families of twenty and upwards. That showed the magnitude of the problem."[41]

As an increasing number of Aboriginal mothers raised children born of unions with white men within their own Aboriginal culture, and the children of these forbidden unions appeared as part of the new nation's demography, people began to fear that the black would not be absorbed into the white after all, but the white into the black.[42] This 'half-caste' problem, as it was known, was experienced as a significant hazard in early-twentieth-century Australia, not simply because of a generalized racism that white Australians shared with their British counterparts, but more particularly because of the fragility of this just emerging and barely independent post-colonial nation. If Aboriginal people could be held remote, both physically (by being kept on reserves) and in the ideation of national identity, they were relatively harmless. Hybridity, however, posed a threat to the very distinction between the civilized (white) and the savage (black), calling into question the all-important boundary that reassured white Australians, themselves so far removed from their imagined heart of civilization, that they were indeed civilized and proven to be so by their unassailable difference from the 'native'.[43] This was in turn reinforced by the place that the two groups played in modernity's temporal imagination; whereas the non-Indigenous nation was set on its progressive march forward, Aboriginal people, understood as peoples belonging to pre-history, were stuck in a timeless past.

This process of national consolidation through racial differentiation was happening not only at the level of the state, but also at the level of civil society. In the nineteenth and early twentieth centuries, as the unifying narratives that had previously provided the glues of civil society (God, natural law, rational morality) lost their hold and societies became increasingly rational and functional, new unifying discourses were required. At this point, as Ernest Gellner

---

[41] Quoted in Toni Buti, "They Took the Children Away," *Aboriginal Law Bulletin*, 3, no. 72 (1995): 35.

[42] In 1936 Cecil Cook, the Chief Protector in the Northern Territory, wrote: "My view is that unless the black population is speedily absorbed into the white, the process will soon be reversed, and in 50 years, or a little later, the white population of the Northern Territory will be absorbed into the black." Commonwealth of Australia, *Aboriginal Welfare: Initial Conference of Commonwealth and State Aboriginal Authorities* (Canberra: Government Printer, 1937), 14.

[43] "Many of such children are so white that, were it not for their presence in camps or in association with blacks, the average individual would characterize them as practically normal. Beneath the skin, however, the taint is more marked, and it is in the correction of degenerate traits and the eradication of demoralised habits that the work of the expert psychologist and educationalist lies . . . . " Extract from State Children Relief Board, Annual Report 1915, *New South Wales Parliamentary Papers* 1915/16, vol. 1: 880.

observed, the strength of ethnicity or other forms of distinguishing identity became mandatory.[44] In the Australian context, where there was little in the way of deep immediate history or long-standing social relations and an otherwise disconnected society of immigrants, Indigenous people became the obvious 'boundary other'. Placed in this context, the fear of hybridity was the analogue of the process of consolidating this new, remote, and fragile nation.

The rising tide of concern about the 'half-caste problem', combined with the growth of the welfare movement and ideas about social engineering in the early part of the century, led to a more aggressive policy approach requiring active intervention to ensure the proper assimilation of 'half-castes'. Assimilation of course by no means implied a meeting of cultures, but quite vehemently meant becoming white.[45] Only to the extent that Aboriginal people could be purified of this backward strain (carried in their black blood) would they be able to enter the social and political order of Australia. Correlatively, as assimilated Aboriginal people became citizens of this new nation, the citizenry, collective memories, and institutional forms of the older (Indigenous) nations would dissipate, and with them, the existence of those nations themselves as viable political entities.[46]

Indigenous people, described by the leaders of assimilation policy as "thousands of degraded and depressed people who crouch on rubbish heaps throughout the whole of this continent" and relics of a "primitive social order" characterized by "ritual murders, infanticide, ceremonial wife exchange, polygamy", were of no value to the political identity or aspirations of white Australia.[47] Their placement on the national map was limited to the field of anthropology, ancient history, and, later, tourism, all of which rendered them objects.

[44] Ernest Gellner, *Conditions for Liberty: Civil Society and Its Rivals* (London: Hamish Hamilton, 1994), 127.

[45] "Assimilation means, in practical terms, that, in the course of time, it is expected that all persons of aboriginal blood or mixed blood in Australia will live like other white Australians do." Paul Hasluck, *Native Welfare in Australia: Speeches and Addresses* (Perth: Paterson, Brokenshaw, 1953), 16.

[46] Paul Hasluck, Minister of the Territories, told Federal Parliament in 1950 that "[t]heir future lies in association with us, and they must either associate with us on standards that will give them full opportunity to live worthily and happily or be reduced to the social status of pariahs and outcasts living without a firm place in the community." He further said: "We recognise now that the noble savage can benefit from measures taken to improve his health and his nutrition, to teach him better cultivation, and to lead him in civilized ways of life." Hasluck, *Native Welfare*, 6, 17.

[47] Hasluck, *Native Welfare*, 9, and Hasluck, "Policy of Assimilation," National Archives of Australia, NTAC 1956/137: 2.

Of the various measures taken to effect assimilation, including tight control over people's movements and tying the provision of basic goods to conformity with 'appropriate' standards of cleanliness and housekeeping, it was the removal of Aboriginal children and their relocation to white society that were thought to be most effective.[48] With A. O. Neville, the Chief Protector in Western Australia, leading the charge, aggressive assimilation of Aboriginal children, effected most radically through systematic removal, became national policy at the first Commonwealth and State Native Welfare Conference in 1937:

> The policy for them must be one of welfare. Improve their lot so that they can take their place economically and socially in the general community and not merely around the periphery. Once this is done, the break-up of such groups will be rapid. . . . [T]his conference believes that the destiny of the natives of aboriginal origin, but not of the full blood, lies in their ultimate absorption by the people of the Commonwealth, and it therefore recommends that all efforts be directed to that end.[49]

In revisiting this verdict, one can see that what was at work here was not simply a morally or aesthetically based racism reflecting abstract cultural predispositions; it was constitutionally *political*, part and parcel of the politics of a post-colonial nation whose legitimacy required that it be detached not only from the British centre, but more importantly from the Aboriginal base. An ideology that deemed Aboriginal people by definition incapable of partaking in the sphere of rights justified the imposition of British sovereignty without negotiation, accommodation, or political recognition. Had Aboriginal peoples been deemed equally human (and thus potential rights holders), the question of their original political rights would have demanded an answer.[50] And this inquiry, which calls into question the very legitimacy of the nation, was taboo.

Historically, the practice of removal had not been interpreted within this broader political frame, but rather understood in welfarist terms. Indeed, the ideology of cultural difference and individual welfare tells a very persuasive story about removal as if it were just an aggregation of ad hoc inter-personal interactions and discrete decisions by white individuals about the worth of black individuals. By the mid-1990s, however, a more structural explanation

---

[48] Robert van Krieken, "The 'Stolen Generations' and Cultural Genocide: The Forced Removal of Australian Indigenous Children from their Families and Its Implications for the Sociology of Childhood," *Childhood* 6, no. 3 (August 1999).

[49] Quoted in James H. Bell, "Assimilation in NSW," in *New Perspectives in the Study of Aboriginal Communities*, ed. Marie Reay (London: Angus and Robertson, 1964), 68.

[50] A similar link between the politics of assimilation and the confiscation of land has been made in Patrick Wolfe, "Land, Labor and Difference: Elementary Structures of Race," *American Historical Review* 106, no. 3 (June 2001).

of racism had already gained significant currency. This was in part because theories of recognition and post-colonial discourses had gained momentum in the intellectual landscape and were available as interpretive frames for intellectuals involved in presenting the material to the public. It was also because the *Mabo* debate had already laid the groundwork for this type of analysis. Both the High Court's decision itself and the subsequent social commentary had made it clear that the stratified theory of race infusing land laws had worked to justify the extinguishment of a pre-existing title and rendered invisible the prior existence of another political order. In the case of child removal, the political import of racist discourse had been rendered more opaque; but now it was coming into view and, with it, the very personal impact of Australia's racialized constitution.

The irony was that this racialized discourse of rights and identity represented a disjuncture at the heart of the Australian constitution and national imaginary. Australia represented itself to itself as a nation committed to political equality, and yet conformity with an implicit racial ideal was a criterion for being a subject of equal rights. Moreover, the disparity was not some type of 'slip up' or aberrant moment. On the contrary, it validated the political salience of a thick line between those who had come to create the (self-conscious) Australian nation and the remnants of the (unconscious) race that had occupied a pre-political and pre-historical land mass. The degradation of Aboriginality was built into the constitution of Australia even as this contradicted an ideal normative commitment to freedom and equality. Ironically, this meant that it was not only Aboriginal people who were damaged by this degradation, but the nation itself, or at least the ideal nation. In a manner that recalls the structural disparity discussed in Chapter Three between the ideal or a-historical norm and the practical, historical norm, removal betrayed the gap between Australia's ideal commitment to equality and its actual practice of systematic inequality. It was testament to the failure of historical Australia to realize the 'ideal' Australia.

Linking this back to my analysis of the injury itself, one can now see how the heart of the injury lay here, at the level of the damage to identity. Because assimilation and the destruction of culturally and politically viable Aboriginal societies was the ultimate motivation of removing children, the transmission of culture and the work of sustaining social bonds were the primary media through which the policy operated. Once placed, Aboriginal children were denied all contact with their original family, all knowledge about their Aboriginal identity or where they came from, and were forbidden to speak their own languages:

Y'know, I can remember we used to just talk lingo. [In the Home] they used to tell us not to talk that language, that it's devil's language. And they'd wash our mouths with soap.

We sorta had to sit down with Bible language all the time. So it sorta wiped out all our language that we knew.[51]

Aboriginal people and culture were held up as objects of condescension, fear, and ridicule, so that children's internalized images of their own Aboriginal identity were a source of contempt and shame. Most were never told directly that they were of Aboriginal descent or were instructed to conceal their Aboriginality by assuming some more 'palatable' ethnic identity (southern European was popular) to explain their darker skin. At the same time, the image of the dirty, inferior black was held over them as an object of fear and threat, ready to drag them into backwardness should they not conform with the behavioural demands of their educators: "I got told my Aboriginality when I got whipped and they'd say, 'You Abo, you nigger'. That was the only time I got told my Aboriginality."[52]

In this sense, no inventory of the discrete damages sustained by the insult to, and loss of, identity tells the whole story. Certainly, there were specific losses such as language, cultural knowledge and experience, access to land, and now potentially to native title rights. But Aboriginal identity cannot be reduced to a sum of these components, because it is embodied in concrete persons and the damage is inflicted at the level of the person's sense of self. Again, however, this is not a private sense of self, but a socially located one and accordingly, the damage also occurred at the level of social relationships and meanings. Nevertheless, general types only appear as embodied individuals; individual Aboriginal people became the site of specific and general annihilation. They were literally placed in an impossible situation: having to be both that which should be eradicated and simultaneously *not* to be it. Understood within this context, their classification as 'half-castes' was less a biological category than a reflection of a racism that needed bodies on which do its work of racial progress and political displacement.

In the debate that ensued after the report was released, people seeking to defend the policy argued that many of the children who had been removed

---

[51] HREOC, *Bringing Them Home*, [3.10] (Confidential Evidence 170). This quote comes from a South Australian woman taken from her parents with her three sisters when the family, who worked and resided on a pastoral station, came into town to collect supplies and placed at Umewarra Mission.

[52] Ibid., [3.10] (Confidential Evidence 139). Another example: "Your family don't care about you anymore, they wouldn't have given you away. They don't love you. All they are, are just dirty, drunken blacks. You heard this daily. . . . When I come out of the home and come to Redfern here looking for the girls, you see a Koori bloke coming towards you, you cross the street, you run for your life, you're terrified." Ibid., [3.10] (Confidential Evidence 8). This quote is from a woman removed to Cootamundra Girls' Home in the 1940s. See also *Royal Commission into Aboriginal Deaths in Custody*, National Report vol. 2, 76.

received economic, educational, and social opportunities that would never have been available to them had they remained with their Aboriginal mothers in remote and deprived communities. High-profile Aboriginal leaders and professionals who had revealed their own stories of removal were held up as paragons of the benefits of removal. Of course, the idea that success depended on people leaving behind their Aboriginal identity ultimately only served to confirm the very bias that was at issue and the contempt in which non-Indigenous Australia held Indigenous culture. But so long as the perspective from the other side was systematically invalidated, and white Australians were only speaking amongst themselves, they were safe in believing that the moral and institutional basis of their nation coincided with universal and untainted justice. Once the voices of Aboriginal people broke through that self-justificatory circle, however, the fault line in the nation started to open up before the eyes of white Australia. What it saw was not only the injury to Aboriginal Australia, but the moral injury to Australia itself. Suddenly, the other, speaking from the other side of the violation, had a legitimate voice – a voice that was also an Australian voice. The Governor General Sir William Deane, a highly sympathetic reader of the report, laid out the new trajectory of identity this made possible and the risk of not taking this path:

[A]ll our citizens are entitled to expect and demand that the mutual respect and tolerance which are of its essence should be encouraged and, in some circumstances, protected. The reason why that is so is that to undermine that mutual respect or to defy or deny that tolerance within our land is to defy or to deny the very basis of our Australian nation ... to hurt or diminish any of us is to hurt or diminish us all.[53]

3. LOCATING A FRAMEWORK FOR REPAIR: THE IDEA OF THE APOLOGY

With the full range of injuries now placed firmly in the public arena, the question became how to identify the means for affecting reparation.[54] Most obviously this had to include reparation for the range of specific injuries to the

---

[53] Governor General Sir William Deane, address given on 26 January 1997 for Australia Day. Partly cited in George Megalogenis, "Governor-General Fears for Future as PM Recognises Stains of Past," *The Australian*, 27 January 1997.

[54] Note here that the choice of a restorative or reparatory justice approach rather than criminal prosecutions was not simply the outcome of its abstract analysis of the situation but was imposed by constraints arising from the constitution of the inquiry. The HREOC is an administrative body, not empowered to prosecute, and although arguably it could have recommended prosecution in some cases, the prospect of indicting and prosecuting individuals who had perpetrated violations was never on the table.

victims, both those removed and the communities left behind. Heads of damage in this category included separation from family, physical and emotional abuse, and loss of cultural, educational, and economic opportunities, as well as possible land rights claims, given that children were also removed from the line of transmission of the now recognized native title. But, consistent with the broader conception of the damage that the report had established, reparation needed to go beyond these specific damages. Indeed, to limit oneself to these would be to buy into the liberal paradigm of justice that begins and ends with discrete rights and omits the dimension of political power and collective recognition that underpinned those specific violations. Indeed, as we shall see when we come to look at the debate that ensued after the report was released, the rhetoric of individual rights, violations, and responsibility can render invisible the manner in which political orders are shaped around questions of recognition and identity. In this sense, a full response had to get to this pre-legal or constitutional wrong.

No doubt in part because Indigenous people had themselves been so intimately connected with the work and direction of the Inquiry, when it came time to think through mechanisms for redress, the Commission was very alive to this more expansive vision. That said, the movement from vision to institution was far from simple. Identifying forms of justice that would address the violation of, and damage to, identity demanded a novel approach to justice for three reasons. First, the injury fell into none of the standard categories; second, it implied a form of collective responsibility; and third, addressing the injuries of the identified Indigenous victims could not take place in isolation from a broader engagement with the identity of the nation.

This last dimension is particularly relevant to the emergence of the apology. Although Indigenous people, individually and collectively, were the principal victims, and the moral imperative provoked by the findings was to attend to their injuries, fully addressing their identity status could not take place in isolation from a broader discourse about the nation. Thus, recalling the discussion in Chapter Two about the inter-penetration of the identity of the perpetrator and victim, and William Connelly's argument that critical responsiveness to relations of violation demands that attention also be paid to the identity of the dominant party, the shifts required had to be located within the nation itself. Indeed, drawing on the religious metaphors of the last chapter, one might say that the illness of the sinner also had to be addressed. In this (carefully circumscribed) sense the Australian nation, most obviously the perpetrator, was also the victim of its own violation. Reparative action thus had to speak to the injury to Aboriginal people, to the nation, and to the relationship in which Indigenous and non-Indigenous Australians stood.

What was required was that those shaping public policy responses to the National Inquiry mould an institutional intervention that went beyond the jurisprudence of direct individual responsibility or discrete heads of damage to encompass issues of collective identity and social meanings. This represented a significant challenge, in the first instance because identities and social meanings do not offer themselves up to simple 'correction' or alteration. Beyond this, traditional liberal conceptions and institutions of justice positively augur against responses that engage this more pervasive and amorphous level of collective identities and circulated meanings. Nevertheless, by mining the conversations it conducted with witnesses, the submissions it received, and international guidelines and practices for compatible situations, the National Inquiry identified a range of broad reparatory strategies, amongst which it included apology as a key means for effecting this type of broader reparation.[55]

As it originally appeared in the report, the apology recommendation seemed to be a relatively modest one, embedded within a broader set of reparative justice strategies. Once it entered the public sphere, however, the apology took on a life and a set of meanings that far exceeded its original articulation. Nevertheless, by looking at the sources of the idea of apology, one can discern some of the original rationale and in this a certain understanding of the distinct role that the National Inquiry believed apology had to play in addressing the past.

Submissions to the Inquiry provided the most immediate impetus, with a number of community-based groups calling for a national apology to Aboriginal and Torres Strait Islander people for the suffering inflicted on them through a history of state-sanctioned removal policies.[56] From their point of view, the heart of apology's work was its official legitimation and acknowledgement of the wrong inflicted by the nation and the subsequent suffering borne by Indigenous people. Importantly, the wrong was not only removal itself, nor even its broader repercussions, but also the continued marginalization of Aboriginal people's experience. Fully addressing the past would be a matter of not just

---

[55] A version of the report commissioned by the Inquiry is published as S. Pritchard, "The Stolen Generations and Reparations," *University of New South Wales Law Journal* vol. 21, issue 1 (May 1998): 259–67. See also Toni Buti and Melissa Parke, "International Law Obligations to Provide Reparations for Human Rights Violations," *Murdoch University Electronic Journal of Law* 6, no. 4 (December 1999).

[56] For example: "ATSIC considers that reconciliation must surely begin with this one elementary condition" (Submission 684). Also: "[T]he assimilation policy that operated in this country [should] be denounced officially by governments across the country" (Aboriginal Legal Rights Movement submission 484, recommendation 18). Other bodies calling for an apology included the South Australian Aboriginal Child Care Agency (submission 347, recommendation 5), Link-Up (NSW) (submission 186), and the Aboriginal Legal Service of Western Australia (submission 127, recommendations 3 and 5). See HREOC, *Bringing Them Home*, [14].

re-introducing certain truths about history into the national narrative, but also facing up to the ways in which the very process of writing the national narrative had systematically excluded Aboriginal people as sites of experience and truth. Thus, the act of apology was to perform two levels of recognition and legitimation: first, of the substance of the truths themselves, and second, of the competence of the ones who told it. This is, of course, outlining what it means to be a recognized as a subject. More relevant than recognition of any particular statement is recognition that one has a legitimate point of view. This was what Indigenous Australians had always been denied, as the various moments of violation so poignantly illustrated.

In this regard, the publicity of the apology and the status of the speaker were both crucial to the reparatory value of the act; they provided the media for transforming the story of removal from the private and marginalized 'perceptions' or memories of Aboriginal people to official and legitimate history. Indigenous people were here demanding that their subject experience and their perspective of history be brought out of the shadows and the realm of untruths and into the well-lit space of the public record. If we recall the potent image of the original *kniefall*, the power of this act lay in its dramatic performance of a change in the organization of power between Germans and Jews. So here, too, Indigenous people wanted the state to address them as people with dignity, with justified grievance, and as important sites of the nation's truth, as distinct from 'untrustworthy' and private sources of dissent. Long placed in a structurally subordinate position to the post-colonial nation, Indigenous people wanted to occupy the position of the one to whom the nation now deferred. Correlatively, they wanted to see the nation appear before them, the international community, and before itself, on its knees and in a position of shame.

The 'Van Boven Principles', recommendations of the United Nations study on the right to restitution, compensation, and rehabilitation for victims of gross violations of human rights and fundamental freedoms, were the second explicit source of the idea of an apology.[57] These principles, designed to expound what a reparatory approach to justice actually entailed, proved particularly useful to the Inquiry because of their expansion beyond a traditional liberal jurisprudential approach. Although Van Boven does not actually elaborate the rationale for apology, or what it is that it is supposed to achieve, one can discern its specific part in the work of reparation by examining the overall approach of the principles and where within that overall approach apology sits.

Van Boven divides the overall task of reparation into four types of intervention – restitution, compensation, rehabilitation, and satisfaction and guarantees against

---

[57] Van Boven Principles. See Chapter Two, note 9.

repetition – each of which is to be effected through concrete interventions. Restitution, defined as seeking to re-establish the situation that existed prior to the violations, includes measures such as restoration of liberty, family life, citizenship, return to one's place of residence, and return of property. The National Inquiry report recommended that this dimension be met by the state's guaranteeing Indigenous Australians full access to files and return to their communities, providing support for members of the stolen generation to benefit from native title claims, giving restitution for property that churches and other agencies had acquired for accommodating Indigenous children, and initiating processes to facilitate admittedly belated family reunions. Compensation refers to monetary compensation for any economically assessable damage resulting from violations. Here, the Inquiry report recommended the establishment of a statutory national compensation fund, with all those who had been removed being guaranteed a minimum lump sum in addition to their being permitted to make further claims under a number of specified heads of damage. The third category, rehabilitation, includes medical and psychological care as well as legal and social services. The Inquiry report recommended the provision of specifically directed counselling and health rehabilitation services including family well-being and parenting skills programs as well as training for healthcare workers to ensure their ability to understand the specific experience of removal.

The last of Van Boven's categories, 'satisfaction and guarantees against repetition', includes verification of the facts and full public disclosure of the truth; official declaration or judicial decision restoring the dignity, reputation, and rights of the victims; apology, including public acknowledgement of the facts and acceptance of responsibility; commemorations and paying tribute to victims; and, finally, inclusion of an accurate account of the violations in human rights training and history textbooks. The Inquiry authors recommended that all Australian school curricula include compulsory and substantial modules on the history of removal and that all undergraduates, trainees, and professionals who work with Indigenous people be educated about removal. Most prominently, it included two specific recommendations specifying that all Australian parliaments, police forces, churches, and relevant non-government organizations should apologize. In a further recommendation, the Inquiry report proposed a national 'Sorry Day' and a range of further commemorations at a local level. Indeed, although this fourth category – satisfaction and guarantees against repetition – appears last on Van Boven's list, in the report, it was presented as the first dimension of reparation.[58]

---

[58] Cf., e.g., the order of provisions 12 to 15 in the Van Boven recommendations with recommendation 3 of the National Inquiry.

Unfortunately, the operational emphasis on this fourth dimension was not accompanied by an elaboration of its meaning, and the Van Boven report is similarly silent on conceptual matters. Indeed, despite the plethora of recent literature on restorative and reparatory justice, there is very little elaboration on what 'satisfaction' means.[59] Nevertheless, by examining the interventions that fall under it, one can discern two distinct characteristics. First, they all emphasize the symbolic dimension of harm and the requirement to publicly establish the wrongfulness of the act and repair the public identity of the victim. Second, whereas the other three dimensions are all clearly concerned with restoration for the victims and make their intervention at the level of doing things for or returning things to the victim, this group of strategies is concerned with the social order more generally and with the perpetrator group specifically. In this sense, these strategies go beyond the conventional view that reparative justice involves attending to the brokenness of the victim of violation to encompass a more capacious understanding of what it is that needs to be repaired.[60]

Justice in this dimension is directed towards healing the damage to the identity of the victim, but with the understanding that the damage to identity occurred through specific forms of social and political relations and in public representations. As such, the restorative action must move through the media of social and political relations rather than be contained in a private victim-centred healing. Moreover, insofar as the interventions demand that the group that has failed to fully recognize the victim group change *its* conceptions of truth, history, and identity, they encode the broadened conception of justice implicated in the type of systematic wrongs discussed in this chapter. That is, while in no way diminishing responsibility, the interventions also recognize that repair of injuries to identity and restoration of relations of respect must include repairing the normative breaks in the responsible community.

---

[59] One article specifically on this question treats satisfaction as a subjective state, in the sense of the various parties being 'satisfied', but does not get at what satisfaction means in this context. Cf. Daniel W. Van Ness and Mara F. Schiff, "Satisfaction Guaranteed? The Meaning of Satisfaction in Restorative Justice," in *Restorative Community Justice: Repairing Harm and Transforming Communities*, ed. Gordon Bazemore and Mara Schiff (Cincinnati, Ohio: Anderson Publishing, 2001).

[60] John Torpey's modified model of different forms of reparation, lying along a two-dimensional continuum mapped across two axes, from symbolic to economic and from cultural to legal, would provide an alternative schema and is not inconsistent with my discussion here. Unlike Torpey, however, I would emphasize the strong interdependence of what he calls symbolic damages and forms of reparation and contemporary economic inequalities. See Torpey, "Introduction," *Politics and the Past*.

Importantly, the fourth dimension of Van Boven's principles is also communicative or discursive strategies, interventions in official narratives about the nation and the nation's history. Continuous with the analysis of the injuries as actions embedded in a more generalized discursive frame that systematically links rights with identity distinctions, they effect their repair through counter-discourses and communicative dynamics. Rather than being interventions that restore legal rights or give back lost property, these are interventions that alter communication by empowering or recognizing the legitimacy of voices, subject positions, and recollections that had previously been marginalized or downgraded. Thus, consistent with the community submissions discussed above, these forms of reparative justice are concerned with the rules of communication and participation themselves and not only with what happens within a political space that is never called into question itself. Located within this dimension of reparation, apology moves beyond the *what* of wrongdoing to encompass the *who* of wrongdoing and the relationships and systems of meaning within which wrongdoing takes place. Put otherwise, it addresses not simply what citizens have done but who they have been, whose voices and experiences have been validated, who has had access to legitimated public speech, and how these differently valued identities have been encoded in law, social norms, and historical narratives.

As we shall see in the next chapter, however, many Australians were not sympathetic to this more radical reconstitutive sense of political justice. Indeed, many saw the attempts to break away from more traditional liberal conceptions and institutions of responsibility and justice as a further affront to their sense of themselves and their sense of justice. An apology seemed to accuse them, when they could not see what they had done wrong.

6

Saying Sorry in Australia

The call for apology powerfully brought together the aspirations of the people who had experienced and suffered the denigration of removal and a more abstract analysis of how to institutionalize reparation for systematic human rights violations. From both perspectives, the apology seemed to take up the distinct level of damage to a social meaning, a dimension of reparation generally omitted in traditional modern (liberal) institutions of justice, despite its analytic centrality and subjective poignancy. Widening the lens, the last chapter illustrated how the apology also stepped onto the political stage at a moment when the country was ripe for this type of reorientation, both because its self-image had been battered by a decade of exposés of human rights violations, and because Australia was on the verge of a new century and the possibility of a new constitution. Yet the multifaceted meaning of apology, and in particular its personal and religious overtones, got in the way of its playing this role without contestation. Even as it gathered significant force in Australian political life, those who saw the apology as a contravention of equally important political and jurisprudential norms – most notably individual liberty and protection from crude collective blame – also fiercely resisted it.

The Australian debate displays several important broader themes concerning political apologies already developed through the previous two lenses. First, it illustrates the two key tensions in which political apologies are caught: between collective and individual responsibility, and between the public, collective trope of apology and the internalized, individual apology. In this living apology debate, one can see how Australians struggled with the idea of collective responsibility, on the one hand looking for some way in which to acknowledge that the violation of the rights of Indigenous peoples was part of the nation's past, while simultaneously resisting being blamed for actions they did not *personally* take.

At the same time, the apology debate folded in with the broader concerns about national identity that had come to the fore as Australia literally sought to reconstitute itself as a nation. Insofar as the apology responded to these politically salient questions of identity and constitution, it offered an appealing and resonant strategy, and one sees how Australians intuited important resources the apology held for dealing with their past *and* opening their future. Still, they struggled with their discomfort with apology's religious and personal resonances, sensing that apology evoked the image of the responsible, private individual repenting his or her sins in a way that was both inappropriate to the sphere of politics and contrary to some other sense of justice. In the way it navigated these tensions, the story of the Australian apology typifies the movement beyond legal paradigms that was characteristic of developments in transitional justice in the latter part of the twentieth century. Finally, in the dénouement of the drama – the actual delivery of the apology as the opening act of the new Parliament and a new government, eleven years after the original call, and the extraordinary public embrace of that act – the Australian story illustrates the remarkable manner in which contemporary secular polities are taken by apology's performative power.

The trajectory of the Australian apology also bears out the idea that political communities become enrolled in apologies because they contribute to future-oriented projects of political reconstitution and not only because they offer a way of dealing with difficult pasts. Admittedly, there is no control case here, but one can still reasonably surmise that had the apology not spoken to broader normative questions with which Australians were already deeply engaged – questions about its identity and the distribution of rights *now* – it would have remained a relatively peripheral suggestion.

Finally, the fact that the apology became such a prominent part of the national political debate reiterates the challenge that contemporary political movements are posing to standard conceptions of the modern (secular) political and the thick line liberal theory draws between the modes of politics and the modes of religion. What this case suggests is that the hybrid nature of the apology as the 'personal political' is not a mistake but a challenge to the scheme that renders this hybrid so problematic. The case of the removal of Aboriginal children illustrates this challenge in a most powerful way, because it was at once a completely political and profoundly personal process. It both reached across to the most publicly and politically salient norms of the Australian nation, and down to touch individual Australians' experience of their identity.

The cynical reader may object that apology's popularity in Australia evidences not the phenomenon's importance but Australians' opportunism.

According to this by no means uncommon interpretation, Australians did not rush to say sorry because apology spoke so deeply to the issues of the moment but because, unlike restitution, compensation, or rehabilitation, it cost nothing and meant little. In fact it gives the one apologizing a rich glow of self-satisfaction at the lowest of costs. Underpinning this interpretation is the assumption we have already parsed, that words are relatively worthless. No doubt there is some truth to this interpretation. Irrespective of the importance of words in religious ritual or Austin's speech act theory, we live in a world where words can be (and frequently are) detached from other forms of substantive political action, from authentic feelings, and from normative orientation. And if this is potentially true anywhere, it is especially true in the political realm. Donning an 'I'm Sorry!' T-shirt (like the now universally consumed Che Guevara T-shirts) may be as much a fashion statement as a political intervention, and apologizing did seem to offer otherwise disengaged Australians a way of cleansing their consciences after they had been sullied by a history about which they might have rather not known. But if this was all there was to apology, why did it matter so much to the people who continued to call for it and why was there so much resistance to it? And why, when it finally came, did the nation come together in unprecedented unity?

Some assumed that objections to apologizing were no more than screen resistance, masking the real fear, which was that it would open the nation to costly compensation claims. In the Australian case, there is evidence that this was at least partially true. Surveys indicated that one reason Australians were concerned about an apology was that they feared it would constitute an admission of liability and be garnered as evidence in support of compensation claims.[1] This explanation goes only so far, however, because as a matter of fact, as distinct from perception, an official parliamentary apology would be immune from further legal proceedings.[2] True enough, this technical legal fact does not discount the fear amongst ordinary Australians, who can be excused

---

[1] Research undertaken in 1999 for the Council of Aboriginal Reconciliation, cited in Parliament of Australia (Senate), the Senate Legal and Constitutional Committee, *HEALING: A Legacy of Generations, the Report of the Inquiry into the Federal Government's Implementation of the Recommendations Made by the Human Rights and Equal Opportunity Commission in Bringing Them Home* (Canberra, November 2000), 115. Available at http://www.aph.gov.au/SENATE/COMMITTEE/legcon_ctte/completed_inquiries/199902/stolen/report/contents.htm.

[2] The Senate Legal and Constitutional Committee similarly points out that the *Parliamentary Privileges Act 1987* (Cth) protects all statements made within the parliamentary chamber from being used as evidence in a court. See *Healing: A Legacy of Generations*, 113–14. This position was confirmed in *Cubillo and Another v. Commonwealth* (No. 2) (2000) 103 FCR 1, 32–4 (O'Loughlin J).

for assuming that an apology would work as an admission of guilt in a court of law. Others, however, and most notably the then Prime Minister, John Howard, who led the charge against the apology, were well aware that apology had no further legal implications, but nevertheless continued to use the compensation argument to bolster their refusal to apologize. Indeed, the Prime Minister had sought legal counsel on this question and received clear advice from his own Solicitor General about legal immunity, but he continued to deploy the argument.[3] This being the case, one might suggest that it was just the opposite: the fear of financial liability was instrumentally held up to mask the resistance to apologizing itself. It was not the financial liability but the taking on of the mantle of responsibility that presented a problem.

So what was it about apology that was so difficult for some, and so appealing for others? How did the different players in the Australian debate interpret the apology, and how did they answer each other's appeals and objections? And what do these understandings tell us about what a political apology is?

I. THE APOLOGY WAVE

The final report, *Bringing Them Home*, recommended that all Australian parliaments, as well as police forces and the churches and other non-government organizations that played a role in removal, officially acknowledge responsibility of their predecessors and that they negotiate an appropriate form of words for public apologies to Indigenous individuals, families, and communities.[4] Although this apparently innocuous suggestion sat amongst far more contentious ones (for instance, that the state pay monetary compensation to all those affected), or inflammatory ones (like the finding that removal constituted genocide), the initial heat these others generated quickly yielded centre-stage to the apology. Within a year the apology movement, like the Sea of Hands, had swept across Australia in a manner unprecedented by any domestic human rights issue previously placed before the public. The scope and effect of the apology movement in Australia exceeded any predictions that social commentators might have had observing the Australian social and political landscape. Saying sorry and performing repentance became a national motif.

Apologies proliferated across the social, geographical, and political landscape. First, there were apologies from groups directly nominated in the

---

[3] "A formal, unqualified apology does, according to legal advice that we have received, have certain legal implications." The Hon. John Howard MP, Transcript of Interview with Paul Lyneham, *Nightline*, 29 May 1997.

[4] HREOC, *Bringing Them Home*, Recommendations 5a, 5b, and 6.

recommendations. All Australian parliaments (with the notable absence of the Commonwealth, until 2008) tendered official apologies staged as part of dramatic performative sequences held in their ceremonial chambers.[5] Aboriginal people were invited into the halls of parliaments as honoured guests to tell their stories; parliamentary representatives responded (often highly emotionally) from the floor; and then official apologies were delivered on behalf of the parliament.[6] Chief Magistrates apologized, and apologies were tendered on behalf of state police forces, as well as on behalf of a range of governmental agencies implicated in the removal process. The official organs of a number of churches apologized, specifically those that were directly involved in the process of removal, but also some with no direct historical role.[7]

Apologies also went well beyond the formal recommendations, issuing from a plethora of groups not specifically mentioned, but which nevertheless felt called to the sorry discourse. In some cases, the groups drew an explicit connection between their role and the practice of removal. The national umbrella body of social services, for example, apologized in view of the direct role of welfare organizations in taking and keeping children.[8] In other cases, groups with no apparent connection with removal nevertheless saw fit to tender formal apologies. These included trade unions, professional associations, civic clubs and associations, schools, and parents' and citizens' associations. Amongst this group, the apology from the Federation of Ethnic Communities Councils of Australia (FECCA, representing immigrant Australians) and the interchange surrounding it were particularly telling. The Prime Minister, who had steadfastly refused to apologize, cited as one of his reasons his commitment to protecting the large number of recently arrived immigrant Australians from this unjust attribution: "you can't really apologize on behalf of people who moved here in the last ten or fifteen years and never knew anything about this."

[5] See Content of Apologies by State and Territory Parliaments, available at http://www.human rights.gov.au/social_justice/bth_report/apologies_states.html.

[6] South Australia: 28 May 1997; Western Australia: 28 May 1997; Queensland: 3 June 1997; ACT: 17 June 1997; New South Wales: 18 June 1997; Tasmania: 13 August 1997; and Victoria: 17 September 1997. The Northern Territory Government has not made a statement of apology.

[7] A number of church apologies can be found on the Reconciliation and Social Justice Online Library at http://www.austlii.edu.au/au/special/rsjproject/rsjlibrary/hreoc/stolen/stolen31.html# Heading112.

[8] "Collectively, we feel a particular sense of responsibility for the consequences of these racist policies because their implementation required the active involvement of community welfare organizations. We unreservedly and wholeheartedly apologize to the individuals, families and communities who have suffered such pain and grief from these terrible acts of injustice." Statement of Apology and Commitment to Aboriginal and Torres Strait Islander People by the Australian Council of Social Services, November 1997.

By way of response, the FECCA President issued a formal apology, adding that "we are part of the current society and society is a continuum."[9]

The one-year anniversary of the release of *Bringing Them Home,* 26 May 1998, was celebrated as National Sorry Day, a commemoration that was conceived from the beginning as a "first annual event", as Jeffrey K. Olick puts it, a commemoration that was intended to endure.[10] The National Sorry Day Committee, schools, churches, and local councils organized public 'sorry' events in cities and towns across the country. Aboriginal people publicly narrated their stories of removal and its repercussions on their lives. Public figures performed ceremonial apologies. 'Sorry Books', compilations of written apologies from individual Australians, were ceremonially handed over to Aboriginal representatives. In Sydney a Welcome Home ceremony was held, during which Aboriginal elders welcomed back the (now adult) stolen children with ritual traditional ritual smoking, dance, and song before the witness of hundreds of Aboriginal and non-Aboriginal Australians.[11] In Melbourne thousands attended a service at the Anglican cathedral and then marched to City Hall where – in a remarkably literal act of political repatriation – the mayor handed over the keys to the city to representatives of the "stolen generation." In Queensland every prison (and, ironically, its disproportionate number of Indigenous inmates) observed a minute's silence.

The following year, this day was officially renamed the 'Journey of Healing', reflecting an attempt to respond to the negative reactions the word 'sorry' had evoked in some sectors.[12] The new name was thought to present the process in a more positive, forward-looking light, a nod of accommodation to those who were uncomfortable with being asked to say sorry for something that, in their words, 'they personally did not do'.

The change from 'sorry' to a trope of healing also reflected the view that, as the movement grew, it should broaden its scope beyond a focus on black victims to healing Australia *in toto*. Whereas the 'sorry' approach seemed to some to divide Australia into two camps, black victims and white perpetrators, the healing narrative told a story in which all Australians bore the scar of

---

[9] *Sydney Morning Herald,* "It Hurts Us, Unapologetic PM Admits," 13 December 1997.

[10] Jeffrey K. Olick, *The Politics of Regret: On Collective Memory and Historical Responsibility* (New York: Routledge, 2007), 58.

[11] Smoking, a ritual form of spirit cleansing, involves burning plants and leaves in the space to be cleansed.

[12] As chair of the National Sorry Day Committee, Carol Kendall, put it, the new day was about "recognition, commitment and unity"; similarly, Lowitja O'Donoghue, a pre-eminent Indigenous leader, said, "Let's try to move on. . . . Some of the people who are nervous about the whole process ought to be able to take this journey with us." Reported in Debra Jopson, "Between the Rock and . . . Nowhere," *Sydney Morning Herald,* 8 June 1999.

removal, and all could benefit from national healing. Pragmatically, this shift also marked an attempt to substitute a harmonious 'win-win' dynamic for the more conflict-ridden 'win-lose' one that some felt apologizing constructed. Though the resonance was by no means made explicit, one may well be reminded here of the early Christian images of the Church as a body where all are infected through sin and healed through repentance, and hear echoes of the collective prayers spoken by the congregation seeking a reconciliation it can achieve only as 'one'.

The ceremonial activities in this second year, 1999, under the banner of the new name, began at Uluru, the symbolic heart of Aboriginal Australia. The traditional owners, the Mutitjulu, handed members of the stolen generation ten pairs of music sticks bearing the symbols of shackles, teardrops above the Aboriginal flag, and a boomerang (a call to return to place and to history), for them to take back to each of the capital cities, where ceremonies were to take place on 26 May.[13] In Adelaide, for example, 1,000 people walked to places important in the story of removal, but largely forgotten in contemporary Australia, such as the site of Piltawodli, a Kaurna school opened by German missionaries in 1839. There, schoolchildren sang in the traditional language, perhaps for the first time since 1845 when troops demolished the buildings and the children living there were moved to an English-language school that banned their language.

As anticipated, public sorry ceremonies continued to take place on 26 May, following a now regular script of testimony, witness, and apology. In 2000, an estimated 1 million people across Australia took part in coordinated reconciliation marches, 250,000 alone crossing Sydney Harbour Bridge. For the 2002 ceremony, one of Australia's legendary bands reunited to perform "Sorry", a song paying tribute to the stolen generation and their families, on the lawn in front of Parliament House.[14] Throughout the year, 'Sorry Books,' open for any Australian to sign, circulated the country. In early anticipation of these books' archival role as record and testimony, specifications were provided for the correct format (size, material, binding) for a Sorry Book.[15] People could also

---

[13] See Debra Jopson, "Radiating from the Rock, Ritual of Hope," *Sydney Morning Herald*, 5 June 1999. The connection between repentance and return, which is so much a part of the drama around removal, is strongly resonant of the meaning of *teshuvah* as return, not simply repentance.

[14] There was even a 'reconcilioke' – a karaoke event dedicated to reconciliation and apology. Details on the activities, including the song lyrics and pictures of the 'I'm Sorry' T-shirts, can be found at the official apology Web site: http://apology.west.net.au/index.html and links.

[15] Many of the Sorry Books are now being held at the Australian Institute of Aboriginal and Torres Strait Islander Studies. A selection is available for viewing online at http://www1.aiatsis.gov.au/exhibitions/sorrybooks/sorrybooks_selection.htm.

register their names on the apology Web site, which in early 2004 contained about 250,000.

Against this tide, the conservative Prime Minister John Howard's explicit long-term and staunch refusal to apologize resounded in its silence. His main objection was that he thought it was wrong for contemporary Australians to apologize for something for which they were not personally responsible, but he also defended the policy of removal as well-intentioned and even occasionally highly successful, albeit perhaps in retrospect mistaken. He was willing to express his sadness for the suffering of individuals, but only in an entirely personal and not a representative capacity. When, at the launch of the report at the National Reconciliation Convention in May 1997, Howard offered a carefully circumscribed expression of personal and deep sorrow, members of the audience rose and turned their backs: a strong mark of contempt and refusal to recognize or respect his authority.[16]

In the face of this refusal, the leader of the opposition party in Federal Parliament apologized, as did numerous other members, including the Prime Minister's own deputy, who also took part in 'sorry' marches. At the same time, Howard's stance attracted support from a significant number of Australians and effectively raised the stakes of the debate, becoming an axis of contention.[17] Outside Parliament, many of the groups that had apologized now turned their public statements to calls to the Federal Parliament and the Prime Minister to apologize. If the apology movement had had some intrinsic half-life, Howard's silence – or more accurately the particular form of words he was willing to enunciate and his deployment of the issue as a rallying point for his version of Australian identity, politics, and history – ensured that the issue would remain on the public agenda, and so it did, right until the change of government ten years later, where it became the staging for the new Prime Minister to announce a change in Australia's political culture.

---

[16] The form of words Howard used was: "Personally, I feel deep sorrow for those of my fellow Australians who suffered injustices under the practices of past generations toward indigenous people." Opening address to the reconciliation convention, May 1997, available at http://www.austlii.edu.au/au/special/rsjproject/rsjlibrary/car/arc/speeches/opening/howard.htm.

[17] Comprehensive studies on the level of support for Howard's position were not done, although one fairly small study conducted in Perth in 2001 found that only 27% of residents supported a political apology. C. McGarty et al., 'Collective Guilt as a Predictor of Commitment to Apology' (unpublished manuscript, Australian National University), reported in Aarti Iyer, Colin Wayne Leach, and Anne Pederson, "Racial Wrongs and Restitutions: The Role of Guilt and Other Group-Based Emotions," in *Collective Guilt: International Perspectives*, ed. Nyla R. Branscombe and Bertjan Doosje (Cambridge: Cambridge University Press, 2004), 269.

Following lengthy negotiations with Aboriginal groups and after the election of an Aboriginal Senator, on 26 August 1999 the Commonwealth Parliament did pass a motion expressing its "deep and sincere regret that Indigenous Australians suffered injustices under the practices of past generations, and for the hurt and trauma that many Indigenous people continue to feel as a consequence of those practices."[18] But for many this was but an incremental improvement of Howard's initial personal apology; it still fell well short of the apology that had been called for, that is, one that did not simply stand by in shared empathy, but rather actively accepted responsibility.

2. INTERPRETATIONS OF APOLOGY IN THE AUSTRALIAN CONTEXT: RESPONSIBILITY AND THE NATURE OF GUILT

Beyond the proliferation of apologies, the debates that ensued provide a fertile source for investigating how different people understand collective apologies and how they actually play out in contemporary political spaces. What is particularly striking about the positions of the advocates and critics is how closely they track the tensions and tropes that I derived in the abstract in the previous chapters. Conflicts over whether a collective could (coherently) apologize, whether it could be held responsible for wrongs in the past, and whether apology was even admissible into the political realm were consistent themes in the national debate.

The Prime Minister's resistance captured the most important components of the argument against apology. The first and initially dominant argument was that contemporary Australians did not *personally* do it and that it was therefore unfair to hold them responsible. Second was the objection that it is wrong to judge the past according to the moral norms of the present. The acts under review, this argument pointed out, had been both legal and, according to most Australians, moral at the time of commission, so it was unfair to retrospectively condemn them. Some supplemented this with the more contentious claim that the policy was developed "for their, Indigenous people's, own good", and as such, far from being condemnable, removal was morally laudable.[19] The third major plank of the argument was that Australia's contemporary public policy should be oriented

---

[18] Commonwealth, Parliamentary Debates, House of Representatives, 26 August 1999, p. 9205 (the Hon. John Howard, MP).

[19] This latter position was most strongly endorsed by the most extreme right-wing One Nation party, but was frequently expressed in letters to the editor and other public commentary. The following is typical: "I then ask the apologetic guilt industry, where would many of these people be today had they not been removed from these sad conditions and given the lives they are now living?" Letters to the Editor, *The Age*, 18 March 1998.

around future goals, not history. Focusing on the present and the future, not dwelling in the past, was what was needed to achieve national reconciliation.

Of course, in the fray of the debate, actors did not articulate their positions in terms of conceptions of responsibility or tropes of apology; theorists, not real people, do that. Nevertheless, with a newly detailed map in hand, one can more clearly discern how the positions in history reiterated distinct conceptions of responsibility (and apology). To this end, Karl Jaspers' original, though imperfect, cartography of guilt, written in the wake of the Holocaust, provides a useful code.[20] Indeed, though addressing a very different set of historical facts, Jaspers was inspired to illuminate different dimensions of guilt precisely because he discerned that they underpinned, and would help to make sense of, apparently irreconcilable views about who could legitimately be held responsible for the wrongs of Nazism. On the one hand, Jaspers was keenly aware of the dangers of attributing guilt to a collective and recognized that it was precisely the failure to apply the principles that would have tamed gross collectivism that had significantly contributed to the aetiology of the very atrocities that were now being addressed.[21] At the same time, he recognized that legalistic definitions of (individual, direct) guilt did not adequately capture his own or others' intuitions about guilt in situations where the wrongs in question had been systemic, long-term, and committed on a national scale. Nevertheless, were the field narrowed to the identification of individuals who could be tied to an *actus reus* with *mens rea*, the only legitimate way to classify the vast majority of Germans would have been as free of responsibility altogether.

Jaspers' strategy to broaden and clarify the map of responsibility so as to justify and explain these apparently contradictory intuitions about guilt's breadth was to articulate a set of conceptual distinctions *within* the relatively undifferentiated category of guilt. The four categories of guilt he set out were criminal, political, moral, and metaphysical. Criminal guilt, the type generally assumed in liberal institutions of criminal justice, applies where there has been a violation of a positive law, and where this violation is established by properly constituted courts. Political guilt is a state of liability attaching to a political community but arising from the actions of political leaders and fellow citizens.[22]

---

[20] Karl Jaspers, *The Question of German Guilt*.

[21] "The mentality which considers, characterizes and judges people collectively is very widespread. . . . This confusion, of the generic with the typological conception, marks the thinking in collective groups. . . . For centuries this mentality has fostered hatred among nations and communities." Ibid., 40–1.

[22] "Es ist jedes Menschen Mitverantwortung wie er regiert wird." (Every person is co-responsible for the way he is governed). Importantly, Jaspers has in mind here a responsibility that exceeds formal mechanisms of democracy, thereby allowing that political guilt also obtains in non-democratic political systems. Ibid., 31.

Moral guilt is the subjective sense of regret that one should feel when one does something that is wrong in an absolute or ideal sense, even if self-defense, duress, or other circumstances provide excuses or justifications from the point of view of the criminal law, and so remove it from the purview of criminal guilt.[23] Finally, metaphysical guilt is a guilt based on our common identity as *human*. It is strongest where the wrong occurred "in our presence or with our knowledge", but because at base it arises through human solidarity, we bear this guilt for all wrongs inflicted by human beings; indeed, to "free themselves [ourselves] from metaphysical guilt, they [we] would be angels."[24] For this reason, it lies beyond the reach of any human institution, or as Jaspers puts it: "jurisdiction lies with God alone."[25]

Despite the encroaching reach of these categories of guilt, right up to the inescapable universal scope of metaphysical guilt, Jaspers insisted that individuals alone are the proper subjects of guilt, save under two circumstances.[26] First, and most obviously, a collective can be liable in the *political* sense, insofar as it is responsible for establishing the political leadership that then sanctions the wrongful acts. Beyond this, Jaspers also suggested that there was a type of political-moral guilt that collectives can bear by virtue of the fact that political conduct not only is the outcome of specific acts of authorization, or even the more general authorization of a government, but are underpinned in a more pervasive way by a society's background morality.[27] His description resonates powerfully with the Australian scene:

Moral failings cause the conditions out of which both crime and political guilt arise. The commission of countless little acts of negligence, of convenient adaptation of cheap vindication, and the imperceptible promotion of wrong; the participation in the creation of a public atmosphere that spreads confusion and thus makes evil possible – all that has consequences that partly condition the political guilt involved in the situation and the events.[28]

---

[23] For an early and comprehensive treatment of how this conflict plays out in the conflict between natural and positive law, see L.H.A. Hart, "Positivism and the Separation of Law and Morals," and Lon Fuller, "Positivism and Fidelity to Law – A Reply to Professor Hart," both in *Harvard Law Review* 71, no. 4 (February 1958): 592, 630. Jaspers insisted that moral guilt was not the appropriate subject of criminal prosecution but rather goes before the tribunal of oneself and those "sharing a common fate." Jaspers, *The Question of German Guilt*, 42–3.

[24] Ibid., 33.

[25] Ibid., 32.

[26] "To pronounce a group criminally, morally or metaphysically guilty is an error akin to the laziness and arrogance of average, uncritical thinking." Ibid., 42.

[27] "The conduct which made us liable rests on a sum of political conditions whose nature is moral." Ibid., 76.

[28] Ibid., 34.

Applying Jaspers' inventory, quite clearly the Australian Prime Minister was assuming that apologizing implied criminal guilt. From his point of view, rejecting both collective and inter-temporal responsibility was a logical corollary of a definition of justice and responsibility appropriate to a modern democratic liberal nation that had progressed to appreciate the dangers of collective attribution; and from within this frame of reference, his stance was undeniably legitimate. The fault is not within the discursive or interpretive field he established; it is with the establishment of the field. Thus, the effect of his pegging guilt at this most demanding and most individualistic level was that the criteria for the types of involvement that could legitimately be the basis of an apology became impossibly narrow. Having thus established the ground rules, it seemed natural to conclude that apology was an inappropriate, even an unjust response. The slippage one has to catch here is that those who advocated the apology were assuming that it implied not criminal guilt, but rather political or political-moral guilt. If one recognises that it was this structural or interpretive difference that was at work, one understands that what entrenched the conflict was not an absurd disagreement about whether contemporary Australians should have been responsible in this criminal sense (clearly, they should not), but rather over whether it was *this* type of responsibility that apologizing implied.[29]

The Senate Committee mandated to examine the implementation of the Inquiry's recommendations remarked on this shift in levels when it assessed the Commonwealth's response.[30] It pointed out that despite the fact that the Commission had recommended a *parliamentary* apology (emphasizing the institutional dimension of the wrong), the Prime Minister had consistently shifted the frame to Australians as an aggregation of individuals. The following statement is typical: "To say to them that they are personally responsible and that they should feel a sense of shame about those events is to visit upon them an unreasonable penalty and an injustice."[31]

This statement is particularly interesting because of what the Prime Minister does with the idea of *injustice*. He draws it away from the original victims, and delivers it to white Australians who, in being blamed for something they did not

---

[29] An alternative way of framing this would be to distinguish, as Mamdani does, between perpetrators and beneficiaries and between the two forms of justice, criminal justice and social justice, that follow from them. Mahmood Mamdani, *When Victims Become Killers: Colonialism, Nativism, and Genocide in Rwanda* (Princeton: Princeton University Press, 2001).

[30] Senate Legal and Constitutional Committee, *Healing: A Legacy of Generations*, 115.

[31] Commonwealth, Parliamentary Debates, House of Representatives, 26 August 1999, pp. 9206–7 (the Hon. John Howard, MP).

do, can now justifiably count themselves as victims of an illegitimate *penalty*.[32] Correlatively, it is now those who would falsely accuse who are guilty of an injustice. This reversal is effected first by assuming that the relevant category underpinning the apology is criminal (direct individual) guilt, and following from this, that the real injustice at work here is the misattribution of responsibility. Once again, one should be clear that this shift was not (or at least not entirely) a matter of bad faith, but emblematic of deeper differences in political and moral philosophy. Howard's line here was fully consistent with the strong ethical individualism that followed from his party's liberal political philosophy, a political philosophy that ardently resists any transfer from the collective to the individual or across generations and that had, under his leadership, moved even more strongly in the direction of a fierce individualism that resisted all structural analyses of injustice or suffering. Similarly, it was consistent (one might even argue co-terminous) with the post-reformation Christian understanding of apology as an individual, personal expression. Both sit uncomfortably with the collective/performative trope of apology.

Thus, consistent with the foundational liberal principle that no individual should be punished for what he or she did not actually do, what was important was to tailor public policy so as to avoid this injustice. From the alternative perspective, what was unjust was the failure to attribute responsibility where it *did* lie.[33] Mapped against these two types of injustice, one can understand the trajectories of the two groups: on one side, the refusal to apologize represented a fear of straying too far towards the first type of injustice (wrongful attribution of criminal guilt); on the other, the impulse towards the apology represented an appeal against the omissions of the second (failure to attribute political guilt). If the Prime Minister stood for protection of the individual at all costs, the apology movement represented an attempt to balance out the excesses wrought by this principle. Depending on which perspective one takes, which definition of

---

[32] A similar reversal was developed in response to the *Mabo* decision and native title legislation, where white Australians were presented as the victims of a new form of land theft. These particular instances should also be understood within the context of the broader phenomenon of 'reverse racism', often accompanied in the Australian context with resentful references to excessive 'government handouts' to Indigenous people. In the survey of Perth residents noted above (note 16), 44% of white respondents saw themselves as disadvantaged when compared with Indigenous Australians. See Iyer, Leach, and Pederson, "Racial Wrongs and Restitutions," 272.

[33] Augoustinos and LeCouteur argued that very few of those who argued in favour did so on the basis of collective guilt, and that acknowledgement and sympathy were their most significant reasons. Their conclusion, however, is based on a narrower understanding of collective responsibility than I employ. Martha Augoustinos and Amanda LeCouteur, "On Whether to Apologize to Indigenous Australians," in Branscombe and Doosje, *Collective Guilt*, 247.

responsibility one assumes, and where one locates apology against the different forms of responsibility, justice demands different responses. The most comprehensive and fullest expression of justice, however, requires a differentiation of forms of justice and responsibility and tailoring appropriate forms of justice for each.

If the disagreement had gone no further than this first objection, then the map of the Australian debate would have been relatively well defined, and the link between the different positions, different theories of responsibility, and different interpretations of apology relatively straightforward. One might imagine the liberals on one side, defending the sanctity of the individual, and the communitarians, or those who adopt a more structural analysis, on the other side, advocating a collective response. The former assume that the apology is individual; the latter accept that it implicates the collective *qua* collective. In truth, however, the field was not so clearly divided.

Critics of the Prime Minister pointed out that his apparently staunch moral and legal individualism was based less on principle than on pragmatics. He did not, for example, seem to have an objection in principle to the notion that contemporary Australians might be linked with other aspects of their collective past. He had never shied away from encouraging Australians to swell with pride when they contemplated the heroism of the Anzacs at Gallipoli or the lauded cricket hero Don Bradman's batting record.[34] Clearly, his brand of conservative liberalism did not prelude all recourse to the thicker notion of the nation, either intertemporally or across bodies. What seemed to be a problem was not inheritance per se but the negative inheritance.[35] When his critics pointed out this asymmetry, they were echoing the same point that Jaspers' student Hannah Arendt had made fifty years earlier when she observed that "we can no longer afford to take that which was good in the past and simply call it our heritage, [and] discard the bad and simply think of it as a dead load which by itself time will bury in oblivion."[36] Of course, Arendt, the critic of nationalism's excesses, was well aware that forgetting, as Renan had pointed out, played perhaps an even more important role than (accurate) remembering when it came to the business of nation building.[37]

---

[34] Stephen Muecke, "No Guilt with Black Armband," *Australian Financial Times Review*, 11 April 1997.

[35] Notably, the lead critic in this regard was the liberal political theorist Robert Manne: "[I]f it is possible to feel pride in the achievements of our forebears, it surely cannot be regarded as impossible or unjust to feel shame about past wrongs." Robert Manne, "Forget the Guilt, Remember the Shame," *The Australian*, 8 July 1996.

[36] Hannah Arendt, *Origins of Totalitarianism* (New York: Harcourt Brace, 1951), ix.

[37] "Forgetting, I would even go so far as to say historical error, is a crucial factor in the creation of a nation, which is why any progress in historical studies often constitutes a danger for [the principle of] nationalism." Ernest Renan, "What Is a Nation?" in *Nation and Narration*, ed. Homi Bhaba (London: Routledge, 1990), 11.

As Edmund Burke, ever the political realist, put it, corporate bodies such as nations "are immortal for the good of the members, but not for their punishment."[38]

As became increasingly evident through the debate, the Prime Minister was in fact not immune to broader discussions about the collective history of the Australian nation. On the contrary, he revealed himself to be heavily invested in protecting a particular understanding of Australia as an honourable, egalitarian nation from the destructive effects of 'black arm-band history'. His refusal to have Australians implicated in removal was thus not simply a refusal to link contemporary debates and political action with a broader engagement with the nation's history and identity. His refusal to apologize was also a representative collective act: he was representing (both in the sense of speaking for and giving a representation to) the Australia that had consistently acted in accord with its morally laudable constitutional principles. Indeed, in his original 1997 speech, he referred to the events in question as "blemishes" in the "overall story of great Australian achievement" and insisted that "the overwhelming majority of Australians who [were] proud" of the country's achievements would repudiate this deliberate distortion of the national narrative.[39] Nevertheless, the Prime Minister's rhetorical stance on the defence of the individual from collective blame proved paradoxically useful in strengthening the case *for* apology, because it forced apology's advocates to develop a far more sophisticated justification for a collective inter-temporal apology and with this a deeper exploration of its meaning.

3. REFRAMING APOLOGY: THE INTRODUCTION OF SHAME

Several moves were deployed to counter the Howard-style objection to wrongful collective attribution. The first, which one might call the 'avoidance of responsibility' move, was to side-step the problem of responsibility altogether by redefining apology as an expression of regret or empathetic sadness rather than an assumption of responsibility in any form.[40] Saying sorry did not mean: 'I/We did this terrible thing, I/we acknowledge my/our wrongdoing and

---

[38] Edmund Burke, *Reflections on the Revolution in France*, ed. Conor Cruise (New York: Penguin Books, 1968), 246.

[39] John Howard, Opening Address to the Reconciliation Convention, 27 May 1997.

[40] The Senate Committee made note of this difference: "An apology, by definition, is a 'frank acknowledgement', by way of reparation, of offence given. . . . By contrast, the intention of an expression of regret may be defined as a 'grievance at', or 'feeling of distress' on account of an event, fact or action. By these definitions, an expression of regret may be seen as something less than an apology as it is only one aspect of a complete apology." Senate Legal and Constitutional Committee, *Healing: A Legacy of Generations*, 112.

apologize', but rather 'I am sorry that this happened to you (or to us)'. This had, of course, been the Prime Minister's own attempt at pragmatic compromise, but it was also adopted by figures on the other side seeking a middle and conflict-free ground. Sir Ronald Wilson, for example, who had jointly headed up the National Inquiry, took this avenue, both by shifting the rhetorical form from 'I am sorry for (our actions or inactions)' to 'I am sorry that/I regret that', and by explaining that apology was an act of solidarity, not an admission of responsibility.[41] But, as the analysis in Chapter Two made clear, shifting from 'I am sorry for' to 'I am sorry that' does not merely affect the degree to which one is apologizing, but structurally changes it from one type of speech act to another. In effect, all this reframing did was at best skirt around the real point of disagreement over what had, after all, made the recommendation so poignant and evocative in the first place, and from where everyone knew it really lay: with hard questions about responsibility. When the Federal Parliament finally issued its muted expression of regret in 1999, for example, it did not pacify apology's by now embittered proponents, but only provoked further scorn.

Far more important were those moves that, in keeping with Jaspers' strategy, attempted to retain the link between apology and responsibility, while altering both how we conceptualise the wrong and the way in which responsibility is attributed. The simplest version was to define the agent of wrongdoing as 'the state', thus attributing responsibility along formal institutional lines, rendering it consistent with liberal principles regarding individual responsibility. Recall, the formulation, legitimation, and implementation of removal policies had all been carried out under the authority of the state and under the colour of law. With this in mind, the Human Rights Commission responded to the Commonwealth's objection to intergenerational responsibility by pointing out that the Commonwealth was well aware that 'the state' is an institution that transcends any particular government in power (located at a distinct time), and as such, the contemporary state inherits the debts (as it does the surfeits) of its earlier incarnations.[42] By way of analogy, the Commission pointed to the arena of international law, where each government inherits the legal commitments, economic debts, and so on of its predecessor governments.

This move does indeed avoid the grosser problems of collective attribution, but only at the price of losing a great deal of the specific type of attribution apology implies. Certainly, I have argued against interpreting political

---

[41] In a letter to *The Australian* written in response to an editorial criticizing the apology on precisely this point, Sir Ronald Wilson wrote: "I hope that your readers will not understand the plea for an apology that comes the Stolen Children Report to be a plea for that kind of apology." *The Australian*, 10 November 1997.

[42] Senate Legal and Constitutional Committee, *Healing: A Legacy of Generations*, 112.

apologies as mere extensions of personal apologies or (as per Trouillot's critique) casting them entirely within the discourse of the modern liberal individual. At the same time, to cast apology as a purely formal and institutional mechanism attributing responsibility to the institution of 'the state' is to miss the active social and cultural dimensions of the constitution of rules of belonging, civility, respect, and participation. It was not just at the level of laws that Indigenous people were accorded lesser rights, but also at the level of social interaction and the meanings that circulated in and organize civil society, the dimension that Jaspers called the moral-political.

Attributing responsibility to 'the state' also relies on the somewhat problematic conceit that the state was acting illegally. If we go back to the analysis of the Australian laws in question, the heart of the claim was precisely that the state was acting according to a legality that was wrong. One could try to characterize that wrongness in legal terms by specifying a higher order law that the laws in question contravened, the likely candidates being constitutional or international law. In the Australian case, however, one would find little joy here. At the time of removal there was (and for that matter still is) no relevant constitutional proscription against such laws. Similarly, the applicable international legal instruments (such as the U.N. Convention on the Elimination of All Forms of Racial Discrimination, ratified by Australia in 1972) attained legal force only after removal had petered out. Even the Genocide Convention, which had come into force in 1948 (and which Australia had ratified in 1949), had been enacted in Australia in a manner so as to preclude domestic violations. Nor would appeals to customary international law get one very far given the contemporaneous practice of states; jurisprudence of human rights bodies and writings of learned experts had hardly provided unambiguous condemnation of racial discrimination – far from it.

The only way to describe the wrongfulness of the laws as a *legal* wrong would be to invoke the existence of natural laws that were not yet embodied in any positive law (or even customary international law).[43] In that case, however, what one is really talking about is a universal, atemporal binding set of *moral* standards. And the subject bound by those standards cannot be said to be the formal institution of the state, but must rather be the people themselves, or their societies. To make sense of the claim, then, one has to assert that the people of Australia, or Australian society, should have prevented these wrongful laws from being enacted. If this is the argument, however, it no longer works to argue that responsibility is transmitted along formal institutional lines. Indeed, the legal and moral inheritances have parted company.

---

[43] This is the substance of the Hart Fuller debate noted above.

This dilemma points to a more comprehensive problem with the assumptions at work here. If one assumes that action can only be *either* formal and institutional *or* individual and personal – an act of the state or an act of the individual (or aggregate of individuals) – then one is forced into one of two characterizations of apology. Either apology adheres to the state in a dry institutional sense, thus in no way engaging the members of the political community, or the apology adheres to each member of the nation in a very personal way. If one chooses the former, one avoids the problem of blaming the wrong individuals, but one is left with a very impersonal characterization that does not fully capture what it means to apologize. One also loses the moral/cultural dimension to which Jaspers pointed and which came through so powerfully in the analysis of the last chapter. If one takes the latter path, one has regained the sense that the apology implicates human subjects and the broader cultural context in which they interact, but has also opened up the habitual problems of inappropriate attribution and collective guilt. Constrained within these permutations one is left with no choice but to conclude that if it is an apology (and hence reflective of the inner subject), it is not political (institutional), and if it is political/institutional, it is not an apology.

But this conclusion is an artefact of the framework, the assumption that there are only two mutually exclusive realms of action: political action, which is collective and institutional, and individual moral action, which is internal and subjective. The complex co-constitution between individuals' identities and subjectively held normative frameworks and formal public institutions means that the concept of 'institutions' falls out of this picture altogether. Elsewhere, most notably in the work of discourse or process theorists, this dichotomous framework has been well and truly taken apart. The problem is that this reframing has not penetrated legal discourses or thinking about mechanisms for dealing with systematic wrongs in the past. The re-emergence of the political apology forces a re-evaluation of this framework as a model for contemporary political action. I return to this in the next chapter.

If one moves outside the officially designated political realm, as it has been defined in modern liberal theory, over to the realm of religious institutions, one does find recognition of this inter-penetration, and indeed one in which apology is central. Recall, in Chapters Three and Four, I elaborated a form of collective apology that was neither a hard institutional mechanism nor an expression of the internal soul. This trope provides a template for conceptualizing the apology *and* political action outside the constrictions of this set of distinctions. The problem is that the *form* of the mechanism has been conflated with the particular substantive content of the normative commitments with which it has historically been associated. This, combined with the problem of carving out a space for individual dissent and divergence within collective forms, has disqualified such a religious source as an appropriate model for contemporary political practice. If, however, we can abstract the form from the content, and work out some of the more serious issues around ensuring individual freedom within this collective framework, this model does seem to offer a framework that breaks through the problematic dichotomous structure identified here.

Returning to the actual terms of the Australian debate, what is fascinating is that when Australians tried to develop their own conceptual scheme to make sense of their political apology in the face of these problems, what they came up with was remarkably similar to the understanding that came through in my analysis of the second religious trope. Participants in the debate made various attempts to explain the link between the state – as the agent with continuous responsibility – and society or the population. First they drew this link through the notion of representation and the institution of democracy. In its response to the Commonwealth's claim that one generation should not inherit the responsibility of the last, for example, HREOC attempted to bring the people back into its institutional argument by framing responsibility not only in horizontal terms across time, from government to government as representatives of the state, but also vertically: from the people to government in its capacity as their democratically elected representative.[44] Insofar as the people are the source of the government's authority, they are then tied in with each government's assumed obligations.[45] The major weakness of this move was that even if it explained the link between society and the government in a single time frame, it did not explain how the vertical and horizontal could combine to link society in one moment with a government in another.[46]

---

[44] "The claim of a current government's lack of any direct responsibility for the actions of past governments overlooks 'a fundamental and enduring feature of Australian democracy, that of continuing responsible government'. That is, the concept that governments are 'responsible' in the sense that they are answerable to the people through an election. This responsibility becomes continuous through being an integral part of the institution of government." HREOC, *Bringing Them Home: Implementation Progress Report, The Report of the Follow Up Project on the Progress of Australian Governments' Responses to and Implementation of the Recommendations Made by National Inquiry into the Separation of Aboriginal and Torres Strait Islander Children from Their Families in Its Bringing Them Home Report (1997)* (Sydney: September, 1998), [7.1].

[45] For elaboration of this conception of responsibility as it came down through Hobbes and Weber, see Hanna Fenichel Pitkin, *The Concept of Representation* (Berkeley: University of California Press, 1967), esp. 19–20.

[46] David Miller's co-operative practice model, which he uses to link members of a collective with acts committed by particular individuals, will similarly only draw in those members who were actively part of a cooperative endeavour and will not persist across time. David Miller, "Holding Nations Responsible," *Ethics* 114 (January 2004).

A variant on this move, developed in part to skirt the temporal restriction, drew on the idea of the idea of the 'name of the people'.[47] According to this argument, the people of the nation should be understood not simply as particular bodies but as a corporate source of authority and legitimacy for the state, much in the same way as one might think of the nation. In this broader capacity, 'the people' is always in some way responsible for actions committed under the stamp of its name, given that it is this name that lends the actions their authority. Like the democratic argument, this is an argument about representation, but one where representation is based on a type of symbolic identity rather than institutional delegation. Precisely for this reason, many Australians remained uncomfortable with this deployment of the idea of the nation as an identity across time, a discomfort that was only heightened by their assumption that apology in particular implicated them in a very personal and individual way.

The richest move adopted a different strategy. Rather than shifting the specification of *who* it was that was responsible (the state, the people, the name of the people), it approached the problem by shifting the specification of what it was that apology implicated about the apologizing subject (apologizer). Thus, instead of accepting that apology implied guilt, as the Prime Minister had insisted, and as conveyed in his use of the term *penalty*, it was suggested that what apology implied was shame, and the criteria for guilt and shame are importantly different.[48] This was despite the fact that they were rhetorically collapsed by the Prime Minister.[49] Specifically, shame does not imply the direct assumption of individual responsibility for past wrongdoing that guilt entails.[50] Accordingly, people can be asked to partake in a shared experience of shame without this implying that they are being blamed for the wrongdoing itself, a blame that provokes the various problems of individual responsibility.[51] This seems like a fertile direction, but to

---

[47] Recall the similar rhetorical device adopted by Adenauer in his 1952 statement concerning responsibility for the crimes of Nazism.

[48] "Guilt is not the same as shame and trying to get out of one doesn't let us out of the other. Guilt ... operates in the realm of personal breach. Shame, on the other hand, operates in the realm of honour and dishonour ... while guilt is often limiting in that it draws down into individual acts of wrongdoing, shame can in a sense be a spur back into our common humanity." Drusilla Modjeska, "A Bitter Wind Beyond the Treeline," address at the 1997 NSW Premier's Literary Awards, excerpt published in the *Sydney Morning Herald*, 18 September 1997.

[49] In John Howard's Reconciliation Conference speech, for example, he identified "a sense of national guilt and shame" as an impediment to reconciliation.

[50] Raimond Gaita, "Genocide, the Holocaust and the Aborigines," *Quadrant* 41, no. 11 (July, August 1997): 18.

[51] "Because guilt for wrongs done is always a matter of individual responsibility an idea of collective guilt genuinely makes no sense. An individual cannot be charged with the crimes of others ... however talk of sharing a legacy of shame is quite another thing." Robert Manne, "Forget the Guilt, Remember the Shame."

make good on the claim that it solved the problems associated with apology, guilt, and responsibility, two links had to be elucidated. First, the specific quality of shame's implications for the shamed people had to be explained, and precisely how it differed from guilt had to be spelled out. Second, a justification had to be provided for why contemporary Australians ought to experience shame for events in their nation's past.

With respect to the first, the basic, distinguishing characteristic of shame is that one can legitimately experience it without having actually committed the wrongful act oneself, a necessary condition for criminal guilt. For shame, a more indirect association with wrongdoing or harm is sufficient. To explain why action is not a necessary condition for shame and to elaborate what the necessary conditions are, shame's proponents argued that guilt and shame correspond to two distinct dimensions of persons: action in the former case, identity in the latter.[52] This move might seem to do little to allay the fears of those who wanted to protect individuals from the dangers of gross collectivism. On the contrary, one of liberalism's fundamental principles is that it is only people's actions and not their ascriptive identities that are relevant for the purposes of public judgements. Blaming individuals for who they are, or the group they belong to, would seem to be the worst form of unjust attribution.

But the advocates of this approach insisted that this unequivocal rejection of any reference to identity involved a denial of the constitutive role that national or cultural context plays in forming individuals and, in turn, a denial of the role that individuals play in perpetuating national cultures. The liberal political theorist Robert Manne, for example, explained the justification for feeling collective shame by arguing that Australia is a place where identity is formed: "To be an Australian is to be embedded or implicated in this country's history in a way outsiders or visitors cannot be."[53] Those defending the apology as an expression of shame argued that for the purposes of political shame, one could legitimately assume an expansive conception of identity. Desmond Manderson, for example, suggested that the subject whose identity is the basis for shame can extend across bodies and time: "because shame is about identity, an identity which extends beyond my body to my society, I can and do feel shame for acts which I did not cause or bring about."[54] Crucial to this understanding, of

---

[52] "Guilt is about taking responsibility for what we did – it stems from our actions ... shame is about *who we are*." Desmond Manderson, "Shame Is Part of Healing Process," *Sydney Morning Herald*, 28 January 1997.

[53] Manne, "Forget the Guilt, Remember the Shame." The constant use of the word 'dwelling' with reference to the past is also interesting here. When objecting to the apology, many critics spoke about not dwelling in the past, thus invoking the conception of the past as a home, an environment.

[54] Manderson, "Shame Is Part of Healing Process."

course, was the claim that shame and guilt were qualitatively different and that apology, *contra* the Prime Minister's definition, was not a form of penalty.

Intriguingly, this was precisely the distinction that Jaspers had used to explain the particular character of moral-political guilt. Again, he was acutely aware not only of the dangers of gross collectivism but more specifically of the link between collectivist political atrocities and late-nineteenth-century German Romanticism, with its emphasis on corporate identity. Nevertheless, he was insistent that there was a connection between the general population of the nation and systematic violations. To elucidate this connection, he played around with a series of terms such as "political culture", "the political conditions", or "the way of life in which the members of a nation are brought up" and which, in turn, "effect political events, and the resulting political conditions in turn place their imprint on the way of life."[55] One can discern in these phrases, and more elaborately in his discussions, how Jaspers was attempting to distinguish his understanding of the collective dimension of identity to more naïve essentialist Romanticism by placing his emphasis on the practices of life that are, in turn, connected with political institutions. He writes, for example:

> By these political conditions . . . all of us Germans have been brought up for ages . . . and these conditions are part of us even if we oppose them. The way of life effects political events, and the resulting political conditions in turn place their imprint on the way of life. This is why there can be no radical separation of moral and political guilt. . . . We are politically responsible for our regime, for the acts of the regime . . . and for the leaders we allowed to rise among us. . . . In addition there is our moral guilt. Although this always burdens only the individual who must get along with himself, there is still a sort of collective morality contained in the ways of life and feeling, which no individual can altogether escape and which has political significance as well.[56]

By way of example, Jaspers argues that Napoleon's leadership was only possible because of the national context in which he emerged, and indeed "his greatness was the precision with which he understood what the mass of the people expected, what they wanted to hear, what illusions they wanted, what material realities they wanted."[57] So, too, the laws sanctioning removal (and the years of silence that followed) were only possible because non-Indigenous Australians failed to see Indigenous Australians as citizens and humans just like themselves, or at least, the continuation of those legalized practices would have been impeded in the absence of this implicit support.

[55] Jaspers, *The Question of German Guilt*, 76–8.
[56] Ibid.
[57] Ibid., 77.

Structurally, shame goes behind the specific wrongs to the basic orientation, to the way in which socially dominant groups constitute their identities and the identities of their *others*, the meanings they ascribe to their own identity and to that of the excluded other. If there is an action to which shame attaches, it is something like that pervasive denigration, a looking down on, that people in marginalized groups experience as the fabric of their lives, but cannot be captured by anti-discrimination laws, as these demand judiciable instances. In this case, the shame of non-Indigenous Australians lay in their failure to recognize the full personhood of Indigenous Australians, in the persistent association between whiteness and civilization and blackness and primitivism, backwardness, or pre-modernism. Shame lay in the fact that it had been so easy to exclude Aboriginal Australians from the human and civil rights that should have been available to all Australians by virtue of their humanity and status as co-nationals.

Once articulated, shame's shift to identity, mediated through a concept like political culture or way of life, certainly struck an intuitive chord. But in a contemporary Western political context, where the idea of the self-creating liberal individual still captivates us all, it was also highly problematic. Nor, to be fair, was this just a matter of staunch neo-liberal individualists refusing to see their connections to a broader national or collective identity; as I stated at the outset, connecting responsibility to any ascriptive identity is a very problematic suggestion when viewed from the perspective of the fundamental normative principles of liberal democracy. And mere assertions about political culture were not going to be sufficient to quell those concerns. Indeed, because existing liberal theories of responsibility cannot easily accommodate this approach, it remained largely untheorized, hanging at the periphery as something that attracted popular support, but could not really justify itself. I take up this task in the next chapter.

4. SHAME, TIME, AND HISTORY

Moving the debate into the arena of shame also provided a framework for addressing a number of objections thematized around time. These were, first, that the whole apology debate was really just dragging us back to dwell in the past, whereas Australia should be forward-looking in its approach to Indigenous issues; second, that one cannot legitimately judge the past according to the moral or legal standards of the present; and third, that contemporary Australians cannot legitimately be held responsible for the actions of their predecessors.[58] Framing the apology as a performative statement about, and active intervention in, ongoing, continuous norms of the Australian nation provided a way of bypassing or blurring the apparently clean distinctions between the past and the present that underpinned all three dimensions of the inter-temporal problem. If shame links people with acts of wrongdoing through the medium of political culture (rather than through individual action), then shame's reach is determined by the lifespan of a political culture, not by the discrete temporal boundaries of the lifespans of individual perpetrators. Shame and its implied responsibility permeate so long as there is continuity in the political cultural propensities that underlay the specific actions.

To this end, proponents of the apology argued that although the bodies had changed, there were strong continuities in the problematic political culture. In Australia, there was no getting away from the conflicts and disparity between Aboriginal and non-Aboriginal people, in the past and in the present. With Indigenous people continuing to occupy the most disadvantaged socio-economic positions, advocates had plenty of ammunition for arguing that the norms that underpinned the horrendous stories and events of the past continued to inform current social and political conditions. They also had the advantage of precedent: the years of exposure of violations against Indigenous Australians had set their stage. More specifically to the issue of removal, *Bringing Them Home* contained an entire section on contemporary forms of removal, pointing out that the hugely disproportionate representation of Aboriginal children in juvenile detention centres and state care was continuous with the more explicit historical forms of removal.

The apology was very quickly connected with a range of contemporary failures of equality and recognition, most prominently the failure to accord full land rights, the poor health status of Aboriginal Australians, and the persistence of over-representation in the penal system and deaths in custody. In this sense, and in contradistinction to those who had insisted that apology dragged Australia back into the past and prevented its movement forward, apology's glance was turned away from the past, and very much towards the

---

[58] In their discursive analysis of the Australian apology, Augoustinos and LeCouteur link these with two of the most common recurring patters of racist discourse, as theorized by Wetherell and Potter. In particular, "You cannot turn the clock backwards", "Present generations cannot be blamed for the mistakes of the past", and "We have to live in the twentieth century." M. Wetherill and J. Potter, *Mapping the Language of Racism: Discourse and the Legitimation of Exploitation* (Hernel Hempstead: Harvester Wheatheaf, 1993), cited in Augoustinos and LeCouteur, "On Whether to Apologize," in *Collective Guilt*, 241.

nation-building project of the future.[59] The particular wrong of removing children became an emblem of a pattern of failure on the part of white Australia to act decently, and apology became emblematic of a change in national orientation. Many Australians recognized that they had to positively distinguish themselves from the past incarnations of white Australia if they were to stand in a different relationship with black Australians, especially now that the story of removal had become a legitimate and undeniable part of Australian history. Silence itself could no longer be mere omission, which is always more difficult to blame in liberal theory, but now became a positive act, a failure to apologize, an act of explicit rejection. As one letter to the editor in Sydney's leading broadsheet framed it: "I stood up ... and said I was sorry ... this was not an admission of guilt but an expression of empathy. I will only feel guilty if now, having learned about the stolen generations ... if I do nothing to help Aboriginal people overcome the past and build a better future."[60]

Indeed, it was undoubtedly the fact that Indigenous inequality continued to be a live social and political issue that made the stories of the past so provocative and compelling. If the normative orientation of contemporary Australia had been radically severed from the normative orientation of the past, then the stories of the past would have struck living Australians as little more than quaint, sad stories. In Australia, the story of removal could not just be a story; as soon as it was told, it stepped into an ongoing narrative, a highly charged commentary on the status of the nation.

This suggests a broader hypothesis about the conditions under which apology is likely to become a socially salient intervention: apologies for past wrongs are most likely to capture the contemporary political community in those cases where it is still engaged with similar normative conflicts. In situations where the apology concerns normative conflicts that are relatively peripheral *vis-à-vis* issues of contemporary identity or the current political agenda, it will attract relatively little attention. I return to consider the applicability of this hypothesis to other cases in Chapter Eight.

Addressing the objection to apology's putative backwards looking and impractical quality, an objection underwritten by the Prime Minister's rhetorical division between practical and symbolic action, apology's advocates insisted that shame was not simply about 'feeling bad', but had a practical, forward-looking import. Indeed, it is precisely the persistence of the norms

---

[59] In their analysis of positive and negative responses to the apology, Augoustinos and Le Couteur note that the whereas for the latter group, the apology prevented the nation moving into the future, for the former, it was seen as the prerequisite of doing so. Ibid., 248.

[60] Letters to the editor, *Sydney Morning Herald*, 15 December 1997.

that underpinned past discriminatory social organization that impede a 'future oriented' reconciliation. As Alex Boraine, former deputy chair of the South African Truth and Reconciliation Commission, said at the Reconciliation Convention the day before the launch of *Bringing Them Home*, "It is wrong to simply say, 'Turn the page'. It is right to turn the page, but first you have to read it, understand it and acknowledge it. Then you can turn the page."[61] This is all the more true when we are, in a sense, still on that same page.

What one sees in this part of the debate brings into history the abstract conceptions of time that I articulated in Chapter Three. Recall that the logic of *teshuvah* rests on the idea that while the line between past events and the present is immutable, the way in which we ethically position ourselves in relation to the past and the judgements we make about it are not. Nor are these judgements about the past irrelevant to our orientations for the future. Far from being passive, recollection and remembering are highly active and productive processes. It is this creative flexibility at the level of ethical evaluation of the past that can alter the trajectory of the future. This is particularly true when it comes to the normative expectations that are inherited from the past but that continue to shape relationships between people and identities.

Here, it is the transformation of the regard that the present has towards the past into one of shameful reception that makes possible a different future. Had the existing narrative remained unbroken, the angle of the line from present to future would be no different from the angle from past to present: one continuous line of social relations. Shame deflects that line and opens a new orientation to the future. As in the *kniefall* when the German Chancellor found himself moved to lower his body and place his head, the head of the German state, at the feet of the persecuted Jew, shame wells up in the first instance when I see the other as a subject accusing me, but then also because I recognize in myself a quality I can no longer stomach. I am moved to shame because I recognize myself as one who has failed to live up to a fundamental norm I embrace and even claim as part of my identity. At the same time, insofar as I face the other and orient myself around his or her experience and subjectivity, I recognize the other as a subject with rights and a source of truth (for me). It is, to paraphrase Adorno, the shudder of recognition that passes through me as it dawns upon me that there is another full subjectivity on the other side of my action.[62] And this, inevitably, shifts my being in the world.

---

[61] Quoted by Andrea Durbach, in "Achieving Reparations for the Stolen Generations," speech given at the Moving Forward conference, Sydney, August 2001, available online at http://humanrights.gov.au/social_justice/conference/ movingforward/speech_durbach.html.

[62] "Shudder is a kind of premonition of subjectivity, a sense of being touched by the other." Theodor W. Adorno, *Aesthetic Theory*, trans. C. Lenhardt (London: Routledge and Kegan Paul, 1984), 455.

The apology, as the relational expression of shame, would then be not simply a constative speech act reflecting internal personal guilt, but rather the performative mechanism for effecting this remapping of identities precisely through the deflection of time's arrow. As a relational expression of shame, the apology would announce the active presence of a different political cultural context: one in which the wrongful actions cannot proceed with the people's stamp of legitimacy. It would be a political and sacramental act, transforming recognition into declaration.

According to this vision, through the apology the Australian nation would be reconstituting itself on the foundation of a normative framework where whiteness was no longer a condition for full citizenship (in terms of both membership and rights) and where substantive respect for the rights of Aboriginal people would be the normative default position. In the words of two Australian commentators: "Shame ignites a healing process in which our changing sense of who we are changes our relationships with others."[63] "Shame can, in a sense, be a spur back into our common humanity."[64]

This understanding also provides a response to the second dimension of the inter-temporal objection, that apologizing means inappropriately judging the past according to standards of the present and as such constitutes an unacceptable form of retroactive justice.[65] When contemporary Australians say that 'we (taking in Australians of the past) were wrong', they are using the past as the story through which to examine and judge the frames of meaning that inform the nation across time and into the present. The judgements that an apology implies about the past are directed not to amending the (dead) past but to reshaping the (living) present and future. They are declarative statements by *and* about Australians in the present and what they continue to believe *now*. In fact, the very inter-temporality that apparently renders the apology illogical (how can *we* apologize for what *other people* in the past did?) is what makes its apparent judgement about the past viable.

In this way, the response to the problem of retroactive justice was also a response to the third temporal objection, that people today cannot take responsibility for actions of people in the past. Those contemporary actors who did not feel constrained by the principle of non-retroactivity were willing to speak across time because they accepted that the true referent of the apology was not

---

[63] Manne, "Forget the Guilt, Remember the Shame,"

[64] Modjeska, "A Bitter Wind."

[65] *Nulla poena sine lege* is a cardinal principle of liberal law and in fact one of the seven nonderogable human rights at international law. See *International Covenant on Civil and Political Rights*, opened for signature 16 December 1966, 99 UNTS 171, art. 7 (entered into force 23 March 1976).

located in a sealed past but in their own living present.[66] Their apology was by way of saying: 'We, here, today as a nation condemn the values and beliefs according to which such laws and actions were seen as acceptable'. Apologizing for an event in the past, particularly one so stark as the forced removal of children, became the dramatic occasion for declaring one's colours. Indeed, apology's internal tension, between assuming responsibility for the wrong, on the one hand, and condemning that wrong, on the other, is what makes it possible to use this speech act to shift identities and move towards the other, a regrouping towards unity and support.

Illustrated here is Austin's theoretical distinction: apology is not a constative speech that labels the past, but performative speech realizing in its own action different norms as the authoritative values of the nation. This is the paradox of the apology: the ones who apologize simultaneously acknowledge their identity as the ones who did wrong *and* establish for themselves a new normative identity as the ones who condemn the wrong. Understood as performance, it is not relevant that the particular individuals alive today who make up the human dimension of the Australian nation did not remove children. It is neither a statement about those dead Australians nor an expression of *their* remorse. It is a public constructive act by those who comprise the nation *now*, about and towards the nation from here on.

Mick Dodson, the Aboriginal man who headed the Inquiry, made explicit this inter-penetration of time in his public presentations of its recommendations:

And it's also not just about our national honour, it's about the legacy we want to leave our children and our grandchildren. Will we be the generation of Australians who go down in history as denying the truth that's been placed in our hands? Are we going to be the generation that will go down in history as being unable to face and amend the wrongs of our past? Are we going to be the generation that's recognised as being complicit in the ongoing dispossession of Indigenous Australians? Or will we be the generation that insists that we move forward into the next century of our nation with honesty, with an acceptance of shame at the parts of our history that fill us with shame? And with courage – are we going to go forward with courage, with pride, and maturity, and above all with honour? [67]

---

[66] Sunder Rajan makes a similar point: "[I]t is today, in the light of what the 'world' knows and accepts differently from the past, that it must condemn the past." Rajeswari Sunder Rajan, "Righting Wrongs, Rewriting History," *Interventions* 2, no. 2 (July 2000): 165.

[67] Michael Dodson, speech at Southern Highlands Community Centre, 2 December 1997, available at http://www.hinet.net.au/~sally/cultures/reconc4.htm.

5. NATIONAL PRIDE AND HISTORY'S DEFENCE

Often to the detriment of the goal, mobilizing shame in this way requires people to recognize their own failure to live up to an ideal self, a requirement that is not always met, particularly where there is a strong and rigid investment in a particular self-image.[68] Shame is one of the most difficult emotions to confront, and the initial experience or inkling of its arrival can provoke a more pronounced defence against recognizing that aspect of oneself of which one might be ashamed. This principle applies no less where the self with which one identifies is the nation. The commentators who advocated shame spoke on behalf of the many Australians who did want to acknowledge that all had not been well in their social home. From where they stood, the years of blatant exposure of systematic violations against Indigenous peoples and the connection between this history of violation and the constitution of the nation left no option than to acknowledge that history both with honesty and shame.

As came through in the native title debate, however, many other Australians vigorously insisted on a very different history: an honourable history untarnished by this stain of racial violation. Indeed, despite the conceit that it was his liberal individualism that led the Prime Minister to insist there could be no connection between individual Australians of today and some dark collective past, it became increasingly apparent that he was leading the defence of Australia's honourable, but equally collective, identity. Just as those demanding pro-active interventions to address Aboriginal disadvantage *now* framed their advocacy in terms of a historical legacy of past violation, so too, the Prime Minister's opposition increasingly became the platform for his lauding the egalitarian political culture of Australia past *and* present. His refusal to apologize crossed time in the same way as the arguments of those supporting it; not apologizing thus became the platform for denying that racism or the systematic denigration of Indigenous people on the basis of their race persisted in contemporary Australia. Indeed, in a reversal structurally similar to the one discussed above, commentators on the extreme right went so far as to argue that the 'myth' of the stolen generation was impeding positive measures of child protection by vilifying constructive welfare as genocide.[69]

From the point of view of my larger inquiry into the significance of political apologies per se, this dimension of the Australian debate provides particularly

---

[68] Nyla Branscombe, Bertjan Doosje, and C. McCarthy, "Antecedents and Consequences of Collective Guilt," in *From Prejudice to Inter-group Relations: Differential Reactions to Social Groups*, ed. D. M. Mackie and E. R. Smith (Philadelphia: Psychology Press, 2002).

[69] Andrew Bonnell and Martin Crotty, "Australia's History Under Howard, 1996–2007," *Anals of the American Academy of Political and Social Science*, 617, no. 1 (2008): 156.

valuable insights. In the first instance, it appeared that the primary disagreement was occurring on the plane of conceptions of responsibility (individual or collective), with the opposing positions lining up with the two different tropes of apology. But as its proponents increasingly linked the apology with shame, the centre of gravity of the debate shifted, and it became apparent that all parties were staking out different conceptions of Australia on the collective plane.

Everyone could see that *Bringing Them Home* had not been narrowly about child removal and Aboriginal suffering. The image of white Australia reflected back through the mirror of child removal was both ugly and remote from the ideal type of the 'fair go' Australia. The Prime Minister's vehement protestation that Australia's history remained at worst slightly blemished and the apology movement's call to repentance represented two responsive postures to the view in the mirror, one swollen with pride, one cowed with shame. On the Prime Minister's side were Australians deeply invested in the belief that Australia had always stood out and continued to stand out internationally as the land of the 'level playing field'. For them the dissonance of the reflected representation was too great to tolerate or accept. Through denying the facts, explaining them away, or insisting that they represented exceptional moments, their commitment was to unflinchingly uphold the nation's honour. On the other side were those who recognized that this image was continuous with the story of violation exposed over the last thirty years. They were willing to recognize and tolerate the dissonance and they saw the apology movement as an institutional opportunity to transform the nation's normative frame and its identity along this racial axis.

Most important, both assumed that the debate was now about the character of the nation. In other words, despite the individualist rhetoric of the Prime Minister, despite his insistence that the problem with apology was that it was a form of unacceptable collective attribution, *in fact* he also understood the apology as an indictment of the nation's political culture. In his case, however, he refused to accept that there was anything of which to be ashamed. He refused to accept that Australia was anything other than a country in which the norm of equality informed what Australians thought and what they did. In the eyes of both its proponents and opponents, apology was now understood as a judgement of the nation and a performative intervention in the national political culture.[70]

---

[70] This became more apparent as the apology became entangled in the "history wars". See Alan Atkinson, "Battle Weary" (Review of *The History Wars* by Stuart McIntyre and Anna Clark)," *Times Literary Supplement*, 29 August 2003, and Peter Kelly, letter to the editor, *Times Literary Supplement*, 26 September 2003. For further links to coverage of this debate, see the *Sydney Line* at http://www.sydneyline.com/Fabrication.htm. For a recent overview of the literature, see Bonnell and Crotty, "Australia's History Under Howard."

At the same time, this war over the words of history was entwined with the battle over representation in the new constitution of Australia, which was to be put to a national referendum in the final year of the millennium. In the lead up to the referendum and the centenary of federation, as Australians were seeking to forge a constitutional foundation to orient themselves for the twenty-first century, the representation of their past took on a particular salience. To paraphrase E. H. Carr's famous observation about the circumstances under which great history is written, here, inflammatory history was written precisely when the historian's vision was illuminated by insights into the problems of the present.[71]

6. APOLOGY'S NARCISSISM?

The focus of this chapter so far has been the debate that took place between apology's advocates and their liberal or conservative critics. In the main, those critics protested that apology exacted too much responsibility for the past and too much divergence in the future. There was, however, another line of criticism altogether, coming from a diametrically opposed political camp and accusing apology of doing just the opposite, that is, exacting too *little* responsibility and requiring too little in the way of radical change.

The problem with apology, according to this line of attack, was not that it constructed or reconstructed the nation's normative orientation, but that in doing so, it ultimately only affirmed a normative orientation that continued to deny the structural rupture at the heart of the nation. If one thinks back to the wording of the French apology, or the Pope's apology, one sees clearly where this criticism draws its ammunition. There, even as the apology acknowledged a historical failure, it nevertheless affirmed a core of goodness, providing assurance that at base, the nation (or Church) did have the right norms; the only problem was that some people had misunderstood or misinterpreted them or failed to realize them in historical time. Thus, it was not those fundamental orienting norms that needed to be corrected, or amended, but rather their historical realization. But what if it is not the failure to realize those foundational norms, but rather the norms themselves that are the source of the violation? If that is the case, then returning to them in however perfect a form will only reinforce the problem. In other words, if the nation is, at core, constituted around inequality or non-recognition of a particular type of other, then

---

[71] The original phrase was: "Great history is written precisely when the historian's vision is illuminated by insights into the problems of the present." E. H. Carr, *What Is History?* (London: Penguin, 1990), 37.

apology's dynamic of return to those fundamental values can never break through the conceit that underpinned the abuse.

To understand the thrust of this critique, it is important to differentiate it from more standard criticisms for which it might be mistaken, that is, those that see apology as hypocritical or worthless because it is a superficial, merely symbolic/rhetorical measure, substituting words for harder forms of 'real' justice, for example, monetary compensation.[72] This analysis accepts the value and importance of the symbolic in the construction of the political field and social relations, but faults the type of symbolic work of reconciliation that the apology does.[73] Apology is seen here as pasting together the political imaginary of the nation in a way that forecloses representation of the very real divisions and inequalities. Because harmonious unification is its ultimate value, the apology renders invisible the differences that persist (in this case those that continue to disadvantage Aboriginal people) without actually addressing them. For these critics, the Australian apology prematurely glossed the 'fractured Australia', whereas Australians needed to keep this fractured image firmly in view as continued incentive for the long road of justice that still lay ahead.

According to Gooder and Jacobs, for example, it was this reassuring discourse of a reconstructed wholeness that led to apology's popularity in Australia and not the fact that it offered genuine recognition to Aboriginal people. Apology may have claimed to affect a form of restorative justice by attending to the losses suffered by Indigenous people (of land, dignity, and sovereign political rights). Indeed, in apologizing it might have sounded like white Australia was returning to *Indigenous people* their lost ideal and objects. In fact, if apology was returning anything, it was white Australia's sense of ease with itself, the 'settlement' that the settler nation had been gradually losing as the story of its own illegitimacy had gained greater and greater currency.[74]

Whereas up to the latter part of the twentieth century, white Australia had been able to slumber in the ignorance of its own illegitimate political heritage, that comfortable slumber had been disrupted by the litany of public rememberings of its violent past. Correlatively, whereas in the early part of the century a

---

[72] "We ... do not attempt to calculate the relative merits for indigenous people of, say, a symbolic gesture as opposed to more materially grounded ones. . . . Rather we reflect specifically upon the 'psychic life' of the apology." Haydie Gooder and Jane Jacobs, "On the Border of the Unsayable: The Apology in Postcolonizing Australia," *Interventions* 2, no. 2 (2000): 231–2.

[73] "The Australian apology ... has the power to form and reform what and who is considered to be legitimate within the reconstituting imaginary. It is an utterance ... which has immense potential as a redistributive force, both material and symbolic." Gooder and Jacobs, "On the Border of the Unsayable," 231–2.

[74] See Attwood, "Setting Histories; Cowlinshaw, "On Getting It Wrong"; and Hage, *Against Paranoid Nationalism*.

range of justifying (cultural, legal, and political) discourses had assured white Australia of its rightful place, the Royal Commission into Aboriginal Deaths in Custody, the land rights movement, the *Mabo* decision, and the unceasing succession of health statistics and international embarrassments had disrupted that narrative. When these were capped by the very intimate and affecting narrative of stealing Aboriginal children, Australians could no longer avoid the ugly reflection in the mirror.

Moreover, the legitimacy they could no longer find in their own post-colonial identity now seemed to be firmly, even eternally, rooted in Aboriginal Australia. If, in the classical colonial narrative, indigeneity had been the mark of illegitimacy, now, as Gooder and Jacobs observe, it "assumed a legitimacy in excess of that which can be claimed by the colonial."[75] Of course, even as they attributed this apparent power to Aboriginal people (or identity), they were doing little more than projecting onto them what Wolfe called the position of "repressed authenticity."[76] Nevertheless, faced with their experience of lack (of a long or dignified history and hence of legitimate sovereignty) and the corresponding projection of Indigenous Australia as abundance (of history and authentic connection to the country), white Australians looked for a strategy to return their lost object. And it was at this juncture that they apologized, turning to Indigenous Australians for forgiveness as a way of restoring the lost ideal of legitimate place and nationhood. If restitution was at work here, what was restored was white Australia's national imaginary: its conception of itself as the principled legitimate sovereign nation.

The argument puts a bitter twist on what had been touted as an act of recognition and respect. The Indigenous other is asked to affirm his or her oppressor as worthy of love after all, even as legitimate in its sovereign claim, despite the very history that this process has brought into view: a history of hatred and disrespect on the part of non-Indigenous Australia. The past, then, does no more than to serve as an earlier stage in a progressive, even a redemptive history. All the threads and perspectives, no matter how disparate, can apparently be stitched together into the grand, national narrative, now in the form of the 'sorry' nation. Ideally, there would be no residues, no experiences, events, perspectives, or patterns of relation that resist integration and remain uncoded, unspeakable, beyond apology. All that would have been left behind.

To illuminate the dynamic at work here, Gooder and Jacobs use the analogy of melancholia, as Freud theorized it, and in particular, the distinction between

---

[75] Ibid., 236.
[76] Patrick Wolfe, "Nation and MiscegeNation: Discursive Continuity in the Post-Mabo Era," *Social Analysis*, 36 (1994): 126–7.

mourning and melancholia.[77] In melancholia, as distinct from true mourning (where the subject gradually, and painfully lets go of the object), the subject refuses to break with the lost object or ideal. Instead, he or she retains it by absorbing it into the ego, albeit with guilt and rage in combination with love. As applied here, the lost object is not a person, but the experience of having a rightful place in the nation or, indeed, the idea of the legitimate post-colonial nation itself. Had it taken the path of mourning, white Australia would have been forced to fully acknowledge the loss and to give up its investment in the legitimate post-colonial nation, thereby making space for a genuine reconstitution of the nation, taking into account the original Indigenous sovereignty. In their melancholic response, however, white Australians hung onto the lost object and the hope of restoring to the nation its lost legitimacy by incorporating Indigenous Australia into its reconciled self.

As theorized here then, apology does not take the subject through a transformative shame at all, where the shudder of recognition demands a reconstruction of the self. Rather, it appropriates the aspect of shame and the language of inclusion only so as to reconstitute the self-same national form and institutional rules, but now with their lost legitimacy returned to the fold. True, it involves the recognition of the historical conflict between the Indigenous and non-Indigenous, but this is only a way-station to blurring the difference between them so that all can become legitimate Australians. By distancing themselves from the acts of dispossession, white Australians symbolically join with the dispossessed and display their allegiance to the rightful values of respect and recognition. With this they can re-settle, but without subjecting those values themselves to the critical evaluation that the Indigenous perspective should be opening up.[78] Cleansed of the sullying sense of itself as the perpetrator of an illegitimate theft (of children, of land, of sovereignty), Australia can now stand proud in its national identity and better carry on the basic neo-colonial project.[79]

---

[77] Sigmund Freud, "Mourning and Melancholia," in *The Standard Edition of the Complete Psychological Works of Sigmund Freud*, vol. XIV (1914–16): *On the History of the Psycho-Analytic Movement: Papers on Metapsychology and Other Works,* ed. James Strachey et al. (London: Hogarth Press, 1958), 237–58.

[78] The Marxist/structural underpinning of the critique of "ideology" is evident here. See Elizabeth Povinelli, "The State of Shame: Australian Multiculturalism and the Crisis of Indigenous Citizenship," *Critical Inquiry* 24 (1998): 581–2.

[79] This critique is structurally similar to critical work on the use of traumatic witnessing in truth commissions. The act of giving testimony of traumatic events is understood not as a liberating process that breaks the relations of violence, but as a mimetic form of violence positioning the witness existing (dominant) structures of juridical and medical employment. See Allen Feldman, "Memory Theatres, Virtual Witnessing and the Trauma Aesthetic," *Biography: An Interdisciplinary Quarterly* 27 (Winter 2004).

In a manner not dissimilar to pity, as theorized by Arendt, apology is then more tailored to the interests of the ones giving than the ones receiving, despite its pretensions to be a project of recognition. Just as Arendt observed that pity "has just as much interest in the existence of the unhappy as thirst for power has a vested interest in the existence of the weak", now the apologizer recognizes the wrong and the other's experience only as far as is necessary to assuage the guilt of white Australians and allow them to reconcile themselves with their own troubled past.[80] As in the original assimilationist vision, where the black blood would be absorbed into the white, now the troubling otherness of indigeneity would be reabsorbed into the national imaginary. Now, however, the wish is not that the black be disappeared because it is worthless, but that it be disappeared because it is worth too much, but is out of the reach of non-Indigenous Australia, an alternative site of legitimacy that sovereignty, being one, cannot tolerate. Indigeneity is thus symbolically revalued, but in a tamed, reappropriated version. It becomes Australia's unique token, the icon it places at the beginning of its 2000 Olympic Games' opening ceremony, the identity it can now use to distinguish itself from an increasingly culturally flat West. In this sense, the apologetic act is ultimately one of narcissism and not recognition.[81]

Stepping back from this argument, one might ask what it would have to say about the overall analysis of the dynamic of apology that I have been developing. At first glance, it no doubt appears to significantly depart from that analysis. It certainly assumes a far more sardonic tone and provides a distinctive analysis of the melancholic motivation of apology. If, however, one sets aside the tenor of its judgement and its proposed aetiology, one sees that at a structural level, it is remarkably similar. In both cases, the claim is that apology's principal target is not, as one might expect, the recipient of apology. Rather, it is directed to doing something to the one giving the apology, even as the rhetorical recipient of the apology is a necessary player in the game of reforming the self. Recall the analysis that emerged when apology was examined from the perspective of speech-act theory in Chapter Two. There, I argued that the principal uptake of apology may not be forgiveness from the one to whom it is rhetorically directed at all, but rather a shift in the identity of the one who gives it.

The two analyses do, nevertheless, part ways in two related respects, first in their evaluation of the scope of the reform apology can effect on the self, and

[80] Hannah Arendt, *On Revolution* (Harmondsworth: Penguin Books, 1973), 89.
[81] "Relatedly, let us remember that the apology is as much an act of narcissistic will and desire as of humility and humanity." Gooder and Jacobs, "On the Border of the Unsayable," 244.

second in their evaluation of the implications of apologizing for the recipient of the apology. According to these left critics, it is assumed that the other is at best an instrument for what amounts to little more than a superficial reformation of the self. To my mind, there is no justification in principle for closing off apology's possibilities in this manner. No doubt there was a certain 'self congratulatory' quality to the apology movement. White Australians, the 'sorry people', could now stand proud before an international community that had of late come to look askance at the old norm of racial discrimination and, by association, at Australia. Similarly, the myth of national harmony had a deeply seductive quality for Australians, enhanced by the compensation this new romantic status offered their long felt sense of cultural lack. No longer the poor replica of Great Britain or the United States, Australia could now stake its claim to distinction as the nation with the oldest civilization on earth, flying the Aboriginal flag and hanging Western desert dot paintings in museums as much for itself as for the prospective tourist market.

Moreover, the very idea that all history, however horrific, might be integrated into the normative framework of the nation seems to presume that the existing culture is sufficiently capacious to include all strands, however disparate. One is rightly suspect of a theory that supposes that it is possible (or even desirable) to integrate all points of experience, or perspectives, leaving no residues. Can this past of abuse, exclusion, and non-recognition, so deeply built into the constitution of the nation, simply shift into recognition and inclusion? The answer is undoubtedly that it cannot. Not every experience or perspective can be written into the story, at least not without doing violence to it and to the people whose experience undergoes translation. The fact that not a single mother whose child had been taken gave testimony before the National Inquiry (even in private or in writing or by representation) poignantly captures the experiences that cannot be integrated. At a more structural level, the comprehensive legal, political, and social forms of organization that had animated the continent before the arrival of the colonizers could not be revived. They were beyond sorry.

The ultimate question is whether the reform of the self can only involve an aesthetic rearrangement of existing norms, or whether it can put those norms into question. Does the voice of the excluded other actually enter into the apologetic discourse to challenge the polity's fundamental rules, or is it admitted only conditionally, through the filter of entrenched norms that will always exclude its most challenging claims or cast them in its own image? Effectively, what this critique does is to throw us back to the problem of how to characterize the norms that orient apology, a problem raised in Chapter Three. More specifically, it demands again that we ask whether an apology can itself force revision of the norms around which a political community has constituted itself or whether it is essentially a conservative act, reinforcing the original norms. Recall, in the context of my argument that the apology in Judaism represented a means of recovenanting, I asked whether this had to mean return to a set of principles identical to those originally articulated, and indeed derived from those principles, or whether the renewed covenant might improve the old one by bringing in the results of historical moral experience. The argument of these critics is that apology, here applied to a secular political community, is always bound to the original norms. No matter how sorry we are, we are always at best affirming our original views about how things ought to be, albeit in a slightly expanded version.

Justice for Indigenous people, however, does not simply require a *quantitative* expansion of norms that are, after all, fundamentally neo-colonial. Full justice for the first and original Australians requires a more radical *qualitative* break with those norms. The issue is not simply one of re-evaluating *who* should be included, but also *what* they should be included in. Indeed, the very assumption that justice for Indigenous people can be done through the expansion of the existing vision of what justice and citizenship has meant in Australia is just another product of the underlying failure to recognize the *different* political culture and social organization of Indigenous peoples. Integrating Indigenous people into the system and norms of post-colonial citizenship will not repair the injury of non-recognition, but simply render the fractures between their perspectives and experiences and those of the one nation invisible. At best, what apology can recognize is that the historical Australia has not been true to its own normative claim to be a liberal egalitarian nation and seek to repair the disparity between the vertical (ideal) and horizontal (historical) norms. It can even expand the conceptualization of those vertical norms themselves: for example, to whom equality applies and what it means. But it cannot fundamentally contradict the essential normative orientation of the neo-colonial state. If it did, it would be affecting an absolute break in its identity and undermining its own legitimacy. And this, these critics contend, is *logically* beyond the limits of apology.

The important point to note here is that this line of criticism is not simply accusing Australians of a lack of political will or of abusing their apologetic discourse so as to conserve their original values and orientations. This is not an empirical critique of the failure of the movement to live up to apology's potential. Rather, it suggests that this type of conservative action is located at the heart of the apologetic dynamic. This is a criticism not of a contingent form of apology but of the logical possibilities of apology itself; apology can never involve a break with the fundamental norms, because logically it is those norms that provide its moral orientation.

What then is the structural or logical reason that apology necessarily entails a return to original values? Why, in apologizing, would the subject necessarily be looking back to its constitutive norms, rather than looking out to other extrinsic sources? In the case of religious communities, where the constitution of the community itself seemed to be based on a thick set of absolute immutable norms, one could understand this insistence (although even there I disputed it); but one might think that by definition liberal democracies allow for the re-evaluation of values in the light of ongoing experience. If not, then in the background is an accusation that despite its apparent normative fluidity, the secular nation is also constituted around certain thick and immutable norms and that its identity is bound up with these to the core. If this is so, then to the extent that its apology is oriented by norms drawn from an extrinsic and new source, they would not be *its* norms. Correlatively, to the extent that the members of the community adopt those new norms now as *their* norms, they would have become a different political community. In so doing, however, the polity would also be breaking with its old self, and so cannot assert the continuity of identity implied by apology.

The appeal of what claims to be a purely structural argument is certainly strengthened by the empirical facts: a country characterized by a continuous thread of structural racism. One is well entitled to expect that the next step in that trajectory will be another version of that theme, albeit in the language of remorse. What this argument fails to allow, however, is that it is precisely this logic of continuous normative identity that the dynamic of apology calls into question, and to this logic of normative continuity that apology offers an alternative. The paradox or tension that apology uniquely holds in place is the assertion of a continuity *and* a break between two conflicting normative positions or identities, and it does so by allowing that the expansion of norms in fact requires historical experience and the encounter with the other.

Recall that when I raised the limits of apology in my discussion of Mishnah Horayot in Chapter Three, I suggested that the continuity in identity in that case was etymologically conveyed in the internal connection between Torah (representing the constitutional pole) and *horah* (representing the laws in history). I circumvented the problem of reconciling continuity with radical change by arguing that although apology *logically* requires that there be some background normative commitment or ground against which historical normative standards are assessed, that ground need not be a set of fixed absolute and immutable laws. Rather, the so-called original normative or 'Absolute' pole (*Torah*) may itself be open-ended and continuously created through a history in which current articulations of the absolute confront their own limitations. In other words, there is an absolute ground, but it is revealed only across historical time. What is more, we only discover the right path when we stray from it and lose our way. What makes it possible for a subject to assert continuity and at the same time break with some of its original and fundamental commitments is precisely the dynamic of apology, where return is to a place that has not yet existed in historical time.

To insist that apology's reconstitutive work is monochromally conservative is to overlook that unique and most powerful quality that Arendt noted when she observed the radical and unique power of forgiveness. Her claim there, and mine here, is that what distinguishes the dynamic of apology is precisely this: it opens the possibility of a different future only because it simultaneously asserts continuity, but it cannot be fully, logically derived from the past. In saying sorry, Australia is indeed asserting that it was the nation that sanctioned removal, even that it is still the nation that fails fully to recognise the rights and dignity of Indigenous Australians. At the same time, apparently paradoxically, it declares that it is not that. Within the apologetic moment, it occupies the conflicting normative identities, and gestures the movement from one to the other.

What this implies is that this apology does not integrate all moments of the abusive past into a grand, harmonious narrative stretching from Australia's beginning to its current incarnation. On the contrary, it allows that there are some things that Australia, as constituted, cannot make right, that the historical Australia has committed wrongs that are beyond repair, beyond redemption, even beyond sorry. Indeed, if we recall the wording of the apologies in Chapter One, many of them said just that, that apology could never make right what was wrong, never repair what is broken. At best, it can create a punctuation point, a moment to take a breath and face the past without explaining it away.

Moreover – and this was Arendt's further point about the plurality inherent in the dynamics of forgiveness – what makes apology's radical break possible is the fact that the one apologizing does not find the source of the condemnation in its existing identity (as a bounded individual or political community), but only by virtue of the perspective of the other. In fact, it is precisely and only an encounter with the other that allows for a development of the existing norms beyond their historical expression.[82] It is no doubt true that, at worst, apology may be a narcissistic, monological act in which I look to the other as a voiceless projection of my own needs (for affirmation, for legitimacy); but at best the

---

[82] This structure of normative progress is already present in Hegel's analysis of the thief in his early Jena papers. I take this up in Chapter Seven.

apology encounter is one in which I judge myself according to a perspective that I could attain only by virtue of being open to the other. It was the other's speech, here literally the testimony of the Indigenous Australians, which tore non-Indigenous Australia out of itself and gave it a different view of itself. Taking on that perspective may, as per Gooder and Jacob's critique, be deemed appropriation, but it may also be the occasion for an expansion of the original identity. Which of these trajectories emerges will depend on the degree to which the perspective of the other actually penetrates the discourse of the nation. And this, I would contend, is a contingent and empirical matter, not a logical one. Whether, in the wake of an apology, there is a shift in political cultural orientation remains to be seen. The final act of the apology drama in Australia did, though, give reason to think that it hit a deep vein.

7. THE APOLOGY

After eleven years of a Howard-led conservative government, at the end of 2007, a new centre-left government was elected, with a national apology explicitly at the top of its political agenda. In a remarkably powerful piece of political performance, on 13 February 2008, at 9 A.M. sharp, as the first piece of business of the new Parliament, and in the presence of members of the stolen generation and their families, the new Prime Minster, Kevin Rudd, tendered a formal apology. Four former Prime Ministers from both sides of politics were also in the House, though the most recent was present only in the form of the new Prime Minister's pointed reference to the "stony, stubborn and deafening silence" of the nation's Parliament for more than a decade. That morning, silence took a different form amongst the members and guests inside, the thousands of people watching giant screens on the lawns outside, the tens of thousands gathered in city squares, and the 1.3 million watching on television as every station in the country simulcast the apology.

The apology itself was a masterful piece of political rhetoric and broadly acknowledged as such.[83] It began with a statement of respect for Australia's Indigenous peoples, briefly moved through reflection on the blemished aspect of Australia's history, and then paused to declare that we had come to a pause in history, the time to right the wrongs. Rudd then enunciated five apologies: for the laws and policies of successive governments and Parliaments that had inflicted profound grief, suffering, and loss on fellow Australians; for the

---

[83] Commonwealth, Parliamentary Debates, House of Representatives, 13 February 2008, 167 (the Hon. Kevin Rudd, MP).

removal of Aboriginal and Torres Strait Islander children from their families, communities, and country; for the pain, suffering, and hurt of the stolen generations, their descendants, and their families left behind; for the breaking up of families and communities; and for the indignity and degradation thus inflicted on a proud people and culture. He then requested that the apology be received in the spirit in which it had been given, and made seven statements about the future: that this moment opens a new page of the future; that by virtue of acknowledging the past, we might lay claim to a future that embraces all Australians; a future where the injustices of the past must never happen again; a future where we harness the determination of all Australians (Indigenous and non-Indigenous together) to close the socio-economic gap; a future of new solutions to enduring problems; a future based on mutual respect, resolve, and responsibility; and, finally, a future of genuine equality.

Following the formal apology, Rudd meticulously described the history of removal, the abuses inflicted, his own encounter with people's resultant suffering, and the reasons why it was critical for the nation to apologize. Occupying both the symbolic body of the representative of the nation and the very human body of a man profoundly affected by shame and sadness for the suffering of particular human beings, his speech navigated the complex territory of apology's personal/political character. His address closed with a call to the nation to bring the two centuries of Australia's racially divided history to a close and to enter the future with new eyes and new forms of mutual recognition. In his closing commissive, he invited all Australians, Indigenous and non-Indigenous, government and opposition, State and Commonwealth, first peoples, the first white arrivals, and the most recently arrived Australians to turn the page and begin to write a new history. The word "covenant" did not appear, but the Prime Minister had spoken one, and there was a palpable sense in the nation that a new future had been laid out before it.

The aspirational national unity was of course imperfect. After much internal struggle, the now opposition party resolved that it would support the apology, but continuous with this ambivalence, the speech that Brendan Nelson (the opposition leader) gave immediately following Rudd's was peppered with qualifications, including references to the often 'well-intentioned' nature of the policy.[84] Also consistent with a decade's battles over history, Nelson went to great pains to

---

[84] For example: "In some cases government policies evolved from the belief that the Aboriginal race would not survive and should be assimilated. In others, the conviction was that 'half caste' children in particular should, for their own protection, be removed to government and church run institutions where conditions reflected the standards of the day. Others were placed with white families whose kindness motivated them to the belief that rescued children deserved a better life." Ibid., 174.

ensure that for every acknowledgement of the wrongs experienced by Indigenous peoples, there was a parallel narrative about the struggle of the non-Indigenous peoples who 'settled' the nation. Like Rudd, he called for an act of imagination whereby we place ourselves in the shoes of others, but his concern was to ensure sympathetic imaginings of those who might be perpetrators. What he saw as balance, however, others experienced as insult; on the lawns outside Parliament House people turned their backs on the screens and in many of the public gatherings throughout the country the sound was turned off altogether. Nevertheless, when the Prime Minister invited the opposition to join a 'war cabinet' on Indigenous disadvantage, the two men reached across the chamber to shake hands, and they walked together into the gallery to embrace the Indigenous witnesses. The opposition speech raised the ire of many people who resented its meanness on a day that seemed to be about unqualified recognition; nevertheless in a relatively short time it fell back to the status of an annoyance, like a fly on a magnificent day.

Those who might have thought that after years of feet-dragging the moment would have passed could not have been more wrong; even people who had expressed cynicism about the apology or who were not sympathetic to the new government found themselves profoundly involved and affected, often despite themselves. Over the following days and weeks, the press, radio, and face-to-face conversations were filled with ordinary Australians' deeply emotional responses to hearing the words, 'I say sorry' given the pride of place by the national government and an unprecedented hope that this might indeed be a turning point in Australia's political culture. As Don Watson, the historian who had penned the famous Redfern address, put it a few days later:

I think it's a different country since Wednesday. . . . It's a bit different in most of our heads, whether we're for or against it. And I think that Kevin Rudd has given a sort of moral compass to the matter of our relations with Aboriginal Australia. . . . It's the sort of thing by which we can steer in future . . . next time a bureaucracy, State government, Federal, or whatever, fails to provide those things they have promised to provide, or are supposed to provide in Aboriginal communities, then they can in some way be held to moral account. That's what words can do for the country, and I think Kevin Rudd's words were of that order.[85]

Stepping back finally to take an overview of the Australian apology debate, one can discern several revealing patterns. First, the two initial dominant and conflicting interpretations of apology coincided with the two tropes of apology we

---

[85] "Reflections on the Apology," *Saturday Extra*, Radio National, 16 February 2008.

traced from its religious history. This religious precedent was of course not made explicit, but resonance between understandings people assumed and those that emerged from the analysis of rituals of repentance in Judaism and Christianity is striking. One might even conjecture that this religious ritual provided the background template out of which this contemporary idea sprung, albeit without attribution or knowledge of its providence.

Second, as the debate deepened, it became evident that all parties assumed that what an apology did was provide a performative summary of the character of the nation. Where they parted company was on the veracity of a shameful representation, but they converged in reading it as constructive performance directed to shifting the normative identity and commitments of the apologizing subject. Thus, *as it played out* the apology was or was broadly understood as a means of collective reconstitution of the normative identity of the apologizing subject. *Contra* an abstract analysis of the nature of modern liberal consciousness that would insist that essentially and necessarily apologetic speech represents inner transformation and thus that it has no place in politics, it is the second trope of apology as reconstitution of the collective (the nation) that gained currency.

That said, the emergence or living currency of this second trope is no simple supplement to modern liberal polities, and this not only is because rituals of repentance seem to belong elsewhere. It is also because they imply a challenging conception of responsibility. The shift of attention apology effected from what particular individuals did to the socially constituted relations in which they could do it sits uncomfortably with contemporary moral and legal theories and institutions of responsibility. Nor is the inclusion of this dimension of responsibility a simple matter of adding another category. On the contrary, it represents a distinctive break with the traditional liberal jurisprudence of responsibility, which vehemently insists that only actions, not identities (especially collective ones), are the proper subject of evaluation when it comes to meting out justice. And yet, as Rajeswari Sunder Rajan pointed out, "wrongs of such magnitude as slavery, genocide and colonialism, as transcendent acts of theft, pillage, murder and dispossession, have overwhelmed the law's grasp and reach."[86] And they have overwhelmed it, structurally, not incidentally, because they take place under the sanction of laws and under the authority of political orders that have been socially, culturally, and nationally defined so as to normalize them.

To expand Stanner's metaphor of the window placed to exclude a certain part of the scene from view, the whole Australian house had been built on the

---

[86] Rajan, "Righting Wrongs, Rewriting History," 165.

foundation of racially based exclusions and forgettings. The title of the report, *Bringing Them Home*, now becomes especially poignant. It is not enough to throw out some aberrant housemates or even to make some minor renovations and open some windows; we must step outside the house, take a look at what its foundations conceal, and assume responsibility for the abuses that have happened. Then they can come home.

As the Australian case has so poignantly demonstrated, however, assuming this dimension of collective responsibility is not something we moderns are comfortable doing for a number of reasons, some good and some not so good. Amongst them is the fact that we are lacking a convincing or coherent framework for explaining how it is that we bear some collective responsibility for systematic wrongs. It is to this task that I now turn.

7

Apology's Responsibility

In recent years, the concept of *constitutive justice* has emerged to theorize the various processes that fall under the rubric of transitional or historical justice. Teitel, for example, thematizes the apparently disparate mechanisms deployed to deal with the past in transitional situations (trials, truth commissions, memorials, compensation, forgiveness, lustration, and compensation) by placing in relief the contribution each makes to constituting the social and political conditions under which all members of the society will be better protected from human rights violations and arbitrary interference.[1] Although apology has received but scant attention in the transitional/ historical justice literature as conceptualized here, it is explicated without difficulty by this model. Nevertheless, this constitutive, future-oriented role does cancel out the fact that in apologizing, contemporary political communities are taking responsibility for past wrongdoing. As we saw in the Australian debate, there was no getting away from that dimension of apology. What this means is that a comprehensive analysis of apology must do more than integrate it into an expanded conception of justice in its reparative and constitutive forms; it must also attend to the dimension of apology that is backward-looking and retains unavoidable implications of collective responsibility.

---

[1] Ruti Teitel, *Transitional Justice* (Oxford: Oxford University Press, 2001). Here I have collapsed liberal and democratic justifications. On the former see Judith N. Shklar, *Legalism: Law, Morals and Political Trials* (Cambridge, Mass., and London: Harvard University Press, 1964), 145; on the latter, see Leora Y. Bilsky, "When Actor and Spectator Meet in the Courtroom: Reflections on Hannah Arendt's Concept of Judgment," *History and Memory* 8, no. 2 (1996): 137. For a different way of thematizing the field, see John Torpey, "Introduction," in *Politics and the Past*.

If this is the case, and we accept that in apologizing contemporary political communities are also acknowledging some form of collective responsibility, we might explain this in two ways. It may be that when they apologize, they are indulging in a form of collective responsibility inconsistent with their commitments to moral individualism; and we might conclude either that they are simply philosophically inconsistent or that the latter commitments are more partial than we thought. Alternatively, it may be that collective apologies *are* consistent with commitments to moral individualism, in which case we need a theory to combine what seem to be incompatible moral frameworks. Apology's proponents in Australia certainly believed that the latter was possible, and they laid the seeds for an alternative theory of collective responsibility by staking out apology's territory in the sphere of shame. In this chapter I water those seeds with the residues of our political theoretical tradition to see what branches they might grow.

This is not the first time I have raised this problem or offered a possible solution. In Chapter Three, I described an ontological and ethical framework within which Judaism (as a religious system) understands the collective responsibility underpinning its collective apologies. Specifically, I pointed to the way in which this framework deconstructs the individual/collective dichotomy by assuming that individuals are normatively embedded in broader ethical systems of meaning. Indeed, although I drew this explanatory system from a religious source, I argued that one can coherently abstract its inter-penetrative normative framework from the thick normative commitments associated with religious systems, thereby also abstracting a more general theory of collective responsibility. It would, however, be naïve to assume that this will suffice. For many contemporary theorists and citizens, any conceptual framework derived from religion will be too tainted with thick morals and 'bad collectivist' ontologies to serve as a generalizable template; my argument will demand too much faith in an alternative reading and imaginative translation. To fill that gap, we still require a theoretical frame articulated in the language of secular epistemology and ontology.

Some of the argument required to develop an alternative conceptual framework was already rehearsed in the last two chapters, and I take this as the starting point for this chapter's inquiry. Chapter Five made it clear that we could comprehensively understand and address the violations against Indigenous Australians only if we looked beyond the particular acts (removing children) to take in the broader context that sustained a pattern of non-recognition and systematic denigration. As a sociological framework this is both fine and familiar. The problem comes when we move from a general sociological interpretation to a liberal jurisprudential framework of responsibility, because the latter can integrate a dimension of responsibility beyond the individual only along strict institutional lines, thereby admitting no space for social, cultural, or identity dimensions in which violations are embedded. Further, what obscures this moral political dimension is not incidental or extrinsic, but rather follows from the combination of liberalism's core and non-negotiable commitment to the moral integrity of the individual, its individualistic ontology, and its formula for deriving responsibility from intentional action.

If one works with liberalism's compass and starts with its ontological assumptions, there is no way of building the broader moral political context into the analysis of responsibility. Either the individual acted and chose freely (in which case he or she, possibly along with other co-actors, is entirely responsible), or he or she acted under duress (in which case the actor who so compelled the individual is responsible), or he or she was not fully rational (in which case he or she did not *act* in the full meaning of that term), or he or she acted as a delegate of an institution (in which case the actors who authorized the institution or the institution itself as a legal person are responsible). Irrespective of which venue we pursue, the gap where we might locate the societal collective lies outside liberalism's jurisprudential gaze.

With this analysis in hand, both what it is we are looking for and where not to look come into relief. On the one hand, any viable conception of collective responsibility will have to be consistent with and leave intact an account of individual responsibility and the principle of individual moral integrity. That means avoiding several common traps: the metaphysical error of reification (the collective as an individual writ large), the ethical error of violating individual integrity, and the affront to justice of punishing individuals for events that they did not bring about.[2] A conception that fails on any of these grounds not only will meet theoretical objections, but also will not satisfy the minimal normative (albeit untheorized) commitments of ordinary citizens in liberal political communities and so will be politically unviable. On the other hand, the conception will have to be developed within a framework that does not have the ontological assumptions and criteria for responsibility underpinning liberal jurisprudence.

Unfortunately, whereas liberalism is the obvious candidate for providing the foundation for individual models of justice, there is no equivalent theoretical

---

[2] In the background here is Plato's image on the good society as an organism that, like the man who hurts his finger and feels it through his whole organism, "will regard the individual who experiences pain or loss as part of itself, and be glad or sorry as a whole accordingly." Plato, *The Republic*, trans. H.D.P. Lee (Middlesex: Penguin, 1955), section 462c–d. The classic refutation, asserting that "human beings in society have no properties but those which are derived from, and may be resolved into, the laws of the nature of individual man," can be found in John Stuart Mill, *A System of Logic, Ratiocinative and Inductive: Being a Connected View of the Principles of Evidence and the Methods of Scientific Investigation* ([1865], London: Longman, Green, 1925), book 6, chapter VII, section 1.

frame obviously offering itself up when it comes to justifying collectivist approaches. As we saw with Jaspers' early attempts to re-theorize guilt in the wake of the Holocaust, coming up with a philosophical justification for our moral intuitions about collective responsibility in a way that remains consistent with the demands of moral individualism presents a significant challenge.[3] That is the challenge taken up in this chapter.

I. RECENT ATTEMPTS TO RECONCEPTUALIZE COLLECTIVE RESPONSIBILITY

Beginning with Joel Feinberg's seminal essay on collective responsibility, a number of contemporary theorists have recognized the inadequacy of the permutations one might draw out of the idea of the responsible individual and have sought to shift their perspective from a hard legalistic analysis of the responsible institution to a more sociological analysis of the political/cultural network.[4] Feinberg's identification of the cultural context of specific violations as the effective link in the chain to the broader collective provides the basic template for a family of theories that ground collective responsibility in discriminatory cultural contexts.[5]

One sees a similar approach in Larry May's contention that what justifies attributing responsibility to a group of people is their *dispositions*, which "create a climate of attitudes in which harm is more likely to occur."[6] Like Feinberg, May identifies the pertinent collective characteristic in this zone of *disposition*, as distinct from decision, action, or even authorization. Building on

---

[3] On the tension in Jaspers' work between his human intuitions and the demands of rational philosophy, see Margaret Gilbert, "Collective Guilt and Collective Guilt Feelings," *Journal of Ethics* 6 (2002). See also Bernard Williams, *Ethics and the Limits of Philosophy* (Cambridge, Mass.: Harvard University Press, 1985), and Jeffrey Stout, *Democracy and Tradition* (Princeton: Princeton University Press, 2004), 162.

[4] In the background is Durkheim's concept of the collective conscience and his attempt to articulate social facts in a manner that mediates between external influence and subjective agency. See the preface to the second edition of 1901 in Emile Durkheim, *The Rules of Sociological Method*, trans. W. D. Halls (New York: Free Press, 1982). Despite Durkheim's awareness of this problem, his work may remain trapped by his original formulation that social facts are "external to individuals", and his correlative insistence that we see them as both external and internal, or internalized by individuals. See Stephen Lukes, *Emile Durkheim: His Life and Work* (London: Allen Lane, 1973), 11–13.

[5] This example comes under what Joel Feinberg calls "contributory group fault, collective and distributive." See Joel Feinberg, "Collective Responsibility," in *Doing and Deserving: Essays in the Theory of Responsibility* (Princeton: Princeton University Press, 1970), 247.

[6] Larry May, *Sharing Responsibility* (Chicago: University of Chicago Press, 1996), 46. May stresses that the attitudes relevant for a story about responsibility are not theoretical, or "*mere* thoughts" but rather affective states in which people are moved to *act* in certain ways.

this notion, David Miller supplements his more institutionally formal "co-op-erative practice" model of collective responsibility with the "like-minded group" model, noting that the latter can capture in its net all those who, even without *acting* or formally assenting, implicitly supported the manifest wrong-ful acts through their shared "general attitude."[7] This shift away from action or even authorization is what permits Miller to trace collective responsibility without having to meet the more onerous conditions required for institutional responsibility, such as fair decision-making procedures.[8] Iris Marion Young's term "social connection" does similar work in casting the net of responsibility over a group of people standing in the background, or off to the side of the actual wrongdoing, but who share a social or cultural space that one senses is the ground for the actual wrongdoing.[9]

Insofar as they point to the space of the cultural field and network of hard and soft institutions that provide individuals with the normative map against which they judge and act, these accounts are on the right track towards expli-cating the dimension of responsibility that is occluded when we tighten our focus to the individual actor. They shift our vision out from the one who wielded the instruments of torture or drove the child away from his or her parental home to the political cultural context and the normative community in which those acts were legitimated, albeit invisibly. However, they fall short in providing fully adequate explications and justifications of a robust conception of collective political responsibility in two important ways.

First, they are somewhat thin, still wanting a characterization of the neces-sary conditions for, and mechanisms of, responsibility at the level of detail theorists have provided for liberal accounts of individual responsibility.[10] The descriptive terms they coin to explain the community's participation con-vey a powerful impression, but remain largely unelaborated. Still missing is a comprehensive elaboration of how those who belong to this 'dispositional

---

[7] David Miller, "Holding Nations Responsible," 253–4.

[8] One should also add a note of caution regarding speaking about a normative community or group as if the outside boundaries were clear and the inside space were homogeneous. This is all the more pertinent under conditions of globalization. See Nira Yuval-Davis, *Gender and Nation* (London: Sage, 1997); Roland Robertson, *Globalizations: Social Theory and Global Culture* (Newbury Park, Calif.: Sage, 1992).

[9] Iris Marion Young, "Responsibility and Global Labor Justice," *Journal of Political Philosophy* 12 (2004). Young deals more squarely with distributive justice, although her attention to issues such as sweatshop conditions entails consideration of wrongful acts.

[10] An exception here is Margaret Gilbert, who explores different explications of the notion of "group belief" in her elaboration of Durkheim's fundamental thesis concerning the col-lective conscience. Her analytic derivation is, however, conducted at a level different from mine. See chapter 5 in Margaret Gilbert, *On Social Facts* (London and New York: Routledge, 1989).

community' are implicated in the aetiology of wrongdoing or how "single-mindedness", "folkways", or "social connection" actually works. Nor is this explanatory gap simply an affront to fastidious theorists; it also has an important practical dimension. If members of contemporary political communities are to be convinced that they have a role to play in addressing past injustice, even when no one can draw a direct line between them (as individuals) and the acts, there needs to be an account at hand to explain how it is that they are implicated in the production of these cultural dispositions and how the dispositions inform particular moral judgements and wrongful actions.

Second, these accounts do not capture the *political* dimension of this collective attribution. Thus, while concepts like "an atmosphere of racism" or a "shared mindset" gain back some of what gets lost when we tag responsibility to the institution of the state, they risk characterizing these patterns of social meaning as something extrinsic or incidental to the political character of the nation. This reactive omission is particularly pertinent in the cases we are concerned with here, where what is at issue is not simply a group of people jointly implicated in some heinous wrong. Rather, more pointedly, the wrongs are embedded in the history of a nation that is now in the process of trying to reconstitute itself as a lawful, peaceful, just, and stable *nation* into the future.

It was this gap that Arendt was pointing to when she originally responded to Feinberg's essay presented at the American Philosophical Association in 1968.[11] Arendt criticized Feinberg for substituting personal/private morality for political ethics and more pointedly objected to what she saw as a slippage from civic virtue (which belongs in the sphere of politics) to moral goodness (which does not) and a danger of grounding responsibility in the latter. Characteristically, the line she draws between social and political identity is too thick to capture the complex relationship between those realms, but her critique does point to the importance of grounding an explanation back into the sphere of the political, or in the constitution of the nation; and again, this is not just a matter of theoretical niceties.[12] From a justificatory point of view, the demand for a *political* response requires more than the mere empirical fact that

---

[11] Arendt argued that Feinberg's position "tries from the beginning to construe all issues according to models which are either legally or morally relevant, so that the political issue appears to be no more than a special case of matters that are subject to normal legal proceedings or normal moral judgments." Arendt, "Collective Responsibility," in *Amor Mundi: Explorations in the Faith and Thought of Hannah Arendt*, ed. James W. Bernauer (Boston, Dordrecht, and Lancaster: Martinus Nijhoff, 1987).

[12] In the background here is the difficult problem of linking what we might call "the nation" or "civil society" on the one hand with "the state" on the other, a linkage conveniently obscured by the term "nation-state". See Jean L. Cohen and Andrew Arato, *Civil Society and Political Theory* (Cambridge: MIT Press, 1992).

the many people who reside in this territory have all been implicated in some wrongdoing or experience some common emotion. The people of the nation can and do share in various emotions, experiences, and aspirations, but these attain the special status of being legitimate occasions for political action only if they are grounded in the political identity of the nation.

Taking Feinberg's notion of the shared disposition of the collective as a starting point, and with Arendt's proviso in mind, the next step is to tell a coherent story that explains the links between this shared disposition, the political identity of the nation, and the particular wrongs. In doing so, one must immediately resist falling back (as we are almost bound to do) on the most familiar narrative structure of stories about responsibility, that is, stories told as a causal sequence, because as soon as we adopt that structure, irrespective of our intentions, we inevitably run into a range of conundrums.[13] As soon as we use the language of cause to tell the story of responsibility, we need a *subject* capable of causing and acting. Attempting to combine this traditional metaphysics with old-fashioned conceptions of the collective leads, as we already know, to problematic reifications of the collective as some type of giant actor. Marrying this with the novel insight that collective responsibility for systematic violations resides in the "shared attitudes" or "dispositions" leads to the absurd propositions like "a cultural disposition caused an action (by the individual)".

Farid Adbel-Nour's attempt to explain how members of the polity are implicated in wrongs they did not personally commit exemplifies the instability of this marriage.[14] Abdel-Nour scrupulously avoids essentializing something like "national character", maintaining rather that what implicates an individual in otherwise remote events is his or her pride in events and achievements of his or her nation, a pride that is connected to the nation's past. When he comes to explain *how* the individual is so implicated, however, the links he draws between pride, the nation, and the specific wrongful acts are again characterized in causal terms. The problem here is not that he locates the link at the imaginary identificatory level but that the imagined relation is not compatible with the logic of causality, and it cannot meet the criteria implied by this logic; if one wants to speak about the relationship between the individual and the nation in abstract terms, one also has to find another logic.

I am not singling out this explanation as particularly incoherent. On the contrary, Abdul-Nour is very much on the right track, and he is attuned to the

---

[13] As Bernard Williams puts it, "cause is primary ... [w]ithout this, there is no conception of responsibility at all." Williams, *Shame and Necessity* (Berkley, Los Angeles, and Oxford: University of California Press, 1993), 56.

[14] Farid Abdel-Nour, "National Responsibility," *Political Theory* 31, no. 5 (October 2003).

impasses one inevitably confronts when trying to engage with what he calls the intractable debates about agency. My point is rather to shed light on the inevitable absurdity or failure of any account that gets drawn into the logical structure of the causal narrative. Here, even given the theorist's explicit care to avoid the problems of collective agency by resorting to a causal narrative to explain his conception of responsibility, he is pulled, whirlpool-like, down into that same dark hole. So long as one locates responsibility as the effect of an intended action, one will inevitably conceptualize the subject of responsibility as a cohesive intentional subject capable of action, self-consciousness, and feeling. And this is precisely the ontological characterization of the collective that violates the metaphysical, moral, and political provisos stipulated above. To use a grammatical analogy, to avoid this, one has to conceptualize a predicate (responsibility) that will not entail the type of substantiation of the subject (the collective) inappropriate to shared disposition (or an analogous term).[15]

To this end, Arendt endorsed but also sharpened Feinberg's distinction between liability and guilt, insisting that unlike guilt, which "always singles out", responsibility (as she translates liability) can legitimately hold for things one has not *done*.[16] This distinction drives a useful wedge between these two concepts, differentiating the necessary conditions in each case and, specifically, the distinct place that *action* plays in legitimate attributions of guilt and responsibility.[17] One sees a similar differentiation in theorists who, echoing the Australian debate, opt for the language of shame over that of guilt because they see the former as entailing less onerous conditions with respect to individual action.[18] The next step then is to explain the link between the

---

[15] In a similar move, Gilbert draws on the concept of members' identification with their group to rethink the common "idea that one's country is something *other* than oneself", thereby providing the path out of the indelible conclusion that nations and individuals stand in some type of causal relationship, where one has logical priority. See Margaret Gilbert, "Group Wrongs and Guilt Feelings," *Ethics* 1, no. 1 (1997): 75.

[16] Arendt, "Collective Responsibility," 147. Note, Arendt's two papers entitled "Collective Responsibility" represent her original response to Feinberg's original paper (as cited above in *Amor Mundi*) and a fuller paper, based on the original remarks but not explicitly mentioning Feinberg's paper, published in *Responsibility and Judgment*, ed. Jerome Kohn (New York: Schocken Books, 2003).

[17] Others have similarly exploited this distinction, for example: "There is no collective guilt. Whoever is guilty must answer for it individually. At the same time, however, there is such a thing as a collective responsibility for the mental and cultural context in which mass crimes become possible. And we are similarly inheritors of past events." Jürgen Habermas and Adam Michnik, "Overcoming the Past," *New Left Review* 203 (January–February 1994): 7.

[18] Larry May and Farid Abdel-Nour both embrace this move to the language of shame. Arendt raises the question of shame, albeit indirectly, in her discussion of the place that Kant accords self-contempt in moral action, and more particularly the effective moral force of self-contempt. "Some Questions of Moral Philosophy," in *Responsibility and Judgement* 63–4.

cultural context and the individual who acts, or, if we use Arendt's terminological distinction, between the responsible collective and the guilty individual, and to do this, we begin with Jaspers' suggested shift from action to
identity.[19]

2. *DASEIN* AND THE SHIFT TO A LOGIC OF IDENTITY

At first glance (and probably even second), this shift seems highly coun-
terintuitive, given that the heart of the objection against collective responsibility lies precisely with the problem of reification. Talking about collective
responsibility in terms of identity seems not only to involve a reification of
the collective (as some*thing* with an identity), but also to characterize it in
the most homogenous and essentialist terms. But we know from Jaspers'
explicit rejection of this type of collectivism that this is far from what he
wanted to capture, and in order to make this subtle differentiation, he used
the notoriously difficult term *Dasein* – that in which – *Ich mein Dasein habe* – I
have my being. *Dasein* does not of course simply denote the physical
dimensions of being, but also comprehends its cultural and political
dimensions.

To understand the way in which this notion had to be carved out to achieve
this mediation, we need to recall that in the background was Hegel's *Sittlichkeit*, a concept that enabled theorists to potentially map the subtle interplay
between individual, collective, and political dimensions, but that also paved the
way for dangerous misunderstandings. As Weber and the *Organschaft* theorists
pointed out, there was a strong drift from Hegel's formulations to a romanti-
cization and essentialization of culture and community that was far from innocent.[20] On the contrary, if *Sittlichkeit* had begun as a remedy to natural law
theory's atomization of individuals, it seemed to end up reverting to the very
logic and ontology Hegel had identified as the source of our habitual failure to
understand the unique relationship between individual and society, simply
flipping the order of priority to privilege a super-entity that subsumed

---

[19] The fact that Arendt uses this distinction while Jaspers differentiates within different types of
guilt may lead to some terminological confusion. I will generally adopt the term "responsibility"
only when referring to the collective dimension, except when I am specifically referring to
Jaspers' conception of political guilt.

[20] See, e.g., Georg Jellinek, *Allgemeines Staatslehre* (Berlin: O. Häring, 1905), and Hans J. Wolff,
Organschaft und Juristische Person (Berlin: Carl Heymanns, 1934). The critique developed
of organic forms of social organization by this group of thinkers is discussed in Pitkin,
The Concept of Representation, 40.

individuals and the spaces between them.[21] More pointedly, in the realm of responsibility, it seemed to lionize an undifferentiated form of social organization in which the actions of any member may become the basis for benefits or blame falling on the rest, justifying exactly the type of collective behaviours that moderns (Jaspers amongst them) wanted to steer clear of: blood feuds, vendettas, reprisals, and collective punishment.

Alive to the perils of pursuing this conceptual route, but still insistent on finding a theoretical basis for his intuition that the broader community was also implicated, Jaspers needed to find a way of catching some aspects of the concept of *Sittlichkeit* in a net that left behind its problematic implications.[22] The alternative path he carved out was to conceptualize *Dasein* as a field of meaning, an ongoing process of political cultural production, through which context is folded into the identity of individual members of the nation, at the same time as the judgements, actions, and aspirations of individuals form the context in which the institutions of the nation take shape.[23] In place of the metaphor of the being in space, one might think of *Dasein* as a melody that organizes those playing the instruments, but has its existence only insofar as they play it, and is transformed as they interpret it within the context of their own lives.[24]

Avoiding the reification of both collective and individual (irrespective of which is privileged) not only removes the problem of having to allocate responsibility either to the individual or to the collective (who must form a zero sum

---

[21] Hegel's work provides a fascinating case for examining how such accounts err because he approached his work with precisely the challenge of mediating the space between communal ethos and individual freedom. See Hegel, *Die Vernunft in der Geschichte*, ed. Johannes Hoffmeister (Hamburg: Meiner, 1955), 112, and *The Philosophy of Right*, ed. and trans. T. M. Knox (Oxford: Clarendon Press, 1965), section 260. Hegel's mistake (in part) was to ascribe to "the state" the type of properties that reinscribed it into an ontological structure where it could not but come into competition with the individual. See *Philosophy of Right*, section 258.

[22] Jaspers was, of course, not alone here, even amongst contemporaries. Ernst Cassirer in particular is associated with the critique of what he labelled "substantialism." See Ernst Cassirer, *Substance and Function, and Einstein's Theory of Relativity*, ed. and trans. William Curtis Swabey and Marie Collins Swabey (New York: Dover, 1953).

[23] Drawing on Jaspers, Larry May characterizes moral values as "action guiding and compelling in that they define initial (or *prima facie*) reasons for behaving in a certain way" and cultures as "both the products of individuals' prima facie actions and attitudes and the producers of new actions and attitudes in the world." May, *Sharing Responsibility*, 77 and 153.

[24] Though predating Benedict Anderson's reconceptualization of the nation by nearly forty years, Jaspers' response to this problem takes the same form as Anderson's observation that the problem with available options for defining "the nation" was that they all operated within a "metaphysics of presence" that forces one to think of these concepts as reified entities. Benedict Anderson, *Imagined Communities: Reflections on the Origin and Spread of Nationalism* (London: Verso, 1983). On the influence of this ontological habit on theories of the nation, see R.B.J. Walker, *Inside/Outside: International Relations as Political Theory* (Cambridge: Cambridge University Press, 1993).

game of responsibility), but also avoids the structural trap of having to place them in a causal relationship with each other, and thus get ensnared in the classical dichotomies of structure and human agency, functionalism and freedom of the will. Indeed, insisting both that the individual is always already operating within a pre-constituted horizon of meaning and that this field of meaning is only ever constituted by the various individuals who share a political-cultural space forces a reconsideration of the ontological status of both terms and the logical structure of their relationship. Both now become co-constitutional dimensions of a broader field of meaning, or *Dasein*. Against this background, the identity to which Jaspers was referring is not a substance that causes individuals to think or do something, but in his words, what imprints a way of life.

One might well recognize here the structure of the solution that interpretive or process theorists developed when they took up the concept of political culture when it became a popular analytic category in the Anglo-American social scientific literature in the 1950s. In a manner typical of the split in the social sciences (then and still now), the most influential theories had conceptualized political culture either in subjective/psychological, agency-based terms or in objective/structuralist terms. According to the former, political culture was just the aggregated effect of the subjective views that existed in individuals' heads;[25] according to the latter it was the result of an underlying set of rules and dynamics embodied in economic, political, and social institutions.[26] Recognizing the limitations of splitting the field in this way, interpretive theorists suggested that political culture was better thought of as the grammar that patterns political action at an individual and institutional level.[27] This does

[25] For example, political culture "consolidated the underlying psychological forces believed to shape civic life and political behaviour." Margaret R. Somers, "What's Political or Cultural about Political Culture and the Public Sphere? Towards an Historical Sociology of Concept Formation," *Sociological Theory* 13, no. 2 (July 1995): 119. Similarly, Walter Rosenbaum defined political culture as "the subjective feelings, attitudes, and consequent behaviors believed to characterize individual and collective political orientations – that is, values – across a political system." Walter A. Rosenbaum, *Political Culture* (New York: Praeger, 1975), 4. The most influential example of this approach is found in the work of Gabriel A. Almond and Sidney Verba, *The Civic Culture: Political Attitudes and Democracy in Five Nations* (Princeton: Princeton University Press, 1963).

[26] For the purposes of this brief schema, I have collapsed a number of quite different approaches here, but what unifies them is the tendency to locate the base of political culture in objective structures, which may be quasi-grammatical rules, in the case of Levi-Strauss, or economic systems, in the case of the structural Marxists.

[27] Reconceptualizations of political culture fall within a broader turn to process orientations principally articulated by Norbert Elias, in particular *What Is Sociology?*, trans. Stephen Mennell and Grace Morrissey (New York: Columbia University Press, 1987); and Pierre Bourdieu, in particular, *The Logic of Practice*, trans. Richard Nice (Cambridge: Polity Press, 1990).

not mean that political culture is an abstract set of beliefs that organizes institutions, nor is it the meaning that emerges from their operation: "meaning is not an effect, a result, a product or a static quality, or something that can be coded out."[28] Rather, the patterning of the political culture exists and can be read in those institutions and at the same time it is patterned as the national identity of the population. Thus, posited neither as free-floating first cause nor as ideological reflection, evaluative schemes, actions, systems of belief, and assumptions about rightful behaviour are sites at which actual people make their judgements and take their actions, and in so doing perpetuate or reform political culture or morality.[29] National culture, the nation, and the individuals who take actions are thus not three distinct entities that stand in a causal relationship, but dimensions that mutually construct and constrain each other, and *Dasein* describes this movement.

Returning to Jaspers, one can now see how far his reference to identity is from the spectre of mega-agent at the start of a causal chain. The German guilt to which he referred was not some Romantic essence deep within *das Volk*. Rather, he wanted to draw attention to the normative categories that organize and saturate the political cultural space in which all Germans locate their *Dasein*, in which "all of us Germans have been brought up for ages."[30] More precisely, by placing his magnifying glass over those conditions, he wants to bring into focus the implicit precepts about right and wrong, inclusion and exclusion, and the meaning of citizen or human that logically precede the moment of individual judgement and action.[31]

If one steps back from the demands of a coherent theory for a moment, this account certainly speaks to our intuitions about how social distinctions actually work in the world. People of colour, or women, or Indigenous people, or people with disabilities know all too well that social distinctions are manifested not simply through what people *do* to each other, but also in who or what they *are*

---

[28] Norman K. Denzin, "Reading Cultural Texts: Comment on Griswold," *American Journal of Sociology* 95, no. 6 (May 1990): 1579. Emphasis added.

[29] "All these routines and scenarios are predicated upon and embody within themselves, the fundamental notions of temporal, spatial and social ordering that underlie and organize the system as a whole. In enacting these routines, actors not only continue to be shaped by the underlying organizational principles involved, but continually re-endorse those principles in the world of public observation and discourse." Sherry B. Ortner, "Theory in Anthropology since the Sixties," *Comparative Studies in Society and History* 26, no. 1 (January 1984): 154.

[30] Jaspers, *The Question of German Guilt*, 70.

[31] Michael Mack has powerfully illuminated what he calls the "ideational paradigms" present and articulated in German idealism that, he argues, underpin the radical othering that became the Holocaust. Michael Mack, *German Idealism and the Jew: The Inner Anti-Semitism of Philosophy and German Jewish Responses* (Chicago, Ill.: University of Chicago Press, 2003).

to each other. This is what people mean when they say that they are constantly made to feel that they *are* less. Yes, they might also be able to point to specific acts of discrimination; but the aggregation of those acts will not capture the pervasive sense of *being*, for example, less valuable, not included, not respected.

At the same time, widening the lens to take in the context of being does not negate the fact that ultimately there must always be an individual actor who causes the wrongful act (this officer of the Chief Protector took these Indigenous children away from their families in 1951 under the authority of this law). All we can extract as positive data is the individual action or others that provide a fuller picture. In this sense, it is *ontological* and not *methodological* individualism that this approach rejects.[32]

No doubt, for those with a particular type of explanatory bent, this logic and its correlative refusal to produce a linear account will appear analytically confused.[33] And given the radical difference in the first principles of the two approaches, there is little point arguing across their logics. But we should not think that the disagreement is uniquely sourced in different ontological commitments or preferences about the aesthetics of theoretical form, or whether we grew up intellectually in positivist or interpretive environments. Rather, this theoretical turn is motivated by a moral and political sensibility of the dangerous drift of using traditional (positivist or substantialist) categories to conceptualize political culture or the collective *in particular*. In this sense, one might go further than Sherry Ortner's methodological observation that this approach "has no need to break the system into artificial chunks like base and superstructure (and to argue which one determines which)."[34] It refuses to do so on ethical and political grounds.

With this broad-brush stroke map in hand, we can now move to fine-tune an alternative narrative of responsibility. To do this, we need to fill out two internal links in the narrative of responsibility. First, we need to explain how the collective is implicated in the creation and perpetuation of moral-political norms. Even if we understand this non-reified pattern of norms as the necessary condition for wrongdoing, how do the citizenry or members of the collective participate in creating, perpetuating, and potentially reforming it? Second, we

[32] The distinction is drawn by Cornelius Castoriadis. See "Individual, Society, Rationality, History," in *Philosophy, Politics, Autonomy*, ed. David Ames Curtis (Oxford: Oxford University Press, 1991), 60.

[33] As Berezin puts it: "the fissures lie between scholars who privilege the possibility of explanation . . . and those who privilege exegesis or interpretation." Mabel Berezin, "Fissured Terrain: Methodological Approaches and Research Styles in Culture and Politics," in *The Sociology of Culture: Emerging Theoretical Perspectives*, ed. Diana Crane (Oxford, U.K., and Cambridge, Mass.: Blackwell, 1994), 94.

[34] Ortner, *Theory in Anthropology*, 148.

need to explain the link between the norms and the individual who judges, decides, and acts.

3. CASTORIADIS, MEAD, AND THE SOCIO-NORMATIVE BASIS OF ACTION

To pry our way inside what has (up to this point) been a relatively dense assertion that the citizenry holds some responsibility for the *Dasein* (or equivalent term), Castoriadis' elaboration of what he calls the social imaginary and, in particular, his explanation of the role of symbolic meaning in social formations prove particularly dexterous. Continuous with the theoretical direction I have been tracing, Castoriadis takes as his starting point the methodological inadequacy of any account that maps social space or explains social phenomena using the building blocks of individuals on the one hand and society on the other.[35] Rather, as he puts it: "the social-historical object is co-constituted by the activities of individuals, which incarnate or concretely realize the society in which they live."[36] The distinctly useful move that Castoriadis makes as he steps away from a causal narrative is to locate *meaning* or *the symbolic* as the mediating term or organizing principle for both the psyche and social and political institutions.[37] What distinguishes a nation would then not be (at least not primarily) a common territory, ascription to law, or the ethnicity of the people who comprise it (and their ancestors and descendants), but its unique form of *organized meaning*. Similarly, the individual is not defined by the bounds of the body or a natural subjectivity, but as a unified psychic field of meaning. Importantly, meaning is not some abstraction that exists in people's heads as ideology, but is always instituted in (*inter alia*) language, law, work, politics, and the reproduction of the individual psyche. Meaning is not added on after primary substances (individuals, societies, institutions) are already constituted, but gives them their being and the form of their inter-relations in the world.[38]

---

[35] On Castoriadis' alternative map, an "instituted society" (as he calls it) and the individuals who compose it stand in an "unprecedented type of relationship which cannot be thought under the categories of the whole and the parts, the set and its elements, the universal and the particular." Castoriadis, "Power, Politics, Autonomy", in *Philosophy, Politics, Autonomy*, 145.

[36] Castoriadis, "Individual, Society, Rationality, History," 60.

[37] "Everything that is presented to us in the social-historical world is inextricably tied to the symbolic." Castoriadis, *The Imaginary Institution of Society*, trans. Kathleen Blamey (Cambridge: MIT Press, 1998), 117. An alternative and equally productive mediating concept would be Bourdieu's *habitus*. Cf. Pierre Bordieu, *An Outline of a Theory of Practice* (Cambridge: Cambridge University Press, 1977).

[38] On the institution of the social subject cf. Castoriadis, "Sublimation and the Socialization of the Psyche", in *The Imaginary Institution of Society*.

Several distinctive characteristics of *meaning* make it enormously useful for elucidating the role that society (or the people who make up society) plays in creating and sustaining institutions and social norms. First, it is multivalent. Thus, whereas on one side structural explanations turn actual people into passive media for the transmission of forms of social organization, and, on the other, agency-based explanations cast the individual as a self-moving source of forms that are then imposed on institutions, meaning is by definition multivalent. It is constituted and it constitutes; and it does so at multiple sites or through multiple media.

Second, meaning is indeterminate and incomplete. Even as meaning is embedded in social structures, symbols are, by their nature, incomplete prior to the act of interpretation: there has to be a subject who relates the symbol to the signified.[39] Thus, though not reducible to any historical instantiation, meaning always implies and already requires the presence of the human subjects who make meaning, and indeed, can and do make meaning in different and changing ways.[40]

Third, and relatedly, the content of meaning is not tied to any particular form. Thus, one can track a common pattern running through and moving dynamically between different levels of the social historical formation. Because what is common are the patterns of meaning, not some substance, we do not need to get stuck at the point of translating between those media or working out how one form (say, a hard institution) can impact or be impacted by another (the psyche). Castoriadis' poetic description merits quoting in the original:

Athenian society is, in a sense, nothing but the Athenians; without them it is only the remnants of a transformed landscape ... worn out statues fished out some place in the Mediterranean. But Athenians are Athenians only by means of the *nomos* of the *polis*. In this relationship between instituted society – which infinitely transcends the totality of the individuals that "compose" it, but which actually exist only by being "realized" in the individuals it manufactures – on the one hand – and these individuals, on the other, we witness an original, unprecedented type of relationship which cannot be thought under the categories of the whole and the parts, the set and its elements, the universal and the particular.[41]

Importing this map of meaning as the mediating and constituting hub of the social world back to the question of responsibility allows us to solve several of

---

[39] "Symbolism can be neither neutral nor totally adequate." Castoriadis, "Individual, Society, Rationality, History," 121.
[40] Castoriadis, "Power, Politics and Autonomy," 145.
[41] Ibid.

the classical dilemmas posed by the idea of collective responsibility across time. First, we can now explain how members of a collective can simultaneously be interpolated into an existing pattern (thus grounding the pole of stability and continuity across time) *and* implicated in the process of recreating it (the pole of history, responsibility, and freedom).[42] Precisely because symbolism and meaning are not self-sufficient, it is possible (and indeed necessary) to locate the active engagement of the people who are part of the social historical formation in its perpetuation and effect. They are given neither a raw 'natural' world awaiting their open interpretation nor a world complete with a closed meaning. Rather they engage with a world endowed with potential meanings, which will be complete (as this historically located world's meaning) only once they have given it meaning *for themselves* (and each other). Prior to their actively taking it up as subjects, there is no meaningful world and no socio-historical institution.

This is tremendously important because explanations that oscillate between structure and agency can explain only either why there is continuity across time and individuals (via structures) *or* why individuals are responsible (via agency), but not both. By adopting this theoretical framework, one can sensibly speak about subjects who are both informed by the social historical formation and *responsible*.

Moreover, the subject of responsibility is *essentially* collective and not, as per the liberal criticism, a sloppy and unethical conglomeration of individuals or what Anthony Quinton calls a *summative*.[43] Because social meaning is what drives the analysis here, and meaning is formed through this interplay of social-historical institutions, it is *necessarily* a collective project and cannot, even hypothetically, be thought of as an aggregation of the meanings that individuals could make on their own. At the empirical or phenomenal level, it is of course only concrete individuals who actively engage as interpreters, but social meaning is uniquely the work of the people who together comprise that society.[44] Correlatively, only together (and with difficulty) can they shift that meaning;

---

[42] One might draw an analogy here with Hannah Arendt's notion that promise and forgiveness are the two faculties that make societal existence possible. See Arendt, *The Human Condition*, 237.

[43] A "summative", following Mill's or Hume's logic, refers to a predicate ascribed to a group that could be broken down to predicates of individuals with no loss of meaning. See Anthony Quinton, "Social Objects," *Proceedings of the Aristotelian Society* 76 (1975).

[44] I am not staking a position here in the Wittgensteinian debate over the possibility of private meaning or the essentially social basis of language. Rather I am making the narrower point that the meaning intrinsic to the being of social and political institutions and norms necessarily involves multiple subject positions, or, put negatively, an individual does not enter into unformed space and make up meaning arbitrarily. Nevertheless, a more considered engagement with the philosophy of language is implicated here. See Margaret Gilbert, *On Social Facts*, chapter 3.

hence Castoriadis' notion that "society and individuals alter themselves together."[45] At a theoretical level, this distinction between the discrete moment of individual interpretation and the collective project of constituting social meanings also speaks to Jaspers' claim that even those who did not approve of (or even protested against) the actions or policies are nevertheless implicated in political guilt.[46] At a practical level, it explains why this form of responsibility is fully consistent with and even demands a collective response.

This then also brings out the *political* dimension of collective responsibility, which had been missing in the original accounts (of Feinberg and others). It does so, first and at a structural level, in the sense that it is an essentially collective, and not an aggregative account, and second, and more substantively, in the sense that what makes the collective responsible is also what makes it (or has made it) the distinct political community that it is. In the types of cases I have been discussing, the collective norms and meanings that inform individual acts of wrongdoing do not occupy some distinct sphere of culture but are woven into the political constitution of the collective, providing not only the contours of personal identity and guiding norms but also underpinning the distributive logics of legal, economic, and political systems.[47]

This schema also allows us to navigate between insisting that there is continuity in the socio-historical formation across its constituent members and across time, and being able to make space for internal dissent, ethical diversity, history, and normative change. This has posed a particular stumbling block for the school of theories I have been discussing here, because if one wants to insist that a society and the individuals who make it up stand in a co-constitutional relationship, it becomes difficult to explain the internal diversity between members (including the fact that some people radically dissent) and to explain how things ever change.

---

[45] Castoriadis, "Power, Politics, Autonomy," 146.

[46] As per Arendt's definition of collective responsibility quoted above, she also insists that individuals are implicated in a certain form of collective responsibility even if they do not agree with what was done. Feinberg makes a brief and largely implicit argument using a Lockean logic of tacit consent, that in cases where wrongful actions are generally sanctioned by a cultural group, all members, even those who oppose the wrongful actions, bear some responsibility for those actions by virtue of "taking respectability and material comfort" from their status as members of the group. See Feinberg, "Collective Responsibility," 247–8. This question is taken up in detail in Juha Raikka, "On Disassociating Oneself from Collective Responsibility," *Social Theory and Practice* 23, no. 1 (1997).

[47] Feinberg also implicitly recognizes this, as is evident in his quoting Dollard's remark that violent acts against African Americans were "instrumentalities for keeping the Negro in his place and maintaining supraordinate position of the white caste." Feinberg, "Collective Responsibility," 247.

Hegel, for example, manages to break through the perpetual reproduction of one-sided ethical life only by building into his argument the transcendental (Kantian) idea that individuals retain access to universal reason (through individual rational will), Herbert: reason that transcends the parochialism of their situated ethical consciousness.[48] George Herbert Mead's solution (in a more Freudian tradition) is also to add something onto the individual self, in his case by drawing a distinction between the socially formed *me* (which is formed in inter-subjective relations) and the spontaneous critical *I,* which exists outside this process. In either case, the possibility of critical distance, dissent, and social/historical change depends on our accepting this bifurcation of the individual self and the assumption that individuals always retain a psychic reservoir (reason for Hegel, unformed energy for Mead) that is not fully subsumed in the process of socialization.

Here, the possibility and source of dissent or change inhere in the social-historical institution itself because meaning (which gives it being) is essentially open-ended and indeterminate. Even as subjects are interpolated into a socio-historical formation with a pool of collective and pre-existing symbols, those symbols await completion through acts of interpretation. The ambiguity and possibility of difference, both within a historical moment and across time, does not require a split between the process of socio-historical production and a projected extra-social world of reason or untamed psychic energy (either in some transcendent realm or inside the individual), but is an inherent feature of socio-historical production.

What we now have at hand is the first piece of the narrative structure of collective responsibility, that is, a (non-causal) way of explaining how the people who belong to a political community are implicated in forming and sustaining the system of meanings within it and its normative principles. Let us now turn to the other side of the puzzle, the link between these socio-cultural norms and the individual who acts wrongfully. On this side, there is certainly no shortage of theories on which one could draw to give a general account of

---

[48] Thus, even while Hegel insists that *Moralität* can become a motor for real social change only when an individual does not withdraw (into alienation, individualism, or idealist religion) but reinvests in his or her concrete community so as to broaden its determinate ethical frame, the source remains individual, not collective, and comes from outside the social formation (or *Sittlichkeit*). There is a similarly directed Talmudic story in which a Rabbi and his son spend twelve years withdrawn from the world in prayer and study, and when they return, catching site of a man ploughing and sowing, they call out in disdain: "[T]hey forsake eternal life and engage in temporal life!" In response, a heavenly voice announces: "[H]ave you emerged to destroy My world? Return to your cave!" and sent them back for another twelve months, upon which time they emerged and remarked with appreciation at the doings of the world. See Talmud, Shabbat 33b.

how social structures shape individual psychic structures; one could select almost at random from a range of approaches informed by the tenets of Levi-Straussian structuralism, Marxism, or psychoanalysis. What we need, however, are theoretical resources to expound how general norms inform individuals' choices and actions specifically for the purposes of expanding the attribution of responsibility. In other words, we need to account, first, for how individuals acquire general (as distinct from local) norms and, second, for how individuals' choices and actions are both informed by general norms and nevertheless remain acts and choices for which they are responsible. For these purposes, George Mead's model of subject formation, which attends both to the acquisition of pre-existing patterns of action and identity and to the subject's agency in the enactment of those norms, proves particularly fertile.[49]

As a basic framework, Mead uses the metaphor of the movement between play and games to explain how individuals acquire a general set of conventions or norms of action and identity that extend well beyond the specific rules or meanings conveyed in their immediate relations and direct interactions.[50] In play the child organizes her activity according to the behaviour of the concrete other with whom she is playing; in the game, she orients her actions according to a generalized set of rules that she understands orient the actions and expectations of the other players in the game. This shift links her sense of herself (and others), what is expected of her (and others), and what she (and others) can do to an abstract set of norms that organize the social field and that flow not from a particular other but from the generalized Other, even as they are only ever manifest in particular interactions. This generalized Other, like the written rules of a board game, takes positive form only in an after-the-fact act of articulation. Only in the boxed version do players read the rules and then play; in the lived version that it mimics, the rules are embedded in actions they join and then take themselves.

The advantage of the game metaphor is that unlike some forms of social structuralism, it is dynamic and always already located in relational action; the "I" which is formed through social interactions is not a type of static being, but a self oriented to act in certain ways, according to certain rules about what is permissible, who can (and is expected to) do what, who deserves what, and so on. At the same time, it is necessarily embedded in a set of similarly structured

---

[49] The key text is G. H. Mead, *Mind, Self and Society: From the Standpoint of a Social Behaviorist*, ed. Charles W. Morris (Chicago: University of Chicago Press, 1934).

[50] Castoriadis similarly recognizes that within an extended pattern of social meaning, any one fragment becomes the entry point to "the interminable reciprocal referrals that link, magmatically, each fragment of this social world to the rest of it." Castoriadis, "Power, Politics, Autonomy," 149; see also "Individual, Society, Rationality, History," 62.

templates for the relationships between other types of identity and correlate expectations.

Both Castoriadis and Mead are making explicit here something already intrinsic to Freud's theory of the construction of gender and the transmission of the significance of sexual difference. That is, what is transmitted through the immediate inter-subjective interaction is not a localized set of meanings about these people, or about the subject per se, but the social-historical formation; indeed, the very notion of inter-subjectivity is problematic insofar as it preserves the ontological priority of a lone subjectivity that might then meet another in a space between.[51] There are two related dimensions to this argument. First, the broader social historical (and its associated normative ordering) is always and only transmitted to the individual through particular and local interactions; and second, those local transmissions are never only local; if they were, they would be deprived of their power to inform the individual or sustain their construction within a world of meaning.[52] The process, in other words, requires both the active participation of concrete persons and the weight of institutionalized meanings; the normative dimension of human subjectivity and the normative shape of the more general social order are folded into each other through patterned inter-subjective relations.

Critically, it is not only the concrete (adult) others who are involved in the process of informing the subject, but also the self under formation. She is not inert material shaped passively by an externally imposed set of norms or values, but is herself an active participant acquiring a subjective sense of self and other. Subjectivity thus arises as much because I recognize the other or recognize myself as a certain type of subject in a map of relations as it arises through the other recognizing me or casting me in an already scripted role.[53] This marks an important move in the argument because it provides the structure for

---

[51] Castoriadis explicitly rejects the term " inter-subjectivity", describing the term as "the fig leaf used to conceal the nudity of inherited thought and its inability to confront the question of the social-historical." Castoriadis, "Power, Politics, Autonomy," 144. Elsewhere: "The *social-historical* is neither the unending addition of inter-subjective networks (although it is this *too*), nor of course is it their simple 'product'." Castoriadis, *The Imaginary Institution of Society*, 108.

[52] One finds in Hegel a similar attempt to overcome the logic of distinct individual and social ontological realms. "The universal does not prevail or achieve completion except along with particular interests and through the cooperation of particular knowing and willing; and individuals likewise do not live as private persons for their own ends alone but in the very act of willing these they will the universal and in the light of the universal." Hegel, *The Philosophy of Right*, section 260.

[53] One thinks here of Lacan's evocative metaphor of the child recognizing and acquiring its self when it spots its image in the mirror. Jacques Lacan, "The Mirror Stage as Formative of the Function of the I as Revealed in Psychoanalytic Experience," in *Écrits: A Selection*, trans. Alan Sheridan (New York: W. W. Norton, 1977), 1–7.

explaining how individuals can both be socially constructed and be freely act-ing or responsible subjects. By acknowledging that the individual is herself an active participant in the process of her subject (and normative) formation, one is not forced into a choice between constructivism and freedom or, in the language of responsibility, between allowing that the background ethical con-text informs individual normative judgements and holding the individual responsible for the judgements she makes. In fact, a genuinely inter-subjective explanation not only allows, but also requires, both dimensions, because even as the generalized norms inform individual consciousness, they do so only by virtue of this consciousness actively grasping and recognizing them as its own. At the same time, this model of the acquisition of subjectivity is far better attuned to our intuitions about what it is to be a person than explanations that cast us as little more than social imprints.

Drawing these insights together, the distinctly *political* dimension of this form of collective responsibility is now apparent, and in a way that goes beyond the Castoriadian insight that the different dimensions of the social-historical formation (including political institutions and the law) co-constitute each other through a common web of meanings. Specifically, Mead's elucidation of the dialogical dynamic of subject formation brings into relief the similarity of, and correspondence between, the structure of normative subjectivity and the struc-ture of legal relations and rights. The formation of both subjectivity and legal relations is always reciprocal, in the sense that they involve more than one party recognizing the subjectivity or rights of the other. Just as it makes no sense to speak of a subject with a normative sense of self and other abstracted from others' normative sense of self and other, so too it makes no sense to think of rights without reference to a community in which one expects to have ones rights honoured *and* is expected to honour the rights of others (not necessarily symmetrically).

This suggests that the structure of legal relations mimics the structure of the relations of normative recognition or, to put it the other way around, that the particular organization of reciprocal recognition in a given social space forms the bedrock of legal and political relations. Differences in how subjects are recognized underpin different forms of political/legal relations. Thus, for example, the egalitarian distribution of rights and membership entailed in a liberal democratic political form would be underpinned by similarly egalitarian patterns of recognition, detached from thick identity markers like race or gender or religion. By contrast, asymmetry at the level of formal rights is embedded in patterns of recognition that are both inegalitarian and shaped by thick identity markers.

From the point of view of trying to understand the basis for rights violations and repairing societies where there has been a systematic failure to respect certain people's rights, this is a very important claim. It draws our attention back from the external legal structure, the set of regulatory laws imposed on subjects (which we call politics), to the 'internal legal structure', the constitution of selves who experience themselves and others as deserving (or not deserving) to have their rights respected. We tend to think of the latter as belonging to the realm of culture or private morality; but in fact the sources of our sense of self and other are the same implicit rules of the game.[54]

The subtle and apparently highly personal dynamics of this process can easily slip by our filter of what belongs to politics. To say, for example, that a person has little self-worth sounds to us like an evaluation of their personal psychology, or at best an effect of inter-personal dynamics. With this more capacious framework, however, one can expand the scene to trace the link between systematic exclusion from the community of persons who can legitimately expect to have generally recognized claims met and the facility with which an individual can develop a sense of self as an equal in the spheres of law, rights, citizenship, and interpersonal relations.[55] Correlatively, and from our point of view more importantly, just as a person develops a sense of herself as having legitimate rights claims (or not), and being a member of the *we* (or not), so too her experience of others includes codes about *their* status in the community of rights-bearers and *their* normative worth. Recall the particular process through which a single subject is "informed" as a particular type of self embedded in a far more comprehensive and extensive grammar of norms. As I enter into this normative system, I acquire not only a sense of where *I* fit in and what I have a right to, but also my sense of where others fit in, what they can legitimately claim. Identity, one might say, is not just who I am, but also who I am that you are.

What needs to be underscored here is that in actual social-historical spaces, identity distinctions are not added onto an identity that is already there, but are rather encoded into the normative orientations that inform individuals' sense of themselves and others and are implicit in their constitution as particular types of selves. The result is that the injustice or immorality of those distinctions often eludes us; they appear natural, part of what a person is. As Jeffrey Reiman

---

[54] Axel Honneth draws on Mead's work in precisely this way to point to the patterns of recognition that organize legal and political relations. See Axel Honneth, *The Struggle for Recognition*, trans. Joel Anderson (Cambridge: MIT Press, 1996); and "Integrity and Disrespect," *Political Theory* 20, no. 2 (1992).

[55] This also helps explain why members of the denigrated group may themselves see members of their own groups as less than co-equals in the political community even as they eschew this norm.

points out, precisely because these patterns define routine, rather than breaking with it, "like the smell of the air or the feel of the ground beneath one, they tend to melt into the background and escape notice."[56] Only in retrospect, or when placed against other normative systems (say, international human rights law) do they come into the foreground.

Thus naturalized, they can be deployed as the justification for the distinctions themselves: Indigenous people are not accorded equal legal rights because they *are* culturally and intellectually backward, women cannot be enfranchised because they *are* essentially oriented to the private sphere, and so on. As we saw, the hypothetical brute reality of Indigenous people's intellectual and cultural deficiencies was brought as incontestable justification for imperial powers insisting that the territory of Australia fell under no property or political regime. If colour is essentialized as a criterion for personal and public value, then every interaction between, and indeed amongst, black and white people becomes the occasion for transmitting and perpetuating this norm. The others' colour will dictate whether I regard them and, if the occasion arises, whether I will treat them as fully fledged legal members of my community. This may or may not result in my violating a particular right, but even if it does not, none of us can claim total innocence.[57] And when it does, none of us is without responsibility for the actual emergence of our common disposition into the world of action.

This significantly expands the sense in which one can say that members of the political community are implicated in systematic violations. Up until this point, I had argued that they can be held responsible for perpetuating the political culture or norms that then underpin *particular* violations, still equating the wrongdoing that justice should address with these particular acts; now, the wrong itself has been enlarged. The injury is not limited to the moment where a particular violation occurs, but includes the more pervasive failure to accord recognition or, more positively, the active disrespect that members of the political community convey in their interactions with persons whose identities are denigrated within that community's normative horizon. There are certainly good reasons for insisting that a manifest public act be a necessary condition for prosecution under criminal or anti-discrimination law, and one can well imagine the danger of allowing people to press charges on the basis of something like their experience of feeling less valued in their society (because of

---

[56] Jeffrey H. Reiman, *Justice and Modern Moral Philosophy* (New Haven: Yale University Press, 1990), 215.

[57] Feinberg makes an analogous point under his category of liability with non-contributory fault where he claims that although only the person who kills someone whilst driving drunk is guilty of that crime, we are all nevertheless guilty of the practice, and the two are not unrelated. See Feinberg, "Collective Responsibility," 241–3.

their colour or gender or religion). Nevertheless, one must not confuse practical institutional requirements with the existence of a phenomenon, and focusing on the visible aberrances may well obscure the background condition.

Let us now piece this together, using the jigsaw puzzle as an (imperfect) analogy. One might imagine that in the middle is the hub piece, the pattern of political cultural relations and meanings (*Dasein*) that organize the distribution of rights and membership according to identity-based rules. Viewed from one perspective, we see on the input side the collective in question, the political community that both generates and is informed by those meanings and rules, giving them life by assuming them as a way (its way) of being in the world. On the other side (the output side) is the individual actor who makes judgements and acts and whose judgements and actions are oriented according to the norms set out in his political cultural space. Now walk around to the other side and you see that as this same person acts, he reinforms those social norms, reconstituting what was first posited as the social collective. He is, if you like, the white Australian who takes an Aboriginal child from her mother and thinks he is (as Howard insisted) "doing the right thing", perhaps even acting "for her own good". That he probably did; and what made that be so is precisely what makes those around him responsible.

Linking this back to the criteria established at the beginning of this chapter for a viable and coherent account of responsibility, this account looks fairly successful. It allows one to speak coherently about collective responsibility, while respecting core commitments to the integrity of individuals and avoiding the problematic reification of the collective. But, one might well ask, has all this been purchased at the cost of giving up anything that actually still looks like responsibility? After all, all of the basic evaluative tools that are normally brought to bear to assess responsibility seem to have been rendered inappropriate because this approach does not partake in the currency of agency, action, or causality. So, for example, the "principle of alternative possibilities", a standard test for responsibility that insists that it makes sense to attribute responsibility only if the subject "could have done otherwise", hits a brick wall here, because there is no doing, "otherwise" or not.[58] Similarly, the very basic demand for a free agent cannot get a look in, because there is no agency.

---

[58] Harry G. Frankfurt, "Alternative Possibilities and Moral Responsibility," in *The Importance of What We Care About* (Cambridge: Cambridge University Press, 1988). Though there is a great deal of disagreement within analytic philosophy about the validity of the principle of alternative possibilities, in the jurisprudence of responsibility, this formulation is generally accepted as a working principle. George Fletcher, *Basic Concepts of Criminal Law* (Oxford: Oxford University Press, 1998).

What this means is that if we are to coherently present and defend this theoretical framework as a viable conception of responsibility, we will need to develop a fresh set of analytic concepts, which do the same type of work as those concepts tailored to the individual model of responsibility, that is, concepts such as agency, the principle of alternative possibilities, and causality. These will have to be amenable to the ontology adopted here, but nevertheless recognizably consistent with a broader concept of responsibility.

As a baseline, the foregoing discussion has already established that one does not need to place the political community and its norms in a causal relationship in order to coherently make the case that the members of the political community collectively played a role in sustaining and perpetuating the normative conditions in which wrongdoing occurred. Within a co-constitutive relationship, one can still assert that it was *this* political community that provided the conditions for the wrongdoing to occur or, more pointedly, that had the community not been the one that it was or sustained the political culture it did, the wrongful acts could not have occurred, or at least not systematically and not without there having been significant and generalized public protest. This is admittedly a minimal form of responsibility, still lacking a moral or evaluative dimension, but it does build the community into the story of how wrongdoing came about, locating it amongst its necessary conditions.

Is it possible to go further than this descriptive claim (this political community is the locus of the normative framework) to also make an evaluative/ moral claim about that normative identity? That is, beyond recognizing that the political community constituted one of the necessary conditions for wrongdoing to occur, can one also attribute what one might call *blame responsibility* to it?[59] The difference at work here is analogous to the one that exists between simply noting that the individual was the one who did something and blaming him for doing wrong. One might distinguish between these two forms of responsibility by pointing to a subtle difference in rhetorical formulations: in the first, one says that "the subject is responsible", but in the second, one says that "the subject can be *held* responsible". Immediately, things are going to get a lot stickier here, because the tests normally brought to bear to make this higher order evaluative claim draw on concepts such as freedom, consciousness, and agency, none of which is available to us here. To see if there is a way of sensibly doing this, let us, as a starting point, take the formulation (the political community) *should have had a different normative framework* or

---

[59] David Miller calls this more minimal form "outcome responsibility" and distinguishes it from "moral responsibility", which involves a moral evaluation and which I call blame. Miller, "Holding Nations Responsible," 244.

should have been a different type of Dasein *or political culture* and substitute it
for the more habitual formulation *should have done otherwise* that is usually
employed as an elaboration of the principle of alternative possibilities.

As per Kant's dictum "ought implies can", getting to *should* requires that
one first pass through the practical claim that it *could have* had such a normative framework. At the most basic level, even before getting to the higher order
demand that it had *that* particular alternative (normative framework), this
implies the possibility of any type of change. Let us call this *alterability*. As
already argued, despite the classical dilemmas social constructivist analyses
pose for explaining historical change, this demand can be modestly met by
reconfiguring social structure as multi-valent, essentially ambiguous, and
always historical (and thus dynamic) meaning.[60] The picture here is not self-
sourced movement (as implied in a full-blown concept of agency), but nevertheless, it breaks the problem of infinite reproduction of the same and thus
fulfils one of the necessary conditions for being able to coherently establish
something like "that the political community should have had a different normative framework". But this is still not sufficient, not only for *should have*, but
even for *could have*. It is not enough to speak about the abstract multi-valence
of the instituted imaginary (it could have moved in some unspecified direction).
The claim here is that it could have moved in a specific direction. Accordingly,
to pay out on the *could have* (*been this*), one must also be able to argue that the
specific alternative normative framework we are holding up as preferable
(Indigenous people are seen as full and equal humans, for example) was in fact
available to the political community. Let us call that *availability*, where availability means that those alternative normative orientations were present somewhere on the normative horizon of the political community.

One might meet this demand in several ways. The norms condemning the
violation may already have been positively codified or embodied somewhere
"outside" the political community, but still within a broader moral or legal
jurisdiction within which the community falls: for example, in international
norms or international law (including both codified and international customary law). For example, apartheid South Africa continued treating blacks as
second-class citizens through the 1980s, even as international custom and
codified international law condemned racial discrimination. No one could have
said that treating blacks as equals was unavailable as an imaginative possibility
to South Africa. The alternative norms may also have been embedded inside the

---

[60] Specifically, Castoriadis' concept of the capacity for self-alteration, whereby "society and individuals alter themselves together, those alterations entailing each other." Castoriadis, "Power,
Politics, Autonomy," 146.

political community, as a possible interpretation of a more general normative principle that it already embraced. For example, the idea of the equal rights of persons had currency in Australia, but the category "persons" was defined in such a way as to exclude Indigenous people and so place them beyond the reach of the principle's practical application. If this is the case, even though the interpretation of the principle that would insist that it should extend to the excluded group was not generally endorsed, it may have been present as minority opinion. It is in this vein, for example, that some Jews criticize contemporary Israel's treatment of Palestinians, claiming that Israel is failing to apply its own (Jewish) principles concerning respect for the stranger or love of the neighbour.

Moving now from *could have* to *should have*, alterability and availability will both be necessary, but they are still not sufficient. To say that the political community *should have* altered its norms in this particular way (from racism towards equality of respect) implies, first, that the norms it did embrace were wrong, with respect to either some absolute moral standard or at least a morally preferable one. Second, it implies the more demanding condition that the political community itself should have made an evaluation that this alternative way of ordering their social world was morally superior to the one they actually adopted; non-Indigenous Australians should have known that it was wrong to see whiteness as a condition of full recognition, for example.[61] This is, of course, a perilous claim to make, especially when one is, as John Howard argued in the Australian debate, making inter-temporal judgements. But claims about what another subject should have been or done are always perilous and not only in the case of a collective and a normative framework. Claiming that an individual who did wrong should have known better, for example, similarly involves enormous assumptions about his moral framework, the social world he occupied, and the way he made judgements. In fact, as is evident if one consults the moral philosophical literature on this issue, there are enormous difficulties in sustaining this type of claim, beginning with the problem of sensibly arguing that something *should have* been other than it was in a universe that can be fully explained.[62]

---

[61] At work here is the principle that the category of the ethical exists only where choice is possible, as articulated succinctly by William James: "An act has no ethical quality whatever unless it be chosen out of several all equally possible." I disagree that "equally possible" is a necessary condition for ethics, but the essential point remains. Cf. William James, "The Stream of Consciousness," in *The Principles of Psychology* (New York: Courier Dover Publications, 1950), chapter IX.

[62] For a discussion of compatabilist arguments, see J. V. Canfield, "The Compatibility of Free Will and Determinism," *Philosophical Review* 71 (1962), and Peter Van Inwagen, "The Incompatibility of Free Will and Determinism," *Philosophical Studies* 27 (1975).

At the same time, even in this case, we are not entirely bereft of tools to make such judgements. Going back to availability, one can, for example, make an evaluation based on the moral frameworks that were around and also had some normative bearing (what other political communities generally deemed to be right). Similarly, if a political community strongly embraces a human rights framework but treats particular groups abominably, this provides a comparative moral framework that is not simply abstract but directly relevant to that political community. The more the moral standard actually adopted is out of keeping with those that were available and endorsed within the community's normative horizon, the more we are justified in judging it as wrong. This matches our intuitions. The more "aberrant" a society is *vis-à-vis* other societies and legal orders to which it is exposed, and the more aberrant the particular norm is *vis-à-vis* its own other norms, the more we think it should not have continued to embrace the wrongful norm. By contrast, where the entire context is more monochrome, where there is no alternative pattern of seeing the world, it is harder to look at this group and condemn it for failing to be otherwise. One would then hold it responsible in the more minimal sense that it is the political community where this norm is affirmed (in Miller's terms, it has outcome responsibility), but without also blaming it in a moral sense for so doing, or so being.

In summary, what this exercise has established is a framework whereby one can evaluate the responsibility of a political community, using a distinct set of analytic tools that do the same type of work as those we would bring to bear were we evaluating individual responsibility. In this case, however, the relevant criteria are not ones like agency, *actus reus,* or *mens rea,* but rather what I have called *alterability* and *availability,* with the latter taking different forms. As these will have internal gradations (in much the same way as *actus reus* and *mens rea* do), this also implies that there is a range of degrees or qualities of responsibility implied in any particular situation. Thus, in those cases where the normative identity or political culture of the political community was entirely in keeping with other similarly located political communities and internally consistent, that is, where there was low availability, one can probably justify no more than the minimal descriptive form of outcome responsibility. By contrast, in those cases where the political community continued to embrace the problematic norms even in the face of a changing world and its own increasing endorsement of human rights principles (high availability), the attribution of responsibility can become more substantial, taking on a moral evaluative dimension.

Finally, and now linking this backward-looking dimension of attributing responsibility with the performative, forward-looking constitutive dimension of reparative acts, one can see that in particular cases, institutions such as apology that may be forward-looking and constitutive or backward-looking and attributive will strike different balances between these two directions. Thus, for example, in the first case discussed above, that is, in those cases where the alternative norms were relatively unavailable, the reparative act will be more inclined in its forward-looking constitutive direction, and involves only a minimal backward-looking attribution. In the latter case, where they were readily available, the balance will be more in favour of the backward-looking responsibility without discounting the forward-looking constitutive dimension.

4. WHAT FOLLOWS?

In closing this exploration of the theoretical underpinnings of collective responsibility, the question that remains hanging is, What institutions would logically follow from or can be justified by this conceptual framework? Asking this question may seem somewhat redundant, given that what motivated this attempt to derive a coherent theory of collective responsibility was the assumption that the collective political apology entailed an attribution of collective responsibility that required justification. Now, at the end point of that exercise, I want to turn around and go back in the opposite direction, reasoning from the theoretical conception back to derive some principles for an appropriate institution to pick up on this distinct form of responsibility. One might think of this as an exercise in reflective equilibrium, as conceptualized by Rawls.[63]

In the Australian debate, we saw how Howard rhetorically equated the apology with punishment and then mounted the quite reasonable argument that punishment is not an appropriate response when one is dealing with a collective across time. His logic may have been both faulty and politically motivated, but his comments illustrate the critical importance of getting the match right between the type of responsibility and the type of institution. Overstepping what can be justifiably done (to people) on the basis of holding them responsible will bring about a further injustice, and, more pragmatically, risks relegating what is already a fragile and novel conception back to the zone of dangerous collectivism.

Starting with the core structural difference between this account and standard accounts of individual responsibility, the fact that there is no question here of isolating a particular agent who freely brought about a certain action or state of affairs immediately rules out any response predicated on free agency.

---

[63] John Rawls, *A Theory of Justice* (Cambridge, Mass.: Harvard University Press, 1971).

We think that it is legitimate to punish someone for doing wrong only because he or she did so freely and with the knowledge that what he or she did was wrong (or unlawful). There is a certain symmetry between what we hold the party responsible for (his or her *doing* something) and the way we respond (*doing* something to him or her). More technically, the justification is both moral and purposive. Morally, one can (at least arguably) justify limiting a person's freedom or inflicting pain on him or her in response to his or her having committed worse or equivalent acts. Because such institutions of justice directly impinge on the liberty of the individual (especially punishment), they require and imply a threshold active involvement in the perpetration of a wrong that is not met in the scenario portrayed here.

From a more instrumental point of view, it makes sense to act on free and conscious agents with a view to influencing agency and thus their future acts. This is not the case, however, when one is talking about a political community and its embedded normative orientations. Responding on the register of agency to a problem that is not located on the register of agency makes little sense.

More positively, to find the correct level or register of the institutional response, one needs to look to the register on which the responsible party is being tied to the wrong. Here, where the site of wrong is the meaning structure of the political culture, the unequal patterns of recognition and unjust norms that orient action, the register of responsibility is not action or agency but rather symbolic or social meanings. As such, one should be thinking of institutions that work at this same level, that is, at the level of the creation or perpetuation of constitutive meanings and norms. If punishment or compensation seeks to right the individual who committed wrong, or restore the correct balance between wrongdoer and victim, what we are looking for here are institutions that will correct or reform the problematic norm, alter patterns of recognition, or reorient the political culture and moreover do so in a manner that actively draws in the persons who comprise the political community.

This presents quite a challenge. How does one correct something that does not have an independent substantive existence but is woven through the practices and psyches of a political community? One might well argue that the very idea of an intervention to effect something that is not a thing but a dimension or the weft of identity through a political community is absurd: one cannot "remake" a political community or act on it in such a way as to alter its identity; this is a process that happens over time and as a result of enormously complex shifts.

Here I find myself back with Jaspers' reflections on this question, which, though schematic and in some ways uncomfortable, suggest a direction that uncannily squares this circle. Jaspers agrees that only criminal guilt (of individuals) can justify punishment. Political guilt forms the basis for liability and hence reparations. But what follows from moral guilt is *penance and renewal*, and from metaphysical guilt *a transformation of human self-consciousness before God*. In the case of these latter two, reparation is necessary but not sufficient. Rather, the individuals and community bearing such guilt have the choice of either bearing it all their lives or undergoing a transformation: "There is no other way to realize truth for the German", he argues, "than purification out of the depth of consciousness of guilt."[64] It is through the confrontation with the past and who we have been that the possibility of a new form of life and a transformed political community emerge.

The fact that in the midst of a piece of political theory Jaspers reaches for a religious metaphor and process should not escape our attention. For some, it will no doubt be a distraction if not the signal to close the book. Again, however, if one reads past a religious language that might disturb a secular sensibility, the process he is recommending involves the political community confronting its actual normative identity (as, say, racially discriminatory) and the gap between its historical identity and its ideal identity (as egalitarian), and declaring its alignment with a corrective identity to which it now aspires (as egalitarian across race).

I would go a step further to suggest that the institution for this dimension of reparation also has to attend to the relational quality of the wrong. In other words, because the wrong was embedded in the relationship, the process should not just be self-confrontation, but should also include confrontation with the other, facing the other with an honest recognition of the wrong and the injury inflicted *on him or her* and a commitment to the right and full recognition. In fact, such a response should not merely speak (theoretically) to what has been wrong, but should actually perform a type of reparation and reconstruction of the normative character of the political community by enacting the very recognition that was missing. In this context, institutions that operate through the media of narrative and symbolic action, including truth commissions, public memorials, representative apologies, as well as legal reform (in its expressive as distinct from its functional dimension), speak well to this form of responsibility. At the risk of this seeming to tie the bows too neatly, there does then seem to be a coherence between the political apology and a theoretically coherent form of collective responsibility, a virtuous circle.

Finally, and to return to my initial observations about the limits of liberalism's jurisprudence and institutions of responsibility, these institutions of symbolic recognition and reparation are fully compatible with the institutions of

[64] Jaspers, *The Question of German Guilt*, 118.

individual punishment and compensation. The collective and individual dimensions and corresponding institutions of responsibility are not in tension with each other – as would be the case were we to place the collective on the same register of action – but fold into each other in a complementary manner. In fact, were we to more fully embrace the viability of this conception of responsibility, the risk that punishing an individual would implicitly excuse the rest of us would be countered by an understanding that even as we condemn the singular individual who wielded the instruments, we recognize ourselves as the ones who placed them in his hands and quietly turned our backs.

8

Apology as Political Action

Stepping back and placing the three lenses through which we have been looking against each other, the apology we now have before us looks quite different from the one we assumed we knew at the beginning. No longer a singular type of speech act whose natural home is personal relationships or the darkened confessional, it now comes into view as a complex repertoire of possible types of speech act. Most importantly, within that repertoire is the 're-covenanting apology'. In this guise, the apology is, in its first movement, an acknowledgement of a collective failure to live up to an ideal ethical principle and, in its second, a public, performative declaration of a new commitment, a new covenant for *now* and into the future.

Still, for apology's (potential) political dimension to be catalysed in real time requires the right context, both at the level of social and political conditions and in terms of people's proclivity to receive it according to this interpretive trope. To this end, we have already identified a canny symmetry between apology's attention to collective responsibility and the deficit or gap in the standard repertoire of strategies for dealing with the systematic violations in nations' pasts bequeathed by a liberal secular political understanding of responsibility. As valuable as the liberal institutions of individual justice have been in pinpointing and prosecuting direct individual responsibility, they have nevertheless occluded the silent and supportive collective from our institutional vision and lacked the emotive theatricality required to bring the polity along into a new political ethic. As the awareness of, and intolerance for, this deficit in justice grew in the latter part of the twentieth century, apology found a waiting audience.

To this one might add a number of other social and political shifts that contributed to the creation of an environment conducive to apology's political reception. First, if part of what set the stage for apology's welcome was an atmosphere of increased self-criticism of national political cultures, this was itself an effect of the unprecedented political and institutional flux in the respective roles and influences of transnational institutions and movements, the nation-state, and sub-national civil society that characterized the latter part of the twentieth century. Although the nation-state remained central to the organization of international space, its firm hold on citizens' identities and normative commitments was shaken from both without and within. One effect of this more open field of political identity or normative evaluation, evident also in the increasing role that international human rights norms played in domestic political debates, has been citizens' developing a more critical gaze towards the previously authoritative claims of the historical nation.

Another effect has been the result of the increasing influence that non-state actors, and religious organizations, in particular, have had on politics. Both would seem to condition citizens towards becoming more open to apology's self-critical message and unusual form. More specifically, religions' expanded salience in public and political life not only, as is now commonly observed, has influenced the *content* of political argument, but also has provided a channel for processes or *forms* of action traditionally at home in the religious sphere to enter the space of politics.[1] If one adds to this the increasing loss of credibility and relevance of those voices traditionally associated with defining political solutions under conditions of globalization and political crisis, these other, novel voices have been especially empowered to suggest new modalities.

Further, though *sui generis*, apology's political ascension also belongs within a more general international trend towards embracing reparative models of justice for past societal violations. As Truth Commissions, reparations schemes, and rituals of public memory inscribed themselves into international political institutional practice and consciousness, supported by a new raft of non-government organizations and scholarly commentary, the institutions and conceptions filling out the formerly vague notion of reparative justice gained legitimacy, also clearing the path for other members of this family of approaches to enter the political scene.[2] In this sense, the trajectory of

---

[1] Amongst the proliferating subject on this topic, see, esp., Jose Casanova, *Public Religions in the Modern World* (Chicago and London: University of Chicago Press, 1994); Douglas Johnston, *Faith Based Diplomacy* (Oxford, New York: Oxford University Press, 2003); and Rajeev Bhargava, ed., *Secularism and Its Critics* (Delhi, New York: Oxford University Press, 2005).

[2] The proliferation of Truth and Reconciliation Commissions and like processes, for example, cannot be dissociated from the formation of the very well-funded and connected International Centre for Transitional Justice, itself a response to the appeal of such strategies, but then a source of their further growth.

particular practices can be neither predicted nor understood through abstract analysis of their potential contribution or even the environmental conditions, but is also path-dependent, rising or falling with the success, failure, and popularity of other related processes and their own historical deployment. Apologies and their cousins also provide the precedent for future apologies.[3] An apology that captured the public imagination, like Willy Brandt's *kniefall*, opened a space for a form of action to crystallize as standard political practice; but so, too, apologies that fall flat can cast a shadow on that path.

Certainly, none of this amounts to an equation, as if apology's arrival on the world stage were but the inexorable product of conjoined forces. Nevertheless, by bringing together the latent trope of the political apology, the growing political legitimacy of reparative justice in general, the heightened intolerance for self-justifying national histories, the expanded political role of religious actors and norms, and the augmented awareness of the shortfalls of individual, liberal institutions of justice, one can tell a convincing story about how apology came to join the repertoire of political action when it did.[4]

And yet, even if the stage and the protagonist in our drama seem well suited to each other, the performance has been halting. We have reached for apology gingerly, and with serious reservations, dubious about its collectivist implications and religious insinuations, uncomfortable with the sentimentality it brings to the space of politics and often cynical about apologists' motivations or intent. From the evidence to date, one has to conclude that even if apology *could* speak the responsibility and commitment of the collective in a manner consistent with our other (liberal, individualist, modern) principles, its other voices and resonances are still too present for it to speak in an unimpeded, political voice. Apology hovers somewhat tentatively in the space of political action, still falling well short of what Austin called a "conventional procedure" and indeed giving rise to a type of interpretive confusion.[5] Even as they are being performed, political apologies are works in progress, introducing novel narratives about responsibility and constituting atypical political forms in the space of contemporary political thinking and practice.

This final chapter assesses this 'work in progress' both practically, with a view to seeing how the practice might fulfil its potential, and normatively, to

---

[3] One might draw a parallel with the establishment of universal jurisdiction, another emergent practice that until recently struck people as confused or nonsensical, but has now taken its place as part of the accepted grammar of international justice.

[4] This is by no means intended as a sufficient historical explanation of the temporality of apology's emergence. Over the body of his work, Jeffrey Olick has developed a very different and extremely rich historical account of the politics of regret. See in particular *The Politics of Regret*.

[5] Austin, *How to Do Things with Words*, 14.

probe the implications of its doing so for our understanding of contemporary politics. As the force of our objections to the 'inappropriate apology' is depleted and we acknowledge that we *have* embraced the apology as a political form, what image of ourselves and what political theory will we see in the mirror?

I. IF WE COULD APOLOGIZE POLITICALLY, HOW WOULD WE?

There are two types of criteria for apology's success as a political act, the first concerning the aptness of context and the second concerning the substance and form of the apologetic act. Attending initially to context, as the inventory in Chapter One illustrated, apologies are in fact deployed under a range of circumstances, though not necessarily equally suited to them all. This book has by no means provided sufficient empirical comparative data on the impacts of apologies in different contexts to ground an assessment of their comparative success, which one might then use as the basis for developing an ideal apologetic context. Nevertheless, one can approach the question from the other side, moving back from the conceptual analysis of apology as a particular type of political act to suggest the circumstances most conducive to its doing this distinct work.

In the last chapter, I argued from the premise that 'the punishment should fit the crime' or, more accurately, that the institutional intervention should fit the appropriate level of responsibility to the conclusion that just as punishment is the appropriate response to criminal responsibility, so too political apology is properly suited to moral-political responsibility. Indeed, one might think of these different forms of responsibility and institutional intervention as nested within each other. Now we can add a temporal or sequential dimension to this analysis.[6] If criminal prosecution (punishment) corresponds to the most direct dimension of responsibility – the responsibility of the people who actually committed specific violations – it also responds to the most acute experience of the violation and is the vehicle for dealing with the most intense emotional and political reactions. If a person has been tortured, then our strongest

---

[6] Jeremy Waldron makes an analogous argument by proposing that rights generate waves of duties, appropriate to the stage of intervention, as distinct from a single duty or conflicting duties. Thus, for example, duties corresponding to the right to be free from torture will come in waves, where each wave requires a certain type of intervention. In the first instance, the right requires that norms against torture be established in the polity. Later on, it requires that those who commit torture be brought to justice, and, finally, that institutions be established to prevent recurrence of the offence. See Jeremy Waldron, "Rights in Conflict," *Ethics* 99, no. 3 (April 1989): 509ff.

reactions are directed towards the people who tortured him or her. Punishment is the vehicle for the emotions of horror, anger, and revenge and the urgent political imperatives of sanctioning the act of torture.

By contrast, apology responds to, and is a vehicle for, less acute emotional and political imperatives. Again, if a person has been tortured, we will have feelings about the political community that allowed this to happen, and it will be important to deal with this normative framework, but both the emotional and the political imperatives to respond at this level are less pressing. Apology is in this sense a 'cool' intervention or mechanism for dealing with the past, as distinct from the 'hotter' intervention of punishment.

Where the conflict remains volatile, the violations are ongoing, and perpetrators are visibly living with impunity in the public space, then apologies are likely to be overwhelmed by demands for the more urgent and passionately felt dimensions of justice. Apology's resonance is not sufficiently sharp to speak to the intensity of felt demands in the living community. In fact, apology under such conditions may, and often does, feel like an insult. It is when these more urgently felt and politically required demands recede that the space for apology becomes available. This is not to say that other forms of justice are no longer on the agenda for victim groups, but rather that some of the heat has gone out of them and the rule of law has become sufficiently strong and stable to ensure that direct violations are condemned, at least formally. Thus, from a negative point of view, one might say that the apology is most appropriate where the pressing demand for bringing perpetrators to (criminal) justice has moved from centre stage.

At the same time, there has to be a positive reason for the apology, or a political imperative to which the apology responds. Given that what the apology does is address normative failures in the political culture, the most appropriate time for it to make its entry onto the political stage will be when the need to address the more deep-seated issues of political/normative orientation is on the political agenda. In the Australia of the 1990s, for example, while there was neither a political imperative from the point of view of the state nor a strong social movement to prosecute the people who had removed children, the structural inequalities that continued to pervade Australian society and the failure to recognize the rights claims of Indigenous Australians were very much part of mainstream political debate. More concretely, as discussed in Chapter Five, at the same time as the apology movement arose, Australians were steeped in a national debate about a new constitution for the Centenary of Federation, about becoming a Republic, and, accordingly, about the type of nation Australia was and wanted to be. The apology, with its orientation to

Australia's normative identity, spoke directly to this contemporary political agenda.[7]

Thus one might say that the most appropriate or conducive circumstances for apology are those where the contemporary political community has some distance from the actual wrongs it addresses *but* the normative breaches and principles to which it speaks resonate with contemporary concerns. This explains why there is often a generational gap between the actual violations and a strong apology movement, a gap in which the experience of injury does not disappear, but loses some of the charge that would render the apology more of an insult than a form of respect.

Turning now from the circumstances most conducive to apology to the substance of the apology itself, one can again distinguish two key dimensions of the act relevant to its success: first, the quality or content of the speech, and second, the status of the speaker. With respect to the former, the most comprehensive apology will achieve all the illocutory functions set out in Chapter Two. That is, it will establish that certain events did in fact occur and give this narrative the state's stamp of legitimacy, declaring that certain acts are wrong and condemning them in the name of the political community; it will take responsibility for the wrong; it will recognize the legitimacy of the subject perspective of the victim by explicitly apologizing; and it will commit to a different approach and normative identity. Let us pause briefly on each of these.

First, the apology should include a comprehensive inventory of the normative failure to which it is responding. The more fully the breach is articulated, including the dissonance between the problematic norm (e.g., blacks do not count) and the political community's ideal normative commitments (e.g., all humans are to be treated with dignity), the more complete it will be. Prime Minister Kevin Rudd's apology, which narrated the entire story of removal as well as the intimate details of its impact on particular Australians, represents a fine example in this regard. Correlatively, an apology that leaves undisclosed the facts of the abuse and leaves opaque the nature of the normative breach will be relatively ineffective, especially if these facts are not widely known or acknowledged. Thus, for example, Clinton's apology to Rwanda was not backed by a comprehensive

---

[7] The contemporary normative concern need not coincide narrowly with the subject of the apology. In the case of European nations' apologies for the Holocaust, for example, the salient contemporary issue was not the position of Jews, but rather those nations' legitimate claim to be constituting the new Europe in the spirit of human rights and non-discrimination. This was made explicit in the Austrian apology, where the President actually said: "Any person who denies or minimizes the Holocaust does not have the basic human qualities that are a precondition for any responsible activity in politics." Address given by President Viktor Klima at the Forum on the Holocaust in Stockholm, *supra* Chapter One, note 20.

narrative of the failure of his nation to respond to the genocide, its suppression of information, and its refusal to use the term genocide, facts of which the majority of U.S. citizens had been, and remained, ignorant.

Second, the apology must explicitly assume responsibility. Expressions of regret that locate the speaker as a sympathetic bystander are not adequate. They must place the collective subject as a protagonist in the drama of violation, not on the sidelines. Ideally, given the complexities of responsibility and the resistance that such an assumption of responsibility is likely to provoke from an individual rights perspective, a political leader should take it upon him- or herself to explain the way in which the polity is responsible and distinguish this responsibility from the problematic model of the guilty collective. This type of sophisticated artic-ulation is certainly beyond what we have come to expect in political rhetoric. Nevertheless, this more nuanced approach would fortify the apology by making explicit that it does not violate other important norms. Moreover, the impact of this type of active construction of the meaning of apology goes beyond the particular apology insofar as any particular apology is both act and precedent, thereby contributing to the viability of the political convention.

Apologies can also fail against this criterion if they do not connect the collective with the wrongdoing, but instead locate responsibility exclusively with particular actors. U.S. Defense Secretary Donald Rumsfeld's apology for the torture of Iraqis by U.S. military personnel poignantly illustrates this failing.[8] Even as he accepted responsibility as part of an institutional chain of command, Rumsfeld was careful to insist that the "acts were perpetrated by a small number of U.S. military" and that the behaviour "was inconsistent with the values of our nation, it was inconsistent with the teachings of the military to the men and women of the armed forces, and it was certainly fundamentally un-American."[9] Nowhere in Rumsfeld's words does one find an acknowledgement that the violations emerged from some broader normative or institutional fail-ure to ensure full and equal respect for Iraqis as the 'other' in an international conflict. On the contrary, the actions are rhetorically defined by Rumsfeld as singular and aberrant and the United States is quarantined from their implica-tions by being held in place as the normative community that *then*, as now,

---

[8] It also demonstrates a number of other failings. For example, Rumsfeld failed to disclose all relevant information, specifically concerning the role of higher authorities. He also refused to define the acts in question as the violations that they were by calling them *torture*. Both would be required to meet the criterion of giving a full account of the wrongs. Further, the apology was not connected with a broader program of systemic changes.

[9] Statement by Defense Secretary Donald H. Rumsfeld before the Senate Armed Services Commit-tee, 7 May 2004, recorded by the Federal News Service and reported in "'My Deepest Apology' from Rumsfeld; 'Nothing Less Than Tragic,' Says Top General," *New York Times*, 8 May 2004.

condemned such violations at the hands of its military personnel.[10] Contrast this with Australian Prime Minister Paul Keating's description of the abuse against Aboriginal people: "[I]t was we who did the dispossessing. We took the traditional lands and smashed the traditional way of life. We brought the disasters. The alcohol. We committed the murders. We took the children from their mothers. We practiced discrimination and exclusion."[11]

Third, the assumption of responsibility and the condemnation of the norms must come together as the explicit and performative expression of apology. The expression of remorse is the way in which the apologizing subject takes responsibility for the wrong, announces that he or she condemns the wrong, displays recognition of the experience of the other, and declares the will to shift normative orientation. The apologizing subject says 'Not only is this wrong and not only did we support the wrong, but in the light of these two facts, we are sorry. We recognize the legitimacy of your grievances. We want to be otherwise'. This is why it is crucial that the representative actually speak the direct words 'I am sorry that (we did 'X')'. This condition of categorical admission explains why formulations like 'I am sorry if (we hurt you)' or 'I am sorry that (you feel a certain way)' or 'I regret (this state of affairs)' will not suffice. 'I am sorry' primarily represents an assumption of responsibility, and an authoritative condemnation of public norms manifests apology's performative quality, where the words bring a state of affairs into being, rather than referring the listener back to something that is already there.

This raises the fourth requirement: envisioning a different future. At its best, apology's performative speech can itself create a new state of affairs, forging or re-forging political relations and covenants. As a successful performative, the apologetic act does not simply announce that condemnation and respect are about to arrive; it condemns and respects. For this to suffice, however, we would have to be operating in a space where, as Arendt put it, "word and deed have not parted company, where words are not empty and deeds not brutal, where words are not used to veil intentions but to disclose realities."[12] And as

---

[10]   In the ensuing years, it has become evident that those supposedly aberrant acts were in fact clear manifestations of a moral environment in which torture was positively sanctioned and that the institutions of the military and executive branches of the state had been directly involved in creating that moral environment. See Dinah Pokempner, "Command Responsibility for Torture," in Kenneth Roth, Minky Worden, and Amy Bernstein, eds., *Torture: Does It Make Us Safer? Is It Ever OK? A Human Rights Perspective* (New York, London: New York Press, 2005).

[11]   See Chapter Five, note 31.

[12]   Arendt, *The Human Condition*, 200. Arendt is not naïve in this regard, but also warns that for all its revelatory potential, speech can always become "'mere talk', one more means toward the end, where it serves to deceive the enemy or dazzle everybody with propaganda." Ibid., 180.

we know, words are not only theoretically detachable from deeds, but have, throughout the career of politics, been radically and cynically detached. Thus, even as one aspires for a situation where apologetic words and reconstitutive deeds are inextricable dimensions of a single turn, any apology, and most especially one to a jaded public, will be most powerful when those deeds are in evidence.

The fact that the New Zealand apology, for example, formed part of modern treaties setting out formal recognition of the territorial and cultural rights of Maori groups substantiated the shift from a norm of non-recognition to one of recognition. Similarly, when Rudd spelled out seven dimensions of the future, he explicitly included actions to address contemporary forms of violation and inequality. By contrast, the revelation that the U.S. administration had sought assurance that its actions in Iraq and Guantanamo Bay would be exempt from the strictures of the Geneva Conventions (and other international and domestic law pertaining to torture) thoroughly undermined Rumsfeld's apology for the abuse of Iraqi prisoners.[13]

There is a strong intuitive appeal to the claim that an apology's success depends in part on other actions being carried out. How can one possibly take an apology seriously as an act of normative condemnation when the apologizing party immediately thereafter fails to act contrary to the condemned norms? As J. M. Coetzee put it so bluntly: "We are all sorry when we are found out. The question is what lesson have we learned? The question is, what are we going to do now that we are sorry?"[14] And yet, acknowledging the importance of actions correlate with apology's reorientation must not be confused with reducing the apology to a constative act, a mere signifier of these harder ('real') institutional shifts.

To retain the validity of the intuition that what happens in tandem with apology matters, and yet stave off the reduction of apology to the herald of events, one has to come back to the logic developed in the last chapter. The normative shifts that apology declares are neither equivalent to nor independent of shifts in hard institutions (the law and distributive systems), but neither do they stand in a causal relationship. Meaning or the symbolic is not a distinct, ideal sphere, but the grammar through which action occurs. Thus, apology's own capacity to effect shifts in the framework of norms will be supported by corresponding changes in other parts of the institutional framework and should in turn support those changes. Indeed, this is precisely what is entailed by both

---

[13] For a complete set of the documents, see Karen J. Greenberg and Joshua L. Dratel, *The Torture Papers: The Road to Abu Ghraib* (New York: Cambridge University Press, 2005).

[14] J. M. Coetzee, *Disgrace* (New York: Viking, 1999).

Van Boven's and Maimonides' multi-dimensional models of reparative action.
Van Boven distinguished apology as a *sui generis* dimension of reparation that
cannot simply be replaced by adding more of the other types of reparation and,
at the same time, located it as part of a complement of acts or forms of justice
that have an intrinsic connection. Though we are thrown to read them as a list,
they are best understood not as discrete acts that simply add together to form a
more or less complete response to the past, but rather as different dimensions of
the higher order requirement of full reparation and recognition. Maimonides
similarly articulated a model of complete *teshuvah* comprising oral confession,
remorse, resolve to act differently, and acting differently, all of which combine to effect transformation.[15] Indeed, if one goes back to the original modes
of repentant action in both Judaism and Christianity, speaking the words of
apology was always implicitly understood as a component of a complex of
reparative acts. Only later were the words shorn off as if they might stand in, or
stand alone, rather than stand with.

Turning now from what to who, we find that the status of the one who
actually speaks the apology has a powerful impact on its performative force.
As per the discussion in Chapter Two, one of the necessary conditions for
any particular apology to do the work of this class of speech acts is that the
speaker actually represent the collective on behalf of which he or she is
speaking. This entails both that he or she be recognized as representing
(having the authority to speak on behalf of) the collective and that he or
she make it explicit that he or she is apologizing in this representative
capacity. Apologies given by someone without the capacity to represent
the polity, as in the case where a senior bureaucrat delivered the apology
to Native Americans, suffer because they fail meet the first of these requirements. Apologies given by someone who *does* have that authority but apologizes in a personal capacity, as in the Howard and Balkan cases, suffer
because they do not meet the second. Moreover, formal delegation from
the head of state to a lesser representative will not substitute status in this
respect, because the speaker is relying on his or her authority and stature to
bring along the polity. One saw this in the Canadian case, where the first
apology was discounted, and only when the Prime Minister apologized did it
register as legitimate.[16]

The contribution of the speaker is reflected not only in his or her current
political status, but also in other aspects of his or her public persona. By way of

---

[15] Maimonides, Mishnah Torah, The Hilchot Teshuva (Treatise Concerning Repentance), Book
I, V, Chapter I.
[16] See Chapter One, notes 64, 65.

a thought-experiment one might ask, for example, whether Nelson Mandela could apologize for the abuses committed against black South Africans. Perhaps one doubts that he could, and if so it would be because he was too deeply associated with the victim group to stand in for the perpetrator group that must be seen to repent. What this points to more generally is the interplay between the representative's identity as an individual and his or her ability to effect apology's work. He or she must literally map the transformation that the apology effects and this requires that his or her representative function be bifurcated: he or she must be able to stand in for the old *and* the new political culture and, by temporalising these two in speech and body, make present a definitive normative shift. He or she must speak and *be* the movement from the old to the new nation.

Going even beyond the role that the leader's political identity plays in effecting apology's work, he or she must also be able to represent authentically the nation's regret. Again, imagine a leader who speaks the words of apology, but clearly without feeling or personal involvement in the meaning of what he or she is doing. Or, perhaps to mark the distinction even more sharply, imagine that apology was delivered by a piece of legislation, published but not spoken by a particular person. Absent the authentic embodiment of shame and sadness, the act would certainly fail. But what is going on here? Much of this book has been devoted to distinguishing the political apology from the individual emotion-laden act with which we are most familiar. So what role can emotional authenticity legitimately play?

It is certainly not the authenticity of the individual *qua* individual that matters; no one really cared that much about whether John Howard was personally sad about Aboriginal children being removed from their homes, because he was unwilling to allow that sadness to speak beyond his own person. Rather, one might say that the singular person of the leader must authentically express the shame of the collective. In saying this, however, it is crucial to avoid reverting to the ontological mistake that led to Trouillot's characterization of the apologizing nation as the giant liberal subject. Thus, in demanding that the authentic expression of the leader stand in for the nation, one cannot take this to mean that his or her emotional, singular, and unified being stands in for an ontologically similar, albeit much larger body with similar feelings, just off-stage: the nation writ large. Rather – and this arises from the *sui generis* character of political representation – the leader's embodiment of authenticity gives form to a dimension of the nation that does not itself have form. It is because – and only because – of his or her ability to embody the aspect of shame and remorse, as Rudd did in Australia, that the leader can *represent* it – in the sense of the original Latin, *repraesentare*, or bring into presence something previously absent.[17] Indeed, political representation is precisely constituted by this ontological difference between the full presence of an actor and the impossibility of full presence of that which he represents. It is only by virtue of the fact that the leader, a person with a body, can stand in for the nation that the nation's repentance can appear.[18]

The ontological tension that is constitutive of political representation takes on a particular poignancy in the case of apology because what is being represented is the soft political-cultural dimension of the nation, and the leader's body, in which humanity and political authority coexist, is uniquely placed to make this present. Even as the force of apology lies in its picking up the *political* identity of the nation, this process is only made possible by virtue of the fact that the leader is *also* a person who can represent shame and regret and humility. The blurring between the political and the personal bodies of the representative leader is precisely what makes it possible for the nation to apologize in a manner that is at once political (but not institutional) and personal, but without suggesting that the nation is a person; the *authentic* expression of apology speaks across this personal/subjective and public/institutional divide.

2. APOLOGY AND THE BOUNDARIES OF THE POLITICAL

At the outset of this journey, I drew attention to various assumptions about rituals of apology, on the one hand, and the nature of modern liberal secular politics, on the other, that led to our seeing them as ill-matched bedfellows. An examination of the former has revealed the extent to which it speaks a political voice, offering transformative possibilities for the constitutive norms of political communities that underpin systematic wrongdoing in a manner that reaches beyond the capabilities of liberalism's justice. But what are the implications for our understanding of contemporary political action? If, indeed, we moderns are reaching for apology, with its attention to collective norms that orient individual actions and its ritual form, what does this tell us about the

---

[17] See Pitkin, *The Concept of Representation*, 3, and more generally Chapter Five.

[18] Donald McEachin, the state legislator who introduced the apology laws in Virginia, and was himself the great-grandson of a slave who moved to Virginia after the Civil War, poignantly illustrated the significance of the double identity of the representative. McEachin described how "his personal history and spiritual journey merged with Virginia's" and then, moving beyond his own body to that of the legislature: "What we had was people with a shared history . . . they're all here in the General Assembly, and we were able to come together for this." Tim Craig, "In Va. House," supra Chapter One, note 73.

way that we are doing politics? And how do we need to recast our political theoretical categories, specifically those that explain responsibility, the relationship between the collective and the individual and the mechanisms for changing the way in which we act?

A simple answer to those questions would be that just as our repertoire of political action has expanded beyond the strategies and mechanisms of justice that we thought were sufficient for, and appropriate to, secular liberal polities, so must our repertoire of theoretical categories. But this does not go far enough. Recall that underpinning a number of the reasons that secular liberals draw on to reject religious processes as appropriate sources for strategies to address wrongdoing in our own context was a dichotomous analytic framework that rendered individual and collective, private and public, the speech of intimacy and the speech of formal institutions, and thin/revisable versus thick/absolutist values as mutually exclusive categories. Moreover, we insisted that our moral and political commitments placed us exclusively on the other side of religious political orders.

And yet we find ourselves engaged in a practice that does not simply operate on the foreign side of these dichotomies, but escapes them altogether. The apologizing polity is neither the institution of the state nor the feeling individual. Rather, it is the people of the nation, constituted both socially and politically and at the level of subjectively held values and identities that have been constituted around certain ways of seeing the world. In its political dimension, apologetic speech reaches not down into the darkness of the heart but out into the grammar that orients the judgements of members of the political community and thus the way in which they recognize and treat each other. Its home is neither the individual heart, nor the rationality of choice, nor the institutions of law and policy, but a shared set of meanings and orientations that pattern each of them. A methodological slant towards positivism combined with an ethical suspicion of anything that bears the hint of collectivism may have prevented our articulating this for ourselves, but in this dogmatic approach perhaps we have blinded ourselves, not only to the complexity of motivation and to the resources ritual offers for reorientation, but also to what we actually do. Perhaps the map of the social and political world is not as we thought; perhaps nor are we.

If human beings were motivated by nothing but reason, then the rule of reason would be sufficient. But we are not, and for that reason politics and political rhetoric have to speak to and speak for all that motivates action and judgement. In the light of overwhelming evidence that human beings are capable of committing horrific violations against each other, even in the face of laws and reason, there is more than enough reason to reach to wherever our tendencies to act well come from; and we are reaching there. In the Jewish and Christian framework, this place of morality was called God: the source of norms that would orient rightful action, if only human beings could align themselves with God and not stray from the path (sin). And the ritual practices of religions, the sacrifices, their substitutes, and the sacraments, were designed to allow human beings to approach this source of rightful action and to undergo the transformations that would bring them to a different orientation. Secular political communities put down that language and disengaged with those practices, often for very good reasons. But in so doing we also deprived ourselves of the resources these concepts and mechanisms offer in achieving exactly what the liberal ideal seeks to achieve: a political community in which the norms of equal recognition and respect increasingly mediate all relations between citizens, and eventually all human beings. The gestures, tonalities, rhythms, and prose of apology may be precisely what we need to break through the patterns of violation that hold us as 'irrationally' as these shunned rituals, and we would do well to remember them in practice.

Moreover, if this ritualized form of re-covenanting seems to be an aberration in the modalities of modern politics, we would also do well to remind ourselves of the forms of political action adopted at the original moments of covenanting our nations. There, as Arendt pointed out in her analysis of the American Revolution, the Founders both made explicit reference to the absolute transcendent principles that were the source of the nation (or Republic) and ritualized their incarnation in the nation. One could interpret this as the legacy of religious irrationalism that still pervaded the worldview of our political forebears, but I prefer Arendt's view that the explicit reference to an absolute source of authority or grounding principles and rituals to incarnate did not reflect religious conviction but was rather a matter of political expediency. The Founders recognized that without this source of a moral order beyond the reach of the mundane and pragmatic business of everyday politics, anything, including any breach of fundamental norms, would ultimately be possible. Reason and the real possibility of a reasonable political community of people who live according to the laws they create sit on top of these truths that they neither create nor hold, but which hold them.[19] Without a pre-rational fidelity to the absolute, the nation or, as Arendt called it, the vicar of God "was liable to do very wrong indeed."[20] The Founders also recognized, as Arendt points out when she references Jefferson's plea that there should be a revolution every twenty years, that it was vanity and

[19] Arendt, *On Revolution*, 193.
[20] Ibid., 190.

presumption to assume that the first covenant had actually approached the true absolute.[21] Only a future of new revolutionary and refounding moments could refresh the 'tree of liberty'.[22]

History has borne out the veracity of their predictions; the vicar *does* do very wrong indeed. We may have covenanted to abstract absolutes like the sanctity of life and the equal dignity of all humans, but in our hands those principles became particularized and narrowed through the projection of our own identity and interests. The absolute that we thought underpinned our actions turned out to be a parochial God after our own image. Certainly, it may take a long time for the citizenry of a nation to notice this. Even in the face of the most horrific politically sanctioned violations, citizens can remain convinced of the moral perfection of their ideal identity and its historical translation. But what happens when this story is interrupted? What happens when the accusing look of the one whose experience was excluded from the closed circle of covenantal respect scars the image in the mirror?

At this crisis point the gap between the identity the nation has embodied through its actions and its ideal identity becomes evident. In covenantal terms, we recognize that our actual law failed the covenantal ideal. Confronting this gap is the occasion for shame. This moment of shame is a critical point; the nation can go either way, and apology can serve both paths. Shocked by the ugly face in the mirror, the nation may look for strategies to convince itself that it is beautiful after all, amongst which it may well reach for 'words that veil intention'. Or it can reflect on the image and remake itself.

Taking this path, the path of re-covenanting, requires something more than the business-as-usual of everyday politics. Just as the moment of covenanting required a ritual to ground identity in an absolute set of commitments, so too the moment of recovenanting will require "some ritual processes through which the ideology [the old regime] embodies . . . can be publicly repudiated."[23] Political repentance is such a ritual: words that disclose a new reality. This is what Lincoln recognized when he proclaimed a Day of National Fasting, Humiliation and Prayer as a ritual process whereby the nation could return to the covenant of liberty and equality, only on this point of the interpretive cycle, recognizing that whites were not the only ones within that covenantal commitment.

---

[21] Ibid., 233.

[22] The words come from a longer phrase in a letter from Jefferson to Colonel William Stevens Smith, 13 November 1787, "the tree of liberty must be refreshed, from time to time, with blood of patriots and tyrants. It is its natural manure." In Julian P. Boyd (ed.), *The Papers of Thomas Jefferson* (Princeton, N.J.: Princeton University Press, 1955), vol. 12: 356–7.

[23] Walzer, ed., *Regicide and Revolution*, 88.

If the religious overtones of self-evident truths and nature's God were not incompatible with the principle of liberal democracy at the founding moment, why should the religious overtones of repentance be incompatible with its improvement or repair thereafter? Secular liberal politics is not, nor can it afford to be, more attached to dogmatic images of itself than to the calls of the day. Far from dismissing the religious overtones of apology as incompatible with the tenets of modern political communities, we can encounter them as new possibilities for apology's expression. There is, admittedly, a utopian aspect of this claim: a notion in the background that as an act of recognition, apology forms part of a movement towards an ever-expanding circle of people whose right to have rights will be recognized. And as we have seen in the case of religion, a universal God is usually a mask for a far more particular God whose definitions of rightful behaviour favour some and exclude others, albeit under the cover of universalism, all the better to exclude the difference that would really challenge those norms.

This tension between the possibility of expanding recognition and the danger of disguising assimilation in the clothes of equality will unavoidably haunt the apology. If, however, one understands that universalism is not an already existent ideal to be discovered but a condition to be achieved through historical movements, movements generated by our recognition of the failure to recognize the other, then one sees that this tension is not a defect, but is rather built into the process. In Hegel's terms, the beautiful soul could never be in the world, could never actually exist in history, because every commitment to action is particular, and so falls short of the universal.[24] It is only the impurity of the commitment, the willingness to fall short of the universal, that brings the universal into a sharper (though always incomplete) focus, and then only because of the damage it brings about and the cry it provokes in the other who becomes my accuser. And it is only my confession, my apology to the other, that drags me past that particularity. The universal cannot be accessed as immediacy, but can only be mediated through my encounter with the other whom I have failed to recognize as a subject who has access to a part of the universal that I do not.[25]

In its determination to ground political relations on a firm foundation of justice, modern political theory has perhaps refused to see that beneath the move to justice (or to injustice) there was already an ethical relation. Justice

[24] See Hegel, *Philosophy of Right*, Preface, 13.

[25] In the case of the apology movement, there are two senses in which the other may provide the opportunity to move beyond the parochial. First, in the apologetic relationship itself, and second, in witnessing the actions of other political communities and thereby recognizing possibilities for moral action.

stabilizes recognition, but justice is not itself fertile. Only the ethical recognition that arises from opening up to the perspective of the one who was not-me, or not-us, can give birth to a movement beyond the justice we already have. Only opening to the perspective of the other can reorient us so as to recognize the injustice of our apparent justice.[26] In the original sense of apology, only when one is called to justify oneself before the other, and most importantly before an other who accuses me of the inadequacies of the justice I was so sure of, only then can occur a genuinely new movement in justice.

[26] In this regard, even while recognizing the importance of trying individuals for the crimes of Nazism, Arendt acknowledges that the speechless horror of the crimes and the refusal to think the unthinkable has "perhaps prevented a very necessary reappraisal of the legal categories." Hannah Arendt, "Some Questions of Moral Philosophy," 56.

Bibliography

Abbott, Walter, ed. *The Documents of Vatican II*. New York: The American Press, 1966.

Abdel-Nour, Farid. "National Responsibility." *Political Theory* 31, no. 5 (2003): 693–719.

Aboriginal and Torres Strait Islander Commission [ATSIC], Monitoring and Reporting Section. *"Five Years On: Implementation of the Commonwealth Government Responses to the Recommendations of the Royal Commission into Aboriginal Deaths in Custody."* Canberra: Commonwealth of Australia, 1997.

Aboriginal and Torres Strait Islander Social Justice Commissioner. "First Annual Report, 1993." Canberra, 1993.

Adorno, Theodor W. *Aesthetic Theory*. Translated by C. Lenhardt. London: Routledge and Kegan Paul, 1984.

Aldrich, Robert. "Colonial Past, Post-Colonial Present: History Wars French-Style." *History Australia* 3, no. 1 (2006): 1–14.

Almond, Gabriel A., and Sidney Verba. *The Civic Culture: Political Attitudes and Democracy in Five Nations*. Princeton, N.J.: Princeton University Press, 1989.

Anderson, Benedict. *Imagined Communities: Reflections on the Origin and Spread of Nationalism*. London: Verso, 1983.

Applebaum, J. *Military Tribunals and International Crimes*. Westport, Conn.: Greenwood Press, 1954.

Arendt, Hannah. *The Human Condition*. Chicago: University of Chicago Press, 1958.

———. *Lectures on Kant's Political Philosophy*. Edited by Ronald Beiner. Chicago: University of Chicago Press, 1992.

———. *On Revolution*. Harmondsworth: Penguin Books, 1973.

———. *Origins of Totalitarianism*. New York: Harcourt Brace, 1951.

———. *The Promise of Politics*. Edited by Jerome Kohn. New York: Schocken, 2005.

———. *Responsibility and Judgement*. Edited by Jerome Kohn. New York: Schocken, 2003.

Atwood, Bain. "Settling Histories, Unsettling Pasts: Reconciliation and Historical Justice in Settler Societies." In *Historical Justice in International Perspective: How Settler Societies Are Trying to Right the Wrongs of the Past*. Edited by Manfred Berg and Bernd Schaefer. New York: Cambridge University Press, 2008.

Atwood, Bain, and Andrew Markus. *The 1967 Referendum or When Aborigines Did Not Get the Vote*. Canberra: Australian Institute of Aboriginal and Torres Strait Islander Studies [AIATSIS], 1995.

Auerbach, Eric. *Mimesis: The Representation of Reality in Western Literature*. Translated by R. Willard. Princeton N.J.: Princeton University Press, 1953.

Austin, J. L. *How to Do Things with Words*. Cambridge, Mass.: Harvard University Press, 1962.

Australian Bureau of Statistics [ABS]. *Deaths* 2004. ABS Catalogue No. 3320.0. Commonwealth of Australia: Canberra, 2004.

———. *Australia's Health* 2004. AIHW Catalogue No. AUS 44; ABS Catalogue No. 8903.0. Commonwealth of Australia: Canberra, 2004.

Australian Bureau of Statistics [ABS] and Australian Institute of Health and Welfare [AIHW]. *The Health and Welfare of Australia's Aboriginal and Torres Strait Islander Peoples* 2005 ABS Catalogue No. 4704.0. Commonwealth of Australia: Canberra, 2005.

Bamford, David. "French General in Algeria Torture Claim." *BBC News Online*, 14 May 2001.

Basil Redlich, E. *The Forgiveness of Sins*. Edinburgh: T & T Clark, 1937.

"Belgian Apology to Rwanda." *BBC News Online*, 7 April 2000.

"Belgrade's Cautious Apology." *BBC News Online*, 13 November 2003.

Bell, James H. "Assimilation in NSW." In *New Perspectives in the Study of Aboriginal Communities*. Edited by Marie Reav. London: Angus and Robertson, 1964.

Bender, Peter. *Die Neue Ostpolitik Und Ihre Folgen: Vom Mauerbau Bis Zur Vereinigung*. Munich: Deutsche Taschenbuch Verlag, 1996.

Benjamin, Walter. *The Arcades Project*. Translated by Howard Eiland and Kevin McLaughlin. Cambridge, Mass.: Bellknap Press, 1999.

———. *Illuminations*. London: Pimlico, 1999.

Bennet, James. "In Uganda, Clinton Expresses Regret on Slavery in U.S." *New York Times*, 25 March 1998.

Bennion, Thomas, ed. "The Tainui Settlement." *The Maori Law Review* (1995).

Berezin, Mabel. "Fissured Terrain: Methodological Approaches and Research Styles in Culture and Politics." In *The Sociology of Culture: Emerging Theoretical Perspectives*. Edited by Diana Crane. Oxford, U.K.; Cambridge, Mass.: Blackwell, 1994.

Bernauer, James W., ed. *Amor Mundi: Explorations in the Faith and Thought of Hannah Arendt*. Boston, Dordrecht, and Lancaster: Martinus Nijhoff, 1989.

Bhargava, Rajeev, ed. *Secularism and Its Critics*. Delhi, New York: Oxford University Press, 2005.

Bilsky, Leora Y. "When Actor and Spectator Meet in the Courtroom: Reflections on Hannah Arendt's Concept of Judgment." *History and Memory* 8, no 2 (1996): 137–173.

Bolt, Robert. *A Man for All Seasons*. New York: Vintage, 1960.

Bonnell, Andrew, and Martin Crotty. "Australia's History under Howard, 1996–2007." *Annals of the American Academy of Political and Social Science* 617 (2008): 149–165.

Bourdieu, Pierre. *The Logic of Practice*. Translated by Richard Nice. Cambridge: Polity Press, 1990.

———. *An Outline of a Theory of Practice*. Translated by Richard Nice. Cambridge: Cambridge University Press, 1977.

Brandt, Willy. *Erinnerungen*. Frankfurt am Main: Propylaen Verlag, 1989.

———. *My Life*. New York: Viking, 1992.

Branscombe, Nyla, Bertjan Doosje, and C. McGarty. "Antecedents and Consequences of Collective Guilt." In *From Prejudice to Inter-Group Relations: Differential Reactions to Social Groups*. Edited by D. M. Mackie and E. R. Smith. Philadelphia: Psychology Press, 2002: 49–66.

Branscombe, Nyla R., and Bertjan Doosje, eds. *Collective Guilt: International Perspectives*. Cambridge: Cambridge University Press, 2004.

Brosnan, Greg. "Kin Get Apology, Cash after Massacre." Reuters, 11 December 2001.

Buchler, A. *Studies in Sin and Atonement in the Rabbinic Literature of the 1st Century*. London: Oxford University Press, 1928.

"Bundestag Apologizes to Homosexual Victims of Nazis." Agence France-Presse, 8 December 2000.

Burke, Edmund. *Reflections on the Revolution in France*. Edited by Conor Cruise. New York: Penguin, 1968.

Buti, Toni. "They Took the Children Away." *Aboriginal Law Bulletin* 3, no. 72 (1995): 35–36.

Buti, Toni, and Melissa Parkes "International Law Obligations to Provide Reparations for Human Rights Violations." *Murdoch University Electronic Journal of Law* 6, no. 4 (December 1999).

Calder v. Attorney General of British Columbia. [1973] S.C.R. 313.

Canfield, John V. "The Compatibility of Free Will and Determinism." *The Philosophical Review* 71, no. 3 (July 1962): 712–36.

Carr, E. H. *What Is History?* London: Penguin, 1990.

Carroll, James. *Constantine's Sword: The Church and the Jews*. Boston: Houghton Mifflin, 2001.

Casanova, Jose. *Public Religions in the Modern World*. Chicago and London: University of Chicago Press, 1994.

Cassel, Douglas. "Lessons from the Americas: Guidelines for International Response to Amnesties for Atrocities." *Law and Contemporary Problems* 59, no. 4 (1996): 197–230.

Cassirer, Ernst. Substance and Theory, and Einstein's Theory of Relativity. Edited by William Curtis Swabey and Marie Taylor (Collins) Swabey. New York: Dover, 1953.

Castoriadis, Cornelius. *The Imaginary Institution of Society*. Translated by Kathleen Blarney. Cambridge, Mass.: MIT Press, 1988.

———. *Philosophy, Politics, Autonomy*. Edited by David Ames Curtis. Oxford: Oxford University Press, 1991.

Charlton, Michael. *The Eagle and the Small Birds: Crisis in the Soviet Empire: From Yalta to Solidarity*. Chicago: University of Chicago Press, 1985.

Coetzee, J. M. *Disgrace*. New York: Viking, 1999.

Cohen, Hermann. *Religion of Reason: Out of the Sources of Judaism*. Translated by Simon Kaplan. New York: F. Ungar, 1972.

Cohen, Jean L., and Andrew Arato. *Civil Society and Political Theory*. Cambridge, Mass.: MIT Press, 1992.

Cohen, Roger. "Wiesel Urges Germany to Ask Forgiveness." *New York Times*, 28 January 2000.

Cohen, Samuel S. "Original Sin." *Hebrew Union College Annual* 21 (1948): 275–330.

Commonwealth of Australia. *Aboriginal Welfare: Initial Conference of Commonwealth and State Aboriginal Authorities*. Canberra: Government Printer, 1937.

Commonwealth of Australia Federal Parliament. *The Case for Yes*. Edited by Federal Parliament. Canberra: Commonwealth of Australia, 1967.

Cornwell, John. *Hitler's Pope: The Secret History of Pius XII*. New York: Viking, 1999.

Council for Aboriginal Reconciliation Act 1991 (Cth).

Cowlinshaw, Gillian. "On Getting It Wrong – Collateral Damage in the History Wars." *Australian Historical Studies* 37, no. 127 (2006): 181–202.

Craig, Tim. "In Va. House, 'Profound Regret' on Slavery; Delegates Unanimously Pass Resolution of Contrition About State's Role."*The Washington Post*, 3 February 2007.

Crichton, James. *The Ministry of Reconciliation*. London: Geoffrey Chapman, 1974.

Cubillo and Another v. Commonwealth (No 2) (2000). 103 FCR 1.

Daley, Suzanne. "For Gandhi (D.1948), a Long Due Apology." *New York Times*, 29 July 1999.

Dallen, James. *The Reconciling Community: The Rite of Penance*. New York: Pueblo, 1986.

Davies, Norman. *God's Playground: A History of Poland*, vol. 2: *1795 to the Present*. Oxford: Clarendon, 1981.

De Leon, Sergio. "Guatemala's Three Branches of Government Apologize for State Role in Human Rights Activist's Slaying."Associated Press, 23 April 2004.

Denzin, Norman K. "Reading Cultural Texts: Comment on Griswold."*American Journal of Sociology* 95, no. 6 (May 1990): 1577–1580.

"Djukanovic Apologized to Croatia."*AIM Zagreb*, 29 June 2000.

Drozdiak, William. "Vatican Gives Formal Apology for Inaction During Holocaust." *Washington Post*, 17 March 1998.

Dumphy, Harry. "De La Rua Apologizes for Nazi Role." Associated Press, 13 June 2000.

Duquoc, Christian. "Real Reconciliation and Sacramental Reconciliation." In *Concilium Religion in the Seventies*, vol. 61: *Sacramental Reconciliation*. Edited by Edward Schillebeeckx. New York: Herder and Herder, 1971.

Durkheim, Emile. "De la definition des phenomenes religieux." *L'Annee Sociologique* 2 (1897–1898): 1–28.

———. *The Division of Labor in Society*. Translated by W. D. Halls. New York: Free Press, 1979.

———. *The Elementary Forms of Religious Life*. Translated by Carol Cosman. Oxford: Oxford University Press, 2001.

———. *The Rules of Sociological Method*. Translated by W. D. Halls. New York: Free Press, 1982.

Elias, Norbert. *What Is Sociology?* Translated by Stephen Mennell and Grace Morrissey. New York: Columbia University Press, 1987.

Federal Parliament of Australia (Senate), Senate Legal and Constitutional Committee. *Healing: A Legacy of Generations. The Report of the Inquiry into the Federal Government's Implementation of the Recommendations Made by the Human Rights and Equal Opportunity Commission in Bringing Them Home*. Canberra: Commonwealth of Australia, 1997.

Fehrenbacher, Don E., ed. *Lincoln: Speeches and Writings 1859–1865*. New York: Library of America, 1989.

Feinberg, Joel. *Doing and Deserving: Essays in the Theory of Responsibility*. Princeton, N.J.: Princeton University Press, 1970.

Feldman, Allen. "Memory Theatres, Virtual Witnessing and the Trauma Aesthetic." *Biography: An Interdisciplinary Quarterly* 27, no. 1 (2004): 163–202.

Fenichel Pitkin, Hannah. *The Concept of Representation*. Berkeley: University of California Press, 1967.

Fletcher, George P. *Basic Concepts of Criminal Law*. Oxford: Oxford University Press, 1998.

Foot Moore, George. *Judaism in the First Centuries of the Christian Era: The Age of the Tannaim*. Cambridge, Mass.: Harvard University Press, 1958.

Frankfurt, Harry G. *The Importance of What We Care About: Philosophical Essays*. Cambridge: Cambridge University Press, 1988.

"French Police Apologize for Jewish Wartime Swoops."Reuters, 7 October 1997.

Freud, Sigmund. *The Standard Edition of the Complete Psychological Works of Sigmund Freud, vol. 14: On the History of the Psycho-Analytic Movement, Papers on Metapsychology and Other Works, 1914–1916*. Translated by J. Strachey, edited by J. Strachey, Anna Freud, and Carrie Lee Rothgeb. London: The Hogarth Press and the Institute of Psychoanalysis, 1957.

Fuller, Lon. "Positivism and Fidelity to Law – A Reply to Professor Hart." *Harvard Law Review* 71, no. 4 (1958): 630–672.

Gadamer, Hans-Georg. *Truth and Method*. Translated by Joel Weinsheimer and Donald Marshall. London and New York: Sheed and Ward, 1975.

Gaita, Raimond. "Genocide, the Holocaust and the Aborigines."*Quadrant* 41, no. 11 (1997): 17–22.

———. *A Common Humanity: Thinking about Love, Truth and Justice*. London: Routledge, 2000.

Gelin, Albert. "Sin in the Old Testament." In *Sin in the Bible*. Edited by Charles Schaldenbrand. New York: Desclee, 1964.

Gellner, Ernst. *Conditions for Liberty: Civil Society and Its Rivals*. London: Hamish Hamilton, 1994.

Gilbert, Margaret. "Collective Guilt and Collective Guilt Feelings."*Journal of Ethics* 6, no. 2 (2002): 115–143.

———. "Group Wrongs and Guilt Feelings."*Journal of Ethics* 1, no. 1 (1997): 61–94.

———. *On Social Facts*. London and New York: Routledge, 1989.

Goldhagen, Daniel. *A Moral Reckoning: The Catholic Church during the Holocaust and Today*. New York: Knopf, 2002.

Gooder, Haydie, and Jane Jacobs. "On the Border of the Unsayable: The Apology in Postcolonizing Australia."*Interventions* 2, no. 2 (2000): 229–247.

Greenberg, Karen J., and Joshua L Dratel. *The Torture Papers: The Road to Abu Ghraib*. New York: Cambridge University Press, 2005.

Gross, Jan T. *Neighbors: The Destruction of the Jewish Community in Jedwabne, Poland*. Princeton, N.J.: Princeton University Press, 2000.

Gunther Plaut W., ed. *The Torah: A Modern Commentary*. New York: Union of American Hebrew Congregations, 1981.

Habermas, Jurgen. *The Structural Transformation of the Public Sphere.* Translated by Thomas Burger.Cambridge, Mass.: MIT Press, 1991.

Habermas, Jürgen, and Adam Michnik. "Overcoming the Past." *New Left Review* 1, no. 203(1994): 3–16.

Hage, Ghassan. *Against Paranoid Nationalism.* Melbourne: Pluto, 2002.

Hanoch, Albeck. *Shisha Sidrei Mishna.* Jerusalem, Bialik, and Tel Aviv: Devir, 1952–1959.

Harmsen, Peter. "History Hinders China's Bid to Play Big Brother in SE Asia." Agence France-Presse, 8 November 2000.

Harnden, Toby. "Blair Apologizes to Ireland for Potato Famine." *Electronic Telegraph,* 2 June 1997.

Hart, L.H.A. "Positivism and the Separation of Law and Morals." *Harvard Law Review* 71, no. 4 (1958): 593–629.

Hartman, David. *A Living Covenant.* Woodstock, Vt.: Jewish Lights, 1997.

Hasluck, Paul. *Native Welfare in Australia: Speeches and Addresses.* Perth: Paterson, Brokenshaw, 1953.

Hegel, George. *The Philosophy of Right.* Edited and translated by T.M. Knox. Oxford: Clarendon Press, 1965.

———. *Die Vernunft in Der Geschichte.* Edited by Johannes Hoffmeister. Hamburg: Meiner, 1955.

Heidegger, Martin. *Basic Writings.* Edited and Translated by David Farrell Krell. San Francisco: Harper Collins, 1997.

Held, Virginia, Sidney Morgenbesser, and Thomas Nagel. *Philosophy, Morality and International Affairs: Essays Edited for the Society for Philosophy and Public Affairs.* New York: Oxford University Press, 1974.

Hellwig, Monika. *Sign of Conversion and Reconciliation: The Sacrament of Penance for Our Times.* Wilmington, Del.: Michael Glazier, 1984.

Henley, Jon. "French Politicians in Firing Line for Role in Algeria."*The Guardian,* 11 May 2001.

Henneberger, Melinda. "The Pope Apologizes for the Catholic Church's 'Errors' in China." *New York Times,* 25 October 2001.

Herf, Jeffrey. *Divided Memory: The Nazi Past in the Two Germanys.* Cambridge, Mass.: Harvard University Press, 1997.

Hillman, James. *The Terrible Love of War.* New York: Penguin, 2004.

Honneth, Axel. "Integrity and Disrespect." *Political Theory* 20, no. 2 (1992): 187–201.

———. *The Struggle for Recognition.* Translated by Joel Anderson. Cambridge, Mass.: MIT Press, 1996.

"Howard Defends Stand on Apology." *The Age,* 28 January 1998.

Human Rights and Equal Opportunity Commission [HREOC]. *Bringing Them Home: Report of the National Inquiry into the Separation of Aboriginal and Torres Strait Islander Children from Their Families.* Sydney: HREOC, April 1997.

———. *Bringing Them Home: Implementation Progress Report.* The Report of the Follow Up Project on the Progress of Australian Governments' Responses to and Implementation of the Recommendations Made by National Inquiry into the Separation of Aboriginal and Torres Strait Islander Children from Their Families in Its Bringing Them Home Report (1997). Sydney: September, 1998.

Humphreys, Margaret. *Empty Cradles.* London: Doubleday, 1994.

"I Would Like to Apologize for the Sins That Have Happened in the Past, to the Victims or the Families of Santa Cruz." *The Straits Times*, 6 March 2000.

"Indonesia Wahid Welcomes Resumption of Timor Air, Sea Link." Associated Press, 1 March 2000.

Inson, G., and R. Ward. "The Glorious Years." *Boomerang*, 17 December 1887.

International Theological Commission. *Memory and Reconciliation: The Church and the Faults of the Past*. Strathfield: St. Paul's Publications, 2000.

"IRA Apology a Building Block." *BBC News Online*, 17 July 2002.

Jacob, E. *Theology of the Old Testament*. New York: Harper, 1958.

James, William. *The Principles of Psychology*. New York: Courier Dover, 1950.

Jaspers, Karl. *The Question of German Guilt*. Translated by E. B. Ashton. New York: Fordham University Press, 2001.

Jellinek, George. *Allgemeine Staatslehre*. Berlin: O. Häring, 1905.

Johnston, Douglas. *Faith Based Diplomacy*. Oxford, New York: Oxford University Press, 2003.

Jopson, Debra. "Between the Rock and Nowhere." *Sydney Morning Herald*, 8 June 1999.

———. "Radiating from the Rock, Ritual of Hope." *Sydney Morning Herald*, 5 June 1999.

Kaesuk Yoon, Carol. "Families Emerge as Silent Victims of Tuskegee Syphilis Experiment." *New York Times*, 12 May 1997.

Kant, Immanuel. *Critique of Pure Reason*. Translated by Paul Guyer and Allen W. Wood. Cambridge: Cambridge University Press, 1998.

Keifer, Ralph, and Frederick R. McManus. *The Rite of Penance: Commentaries*, vol. 1: *Understanding the Document*. Washington, D.C.: The Liturgical Conference, 1975.

Kidd, Rosalyn. *Trustees on Trial: Recovering the Stolen Wages*. Canberra, Australian Capital Territory: Aboriginal Studies Press, 2006.

Kirk, Kenneth E. *The Vision of God, the Christian Doctrine of the Summum Bonum: The Bampton Lectures for* 1928. London, New York: Longman, Green, 1941.

Kleist, James, trans. *The Epistles of St. Clement of Rome and St. Ignatius of Antioch: Ancient Christian Writers*. New York: Newman Press, 1946.

Koselleck, Reinhart. *Futures Past: On the Semantics of Historical Time*. Translated by Keith Tribe. New York, Chichester, West Sussex: Columbia University Press, 2004.

Kwabena-Essem, Adu. "A New Look at Ju-Ju: The Pope's Apology to Africans." *Djembe Magazine*, July 1995.

Lacan, Jacques. *Ecrits: A Selection*. Edited and translated byAlan Sheridan. New York: W. W. Norton, 1977.

Laclau, Ernesto. *Emancipations*. London: W. W. Norton, 1996.

Lake, Marilyn. "Citizenship as Non-Discrimination: Acceptance or Assimilationism? Political Logic and Emotional Investment in Campaigns for Aboriginal Rights in Australia, 1940 to 1970." *Gender and History* 13, no. 3 (November 2001): 566–592.

Lambert, W. "Three Literary Prayers of the Babylonians." *Archiv fur Orientforschung* 19 (1959–1960): 55–60.

Lang, P.H.D. "Private Confession and Absolution in the Lutheran Church: A Doctrinal, Historical, and Critical Study." *Concordia Theological Quarterly* 56, no. 4 (October 1992): 241–263.

Laub, Karin. "Austrian President: No Apology Can Expunge Agony of Holocaust." *Associated Press*, 15 November 1994.

Lawler, Michael G. *Symbol and Sacrament: A Contemporary Sacramental Theology.* New York: Paulist Press, 1987.

Leach, Barbara, ed. *The Aborigine Today.* Sydney: Paul Hamlyn, 1971.

Levinas, Emmanuel. *Nine Talmudic Readings.* Edited by Annette Aronowitcz. Bloomington and Indianapolis: Indiana University Press, 1994.

———. *Totality and Infinity: An Essay on Exteriority.* Translated by Alphonso Lingis. Pittsburgh: Duquesne University Press, 1969.

Locke, John. *Two Treatises on Government.* Edited by Peter Laslett. London: Cambridge University Press, 1967.

Lods, A. "Éléments anciens et éléments modernes dans le rituel du sacrifice israélite." *Revue d'histoire et de Philosophie Religieuses* 8 (1928): 399–411.

Lowe, D. *Forgotten Rebels: Black Australians Who Fought Back.* St. Kilda: St. Kilda Permanent Press, 1994.

Lukes, Stephen. *Emile Durkheim: His Life and Work.* London: Allen Lane, 1973.

Lyneham, Paul. "Interview with John Howard M.P." *Nightline.* Broadcast Channel 9, 29 May 1997.

Mabo and Ors v. The State of Queensland (1992). 175 CLR1 (3 June 1992).

Mack, Michael. *German Idealism and the Jew: The Inner Anti-Semitism of Philosophy and German Jewish Responses.* Chicago: University of Chicago Press, 2003.

Mamdani, Mahmood. *When Victims Become Killers: Colonialism, Nativism, and Genocide in Rwanda.* Princeton, N.J.: Princeton University Press, 2001.

Manderson, Desmond. "Shame Is Part of Healing Process." *Sydney Morning Herald*, 28 January 1997.

Manne, Robert. "Forget the Guilt, Remember the Shame." *The Australian*, 8 July 1996.

Manne, Robert, ed. *Whitewash: On Keith Windschuttle's Fabrication of Aboriginal History.* Melbourne Black Inc. Agenda, 2003.

Marcus, Joseph. "Confession." In *The Universal Jewish Encyclopaedia.* Edited by Isaac B. Landman. New York: Universal Jewish Encyclopaedia, c. 1939–1944.

Margalit, Natan. "Life Containing Texts: The Mishnah's Discourse of Gender, a Literary/Anthropological Analysis." Ph.D. diss., U.C. Berkeley, 2001.

Markus, Andrew. *Australian Race Relations* 1788–1983. Sydney: Allen and Unwin, 1994.

Martos, Jose. *Doors to the Sacred.* New York: Doubleday, 1981.

May, Larry. *Sharing Responsibility.* Chicago: University of Chicago Press, 1996.

McGarty, C., A. Pedersen, C. W. Leach, T. Mansell, J. Waller, and A. M. Bliuc. "Group-Based Guilt as a Predictor of Commitment to Apology." *British Journal of Social Psychology* 44, no. 4 (2005): 659–80.

McGrory, Mary. "Apologies Are U.S." *The Washington Post*, 14 March 1999.

McNeill, John T. "Medicine for Sin as Prescribed in the Penitentials." *Church History* 1 (1932): 14–26.

Mead, G. H. *Mind, Self and Society: From the Standpoint of a Social Behaviorist.* Edited by Charles W. Morris. Chicago: University of Chicago Press, 1934.

Megalogenis, George. "Governor-General Fears for Future as PM Recognises Stains of Past." *The Australian*, 27 January 1997.

"Megawati's Apology for Rights Abuse in 2 States." The Tribune Online, 17 August 2000.

Mercer, Jeannine. "'Better Late Than Never' for Crusades Apology." *The Jerusalem Post*, 18 July 1999.

Mierzejewski, Marcin. "A Bishop's Apology." *The Warsaw Voice*, 3 June 2001.

Milgrom, Abraham. *Jewish Worship*. Philadelphia: Jewish Publication Society of America, 1971.

Milgrom, Jacob. *Cult and Conscience: The Asham and the Priestly Doctrine of Repentance*. Leiden: E. J. Brill, 1976.

Milgrom, Jacob, ed. *Leviticus 1–16: A New Translation with Introduction and Commentary, vol. 3 of Anchor Bible*. New York: Doubleday, 1991.

Milirrpum v. Nabalco Pty. Ltd. (1971). 17 FLR 141.

Mill, John Stuart. *A System of Logic, Ratiocinative and Inductive: Being a Connected View of the Principles of Evidence and the Methods of Scientific Investigation*. London: Longman, Green, 1925.

Miller, David. "Holding Nations Responsible." *Ethics* 114 (January 2004): 240–268.

Modjeska, Drusilla. "A Bitter Wind Beyond the Treeline: Address at the 1997 NSW Premier's Literary Awards." *Sydney Morning Herald*, 18 September 1997.

Mody, Anjali. "Mr. Chirac Honors the Truth." *New York Times*, 18 July 1995.

———. "Queen Not Welcome in Amritsar, Says Gujral." *The Indian Express*, 18 August 1997.

Moses, Dirk, ed. *Genocide and Settler Society: Frontier Violence and Stolen Indigenous Children in Australian History*. Oxford and New York: Berghan, 2004.

Muecke, Stephen. "No Guilt with Black Armband." *Australian Financial Times Review*, 11 April 1997.

Murphy, Jeffrie G., and Jean Hampton. *Forgiveness and Mercy*. Cambridge: Cambridge University Press, 1998.

Murphy-O'Connor, J. "Pêche et communauté dans le nouveau testament." *Revue Biblique* 74 (1967): 161–93.

"'My Deepest Apology' from Rumsfeld; 'Nothing Less Than Tragic,' Says Top General." *New York Times*, 8 May 2004.

Ness, Daniel W. Van, and Mara F. Schiff. "Satisfaction Guaranteed? The Meaning of Satisfaction in Restorative Justice." In *Restorative Community Justice: Repairing Harm and Transforming Communities*. Edited by Gordon Bazemore and Mara F. Schiff. Cincinnati, Ohio: Anderson, 2001.

New South Wales. State Children Relief Board Annual Report 1915. Parliamentary Papers, vol. 1, 1915 (851–933).

Noailles, Martina, and Alfredo Ves Losada. "Godoy Mandó descolgar un retrato de Emilio Massera."*Pagina* 12, 7 May 2004.

Nobles, Melissa. *The Politics of Official Apologies*. New York: Cambridge University Press, 2008.

Novick, Peter. *The Holocaust in American Life*. Boston: Houghton Mifflin, 1993.

Oates, Whitney J., and Eugene O'Neill, Jr., eds. *The Complete Greek Drama: All the Extant Tragedies of Aeschylus, Sophocles and Euripides, and the Comedies of Aristophanes and Menander, in a Variety of Translations*. vol. 1. New York: Random House, 1938.

Olick, Jeffrey K. *The Politics of Regret: On Collective Memory and Historical Responsibility*. London: Routledge, 2007.

Ortner, Sherry B. "Theory in Anthropology since the Sixties." *Comparative Studies in Society and History* 26, no. 1 (1984): 126–166.

Osborne, Kenan B. *Reconciliation and Justification: The Sacrament and Its Theology.* New York: Paulist Press, 1970.

Parker, Ned. "*Barak Offers Strong Apology to Arab Israelis for Deaths in October.*" Agence France-Presse, 24 January 2001.

Plato. *The Republic.* Translated by H.D.P. Lee. Middlesex: Penguin, 1955.

Poachmann, Bernard, ed. *Penance and the Anointing of the Sick.* New York: Herder, 1964.

Pokempner, Dinah. "Command Responsibility for Torture." In *Torture: Does It Make Us Safer? Is It Ever Ok? A Human Rights Perspective.* Edited by Kenneth Roth, Minky Worden, and Amy Bernstein. New York and London: The New Press, 2005.

"Poland Apologizes to Jews." *BBC News,* 10 July 2001.

Pope John Paul II. "Address to the New Ambassador of the Federal Republic of Germany to the Holy See." *Acta Apostolicae Sedis* 83, no. 2 (1991): 587–588.

Povinelli, Elizabeth. "The State of Shame: Australian Multiculturalism and the Crisis of Indigenous Citizenship." *Critical Inquiry* 24, no. 2 (Winter 1998): 575–610.

"Presidents Apologize over Croatian War." *BBC News Online,* 10 September 2003.

Price, Adrian Hyde. *Building a Stable Peace in Mitteleuropa: The German Polish Hinge.* Birmingham: University of Birmingham, Institute for German Studies, 2000.

Pritchard, S. "The Stolen Generations and Reparations." *UNSW Law Journal Forum* 4, no. 3 (1997): 28–29.

Quinton, Anthony. "Social Objects." *Proceedings of the Aristotelian Society,* no. 76 (1975): 67–87.

Rahner, Karl. *Theological Investigations,* vol. 2: *Man in the Church.* Baltimore: Beacon Press, 1963.

Raikka, Juha. "On Disassociating Oneself from Collective Responsibility." *Social Theory and Practice* 23, no. 1 (1997): 93–108.

Raitberger, Frances. "France, Algeria Struggle to Put Past Behind Them." *Reuters,* 17 June 2000.

Rajan, Rajeswari Sunder. "Righting Wrongs, Rewriting History." *Interventions* 2, no. 2 (2000): 159–170.

Rawls, John. *A Theory of Justice.* Cambridge, Mass.: Harvard University Press, 1971.

Reiman, Jeffrey H. *Justice and Modern Moral Philosophy.* New Haven: Yale University Press, 1990.

Renan, Ernest. "What Is a Nation? [1882]." In *Nation and Narration.* Edited by Homi Bhaba. London: Routledge, 1990.

Repa Jan. "Analysis: Poland Divided on Massacre." *BBC News Online,* 10 July 2001.

Reynolds, Henry. *Dispossession: Black Australians and White Invaders.* St. Leonards: Allen and Unwin, 1989.

Rice, Xan. "Germans Sorry for Genocide." *The Times,* 16 August 2004.

Ricoeur, Paul. *Symbolism of Evil.* Translated by Emerson Buchanan. Boston: Beacon Press, 1967.

Robertson, Roland. *Globalizations: Social Theory and Global Culture.* Newbury Park, Calif.: Sage, 1992.

Rosenbaum, Walter A. *Political Culture.* New York: Praeger, 1975.

Roth, Cecil, ed. *Encyclopaedia Judaica.* 16 vols. New York: Macmillan, 1971.

Rousso, Henry. *Le syndrome de Vichy de 1944 à nos jours.* Paris: Éditions du Seuil, 1990.

Rowley, James. "Japanese American Internees Get Apologies, $20,000 Checks." Associated Press, 9 October 1990.

Sanders, W. "Towards an Indigenous Order of Australian Government: Rethinking Self-Determination as Indigenous Affairs Policy." In Discussion Paper No. 230/2002. Canberra: Centre for Aboriginal Economic Policy Research, ANU, 2002.

Schillebeeckx, Edward, ed. *Sacramental Reconciliation (Concilium* Vol. 61). New York: Herder, 1971.

Scholem, Gershom. *Origins of the Kabbalah.* Translated by A. Arkush. Princeton, N.J.: Princeton University Press, 1987.

Seeskin, Kenneth. "Ethics, Authority and Autonomy." In *Cambridge Companion to Modern Jewish Philosophy.* Edited by Michael Morgan and Peter Eli Gordon. Cambridge: Cambridge University Press, 2007.

Shaviv, Miriam. "Croatian President Mesic Apologizes to Jews from Knesset Podium." *The Jerusalem Post,* 1 November 2001.

Shklar, Judith N. *Legalism: Law, Morals and Political Trials.* Cambridge, Mass., London: Harvard University Press, 1964.

Sifton, Elizabeth. *The Serenity Prayer.* New York and London: W. W. Norton, 2003.

Sims, Calvin. "After 90 Years, Small Gestures of Joy for Lepers." *New York Times,* 5 July 2001.

"Sinn Fein Leader Visits Ct." *Yale University Daily,* 20 October 1998.

Somers, Margaret R. "What's Political or Cultural About Political Culture and the Public Sphere? Towards an Historical Sociology of Concept Formation." *Sociological Theory* 13, no. 2 (1995): 113–144.

Stanner, William. *After the Dreaming: Black and White Australians. The Boyer Lectures.* Sydney: ABC Press, 1969.

Steiner, Franz Berman. "Elephant Capture." *Modern Poetry in Translation* 2 (1992):31.

Stephenson, M. A., and S. Ratnapala, eds. *Mabo: A Judicial Revolution.* Brisbane: University of Queensland Press, 1993.

Stern, Chaim, ed. *Shaarei Teshuvah: Gates of Repentance: The New Union Prayer Book for the Days of Awe.* New York: Central Conference of American Rabbis, 1978.

Stern, Frank. *The Whitewashing of the Yellow Badge: Anti-Semitism and Philosemitism in Postwar Germany.* Translated by William Templer. Oxford: Pergamon Press, 1992.

Stone, Susan. "The Jewish Tradition and Civil Society." In *Alternative Conceptions of Civil Society.* Edited by Simone Chambers and Will Kymlicka. Princeton, N.J.: Princeton University Press, 2001.

Stout, Jeffrey. *Democracy and Tradition.* Princeton, N.J.: Princeton University Press, 2004.

Strauss, Julian. "Pope Seeks Forgiveness." *The Daily Telegraph,* 6 May 2001.

Swindler, Leonard. *Aufklärung Catholicism, 1780–1850: Liturgical and Other Reforms in the Catholic Aufklärung.* AAR Studies in Religion, vol. 17. Missoula, Mont.: Scholars Press, 1978.

Tavuchis, Nicholas. *Mea Culpa: A Sociology of Apology and Reconciliation.* Stanford: Stanford University Press, 1991.

Taylor, Charles. *Sources of the Self: The Making of the Modern Identity*. Cambridge, Mass.: Harvard University Press, 1989.

Teitel, Ruti. "Human Rights in Transition: Transitional Justice Genealogy." *Harvard Journal of Human Rights* 16 (2003): 69–94.

———. "The Transitional Apology." In *Taking Wrongs Seriously: Apologies and Reconciliation*. Edited by Elezar Barkan and Alexander Karn. Stanford: Stanford University Press, 2006: 101–114.

———. *Transitional Justice*. Oxford: Oxford University Press, 2001.

Thorson, Lucy. "A Call to Communal Repentance, Jewish and Christian Liturgical Experiences: A Dialogical Approach." M.A. diss., University of St. Michael's College, 1993.

Tindale, Norman B. "Survey of the Half-Caste Problem in South Australia." In *Proceedings of the Royal Geographical Society, SA Branch, Session* 1940–41. Edited by Royal Geographical Society. Adelaide Royal Geographical Society: S. A. Branch, 1941.

Torpey, John C., ed. *Politics and the Past: On Repairing Historical Injustices*. Oxford: Rowman and Littlefield, 2003.

"Trial to Revisit French Role in Holocaust." *CNN News Online*, 7 October, 1997.

Trouillot, Michel-Rolph. "Abortive Rituals: Historical Apologies in the Global Era." *Interventions* 2, no. 2 (2000): 171–186.

United Nations General Assembly. United Nations Basic Principles and Guidelines on the Right to a Remedy and Reparation for Victims of Gross Violations of International Human Rights Law and Serious Violations of International Humanitarian Law. GA Res 60/147, GAOR on the report of the Third Committee (A/60/509/Add.1). UN Doc A/Res/60/147.

United States Congress. The Apology Resolution, United States Public Law 103–150, 103d Cong., Joint Resolution 19 (23 November 1993).

"US to Pay Japanese Latin Americans Held During WWII." *CNN News Online*, 12 June 1998.

Vacant, A., and E. Manganot, eds. *Dictionaire de théologie catholique*. Paris: Letonzey et Ané, 1911.

Van Boven, Theo. "The Administration of Justice and the Human Rights of Detainees." Revised Set of Basic Principles and Guidelines on the Right to Reparation for Victims of Gross Violations of Human Rights and Humanitarian Law. In 1995/117, UN Doc E/CN4/Sub2/1996/17, 24 May 1996. United Nations, 1995.

Van Inwagen, Peter. "The Incompatibility of Free Will and Determinism." *Philosophical Studies* 27 (1975): 185–199.

Van Krieken, Robert. "The 'Stolen Generations' and Cultural Genocide: The Forced Removal of Australian Indigenous Children from Their Families and Its Implications for the Sociology of Childhood." *Childhood* 6, no. 3 (August 1999): 297–311.

Von Rad, Gerhard. *Old Testament Theology*. Translated by D.M.G. Stalker. San Francisco: Harper, 1967.

Waldron, Jeremy. "Rights in Conflict." *Ethics* 99, no. 3 (1989): 503–519.

Walker, R. B. J. *Inside/Outside: International Relations as Political Theory*. Cambridge: Cambridge University Press, 1993.

Walzer, Michael, ed. *Regicide and Revolution: Speeches at the Trial of Louis XVI*. New York: Cambridge University Press, 1974.

Warner, Marina. "Who's Sorry Now: The Meaning of Apology in the Modern World." *Times Literary Supplement*, 1 August 2003.

Watkins, Oscar Daniel. *A History of Penance: Being a Study of the Authorities*. New York: B. Franklin, 1961.

"We Must Find Bloody Sunday Truth – Blair." *BBC News Online*, 29 January 1998.

Weber, Max. *Max Weber: Essays in Sociology*. Edited by H. H. Gerth and C. Wright Mills. New York: Oxford University Press, 1946.

Weisbrot, Mark. "Guatemala Not the Only Dark Side of U.S. Policy." *Times Union*, 20 March 1999.

Wetherill, M., and J. Potter. *Mapping the Language of Racism: Discourse and the Legitimation of Exploitation*. New York: Columbia University Press, 1992.

Williams, Bernard. *Ethics and the Limits of Philosophy*. Cambridge, Mass.: Harvard University Press, 1985.

Williams, Bernard, and Arthur Owen. *Shame and Necessity*. Berkeley, Los Angeles, and Oxford: University of California Press, 1993.

Williams, Raymond. *Key Words*. New York: Oxford University Press, 1983.

Windschuttle, Keith. *The Fabrication of Aboriginal History*, vol. 1: Van Diemen's Land 1803–1847. Sydney: Macleay Press, 2002.

Wolfe, Patrick. "Land, Labor and Difference: Elementary Structures of Race."*American Historical Review* 106, no. 3 (2001): 866–905.

———. "Nation and Miscegenation: Discursive Continuity in the Post-Mabo Era." *Social Analysis* 36 (1994): 93–152.

Wolff, Hans J. *Organschaft und juristische Person*. Berlin: Carl Heymanns, 1934.

World Jewish Congress. "Vichy France and the Jews: After Fifty Years, Regrets Emerge." *Policy Dispatches* 20 (1997).

"World News Briefs." *CNN News Online*, 4 November 1995.

Young, Iris Marion. *Justice and the Politics of Difference*. Princeton, N.J.: Princeton University Press, 1990.

———. "Responsibility and Global Labor Justice." *Journal of Political Philosophy* 12 (2004): 365–388.

Yuval-Davis, Nira. *Gender and Nation*. London: Sage, 1997.

Zarader, Marlene. *The Unthought Debt*. Translated by Bettina Bergo. Stanford: Stanford University Press, 2006.

Zuccotti, Susan. *Under His Own Window: The Vatican and the Holocaust in Italy*. New Haven: Yale University Press, 2002.

Index